JAMES RENDEL HARRIS

New Testament Monographs, 7

Series Editor
Stanley E. Porter

James Rendel Harris

JAMES RENDEL HARRIS

NEW TESTAMENT AUTOGRAPHS AND OTHER ESSAYS

Edited by
Alessandro Falcetta

SHEFFIELD PHOENIX PRESS

2006

Copyright © 2006 Sheffield Phoenix Press

Published by Sheffield Phoenix Press
Department of Biblical Studies, University of Sheffield
Sheffield S10 2TN

www.sheffieldphoenix.com

All rights reserved.
No part of this publication may be reproduced or transmitted in any form or by any means, electronic or mechanical, including photocopying, recording or any information storage or retrieval system, without the publishers' permission in writing.

BWHEBB, [Hebrew]; BWGRKL, [Greek] Postscript® Type 1 and TrueType fonts Copyright © 1994–2002 BibleWorks, LLC. All rights reserved. These Biblical Greek and Hebrew fonts are used with permission and are from BibleWorks, software for Biblical exegesis and research.

A CIP catalogue record for this book
is available from the British Library

Typeset by ISB Typesetting
Printed on acid-free paper by Lightning Source UK Ltd, Milton Keynes

ISBN 1-905048-15-7

ISBN-13 978-1-905048-15-1

Contents

Acknowledgments	vii
Preface	ix
Editorial Note and Abbreviations	xiii
Publication Credits	xv

Introduction
JAMES RENDEL HARRIS: A SKETCH OF HIS LIFE AND WORK 1

Chapter 1
NEW TESTAMENT AUTOGRAPHS 17

Chapter 2
METHODS OF RESEARCH IN EASTERN LIBRARIES 72

Chapter 3
THE RATE OF PROGRESS IN NEW TESTAMENT RESEARCH 83

Chapter 4
THE BOOK OF TESTIMONIES 98

Chapter 5
THE ORIGIN OF THE PROLOGUE TO ST JOHN'S GOSPEL 117

Chapter 6
THE FIRST TATIAN READING IN THE GREEK NEW TESTAMENT 185

Chapter 7
JOSEPHUS AND HIS TESTIMONY 192

Chapter 8
NICODEMUS 217

Chapter 9
CORRESPONDENCE WITH HERBERT G. WOOD 232

Bibliography	240
Index of References	248
Index of Authors	255

Acknowledgments

The completion of this book was made possible through the help of several people. I express my gratitude to Ian C. Jackson, librarian of Woodbrooke Quaker Study Centre, Birmingham, Meline Nielsen of the Special Collections Department of the University of Birmingham, Les Gray of the John Rylands University Library of Manchester, Cristina Chersoni of the Biblioteca dell' Archivio Storico, Bologna, my friend Chloé Ragazzoli. They generously spent their time in order to meet my tiresome requests. Tina Dykesteen Nilsen encouraged this project all the way through: being a Bible scholar herself, she offered advice and editorial support and rescued her husband from many pitfalls. Obviously, I am responsible for all the shortcomings.

I would also like to express my most sincere gratitude to the Trustees of Woodbrooke Quaker Study Centre for granting permission to publish Rendel Harris' correspondence, the notes to his personal copy of *The Origin of the Prologue to St John's Gospel* and the essays 'Methods of Research in Eastern Libraries' and 'The Book of Testimony.' Thanks also to the Special Collections Department of the University of Birmingham, which gave permission to reproduce the photograph of Rendel Harris in the frontispiece, and to my friend and editor of *Quaker Studies*, Ben Pink Dandelion, who granted permission to publish in this collection my article on Rendel Harris.

This book is part of a project on James Rendel Harris' life, which I began in 1995 thanks to Prof. Pier Cesare Bori (University of Bologna). The final part of it, a full-fledged biography, is nearing completion. Proper acknowledgment of the tremendous help I have received from individuals and institutions during this project will be made in the biography.

A final note: every effort has been made to ensure permission to reproduce copyright material. In case of oversight, I would be grateful if copyright holders would inform me.

Preface

In his own time, James Rendel Harris was internationally famous for his scholarship, his travels and his public life. When, during the First World War, he safely reached the shores of Corsica after a submarine attack, upon hearing his name the priest of Calvi exclaimed: 'It is the Orientalist!' It was a definition typical of the day, but also an illustration of his fame. Today the name of Rendel Harris may not prompt the same immediate reaction as that of Father Angeline. However, the influence of his works and discoveries was lasting. His *testimonia* research is the object of unfailing interest, his studies in Codex Bezae set the scholarly agenda for decades, and without his finds our library of early Christian literature would not boast the *Apology of Aristides* or the *Odes of Solomon*, nor would Harvard, Haverford, Manchester and Birmingham boast their fine collections of Semitic and Greek manuscripts. These are only a few examples among many.

The interest of Rendel Harris's studies does not reside only on what subsequent research has confirmed. His scholarship was striking for its scope, variety, and freshness. He was able to tackle problems in new ways as his mathematical mindset and formidable memory enabled him to open unexpected paths. Often his theories are controversial and sometimes patently wrong, but they always provide the student with a wealth of insights which can be developed in new directions.

This collection aims at making readily available a number of essays covering almost the entire scholarly life of Rendel Harris and offering a comprehensive specimen of his remarkable output. This selection has favoured unpublished material and those studies that are either little known or of difficult access. It also includes more famous works such as *The Origin of the Prologue to St John's Gospel*, which is here presented with Rendel Harris's notes for a second, never published, edition.

In the first essay, 'New Testament Autographs', Rendel Harris tried to establish the quantity of text per page in the apographs of the leading New Testament uncials and ultimately in the autographs of the New Testament. Subsequent manuscript discoveries did not confirm his hypothesis. His intuition, however, can be successfully applied to other fields. I have proposed that some patristic collections of *testimonia* may still bear traces of the format of their sources. The reason is that writers gathering scriptural citations around a particular theme tried to fill up the page.[1]

The second essay, 'Methods of Research in Eastern Libraries', is published here for the first time. It is a lively lecture in which Rendel Harris writes about Christian works awaiting discovery and about the skills required of a manuscript hunter.

The third essay features 'The Rate of Progress', once again a lecture, in which Rendel Harris recalls his conversion from mathematics to textual criticism, explains the significance and shortcomings of the Revised Version and of the Westcott and Hort New Testament, and gives a lively account of the Burgon controversy. Subsequent research has confirmed his insight that the Gospel text has suffered from theological manipulation.[2]

The fourth essay is 'The Book of Testimonies', a hitherto unpublished paper, which provides the clearest exposition I have found of Rendel Harris's *testimonia* research, including the first steps of its formulation.[3]

The fifth essay, 'The Origin of the Prologue to St John's Gospel', was written in the wake of the *testimonia* studies. Rendel Harris considered the Old Testament background of the prologue and proposed that this derives from a hymn based on wisdom literature. It was one of the first fully developed proposals of this kind.[4]

The title of the sixth essay, 'The First Tatian Reading in the Greek New Testament', is self-explanatory. Rendel Harris found the only *Diatessaron* reading known to us in a Greek Gospel. The codex belonged to him.

The last two essays are entitled 'Josephus and his Testimony' and 'Nicodemus'. These studies contain a wealth of intriguing and controversial

1. See 'A Testimony Collection in Manchester: Papyrus Rylands Greek 460', *BJRL* 83 (2001), pp. 3-19.

2. For instance, Bart D. Ehrman, *The Orthodox Corruption of Scripture: The Effect of Early Christological Controversies on the Text of the New Testament* (New York: Oxford University Press, 1996); David C. Parker, *The Living Text of the Gospels* (Cambridge: Cambridge University Press, 1997).

3. *Testimonia* research is the object of a monograph: Martin C. Albl, *'And Scripture Cannot Be Broken': The Form and Function of the Early Christian Testimonia Collections* (NovTSup, 96; Leiden: E.J. Brill, 1999). See also Albl's recent translation and commentary of a testimony collection (*Pseudo-Gregory of Nyssa: Testimonies against the Jews* [Society of Biblical Literature Writings from the Greco-Roman World, 5; Leiden: E.J. Brill, 2004]) and my article, 'The Testimony Research of James Rendel Harris', *NovT* 45 (2003), pp. 280-99.

4. Cf. Walter Schmithals, *Johannesevangelium und Johannesbriefe: Forschungsgeschichte und Analyse* (BZNW, 64; Berlin: W. de Gruyter, 1992), p. 126. In subsequent essays Rendel Harris drew attention to the influence of Greek thought: 'Stoic Origins of the Prologue to St John's Gospel', *BJRL* 6 (1922), pp. 439-51; 'Athena, Sophia, and the Logos', *BJRL* 7 (1922), pp. 55-72.

suggestions on the *Testimonium Flavianum* and on the *testimonia*. On the basis of one of these proposals it was possible to detect a *testimonia* collection behind an addition to the Slavonic version of the *Jewish War*.[5]

The closing pages present five letters from the correspondence of Rendel Harris with Herbert G. Wood, future professor of theology at the University of Birmingham. The letters tackle dogmatic questions, Albert Schweitzer's *Quest of the Historical Jesus*, and offer a dispassionate assessment of Rendel Harris's *testimonia* research.

The essays and the correspondence are introduced by an article in which I sketch the main episodes in Rendel Harris's eventful life.

I hope that this collection can achieve the same goal aimed at by Rendel Harris's studies: to stimulate debate and provoke fresh research that may yield 'daily discoveries'.

---

5. This is the conclusion I came to in 'The Logion of Matthew 11.5f from Qumran to Abgar', *RB* 110 (2003), pp. 222-48, 238-43.

Editorial Note and Abbreviations

In the process of editing, some harmonisation among the essays has been necessary, since Rendel Harris is not consistent in such matters as italics or quotation marks. Spelling mistakes and wrong or missing diacritical marks in the Greek quotations have been corrected. Biblical references have been conformed to a consistent pattern.

Bibliographical references in Rendel Harris's essays follow the contemporary custom of being wanting. Whenever possible I have given full reference of the works he cites. If several editions of the same book were published, I give only the first one unless the context requires more precision. I have checked the references mostly on library catalogues and, with the exception of Rendel Harris's works, only on few occasions have I been able to validate them. References to biblical and patristic passages have been completed or inserted when Rendel Harris provided insufficient or incorrect information. Biblical references follow the NRSV, even in the case of the Septuagint version of the Psalms. All my additions are in footnotes between square brackets. These are followed by 'AF' with the exception of Rendel Harris's notes to the fifth essay.

The abbreviations follow *The SBL Handbook of Style*[1] with these additions:

Dialogus Athanasii et Zacchaei: *Dial. Ath.*
Ephrem, *Commentary on the Diatessaron*: *Comm. Diat.*
Ps. Gregory of Nyssa, *Testimonia adversus Judaeos*: *Jud.*
Methodius, *Convivium Decem Virginum*: *Conv.*
Odes of Solomon: *Odes*

It should also be noted that 'Woodbrooke' is short for 'Woodbrooke Quaker Study Centre, Birmingham'.

---

1. Patrick H. Alexander *et al.* (eds.), *The SBL Handbook of Style: For Ancient Near Eastern, Biblical and Early Christian Studies* (Peabody, MA: Hendrickson, 1999).

Publication Credits

James Rendel Harris: A Sketch of his Life and Work
Revised text of Alessandro Falcetta, 'James Rendel Harris: A Life on the Quest', *Quaker Studies* 8 (2004), pp. 208-25.

1. New Testament Autographs
Supplement to the *American Journal of Philology* 12 (1882), Baltimore. ii + 54 pp.

2. Methods of Research in Eastern Libraries
Lecture no. 4, Haverford College Library Lectures, Haverford, PA, 1895; typescript, Rendel Harris Room, Woodbrooke Quaker Study Centre, Birmingham. 19 pp.

3. The Rate of Progress in New Testament Research
In *Side-Lights on New Testament Research: Seven Lectures Delivered in 1908, at Regent's Park College, London* (London: The Kingsgate Press, James Clarke, 1908), pp. 1-35.

4. The Book of Testimonies
Revised text of one of the Haskell Lectures for 1909–1910, which Rendel Harris delivered on May 1910 at Oberlin College, Oberlin, Ohio, and which were entitled 'Some Lost Books of the Early Church'. The typescript is kept in the Rendel Harris Room, Woodbrooke Quaker Study Centre, Birmingham. 35 pp.

5. The Origin of the Prologue to St John's Gospel
Cambridge: Cambridge University Press, 1917. 65 pp. The present publication includes the handwritten additions Rendel Harris penned in his personal copy, which is kept in the Rendel Harris Room, Woodbrooke Quaker Study Centre, Birmingham.

6. The First Tatian Reading in the Greek New Testament
Expositor, 8th series, 23 (1922), pp. 120-29.

7. Josephus and his Testimony
Evergreen Essays, 2; Cambridge: Heffer, 1931. 35 pp.

8. Nicodemus
Evergreen Essays. 4; Cambridge: Heffer, 1932. 22 pp.

Correspondence with Herbert G. Wood
Woodbrooke Quaker Study Centre archives, Birmingham.

JAMES RENDEL HARRIS:
A SKETCH OF HIS LIFE AND WORK

'Give us, Lord, our daily discovery'.[1] This is how James Rendel Harris used to pray. His prayers were fulfilled on an unusual number of occasions. Some of those events are reported in the following biographical essay.[2]

Education and Religious Experiences

James Rendel Harris was born to a Congregationalist family on 27 January 1852 in Plymouth, one of eleven children. The name of his mother was Elisabeth Corker. His father, Henry Marmaduke Harris, was a house decorator. One of his aunts, Catherine Jane, had married a famous engineer, Meadows Rendel, from whom James took his middle name, while another, Augusta Harris, was the mother of the poet Henry Austin Dobson.[3] After completing grammar school, Rendel Harris studied mathematics at Clare College, Cambridge, where in 1874 he was third wrangler in the mathematical tripos. At this stage of his life, he was particularly influenced by the meetings of Dwight L. Moody and Ira D. Sankey, leaders of the second evangelical revival who toured Britain in 1873, as well as by the holiness movement

---

1. Letter of Rendel Harris to Irene Speller, 28/5/1919 ('Correspondence with Irene Speller Pickard 1912–39', G Har 13, Woodbrooke).
2. The main biographical sources are: Alessandro Falcetta, *James Rendel Harris (1852–1941): Uno studioso del cristianesimo delle origini ed un uomo spirituale* (B.A. dissertation, Università di Bologna, 1996); Irene S. Pickard, *Memories of J. Rendel Harris* (private publication, 1978); Herbert G. Wood, 'The First Director of Studies', in *Woodbrooke 1903–1953: A Brief History of a Quaker Experiment in Religious Education* (ed. Robert Davis; London: The Bannisdale Press, 1953), 19-30; Wood *et al.*, 'The Doctor', *The Woodbrooke International Journal* no. 41 (1941), pp. 2-15; Wood *et al.*, 'James Rendel Harris: 1852–1941', *The Friend* 99 (1941), pp. 115-19. The major collections of Rendel Harris's papers are at Woodbrooke, at the University of Birmingham, and at Haverford College (Pennsylvania). There is an almost complete bibliographical list that also takes into account unpublished writings: L. Sinclair, 'A List of Writings, etc., of James Rendel Harris (1852–1941)' (typescript, 1956, Rendel Harris Room, Woodbrooke).
3. On Rendel Harris's family, see the autobiography of his nephew: Henry W. Harris, *Life So Far* (London: Jonathan Cape, 1954), 11-28.

preached by the Quaker couple Robert Pearsall and Hannah Withall Smith.[4] As a consequence, he had a sort of second conversion, which, in the words of his closest friend Herbert G. Wood, was 'an experience of sanctification over and above the realisation of the forgiving love of God which had come to him earlier'.[5] Trust in a loving and directly accessible God and mistrust of creeds were probably the foundations of his Quaker faith. His wife, Helen Balkwill, was already a Quaker.[6] He married Helen, who was from Plymouth and ten years his senior, in 1880.

Rendel Harris became a member of the Society of Friends on 5 October 1885,[7] as he attended the Cambridge, Huntingdon and Lynn Monthly Meeting at Wisbech. A master from Ackworth, G. Satterthwaite, 'spoke of those who worked for the Lord, unattached, without taking their share of responsibility for the business and life of the organised church',[8] or, to put it otherwise, the master convinced him of the importance of accepting the duties of membership. Rendel Harris said that if Friends thought he would be more serviceable if in outward connection with the Society, he was willing to apply for membership. He was asked to go out into the graveyard, and three Friends were requested to visit him and to report at a further stage of the meeting. Their report was entirely satisfactory, and thus he was united at once in membership.

The First Academic Positions

Starting from 1875, Rendel Harris was lecturer and tutor in mathematics at Clare College.[9] However, in 1881 he decided to change his field of work to biblical studies. This was partly a consequence of the publication of the Greek New Testament edition by Westcott and Hort.[10] Rendel Harris had already

---

4. See Melvin E. Dieter, *The Holiness Revival of the Nineteenth Century* (Lanham, MD: The Scarecrow Press, 2nd edn, 1996), pp. 129-69.

5. Wood, 'Director', p. 21.

6. On Helen Balkwill, see the obituary in *The Annual Monitor for 1915* (Gloucester: John Bellows, 1914), pp. 106-16.

7. Rendel Harris's application for membership is recorded in 'Cambridge, Huntingdon & Lynn Monthly Meeting, Minute Book', and 'List of Members' (respectively R59/26/5/1 and R59/26/5/8, Cambridgeshire County Record Office, Cambridge). See also Margaret A. Backhouse, 'James Rendel Harris', in *London Yearly Meeting of the Society of Friends 1942: Reports and Documents Presented to the Yearly Meeting together with Minutes and Index* (London: Headley Brothers, 1942), pp. 182-84.

8. Anonymous handwritten note, probably by Herbert G. Wood, dated 6 August 1936, reporting a conversation with Rendel Harris on how he joined the Society (folder 1, G Har 14, Woodbrooke archives).

9. 'J.R. Harris' (Harrison Index, Clare College archives, Cambridge).

10. Brooke F. Westcott and Fenton J.A. Hort (eds.), *The New Testament in the Original Greek* (2 vols.; Cambridge: MacMillan, 1881). The first volume presents the text, the second

been studying Scripture with Hort. Bible studies may even have been his first interest, but it took him some time to make up his mind, probably because of the British bias against nonconformist Bible scholars.

In 1882 Rendel Harris left Clare College and accompanied Helen to the northeast coast of the USA, where she led campaigns in a temperance movement. Through influential American Friends he met D.C. Gilman, the president of the Johns Hopkins University in Baltimore, who eventually arranged his appointment as lecturer in New Testament Greek.[11] Rendel Harris worked with enthusiasm, and proved to be a very promising scholar. However, in 1885 he left Baltimore. In a letter sent to a local newspaper he had criticized Pasteur's experiments on animals.[12] This critique was felt as an attack on the biology department of the Johns Hopkins, which practised vivisection. Gilman remarked that the letter was out of place. Rendel Harris replied that he could not admit his freedom of speech being limited in the least degree.[13] Thus, he and Helen went back to Cambridge. They remained in Britain only for a short time since there were no vacant positions for him. Returning to the USA, they were welcomed at Haverford College, a Quaker institution near Philadelphia. For six years Rendel Harris taught biblical languages and Church history, and he deeply influenced the college with his spiritual leadership and scholarly achievements. Rufus M. Jones, a leading Quaker thinker and scholar, wrote about Rendel Harris at Haverford:

> His method of teaching was unique and peculiar to himself. The students never knew in advance with what the next lecture would deal, and the marvellous man carried them on wings as eagles from one peak of truth to another across continents and athwart the centuries as though he were at home in all ages and in all lands.[14]

Eventually, the favourable reception of his essays on New Testament textual criticism persuaded him that the climate was ripe to return to Cambridge,

---

volume is an introduction written by Hort. Rendel Harris refers to this conversion in *Side-Lights on New Testament Research: Seven Lectures Delivered in 1908, at Regent's Park College, London* (London: The Kingsgate Press; James Clarke, 1908), pp. 8-9. See below p. 86.

11. On Rendel Harris and the Johns Hopkins University, see Hugh Hawkins, *Pioneer: A History of the Johns Hopkins University, 1874–1889* (Ithaca, NY: Cornell University Press, 1960), pp. 152-54.

12. *The Sun*, 13 February 1885.

13. The official reason for Rendel Harris's resignation concerned the issue of freedom of speech, whereas all the biographical notices mistakenly point to his protest against vivisection. The documentation on this story is kept in 'James Rendel Harris Vertical File', Special Collections, Johns Hopkins University, Baltimore.

14. *Haverford College: A History and an Interpretation* (New York: MacMillan, 1933), p. 95.

where in 1892 he was appointed a fellow at Clare College and University lecturer in palaeography.

Textual Criticism and the Search for Manuscripts

The core of Rendel Harris's work was the study of New Testament manuscripts as objects presenting a number of features that point to a specific history.[15] He studied Codex Bezae and proposed that the Greek text had been reworked on the basis of the parallel Latin text.[16] Moreover, he studied several other manuscripts, such as the Leicester codex,[17] and considered the origin of the group to which it belongs, the Ferrar group.[18]

For Rendel Harris, the most fascinating aspect of textual criticism was the number of variants which have come down to us. He was convinced that these played an important role in the early history of the text of the New Testament and that editors should not feel too confident when trying to reconstruct an original text on the belief of a somewhat fixed transmission.

Rendel Harris's research was not limited to working on known manuscripts. Over the course of thirty years he travelled to the Near East in search of lost or neglected ancient documents. In the autumn of 1888, while still teaching at Haverford, he undertook an expedition to Lebanon, Palestine and Egypt.[19] Together with Helen, he spent some time in Brummana, a Lebanese village with a Quaker mission. From there they travelled to Jerusalem, where Rendel Harris quickly became acquainted with the Greek Orthodox patriarch as well as with leading westerners. After six weeks of research he discovered in the library of the Greek Orthodox Patriarchate the Greek text of the *Acts of the Martyrdom of Perpetua and Felicitas*.[20] This work, which was already known

---

15. *New Testament Autographs* (Supplement to the *American Journal of Philology* 12 [1882], Baltimore), which is reprinted in this book; 'Stichometry', *American Journal of Philology* 4 (1883), pp. 133-57, 309-31; repr. with additions in *Stichometry* (Cambridge: Clay, 1893).

16. Rendel Harris's chief works on Codex Bezae are: *Codex Bezae: A Study of the So-Called Western Text of the New Testament* (TS, 2.1; Cambridge: Cambridge University Press, 1891); *The Annotators of Codex Bezae (with Some Notes on* Sortes Sanctorum*)* (London: Clay, 1901). An assessment of Rendel Harris's contribution is found in David C. Parker, *Codex Bezae: An Early Christian Manuscript and its Text* (Cambridge: Cambridge University Press, 1992), pp. 187-88.

17. *The Origin of the Leicester Codex of the New Testament* (London: Clay, 1887).

18. *On the Origin of the Ferrar Group* (London: Clay, 1893); *Further Researches in the History of the Ferrar-Group* (London: Clay, 1900).

19. 'Diary kept during a visit to the Middle East' (DA21/2/1/1/1, Special Collections, University of Birmingham).

20. Rendel Harris edited it with Seth K. Gifford: *The Acts of the Martyrdom of Perpetua and Felicitas: The Original Greek Text Now First Edited from a MS. in the Library of the Convent of the Holy Sepulchre at Jerusalem* (London: Clay, 1890).

in Latin, tells the story of Montanist martyrs eaten by wild beasts in Cartage in 203. In February 1889 Rendel Harris set out for Egypt. Starting from Cairo, he reached the Monastery of Saint Catherine on Mount Sinai. Rendel Harris soon became fast friends with the librarian, Galakteon, and eventually discovered a Syriac version of the hitherto lost text of the *Apology* of Aristides, an address in defence of Christians written in the first half of the second century.[21]

In 1891–1892 and 1901 Rendel Harris was commissioned by the University of Cambridge to survey the manuscripts of the Septuagint in Greece and in other European countries for Henry B. Swete's edition of this text.[22] In 1893 he undertook another expedition to Saint Catherine in order to study what was to be called Codex Syriacus Sinaiticus. Rendel Harris was part of a team including Robert L. Bensly, Francis C. Burkitt, their respective wives Agnes and Amy, and twin sisters Margaret S. Lewis and Agnes D. Gibson.[23] The two sisters had found the codex during a visit made to the monastery in 1892. They had undertaken the journey after knowing about Rendel Harris's, 1889 visit. In the subsequent journey of 1893 the group did not get on well because of mutual suspicion, copyright concerns and differences in personality. Rendel Harris acted as intermediary between the twin sisters, Bensly and Burkitt, and the monks. The *editio princeps* of the manuscript was published the following year.[24]

Armenia Relief

Near the end of the nineteenth century the massacre of Armenians in the Ottoman Empire roused considerable indignation in Britain and other Western countries. With the help of the 'Friends' Armenia Relief Committee'[25] Rendel Harris and Helen travelled to Asia Minor in March 1896. After stopping in Constantinople, they visited Armenian and Syriac villages between

---

21. *The Apology of Aristides* (TS, 1; Cambridge: Cambridge University Press, 1891).

22. *The Old Testament in Greek according to the Septuagint* (3 vols.; Cambridge: Cambridge University Press, 1887–1891). Several more editions followed.

23. See the biography of the two sisters by Allan W. Price, *The Ladies of Castlebrae: A Story of Nineteenth-Century Travel and Research* (Gloucester: Alan Sutton, 1985). A new biography by Janet Soskice is due for the year 2007. The two sisters's account of the travel has recently been republished: Margaret D. Gibson, *How the Codex Was Found: A Narrative of Two Visits to Sinai from Mrs. Lewis's Journals, 1892–1893* (Cambridge: MacMillan and Bowes, 1893; repr., Piscataway, NJ: Gorgias Press, 2001).

24. Rendel Harris, Francis C. Burkitt and Robert L. Bensly (eds.), *The Four Gospels in Syriac Transcribed from the Sinai Palimpsest* (Cambridge: Cambridge University Press, 1894).

25. 'Armenia Relief Committee (1896–1899)' ('Central Organisation Volume', Friends House archives, London).

Alexandretta and Samsoun, facing every sort of difficulty and peril along the way.[26] The relief work they undertook among a population which had suffered horrific atrocities of torture, maiming and murder, was aimed at restoring life to the Armenian communities by building schools, orphanages and small manufacturing industries. Rendel Harris remained active in assisting these enterprises for many years. While in Armenia he obviously spent some time looking for manuscripts, many of which were being destroyed by the Turks and the Kurds.[27] He left the region in August 1896 and went back to his academic duties in Cambridge, while Helen remained behind to carry on the work. Between November 1896 and January 1897 she went to Berlin and to Saint Petersburg trying unsuccessfully to meet both the German emperor and the tsar in order to plead for some intervention on behalf of the Armenians.[28]

The Leiden Appointment

In the spring of 1903 Rendel Harris returned to Armenia in order to check on and to support the initiatives undertaken seven years earlier. While he was there, a telegram reached him with the offer of the chair of Early Christian Literature and New Testament Exegesis at the University of Leiden. To the surprise and disappointment of A. Kuyper, the Dutch Secretary of Internal Affairs, who had chosen his name from a list including W. Bousset, J.M.S. Baljon and H. Weinel, Rendel Harris turned down the offer. His refusal seems inexplicable since he had no chances of upgrading his Cambridge lectureship into a permanent position.[29] However, in his reply to the University he made clear that he would have accepted the appointment, had he not promised to direct a Quaker settlement for religious and social work in Birmingham.[30] The Dutch Secretary made every effort to persuade Rendel Harris to change his mind, but it was all in vain.

---

26. Rendel Harris and Helen gathered the letters they wrote to friends at home in *Letters from the Scenes of the Recent Massacres in Armenia* (London: Nisbet, 1897).

27. Rendel Harris has not left any information about his purchases except for a few hints in *Letters from Armenia*.

28. See 'Helen Balkwill Harris's petitions to the Emperor of Germany and the Empress of Russia' (DA21/1/1/25/3, Special Collections, University of Birmingham).

29. On Rendel Harris's university lectureship, see the minutes of the senate in the *Cambridge University Reporter* no. 936 (1892), pp. 854-56. Serious resistance was made against creating a permanent lectureship *ad personam*.

30. See the correspondence in 'Letters written from the Near East by James Rendel Harris to Kitty Whibley', and in 'Letters to James Rendel Harris from the University of Leiden, offering him a post', DA21/1/1/25/6 and DA21/1/5/4 respectively, Special Collections, University of Birmingham. I also draw on the research kindly carried out for me by the late Professor J. van den Berg in the archives of Leiden University (personal correspondence, September 1995–May 1996). It has been proposed that the appointment might

Woodbrooke

The settlement was Woodbrooke. Before going further, it is better to take some steps backwards, and to consider Rendel Harris's involvement with the Society of Friends and the origins of the college. Rendel Harris was a leader of the Quaker liberal movement. This movement aimed at reforming Quakerism in the light of the innovations and discoveries in contemporary Bible scholarship, theology, philosophy and social sciences. Stress was placed upon understanding faith and Scripture in the light of reason and historical research.[31]

Liberal Friends like John W. Rowntree were the promoters of the Manchester Conference of 1895, in which the liberal and the evangelical members laid out their positions. Rendel Harris took part in the conference with an important speech. It dealt with the necessity of keeping together religion and modern thought, and of using the instruments of the latter to study the former.[32] Concerning Scripture and truth he said:

> No other century since the beginning has cared for Him enough to try to write His history. But perhaps it is the Scriptures that they are going to steal; they cannot steal from us the truth of immediate Revelation and direct communication with God, which was before the Scriptures, and was the cause of them. We have been told in these meetings that the Scriptures are the ultimate test of truth; if that un-Quakerly proposition be true, the criticism of them is a gross impertinence; but the internal discords of all Scriptures, and of all explanations of Scriptures, ought to be enough to convince us that we have no infallibility in the house, not a drop [...] But while we have no infallibility we have some splendid probabilities, and one of them in particular is of such high order that we call it 'The certainty of love, which sets our hearts at rest'.[33]

have been favoured by Helen's pro-Boer work in the British concentration camps in South Africa in 1901, where Boer families had been confined (so Wood, 'Director', p. 21). A different proposal comes from Hope H. Hewison (*Hedge of Wild Almonds: South Africa, the Pro-Boers and the Quaker Conscience, 1890–1910* [London: James Currey, 1989], p. 223). Helen, after visiting the camps, allegedly softened her position towards the British government, and, therefore, she could have been an object of resentment in the Netherlands. This would have prompted her husband's refusal. However, this proposal is farfetched since we know very little as to Helen's attitude towards the camps and since Helen and Rendel Harris were convinced pacifists. Moreover, if such resentment did exist, why did Kuyper select Rendel Harris? The official reason is to be preferred.

31. See Thomas C. Kennedy, *British Quakerism 1860–1920: The Transformation of a Religious Community* (Oxford: Oxford University Press, 2001).

32. *Report of the Proceedings of the Conference of the Society of Friends Held by Direction of the Yearly Meeting, in Manchester from the Eleventh to the Fifteenth of Eleventh Month, 1895* (London: Headley Brothers, 1896), pp. 218-26.

33. *Report*, pp. 222-23.

After the conference the liberal Quakers kept promoting their ideas within the Society. In August 1897 Rowntree and others organized the first Quaker Summer School, which was held in Scarborough. The tutors, many of whom were Cambridge and Oxford scholars, taught Old Testament, New Testament, Church history, and social subjects. The pupils got acquainted with facsimiles of ancient manuscripts, and were introduced to the most recent discoveries in textual criticism. Rendel Harris was one of the most successful teachers. In 1899 Rowntree proposed the establishment of a permanent summer school in order to train Quakers for ministry.[34] Eventually, this project was combined with an idea conceived by George Cadbury, who was a Quaker and a chocolate manufacturer like Rowntree. In 1902 Cadbury thought of dedicating Woodbrooke, a villa of his in Selly Oak, Birmingham, to train young men and women for service in the Society. Cadbury joined hands with Rowntree in order to found an educational settlement at Woodbrooke.

A problem of paramount importance was the appointment of the first director of studies, so that the right atmosphere could be created from the outset and criticism silenced. Considering the concern being expressed by many weighty evangelical Friends, an initial mistake would have been difficult to outlive. In May 1902 John W. Rowntree, on behalf of the small team working on the project, asked Rufus M. Jones to come to England and to become the head of Woodbrooke. Jones refused. Woodbrooke was a very daring and uncertain educational experiment, while Jones was already committed to the College of Haverford and to US Quakers. Cadbury received the decision with some dismay. According to his plans, after only two years Jones would have been free to go back to the USA and would have been replaced by Rendel Harris. On 12 December 1902 Cadbury contacted Rendel Harris, who accepted.

There may have been several reasons why Rendel Harris decided to move to Birmingham. First, Woodbrooke was a centre through which he could make a serious contribution to the life of British Quakerism. Second, he could shape the settlement according to his own wishes. Third, this position was less time-consuming than a university appointment.

Woodbrooke opened on 13 October 1903. The teaching staff was of the first rank, as the director felt bound to keep the standard at least as high as that of the recently founded University of Birmingham. Cadbury did not want anything less than the best for the institution, no matter what it took. However, Rendel Harris's ideas about the settlement did not coincide with the plans of Rowntree and Cadbury. According to Rendel Harris, the aim of the settlement was 'to help young men and women to think things out, to

---

34. On Woodbrooke's beginnings, see Herbert G. Wood, 'Origins', in Davis, *Woodbrooke 1903–1953*, pp. 13-18. Copies of the letters written by Cadbury, Rowntree and Jones about the founding of Woodbrooke are kept in the file 'Woodbrooke History I', C 4, Woodbrooke archives.

study social and religious problems, to prepare them for practical service'.[35] He did not consider it only as a centre for training Quaker ministers and promoting the liberal side of the Society.[36]

The high level of the teaching entailed that only a small number of students were able to understand fully the lectures. The majority of British Friends who attended Woodbrooke had no academic training in biblical studies, whereas Rendel Harris laid stress on biblical Greek, Hebrew and Syriac. Especially difficult were the classes he gave on New Testament textual criticism, patristic literature, and Church history. These classes were mistakenly based on the assumption that the pupils had the necessary background knowledge. Moreover, before lecturing Rendel Harris apparently made little or no preparation at all.[37] At any rate, Rendel Harris's wide erudition and ingenuity produced a most unconventional manner of teaching, so that the number of anecdotes and tales about his classes grew fast. His students used to say: 'When the Doctor gives a title to a lecture, you may be sure of one thing he won't lecture about'.[38] One day Rendel Harris announced an unscheduled lecture on the Epistle to the Ephesians. At the end of it a young student approached to congratulate him on the class, but she could not help asking why he did not even mention the Epistle. He said: 'My dear child, why ever should I?'[39]

Among the pupils there was for many years a group from the Netherlands with a solid academic training. Since Rendel Harris had not gone to Leiden, the Leiden students came to him.

The Spiritual Works

At Woodbrooke Rendel Harris wrote most of his devotional books.[40] The heart of his spiritual beliefs was the idea of direct communication with God.

---

35. Anon, 'Dr Rendel Harris at Home', *The Christian Commonwealth* (7 March 1907).

36. 'You see the straits I am reduced to in trying to save Woodbrooke from becoming a Friends Boarding School' (Rendel Harris's letter to William C. Braithwaite, 2/3/1906 ['Letters from J. Rendel Harris 1899–1923', G Har 12, Woodbrooke archives]).

37. Particularly scathing were the letters sent by the warden William Littleboy to William C. Braithwaite and the reports he submitted to the Woodbrooke Committee ('William Littleboy. Letters written by W. L. 1905-1907', G Litt, Woodbrooke archives).

38. Anon, 'Dr Harris' Angus Lectures', *The Old Woodbrookers Magazine* no. 9 (1909), p. 68.

39. George R. Howe, 'The Lighter Side of a Weighty Friend' (typescript, 'Biographical Material', G Har 4, Woodbrooke archives [p. 3]).

40. Rendel Harris's devotional books are: *Memoranda Sacra* (London: Hodder & Stoughton, 1892); *Union with God* (London: Hodder & Stoughton, 1895); *The Guiding Hand of God* (London: National Council of Evangelical Free Churches, 1905); *Aaron's Breastplate* (London: National Council of Evangelical Free Churches, 1908); *The Sufferings and the Glory* (London: Headley Brothers, 1914); *As Pants the Hart* (London: Hodder

Rendel Harris wrote: 'As we learn to live the life of dependence upon the Lord, we must be not surprised if a great deal of our early theology drops off ... I am amazed to find how much of true religion may be resolved into that one word "dependence"'.[41] 'Dependence' was a daily experience. He thought that this experience, which goes beyond the limits of a particular Church, brings Christians towards an ever-increasing faith. The believers must think their relationship with Christ on the highest possible planes, without false modesty: 'Hyperbole on the experimental side is one of the characteristics of a Divine revelation ... Let God promise like God, and do you believe like a child of God. Make a collection of the hyperbolic promises of God, and you have the materials for the dogmatic statement of a full salvation'.[42] Rendel Harris fully relied on God's direct guidance, as he found evidence of it in his own life. He was convinced that this guidance brings about tangible results:

> Some may be content with scoring an occasional success: the true prophet aspires after a communion with the Lord, according to which his Master will be with him and *let none of his words fall to the ground*, although he knows that this means not only previous instruction, but also a wary walking and a constant watching.[43]

Not even death can hinder the achievement of a full experience of life; death is not a terminus, but a starting point.[44]

The process of spiritual growth begins with obedience and dependence, passes through divine guidance and the development of one's own personality, and moves towards life beyond death. Rendel Harris held fast to these principles even when, after the death of Helen and the trauma of the Great War, he had to come to terms with the presence of noise in the music of the world.[45]

Public Life

Rendel Harris's spiritual works in addition to his scholarly achievements and his engagement for Armenia were probably among the reasons why he was

& Stoughton, 1924). Though variations occurred, I give a synchronic account of Rendel Harris's spiritual tenets, as they kept recurring throughout his life.

41. *Memoranda Sacra*, p. 40.
42. *Aaron's Breastplate*, p. 39.
43. *Guiding Hand*, pp. 101-102.
44. *Guiding Hand*, p. 106. There is a nice anecdote about Rendel Harris's understanding of death. One day during a funeral, a nine-year old girl was sobbing in a corner of the graveyard for the death of her parent. Rendel Harris took her hand and, without saying anything, walked the little girl around the graveyard. Only when she calmed down did he speak: 'Never be afraid of the Road to Paradise, dear. It's a conducted tour'. The anecdote is in Howe, 'The Lighter Side' (p. 3).
45. This is one of the themes of *As Pants the Hart*.

appointed president of the National Council of the Evangelical Free Churches from 1907 to 1908. Moreover, some years earlier, he had written a widely circulated letter[46] and promoted tax objection against the 1902 Education Act, which was considered to discriminate against nonconformists.

Research on Testimonia *and on Twin Cults*

During the first quarter of the twentieth century Rendel Harris's scholarly output was remarkable. One of his most enduring contributions to scholarship is the *testimonia* hypothesis. Studying early patristic literature he noted the habit of quoting a number of Old Testament passages around a certain theme or a catchword. He found that different writers without apparent connections quoted the same or similar clusters of passages, and made similar errors in attributing them or in the wording of the texts. The most likely explanation was that these authors employed common sources. Initially he thought that, starting from the second century, Christians produced many collections of those Old Testament passages, or *testimonia*, which they believed to have prophesied about Jesus and the Church. However, Rendel Harris is best known for the subsequent theory that Christians produced, soon after Jesus' death, only one collection, the *Testimony Book*, which was modified in the course of time and drawn on by the writers of the New Testament and by the Fathers.[47] The *testimonia* question has been an object of study, with changing fortunes, for over a hundred years. Consensus is growing around the hypothesis that there were many collections circulating among Christians starting from the second and probably even the first century. It is interesting to remark that the freedom with which Christians handled the Old Testament, extrapolating passages, associating different quotations, and sometimes altering texts, has been explained in more recent scholarship with words recalling George Fox's journal: these collectors believed that they had the same spirit which produced the Scriptures, and therefore felt justified in working on them as they saw fit.[48] It is also interesting to note that a similar explanation has

---

46. 'Passive Resistance: A Letter from J. Rendel Harris to the Nonconformists of the County of Cambridge and the Isle of Ely', *The British Weekly* (1 December 1902).

47. His classic work is *Testimonies* (2 vols.; Cambridge: Cambridge University Press, 1916–20). It is mostly a collection of articles published over nearly twenty years, with the addition of some chapters written by a collaborator, Henry V. Burch. For a close analysis, see Falcetta, 'Testimony Research'.

48. Regarding a priest who, expounding 2 Pet. 1.19, had said that the Scriptures were 'the touchstone' of all doctrines, Fox wrote: 'Oh no, it is not the Scriptures ... But I told them what it was, namely the Holy Spirit, by which the holy men of God gave forth the Scriptures, whereby opinions, religions and judgements must be tried' (John L. Nickalls [ed.], *The Journal of George Fox* [London: London Yearly Meeting of the Religious

been provided for the unusual readings of Codex Bezae and in general for a certain freedom in the transmission of the text of the New Testament in the first two or three centuries.[49]

Rendel Harris also made enquiries into other fields of research. Between 1903 and 1913 he published three books on the phenomenon of the cult of twins.[50] While working on liturgical calendars, he had accidentally discovered that many saints were actually twins. He then suspected that this cult had deliberately been used to displace the worship of the most famous pagan twins, Castor and Pollux. This discovery led him to find traces of twin cults in a number of different cultures. In later years, he carried on research on folklore with the study of the Greek pantheon. He proposed that several Greek gods were originally associated with the cult of plants.[51]

The Last Journeys to the Near East

Amidst his continuing scholarly and spiritual activities, Rendel Harris found time to travel. In 1912–1913 he spent some months in Constantinople, offering assistance to the Christian war refugees fleeing from the Balkans. Three years later he set off on a new trip.[52] The death of Helen in 1914 and the outbreak of the First World War may have brought about the feeling that his scholarship was inadequate to the immediate necessities of the conflict. This is probably why in 1916 he accepted a warm invitation from his friend James Hope Moulton to support his missionary work in India. On 17 November 1916 Rendel Harris left from Liverpool on the 'City of Birmingham' in order to reach Bombay via the Mediterranean Sea. Ten days later, not far from Malta, a German submarine torpedoed the steamer. The passengers were rescued by a ship after three and a half hours and brought to Alexandria. Rendel Harris recovered quickly and then went off looking for manuscripts. He explored the countryside and contacted the local farmers, who sometimes dug up scraps of papyri, which, if they managed to escape the surveillance of the authorities, they would sell to western buyers.[53] After gathering a remarkable collection,

---

Society of Friends, 1986], p. 40). On the freedom in quoting *testimonia*, see Prosper Grech, 'Testimonia and Modern Hermeneutics', *NTS* 19 (1973), pp. 318-24.

49. See Parker, *Living Text*, pp. 202-13.

50. *The Dioscuri in Christian Legends* (London: Clay, 1903); *The Cult of the Heavenly Twins* (Cambridge: Cambridge University Press, 1906); *Boanerges* (Cambridge: Cambridge University Press, 1913).

51. The articles were collected in one volume: *The Ascent of Olympus* (Manchester: John Rylands Library, 1917).

52. Rendel Harris, *Ulysses to his Friends* (private publication, 1917).

53. Some information on Rendel Harris's manuscript dealings is in his correspondence

he decided to return to England with Moulton, who, in the meantime, had come to Egypt. On 30 March 1917 the 'City of Paris' set off from Port Said for Marseilles. On 4 April a German submarine destroyed the ship. Rendel Harris and Moulton boarded the same lifeboat and, after four harrowing days, Corsica came into sight and a boat from the island saved the survivors. Moulton was not among them. The manuscript collection had been left in the Museum in Cairo, and was safely shipped to Britain at a later stage, where it found its way to the Rylands Library in Manchester.

Despite these frightening experiences, in 1922–1923 Rendel Harris returned to Mount Sinai. He had read in a report on the monastery library the description of a manuscript that seemed to be the *Diatessaron* of Tatian. Eventually, the manuscript turned out to be a valueless text. The disappointment was probably mitigated by the acquisition of papyri in the Egyptian countryside. The papyri are now at the University of Birmingham.[54]

The Odes of Solomon *and the Mingana Collection*

Since 1915 Rendel Harris had been Emeritus Director of Studies of Woodbrooke, turning over the leadership of that institution to Herbert G. Wood, whose fresh enthusiasm was more appropriate for conducting the college through the new problems caused by the war. In 1918 Rendel Harris left Birmingham and moved to Manchester, where he had been appointed curator of eastern manuscripts at the John Rylands Library. This appointment reflected his worldwide reputation as a scholar and allowed him to work on his most famous discovery. On 4 January 1909 Rendel Harris had picked up from his library a little Syriac manuscript, which had been in his possession for two years. It probably belonged to a lot of Syriac manuscripts, which Alpheus N. Andrus, a Mardin missionary and Rendel Harris's agent, had gathered and sent him.[55] A rapid survey proved it to contain the hitherto lost *Odes of Solomon*.

---

with his secretary Irene Speller ('Correspondence with Irene Speller Pickard 1912–39', G Har 13, Woodbrooke).

54. Rendel Harris described the expedition in the letters he sent to his secretary ('Correspondence with Irene Speller Pickard 1912–39', G Har 13, Woodbrooke).

55. Rendel Harris gave the first account of the discovery in 'An Early Christian Psalter', *Contemporary Review* 95 (1909), pp. 414-28. He never said where the manuscript exactly came from, except that it was from 'the neighbourhood of the Tigris' (*The Odes and Psalms of Solomon: Now First Published from the Syriac Version* [Cambridge: Cambridge University Press, 1909], p. 3). As far as I have been able to ascertain, at that time Rendel Harris had two major sources of Syriac manuscripts. One of them was the mission in Urmia (Moshe H. Goshen-Gottstein, *Syriac Manuscripts in the Harvard College Library: A Catalogue* [HSS, 23; Missoula, MT: Scholars Press, 1979], pp. 16-18). The other was Andrus in Mardin, which is near the Tigris ('Letters from American Missionaries in the

This discovery appeared in the major newspapers, and many translations were made of Rendel Harris's edition. Later on the Rylands Library entrusted him and Alphonse Mingana with the task of re-publishing the manuscript with commentary.[56]

More manuscripts were found by Mingana.[57] Mingana had arrived at Woodbrooke in 1913. Coming from Iraq, and fluent in Arabic, Hebrew, Syriac, Persian, Kurdish, Latin and French, but not in English, he was looking for support, a step suggested to him by Andrus in Mardin. Rendel Harris immediately recognized that a scholar of the first rank was at his disposal. In 1924, 1925, and 1929 he sent Mingana to the Near East with the financial backing of Edward Cadbury, George's son. The outcome of these expeditions is the outstanding Mingana collection, including Syriac, Arabic and Persian manuscripts.

In 1925 Rendel Harris returned to Selly Oak. His personal library became the Rendel Harris Library, near Woodbrooke, of which he was appointed head. To house the priceless collection gathered by Mingana a new library was built.[58]

The Holy Grail

Rendel Harris was not only a successful finder of precious manuscripts. After the war, his friend Adolf Deissmann had sent him a first century CE chalice. This cup presented a Greek inscription around the rim reading: 'Friend, what are you here for? Be merry!' The Greek of the first sentence corresponds exactly, but without the question mark, to the Greek of Matthew 26.50, according to which Jesus said to Judas in Gethsemane: 'Friend, you are here for this'. According to Rendel Harris, Jesus quoted to Judas words that were inscribed on the cup they had just used to drink. Several other cups of the same type have been found. From a cup of this sort, which Rendel Harris called 'the Holy Grail', Jesus may have drunk.[59]

Middle East', DA21/1/1/27, Special Collections, University of Birmingham). It is therefore very likely that the manuscript comes from Andrus. A detailed study of this question will appear in the biography of Rendel Harris.

56. *The Odes and Psalms of Solomon* (2 vols.; Manchester: Manchester University Press, 1916–1920).

57. Samir K. Samir, *Alphonse Mingana 1878–1937 and his Contribution to Early Christian Studies* (Birmingham: Selly Oak Colleges, 1990).

58. The library has in recent years moved to a new building and it is now the Orchard Learning Resources Centre, part of the University of Birmingham.

59. See 'Deissmann and the Holy Grail', *Expository Times* 35 (1924), pp. 523-24; 'Glass Chalices of the First Century', *BJRL* 11 (1927), pp. 286-95.

The Last Years

Progressive blindness no longer allowed Rendel Harris to study his beloved manuscripts, so that by the end of the twenties he turned his interest in other directions. In particular, he studied the migration of cultures and peoples in the most remote past.[60] For instance, he proposed evidence that the Egyptians colonized Europe and other continents. His hypotheses were most speculative, but they witness to a genius that did not fear to enjoy himself in daring scholarly adventures. Rendel Harris carried on research until he died in Birmingham on 1 March 1941.

---

60. See the collections of essays: *Woodbrooke Essays* (Cambridge: Heffer, 1927–28); *Caravan Essays* (Cambridge: Heffer, 1929); *Sunset Essays* (Cambridge: Heffer, 1930–31); *Evergreen Essays* (Cambridge: Heffer, 1931–32); *The After-Glow Essays* (London: University of London Press, 1933–35). See also *The Migration of Culture: Two Essays, with Maps* (Oxford: Blackwell, 1936).

ΙΩΑΝΟΥ Β

ο πρεσβυτερος εκλε
κτη κυρια και τοις
κνοις αυτης ους εγω
αγαπω εν αληθεια και
ουκ εγω μονος αλλα
και παντες οι εγνωκο
τες την αληθειαν δια
την αληθειαν την με
νουσαν εν ημιν και
μεθ ημων εσται εις
τον αιωνα εσται με
θ ημων χαρις ελεος
ειρηνη παρα θυ πατρος
και παρα ιυ χυ του υι

ου του πατρος εν αλη
θεια και αγαπη εχα
ρην λιαν οτι ευρηκα
εκ των τεκνων σου
περιπατουντας εν α
ληθεια καθως εντο
λην ελαβομεν παρα
του πατρος και νυν ε
ρωτω σε κυρια ουχ ως
εντολην γραφων σοι
καινην αλλα ην ειχο
μεν απ αρχης ινα α
γαπωμεν αλληλους και
αυτη εστιν η αγαπη ινα

περιπατωμεν κατα
τας εντολας αυτου
αυτη η εντολη εστιν
καθως ηκουσατε απ
αρχης ινα εν αυτη
περιπατητε οτι πολ
λοι πλανοι εξηλθον
εις τον κοσμον οι μη
ομολογουντες ιην χρν
ερχομενον εν σαρκι
ουτος εστιν ο πλανος
και ο αντιχριστος
βλεπετε εαυτους ι
να μη απολεσητε α ηρ

γασαμεθα αλλα μισθο
πληρη απολαβητε πας
ο προαγων και με
νων εν τη διδαχη του
χυ θν ουκ εχει ο μενων
εν τη διδαχη ουτος και
τον πατερα και τον
υιον εχει ει τις ερχετ
αι προς υμας και ταυ
την την διδαχην ου
φερει μη λαμβανετε
αυτον εις οικιαν και
χαιρειν αυτω μη λεγ
ετε ο λεγων γαρ αυτω

χαιρειν κοινωνει τοις
εργοις αυτου τοις πο
νηροις πολλα εχων
υμιν γραφειν ουκ εβου
ληθην δια χαρτου και
μελανος αλλα ελπιζω
γενεσθαι προς υμας
και στομα προς στομα
λαλησαι ινα η χαρα
ημων πεπληρωμενη
ασπαζεται σε τα
τεκνα της αδελφης
της εκλεκτης

Chapter 1

New Testament Autographs

Preface[1]

A few words of introduction are necessary to the investigations contained in the following pages, in order to remove some of the perplexity which may hang around the enunciation of the theory which they contain.

In the course of an examination of the columnar arrangement of the text of the oldest MS of the New Testament, my attention was drawn to a remarkable numerical peculiarity in the arrangement of the lines and columns of the several books, and from this my mind was forced to the conclusion that the scribes of the New Testament produced Epistles more uniformly written and at the closing page more frequently filled than is the custom at the present day; and that it was, in fact, possible to reproduce the original pages by a simple process of numerical subdivision, if only the MS had preserved the lines of the original writing. Further study of the Vatican Codex showed that a large number of the books of the New Testament were capable of this subdivision (by the very simple process of dividing the column of the MS into three equal parts), and that the pages resulting from the subdivision were very closely related to the original pages.

Perhaps this will become easier to apprehend by a simple variation of the statement. Imagine a printed book, in which there are, let us say, ten equal pages, of thirty lines to each page, printed uniformly. If a reprint be made of this book in any other form, i.e. on pages and with lines of a different size to the copy, it is evident that the original arrangement of the book will be lost, and it is very unlikely that the last page of the new book will be a complete one. If, however, the printer adheres to the original lines, no matter how he may change his pages or his type, we shall always be able to restore the book to its original shape by simple subdivision of its 300 lines into ten pages, although, of course, the subdivision may not be easy to detect, nor to demonstrate. This is what has happened in the Vatican MS; the scribe has retained

---

1. [The corrections listed in the "Errata" at the end of the essay have been transferred to the text. AF]

the original line, and in a certain sense has preserved the original page also, since he made his column (as the investigation will show) by placing three of the original pages in a vertical line. This fundamental fact is the key to the method of textual criticism to which these pages form an introduction.

New Testament Autographs

A. 1. In the course of the first lecture, which I had the honor of delivering in this University,[2] on the Textual Criticism of the New Testament, I pointed out that the material of the Second and Third Epistles of St John was probably a sheet or series of sheets of papyrus; and not only so, but that in the two documents mentioned, the sheet of paper was of a given size, capable of holding a given quantity of uncials. The first of these statements was based upon the allusion which the writer makes to paper, pen, and ink (διὰ χάρτου καὶ μέλανος, 2 John 12; διὰ μέλανος καὶ καλάμου, 3 John 13); while the second statement was an inference from the equality in the contents of the two Epistles, which in Westcott and Hort's edition of the New Testament occupy twenty-nine lines of type apiece, and from the evidence that in each case the writer had completely filled the sheet on which he was writing, since he complains of the insufficiency of his writing materials (πολλὰ ἔχων ὑμῖν γράφειν, πολλὰ εἶχον γράψαι σοι).[3] From this point we are led to the enquiry as to the usual size of the sheets of paper employed in the New Testament documents, and the number employed in the autographs of the several books.

2. In order to make the enquiry carefully, we will first tabulate the number of columns and lines occupied by the uncial letters of the separate texts, as they are presented in the oldest known manuscripts. We begin, then, with the Vatican Codex, B. This manuscript is written in columns, three to the page, and each column contains 42 lines of uncial writing. Omitting the Epistle to the Hebrews, the latter part of which is in a later cursive hand, and the Apocalypse which is also supplied in cursive character,[4] we construct the following table:

---

2. [Johns Hopkins University, Baltimore. AF]
3. [2 John 12; 3 John 13. AF]
4. Scrivener adds the Pastoral Epistles (*Introduction*, p. 96 [Frederick H.A. Scrivener, *A Plain Introduction to the Criticism of the New Testament for the Use of Biblical Students* (Cambridge: Deighton, Bell, 1861). AF]), apparently following Cardinal Mai, but I can find no trace of them in the Roman edition [Angelo Mai (ed.), *Vetus et Novum Testamentum ex antiquissimo Codice Vaticano* (Rome: Josephus Spithöver, 1857). AF]. The Palaeographical Society, in the description accompanying their facsimile, follow Scrivener.

1. *New Testament Autographs*

Table I.

	Columns	Lines	Total Lines
Matthew	127	9	5343
Mark	77	31	3265
Luke	136	41	5753
John	97	6	4080
Acts	130	3	5463
Romans	49	16	2074
1 Corinthians	46	6	1938
2 Corinthians	31	28	1330
Galatians	15	27	657
Ephesians	16	22	694
Philippians	11	0	462
Colossians	11	15	477
1 Thessalonians	10	28	448
2 Thessalonians	5	34	244
James	12	26	530
1 Peter	12	30	534
2 Peter	8	32	368
1 John	13	27	573
2 John	1	27	69
3 John	1	27	69
Jude	3	27	153

The first thing that strikes us on examining this table is that the compositions do not end, as one might suppose, at different points of the page according to random distribution, but they show a preference for ending at particular points, and especially at the 27th line. Out of the 21 documents cited, five end on the 27th line of the page, two on the 28th and one on the 26th. This is very remarkable.

3. If the compositions were of arbitrary length, the probability that five out of the twenty-one should end on the same particular line is small indeed. Unless I am mistaken, it would be represented by the fraction

$$\frac{21 \cdot 20 \cdot 19 \cdot 18 \cdot 17}{1 \cdot 2 \cdot 3 \cdot 4 \cdot 5} \cdot \left(\frac{1}{42}\right)^5 \cdot \left(\frac{41}{42}\right)^{16}$$

which is evidently much less than ($1/_{1 \cdot 2 \cdot 3 \cdot 4 \cdot 5} \cdot 1/_{32}$) or $1/_{3840}$. We may be sure then that the odds are at least four thousand to one against such a conjunction of endings being the work of *chance*.

It is evident that the eight compositions alluded to, viz. 2 Corinthians, Galatians, 1 Thessalonians, James, the three Epistles of John, and Jude, are each written on an integral number of sheets of a given size; and further, this sheet of given size must bear a peculiar relation both to the whole column of the Vatican Codex consisting of 42 lines, and to the fractional column of 27 lines; for, otherwise, it would not be possible for documents of different length, even though written on sheets of given size, to end at the same place on the Vatican page. If we allow a line for the subscription of those Epistles which end at the 27th line, we have to seek a submultiple of 28 and 42; and we at once see that 14 lines of the Vatican Codex bears some multiple proportion to the size of a page of the original writing, and in all probability, in the cases referred to, we may say that 14 lines of the Vatican Codex represents exactly the page of the autograph, the only submultiples of 14 being 7 and 2. This provides us with a unit upon which to base our calculations, which for convenience we will denominate a V-page.

4. We see, then, that of the Epistles especially referred to,

2 Corinthians	= 95 V-pages exactly.
Galatians	= 47 V-pages, wanting one line.
1 Thessalonians	= 32 V-pages exactly.
James	= 38 V-pages, wanting two lines.
1 John	= 41 V-pages, wanting one line.
2 John } each 3 John	= 5 V-pages, wanting one line.
Jude	= 11 V-pages, wanting one line.

With regard to these conclusions, the single line left blank in the letter is probably left for subscription; in the case of the Epistle to the Galatians we have the additional explanation that there was a passage in it written in large letters by the Apostle Paul's own hand, and when this sentence is copied there is a slight contraction in the copy as compared with the original.

With regard to St James, we find two lines wanting; either, therefore, his handwriting is larger than ordinary, or we may assume that he actually left a somewhat larger blank space than was usual with the other writers, who evidently economized every inch of paper. The sheet of paper, too, is noticeably a small one; it is only capable of containing 14 lines of average length, about 17 letters each: this also is explicable by the supposition of economy, for the cost of a sheet of papyrus increases with the size of a sheet, but in a much greater ratio than the sheet, on account of the difficulty of finding plants or reeds of a very great length and section. We can see, then, that the cheapest paper is used, and no space spared.

Now turn to the table again, and observing that our manuscript-unit is fourteen lines of the Vatican Codex, we see that in the autograph

Philippians = 33 V-pages exactly.

We come, then, to a group of three Epistles which run slightly over an exact number of pages; thus:

1. *New Testament Autographs*

Romans occupies	148	V-pages and two lines.
Colossians	33	V-pages and one line.
1 Peter	38	V-pages and two lines.

With regard to the Epistle to the Romans, it is not inconceivable that in 148 pages the copy should have gained two lines on the autograph; the study of the Epistle is, however, complicated by the existence of important various readings, and by the doubtful character of its concluding portion, which seems rather to be addressed to an Ephesian than a Roman community, and by the questionable authenticity of its doxologies. We content ourselves, for the present, by saying that the Epistle, as it stands in Codex B, probably represents 148 pages of the autograph.

With regard to the Epistle to the Colossians the question is more simple, as the document is shorter. Four lines of this Epistle, at least, are from the hand of Paul himself, and would therefore be in larger characters than usual; this would make the original document longer than 33 V-pages and one line. Either, therefore, the greater part of a page was left blank, which is unlikely; or Codex B has inserted words in the text, or the amanuensis of Paul (Tychicus, Onesimus?) must have written a smaller hand than was normal.

We leave the matter for the present undecided.

Similar remarks will apply to the First Epistle of Peter.

We annex the Second Epistle of John, as we imagine it to have stood on the original sheets.

When we turn to the Gospels we have a much more difficult question to examine, on account of the multitude of various readings. We shall simply remark that the Gospel of Luke, in Codex B, is within a line of the end of a column, so that

Luke = 411 V-pages, wanting a single line.

In the Gospel of St John, if we omit the last verse, we find ourselves at the end of a page, and

John = 291 V-pages exactly.

It will have been noticed that the number of V-pages occupied by the documents discussed is more often odd than even, which is more consistent with the hypothesis of papyrus sheets written on one side only, than with the supposition of a material capable of being written on both sides.[5]

---

5. The more delicate papyri are quite unsuited to the reception of writing on both sides: that species, in particular, which was held in the highest Roman estimation, and honored with the name of Augustus, was so fine as to be almost transparent, so that its extreme tenuity came to be regarded as a defect.

For a document to be written on both sides seems to be a mark of the poverty of the writer or the over-productiveness of his brain: thus we find in Juvenal I 5 [*Sat.* 1.4-5. AF]:

5. We shall now turn our attention to the Sinaitic Codex, which is written in columns, four to each page, and in lines, 48 to each column.[6] The difficulty in this case will arise from the fact that the lines of the text are not nearly so uniform as in the Codex Vaticanus, and in the first two Gospels in particular the text is broken up into paragraphs, and the recurrence of short lines, unless it be a genealogical feature of the successive MS, will prevent us from tracing the structure of the original documents. We proceed, however, to form our second table, constructed in the same way as the previous one, and containing a larger collection of books. The lines in this manuscript are shorter than in B, by several letters.

Table II

	Columns	Lines	Total Lines
Matthew	139	1	6672
Three letters only in the residual line.			
Mark	85	4	4084
Luke	149	24	7176
John	107	35	5171
Acts	146	10	7018
Romans	53	6	2550
1 Corinthians	51	12	2460
2 Corinthians	35	6	1686
Galatians	16	45	813
Ephesians	18	5	869
Philippians	12	9	585
Colossians	12	13	589
1 Thessalonians	11	21	549
2 Thessalonians	6	3	291
Hebrews	40	24	1944
1 Timothy	13	40	664
2 Timothy	10	3	483

Summa pleni jam margine libri
Scriptus et in tergo, necdum finitus Orestes.

Lucian, *Vit. Auct.* 9, represents Diogenes as saying ἡ πήρα δέ σοι θέρμων ἔστω μεστὴ καὶ ὀπισθογράφων βιβλίων.

Scripture students will call to mind an illustration of a similar kind in the Apocalypse, where the plenitude of coming judgments and tribulations is represented by a book or paper-roll written both outside and inside (Rev. 5.1).

6. This is not always true; in the Catholic Epistles the scribe has frequently contented himself with a column of 47 lines. I do not know whether this peculiarity has ever been noted. Scrivener, in his collation of the Sinaitic MS, does not seem to allude to it. Our results, as given in the table, must be corrected for the aberration of the scribe, when we come to analyse the documents more closely.

1. *New Testament Autographs*   23

	Columns	Lines	Total Lines
Titus	5	37	277
Philemon	2	24	120
James	13	33	657
1 Peter	14	9	681
2 Peter	9	24	456
1 John	15	12	732
2 John	1	39	87
3 John	1	39	87
Jude	4	6	198
Revelation	68	12	3276
Barnabas	53	18	2562

The first thing we notice is that the distribution of the concluding lines of the books is much more varied and irregular. The only thing that is remarkable is the recurrence of the multiples of twelve; three books end at the twelfth line, viz. 1 Corinthians, 1 John, Revelation; four end on the 24th line: Luke, Hebrews, Philemon, and 2 Peter; the Gospel of John ends on the 35th line, which may practically be counted as the 36th.[7] This, again, can hardly be

---

7. It may be asked why, in discussing this table, we pay no attention to the repetition of the sixth line as an ending of three books, nor to the double recurrence of the number three. I have no theoretical objection to urge against either of these numbers, seeing that they are both submultiples of the whole column of 48 lines; but practically they are too small subdivisions, and their recurrence is accidental. The probability that out of 28 books, one number should recur in the line-endings three times (I do not say this time a particular number) is roughly represented by

$$48 \cdot \frac{28 \cdot 27 \cdot 26}{1 \cdot 2 \cdot 3} \cdot \left(\frac{1}{48}\right)^3 \cdot \left(\frac{47}{48}\right)^{25}$$

whose value is nearly $21/25$.

It is almost certain, then, that such an event as the recurrence alluded to will be found in our table. Those who are interested in observing these occurrences may study the following table from the Codex Sinaiticus:

Tobit	ends on line	3	Jonah	ends on line	45
Judith	"	" 23	Nahum	"	" 15
1 Macc	"	" 38	Habakkuk	"	" 21
4 Macc	"	" 37	Zephaniah	"	" 16
Isaiah	"	" 14	Haggai	"	" 3
Joel	"	" 19	Zechariah	"	" 38
Obadiah	"	" 28	Malachi	"	" 20

Here every ending is formed by random distribution (unless we except the book of Judith and the Maccabees), for the works referred to are translations, and have therefore no pattern; yet there is a double recurrence of the 3, and of the 38 with its submultiple 19. These accidental; we may assume that in the cases alluded to, with the exception of the First Epistle of John, which, on account of the irregular length of the columns, furnishes an accidental coincidence, there is a unit sheet of paper employed, capable of containing 12 lines of the Sinaitic Codex; we shall therefore have a new leaf of paper (for reference to which we adopt the expression S-page, in order to distinguish it from the previous V-page), by means of which to measure our documents.

With regard to the comparative sizes of the two pages, it is evident at a glance that the S-page is smaller than the V-page, for it contains twelve lines where the other has fourteen, and has a smaller number of letters to the line.

6. We thus get the key to the method by which the text of the papyrus leaves was reduced into the shape in which we find it in the oldest manuscripts. Codex B selects the larger type of page, and arranges them nine on a page, or three in a side; while the Sinaitic Codex selects the smaller leaf, and arranges them sixteen on a page, four in a side. And it is this arrangement which Eusebius[8] describes when he says that the accurate MSS, prepared by order of Constantine, were written τρισσὰ καὶ τετρασσά; i.e. as we should say, in a square whose side is three, or in a square whose side is four. The V-pages, then, are arranged τρισσά, and the S-pages τετρασσά.

7. Now, examining our second table, we see at once that the Sinaitic Codex gives

Gospel of Matthew	=	556	S-pages, and three letters.
Gospel of Luke	=	598	S-pages.
1 Corinthians	=	205	S-pages exactly.
Hebrews	=	162	" "
Philemon	=	10	" "
2 Peter	=	38	" "
Revelation	=	273	" "

We may perhaps conjecture that Titus should be added to the list, as containing 23 S-pages and one line; while the Epistle to the Colossians is again doubtful, comprising 49 leaves and one line. We have thus deduced the type of almost all the Epistles, some of them with great exactness; and we observe that they fall into two groups, with the exception of some four or five Epistles, which either are not written so as to fill the paper, or are written on paper of a different size to the two sorts we have been considering, or on a different pattern.

8. When we turn to the Gospels we have a harder problem to solve, but I think we may say that if the two principal types of the early MSS are those

---

are, of course, purely accidental. The recurrence would have to be more frequent before we should notice it, or look for any concealed cause at work to produce such a result.

8. Eusebius, *Vit. Const.* IV 37 [4.37.1. AF].

indicated as τρισσά and τετρασσά, then it is far more likely that those types were found in the Gospels than that they were merely adopted from the Epistles. We may therefore expect to find some of the Gospels written τρισσά and some τετρασσά, or rather some on the V-page and some on the S-page. The question is, how shall we determine the type of the autograph for any particular Gospel? And here an important remark must be made. I am aware that every one of these results and suggestions is subject to a disturbing factor of the greatest moment, viz. the question of various readings in the text, and of accidental omissions or insertions of passages or lines in the great Codices. The disturbance will be most to be apprehended in the case of the longer compositions, and with regard to these all our results must be looked upon at first as tentative. But in the smaller writings the various readings are generally so few and unimportant that the majority of our results may be regarded as unaffected by them. We will, however, examine the effect of these various readings in each of the separate books. It is the more important to do this carefully, because the Sinaitic and Vatican Codices are known to contain a number of apparent insertions and omissions and repetitions, which have been held up by a certain school as convincing proof of their unreliable character as witnesses to the text of the New Testament.

Dr Dobbin gave in the *Dublin University Magazine* for November, 1859,[9] a calculation of the omissions of Codex B in the different books of the New Testament, in which we find for

Matthew	330 omissions.	Jude	11 omissions.
Mark	365 "	Romans	106 "
Luke	439 "	1 Corinthians	146 "
John	357 "	2 Corinthians	74 "
Acts	384 "	Galatians	37 "
James	41 "	Ephesians	53 "
1 Peter	46 "	Phillippians	21 "
2 Peter	20 "	Colossians	36 "
1 John	16 "	1 Thessalonians	21 "
2 John	3 "	2 Thessalonians	10 "
3 John	2 "		

An appalling table, certainly, and one which, if we did not remember that the figures are the result of a collation with the Textus Receptus, and that the majority of them refer to wholly insignificant readings, would almost make us despair of finding in the Vatican or Sinaitic MSS any traces of the original style and size of the books of the New Testament. We will, however, discuss any important readings that may occur, and after having first carefully dissected the text of St John, and examined the bearing of our investigation

---

9. [Orlando T. Dobbin, "The Vatican Manuscript," *Dublin University Magazine* 54 (1859), pp. 614-29. AF]

upon the stichometry of the New Testament, we will proceed to the Epistles, beginning with the smaller ones, and so working up to the longer Epistles, the Acts and the Gospels. And no result of the previous tentative examination is to be allowed to pass unchallenged or unverified.

9. We begin with the Gospel according to John. In the Vatican Codex this occupies 97 columns and six lines. In the Sinaitic Codex it occupies 107 columns and 35 lines. At first sight, therefore, it seems that the Gospel is written on the S-page, with only a deficiency of one line from a total of 431 S-pages. But here comes in the question of the last verse of the Gospel,[10] which Tischendorf observed to be written in the Sinaitic MSS by a different hand, and many scholia to different MSS affirm to be an addition. Removing this verse, eight lines of the Codex, the S-page is of course no longer apparent. But strange to say, when the verse is also removed from Codex B, in which it occupies six lines at the top of a page, we are left with a Gospel terminating at the end of a page, and in our notation occupying exactly 291 V-pages. The Gospel of John is, therefore, probably written on the V-page, and the apparent contradiction of this statement by the Sinaitic Codex may be due to the fact that in the type of MSS which that Codex has been following some one has utilized part of the blank space at the latter half of a column for the insertion of a sentence as to the number of books that might have been written. The addition must have been earlier than the age of vellum MSS, and may have arisen in the transcription of the Gospel of John from the larger-sized paper to the smaller, since it nearly fills the blank in a smaller sheet, and that sheet not the lowest in a Sinaitic column.

10. This conclusion with regard to the autograph of St John leads to very important consequences with regard to the celebrated pericope of the woman taken in adultery.[11] An examination of this passage shows that there are 908 letters either inserted in the text or dropped from it. Now the average number of letters to the line in St John's Gospel in the Codex Vaticanus is 16.4, from whence we conclude that the passage in question is equivalent to about 56 lines of Codex B, i.e. to four V-pages exactly. Now it is obvious that four such pages could not by any possibility have been excised from a document in which the V-pages are arranged nine in a square. They must, therefore, have been lost from the original document before it came into the shape represented by Codex B. Their reinsertion has been characterized by great awkwardness in later manuscripts, and breaks the continuity of the narrative. They have been, in fact, restored to a place which they did not previously occupy.

Before going further we insert a reproduction of the four pages which we have reason to believe the lost passage to have occupied.

10. [John 21.25. AF]
11. [John 7.53-8.11. AF]

1. *New Testament Autographs*

As a restoration of the text of B, it is not quite a successful effort. I have not, I find, done justice to the syllabic division followed by the scribe, who has a distinct custom in ending his lines and dividing his words, and prefers, if possible, to write a seven-syllabled line. Moreover, some of the most capriciously concluded lines are meant to be syllabically divided, such as those which end with ου and leave the κ of the οὐκ to be carried to the next line. This division occurs so frequently that it is evident that the scribe, in writing such words as οὐκ ἔστιν, really regards the κ as a sort of prefix to the verb.

We may now proceed to determine the place where the celebrated pericope should be reinserted. Turning to the end of the fifth chapter, we find that it closes with the words: "There is one that accuseth you, even Moses on whom ye trust. For if ye had believed Moses, ye would have believed me; but if ye do not believe his writings, how can ye believe my words?" The scene then changes abruptly to Galilee: "After these things Jesus departed to the other side of the sea of Galilee from Tiberias."[12] It is between these chapters that I would locate the pericope. The fifth chapter narrates how Jesus found in the temple the man whom he had healed at the pool of Bethesda; it describes the long subsequent discussion with the Pharisees, which must have taken nearly all day, after which they depart, each man to his own house, but Jesus to the Mount of Olives. Appropriately the Pharisees bring him next morning the woman for judgment, with the remark that "Moses in the law said ... but what sayest thou?"[13] Codex D, which gives the pericope in somewhat shorter form, is even more forcible, τί δὲ νῦν λέγεις; we conclude, then, that this is a far more likely place to locate the pericope than at the end of the seventh chapter.

This readjustment of the text at once removes many of the objections urged against its authenticity, and it also helps to fill up that unsightly chasm at the close of the fifth chapter. It is unnecessary to discuss in detail the objections which had been raised by critics to the passage as it originally stood, but we will quote a single one out of many difficulties urged, as given by Davidson in his *Introduction to the New Testament*, I 363.[14] He says: "The greatest perplexity connected with the passage lies in the reason for bringing the case before Jesus. No adequate motive appears to induce the Scribes and Pharisees to employ this woman for the purpose of embarrassing the Redeemer, and thence extracting a ground of accusation against him. It is evident that they wished to entrap him; the narrative itself states that they tempted him in order

---

12. [John 5.45–6.1. AF]
13. [John 8.5. AF]
14. [Samuel Davidson, *An Introduction to the New Testament: Containing an Examination of the Most Important Questions Relating to the Authority, Interpretation, and Integrity of the Canonical Books, with Reference to the Latest Inquiries* (3 vols.; London: Samuel Bagster, 1848–1851). AF]

1. *New Testament Autographs*

to procure a tangible charge, but how they expected to do so by means of the adulteress is exceedingly obscure." I hope the obscurity disappears in the new arrangement of the text, and that the passage is more harmoniously placed with regard to the context than previously.

Moreover there is this difficulty, that in the ordinary supposition these lost V-pages would begin four lines from the top of the page, and we should have to assume that Codex B had either added four lines to the autograph, or lost ten lines in the first seven chapters, before we could rectify the pages so as to reintroduce the lost columns of the papyrus. Neither of these suppositions seems likely, as the text of John in these chapters is remarkably good, and the text of B is more likely to be marked by omissions than insertions.

On our hypothesis they begin on the last line of the left-hand column of the page, and we have only to assume that a single line has been lost from Codex B in the first five chapters. We proceed to go in search of this lost line. The Gospel of John in B has comparatively few various readings in the shape of insertions or omissions. The majority of them consist of transpositions and changes of merely verbal importance. We proceed to tabulate those of them which affect our enquiry, from the principal editors and MSS.

	Letters	Text. Rec.	ℵ	B.	W. H.	T.	Tr.[15]
1.5. τῶν ἀνθρώπων	11	+	+	–	+	+	+
1.13. οὐδὲ ἐκ θελήματος ἀνδρός	21	+	+	–	+	+	+
1.27. ὃς ἔμπροσθεν ...	21	+	–	–	–	–	–
2.2. A long variant in the Sinaitic, but very doubtful.							
3.13. ὁ ὢν ἐν τῷ οὐρανῷ	13	+	+	–	–	+	+
3.31. ἐπάνω πάντων ἐστίν	16	+	–	+	+	–	+
4.9. οὐ γὰρ συνχρῶνται ...	34	+	–	+	+	+	+
4.14. οὐ μὴ διψήσῃ ...	40	+	+	+	+	+	+
5.12. τὸν κράβαττόν σου	15	+	+	–	–	–	[+]
5.16. καὶ ἐζήτουν ...	25	+	–	–	–	–	–
5.45. πρὸς τὸν πατέρα repeated	13	–	–	+	–	–	–

Reviewing the variants of the text of B thus far, we find four cases of probable omission, and two of insertion. If we allow that B is right in omitting τὸν κράβαττόν σου, the result is a balance of a line to be added, which suits our case exactly.

11. We must now examine the remainder of the Gospel in the same manner.

---

15. [Textus Receptus; Codex Sinaiticus; Codex Vaticanus; Westcott and Hort, *New Testament*; Konstantin von Tischendorf (ed.), *Novum Testamentum Graece ... Editio octava critica maior* (3 vols.; Leipzig: Giesecke & Devrient, 1869–1894); Samuel P. Tregelles (ed.), *The Greek Testament: Edited from Ancient Authorities with their Various Readings in Full and the Latin Version of Jerome* (7 vols.; London: Samuel Bagster, C.J. Stewart, 1857–1879). AF]

	Letters	Text. Rec.	ℵ	B.	W. H.	T.	Tr.
6.11. τοῖς μαθηταῖς ...	23	+	–	–	–	–	–
6.22. ἐκεῖνο εἰς ὅ ...	27	+	+	–	–	–	–
7.30. ἅγιον δεδομένον	14	+	–	–	–	–	[+]
7.46. ὡς οὗτος ὁ ἄνθρωπος	16	+	+	–	–	+	[+]
8.52. B reads incorrectly, but the passage is of the same length as the ordinary reading.							
8.59. διελθών ...	34	+	–	–	–	–	–
9.7. B has dropped a line by ὁμοιοτέλευτον.							
9.36. ἀπεκρίθη ...	23	+	+	–	[+]	–	+
10.13. τὰ πρόβατα ...	26	+	–	–	–	–	–
10.26. καθὼς εἶπον ὑμῖν	14	+	–	–	–	–	–
11.40. οὗ ἦν ὁ τεθνηκώς	21	+	–	–	–	–	–
13.10. εἰ μὴ τοὺς πόδας	13	+	–	+	[+]	–	+
13.14. B repeats two lines and a half.							
13.24. B has a slightly longer reading.							
13.32. εἰ ὁ θεός ...	21	+	–	–	–	+	[+]
14.4. καὶ οἴδατε	9	+	+	–	–	–	–
14.5. δυνάμεθα	8	+	+	–	–	–	–
16.16. ὅτι ὑπάγω ...	21	+	–	–	–	–	–
17.15. (κ)όσμου ἀλλά ... omitted	35	+	+	–	+	+	+
17.18. κἀγὼ ἀπέστειλα repeated	31	–	–	+	–	–	–

The total result of our examination of this passage is that perhaps one or two lines might be added to the text of B, but the text has repeated more than five lines and dropped only three, so the total result is hardly affected.

It will be seen that we have made no allusion to the account of the troubling of the waters at Bethesda,[16] which does not occupy a distinct number of V-pages.

But we must not altogether pass the passage by, for it enables us to see why the pericope *de adultera* came to be inserted in the wrong place. There is no doubt whatever that the gloss in question is very early, seeing that we find a striking reference to it in Tertullian, *De Baptism.* 9.[17] Written on the V-pattern, the passage John 5.3-4 would occupy about 10 lines of manuscript. Bearing in mind that the passage to which the pericope *de adultera* has been wrongly restored is four lines from the beginning of a column, and adding the gloss on the Troubling of the Water to the fifth chapter, we have now moved the inserted pericope to the beginning of a V-page. Each of the three errors, viz. the omission of the pericope, its reinsertion, and the insertion of the gloss in chapter V, is therefore anterior to the age of vellum manuscripts, and we can even arrange the errors in their proper chronological order. Perhaps we

16. [John 5.4. AF]
17. [*Bapt.* 9.4. AF]

ought to have added that in the same interval of time a balance of a single line was lost from the first five chapters of B.

The majority of the errors are of the V-type, that is, there are more V-lines than S-lines inserted or omitted. And this is just what we should expect, if the MSS were originally of the V-pattern; and we may lay down the following general principle: *A manuscript originally written on a certain pattern will generally show a majority of errors of the pattern on which it is written.* The advantage of this proposition is that it will help us to determine the original character of a MS, whether the MS occupy an exact number of pages of its pattern or not. We are now in the position to print the Gospel of John, approximately, from the original sheets.

No one can study the Gospel carefully without noticing the discontinuity of many of its sequences. The probability is that some passages are still lost from the 500 original sheets of the Gospel.

12. Now let us turn to the close of the Gospel and examine the endings of the 20th and 21st chapters: the similarity of the 30th verse of the 20th chapter to the last verse of the 21st chapter is unmistakable.[18] The Gospel has apparently two endings. And here comes in the remarkable fact that Tertullian calls the 30th verse of the 20th chapter the close of the Gospel, although he quotes from the 21st chapter in at least two places: "Ipsa quoque clausula Evangelii propter quid consignat haec scripta, nisi, ut credatis, inquit Iesum Christum filium Dei?"[19] The proper place for the two closing verses of the 20th chapter is most likely at the end of the 21st chapter.

For the expression that there were "many other signs not recorded which Jesus wrought"[20] implies (just as the expression "I had many things to write to you" in the Second and Third of John[21]) an insufficiency of writing material; we are close to the end of the roll of paper.

In the next place, the restoration of the closing verses of the 20th chapter to the end of the 21st is strikingly harmonious with the introduction of the Gospel, to which it returns as a keynote, and with the 24th verse of the 21st chapter which precedes it.

And thirdly there is room for a single conjectural emendation which adds vividness to the narrative. In 21.30,[22] after ἐνώπιον τῶν μαθητῶν, many important MSS, especially those which exhibit a Western text, insert αὐτοῦ. It is a lawful suggestion that the original reading was simply ἐνώπιον αὐτοῦ, which was altered as soon as the verse had become severed from its proper connection.

18. [John 21.25. AF]
19. Tertullian, *Adv. Praxeam*, 25 [25.4. AF].
20. [John 20.30. AF]
21. [2 John 12; 3 John 13. AF]
22. [John 20.30. AF]

The Gospel now closes as follows:

> Οὗτός ἐστιν ὁ μαρτυρῶν τούτων καὶ ὁ γράψας ταῦτα, καὶ οἴδαμεν ὅτι ἀληθὴς αὐτοῦ ἡ μαρτυρία ἐστίν· πολλὰ μὲν οὖν καὶ ἄλλα σημεῖα ἐποίησεν ὁ Ἰησοῦς ἐνώπιον αὐτοῦ ἃ οὐκ ἔστιν γεγραμμένα ἐν τῷ βιβλίῳ τούτῳ· ταῦτα δὲ γέγραπται ἵνα πιστεύητε ὅτι Ἰησοῦς ἐστιν ὁ Χριστὸς ὁ υἱὸς τοῦ Θεοῦ καὶ ἵνα πιστεύοντες ζωὴν ἔχητε ἐν τῷ ὀνόματι αὐτοῦ.

13. We now proceed to state the further results at which we have arrived for the several books of the New Testament, postponing the critical details to a subsequent page. It will be convenient to tabulate, as far as possible, the whole of the results in a form suitable to a critical comparison.[23]

We have, on the basis of the previous investigation, constructed a column in the table showing the ratio of the V-line to the S-line for different books.

If a book contains m lines in the Sinaitic and n in the Vatican Codex, we have, other things being equal, $mS = nV$, or

$$\frac{V}{S} = \frac{m}{n}$$

where V and S represent the V- and S-line respectively. But this ratio must be corrected for omissions and insertions; if, for example, B omits q lines of the original, the ratio ought to be $m/(n+q)$, or it is diminished in the ratio $n : n + q$, or giving p either sign, and reserving the + sign for omissions, the ratio is altered by the fraction $n/(n \pm q)$. Similarly, if the Sinaitic Codex omits p lines, the ratio is altered by $(m \pm p)/m$. Change in the style of a writer will also affect the number of lines, etc., but at any rate we can see that, as a general rule, *books written in the same style and by the same author will be similarly affected by the processes of transcription.*

Referring to our table we have ratios as follows:

John 1:267	1 John 1:277
2 John 1:260	3 John 1:260

results so nearly coincident that they suggest the same hand in the original documents.

But this remark must not be unduly pressed; for, strictly speaking, if any book is written out on the same two given patterns, the ratio of the lines is fixed, for V and S are fixed, and $m/n = V/S$.

---

23. [See Table III, opposite. AF]

Table III

	Sinaitic			Vatican				Probable number of S-pages	Probable number of V-pages	Probable number of sheets bought	Ratio of V-line to S-line, uncorrected for omissions, etc.	Average Letters to the line	
	Col.	Line	Total	Col.	Line	Total	S or V					S	V
Matthew	139	1	6672	127	9	5343					1.249	13.24	16.8
Mark	85	4	4084	77	31	3265					1.250	13.04	16.4
Luke	149	24	7176	136	41	5753					1.247	13.6	16.5
John	107	35	5171	97	6	4080					1.267	13.3	16.7
Acts	146	10	7018	130	3	5463	S				1.284		
1 Thessalonians	11	21	549	10	28	448	V				1.225		
2 Thessalonians	6	3	291	5	34	224	S	600		600	1.192		
1 Corinthians	51	12	2460	46	6	1938	SV	578	295	300	1.269		
2 Corinthians	35	6	1686	31	28	1330	S	46		600	1.267		
Galatians	16	45	813	15	27	657	S	24	32	50	1.236		
Romans	53	6	2550	49	16	2074	V	205			1.229		
Ephesians	18	5	869	16	22	694	V		95	100	1.252		
Philippians	12	9	585	11	0	462	V	73	47	50	1.266		
Colossians	12	13	589	11	15	477	S	49	147	150	1.232		
Philemon	2	24	120				SV	49	33				
1 Timothy	13	40	664				S	10		50			
2 Timothy	10	3	483				S			50			
Titus	5	37	277										
Hebrews	40	24	1944										
James	13	33	657	12	26	530	V		38	40	1.237		17.2
1 Peter	14	9	681	12	30	534	S	57		60	1.275		
2 Peter	9	24	456	8	32	368	S	38		40	1.239		
1 John	15	12	732	13	27	573	V		41		1.277		16.4
2 John	1	39	87	1	27	69	V		5		1.260		16.5
3 John	1	39	87	1	27	69	V		5		1.260		15.2
Jude	4	6	198	3	27	153	V		11		1.294		
Revelation	68	12	3276				S?	273					

Hence, when the text has been corrected, the column of ratios ought to be the same for all books. And the normal value of the ratio, if we allow 36 letters to the V-type for 28 to the S-type, is $9/7$, or 1:285. The first use of this table is to show, or rather suggest, omissions or insertions in a codex. When these are corrected for, there remains a residual effect upon the ratio produced by the variation in the hand of a scribe, induced by his copy being somewhat different from his normal style. And this residual effect may perhaps help us to classify the scribes of the different books.

We have grouped the Pauline Epistles in chronological order, and it is interesting to observe that those Epistles written at the same time show traces of being written in the same manner. Thus Galatians and Romans are both written on the V-page; between them they occupy 200 sheets of paper.

Ephesians, Philippians, Colossians, and Philemon are all written on the S-page (unless we must except Philippians). And the four Epistles together occupy 200 sheets of paper. The three Pastoral Epistles show traces of being written in the same style, but we have not been able to identify it. The two Epistles of Peter agree in this, that they are both written on the S-page.

B. 1. The resolution of the books of the New Testament into two main groups, characterized as the S-type and V-type respectively, has an important bearing upon the stichometry of the New Testament.

Professor Gildersleeve has drawn my attention to the analysis by which M. Ch. Graux showed in the *Revue de Philologie* for April, 1878,[24] that the στίχος, both in sacred and profane writers, represented not a verse, nor a clause, nor sentence, *but a fixed quantity of writing*. Evidence is offered in this article that copyists were paid at a fixed legal rate per 100 lines. Such a law would have been vain and illusory if early and constant tradition had not established what was to be understood by the length of the line. M. Graux estimates as nearly as possible the number of letters contained in a given work of some sacred or profane author, and divides this number by the number of στίχοι which the manuscript of the work declares it to contain. The results at which he arrives are very remarkable, being almost all of them included between 35 and 38 letters to the στίχος. From 50 consecutive lines in the *Iliad* opened at random, he deduces that the average Homeric line contains 37.7 letters.

The significance of these results can hardly be mistaken: they imply that the στίχος is equivalent to the Homeric line. Now if we apply this result of M. Graux to the case of the Codex Vaticanus, it is almost impossible to resist the conclusion that two lines of the Codex Vaticanus are meant to represent the same quantity; we have found by selecting 25 lines at random in Codex B

---

24. [Charles Graux, "Nouvelles recherches sur la stichométrie," *RevPhil* 2 (1878), pp. 97-144. AF]

that the average for a single line is nearly 17 letters; two such lines come very near to the average obtained by M. Graux. But if this be correct, what shall we say of the much shorter lines of the Sinaitic Codex? We are inclined to believe that they represent the half of an iambic line. Taking the average of 25 lines from the *Medea* of Euripides, we have 29.96 letters; but we have already found for the Codex Sinaiticus the number of letters to be nearly 14, which is not far from the half of the iambic line. These must therefore be two of the principal types of writing employed both before and after the time of the composition of the books of the New Testament: and these are the two principal types employed in the New Testament. The origin of what we have called the S-page and V-page respectively is therefore to be found in the iambic and hexameter lines.

These results admit of a very simple test. In the Epistle of James 1.17 we have an almost perfect hexameter:

πᾶσα δόσις ἀγαθὴ καὶ πᾶν δώρημα τέλειον.

Now this occupies exactly two lines in Codex B, as the following transcript will show:

ΠΑΣΑΔΟ
ΣΙΣΑΓΑΘΗΚΑΙΠΑΝΔΩ
ΡΗΜΑΤΕΛΕΙΟΝΑΝΩΘΗΝ

In the same way the iambic which St Paul quotes in 1 Cor. 15.34[25] from Menander:

φθείρουσιν ἤθη χρηστὰ ὁμιλίαι κακαί,

is exactly two lines in the Sinaitic Codex.

It will be noticed that our lines, as a general rule, fall a little short of the average hexameter and iambic. The reason for this lies in the fact that a scribe paid at so much a hundred lines, when copying some other work than Homer, selected a short line of Homer for his pattern. By this means the conventional στίχος is a little smaller. These στίχοι must not be confounded with the divisions of the text made by Euthalius, an Alexandrian deacon, in the fifth century, which does not proceed by letters, but apparently by words and sentences.

2. The allusion which we have made to the existence of an iambic στίχος explains a difficulty in Josephus. At the close of the *Jewish Antiquities* the writer says, Ἐπὶ τούτοις τε καταπαύσω τὴν ἀρχαιολογίαν, βίβλοις μὲν εἴκοσι περιειλημμένην, ἐξ δὲ μυριάσι στίχων.[26] M. Graux remarks on this that if we were to take the assertion of Josephus literally, that his work contained 60,000 στίχοι, we should find for the value of the στίχος the inadmissible

25. [1 Cor. 15.33. AF]
26. [*A.J.* 20.267. AF]

quantity 28 or 29 letters. He therefore proceeds to explain away the statement of Josephus, as being a rough expansion of the assertion that each of the twenty books of the *Antiquities* contained 2000 to 3000 στίχοι.

Birt, on the other hand (*Buchwesen*, p. 204),[27] attempts to evade the difficulty by changing ἐξ δὲ μυριάσι into ἐ δὲ μυριάσι, by means of which he deduces the Josephus-line to be 34.2 letters.

We have only to assume, however, that Josephus employs the iambic verse as his model, and the result arrived at by M. Graux needs no further explanation.

A singular corroboration of this assumption will be found by examining the lengths of some of Josephus' own letters as given by himself. I will here only briefly allude to one result out of many. If we examine the six letters contained in the life of Josephus, we shall find that the

Letter of	Jonathan to Josephus (*Vita* 44) contains	26	S-lines.
"	Josephus to Jonathan (*Vita* 44)	"	33	"
"	Jonathan to Josephus (*Vita* 45)	"	12	"
"	Josephus to Jonathan (*Vita* 45)	"	12	"
"	Agrippa to Josephus (*Vita* 65)	"	12	"
"	Agrippa to Josephus (*Vita* 65)	"	12	"

The recurrence of the number 12 is very remarkable, and four out of the six letters reduce at once to the S-pattern, while one of the remaining letters is only two lines in excess.

A similar remark will possibly apply to one or two other results of M. Graux. In calculating the value of the στίχος for the *Epistles of Clement*, as given in Gebhardt's editio minor,[28] by means of the data supplied by Nicephorus and Anastasius, he comes to the conclusion that the στίχος is 29 letters to which he affixes the mark of doubtfulness. We need only assume that the writing is based on the iambic στίχος and all is clear. M. Graux appears to accept as the mean result for the στίχος based on the Homeric line, a number of letters between 34 and 38 as limits, and with 36 for the normal type. If we allow the same latitude of limits, say take the normal iambic στίχος at 28 or 29 letters and allow limits 27 to 31 letters, we can at once explain several other results which were rather rejected by M. Graux as inconsistent with his theory, or were marked by him with a query.

3. But now let us return for a moment to M. Graux's estimate of 36 letters to the στίχος. The following passage from Eustathius, Bishop of Antioch in

---

27. [Theodor Birt, *Das antike Buchwesen in seinem Verhältnis zur Literatur: Mit Beiträgen zur Textgeschichte des Theokrit, Catull, Properz und anderen Autoren* (Berlin: Hertz, 1882). AF]

28. [Oscar von Gebhardt *et al.* (eds.), *Patrum apostolicorum opera ... Editio minor* (Leipzig, 1877). AF]

1. New Testament Autographs

the fourth century, will perhaps be a good test as far as the New Testament is concerned. In his treatise *De Engastrimytho*[29] we read as follows: ἦραν οὖν λίθους ἵνα βάλωσιν ἐπ' αὐτόν· ὡς δὲ ταῦτα προὔγραψεν ἐν τῷ μεταξὺ πέντε που καὶ τριάκοντα πρὸς τοῖς ἑκατὸν στίχους ὑπερβὰς ἐπιφέρει προσθείς· ἐβάστασαν οὖν οἱ Ἰουδαῖοι λίθους ἵνα λιθάσωσιν αὐτόν, that is to say, between two given passages of the Gospel of John, 8.59 and 10.30,[30] Eustathius reckons about 135 στίχοι. Now if we count these intervening lines in Codex B we have 326 lines, which is more than twice 135, and in the Sinaitic Codex the passage occupies 414 lines. If, however, we count the actual letters in the passage, we find from the Sinaitic Codex 5375 letters, which when divided by 135 gives us 39.9 letters to the στίχος, a result somewhat too large, but still confirmatory of M. Graux's conclusion. It will be noticed that Eustathius is approximate.[31] Probably he mistook 135 for 145. The number of intervening στίχοι is really nearer to 150, and at 36 letters to the στίχος is almost exactly 149. From this last result it will be easy to express any book in the New Testament in στίχοι, for we may say approximately:

326 Vatican lines = 414 Sinaitic lines
= 149 στίχοι of 36 letters each.

The calculations are given in a subsequent table, and are compared with estimates derived from various codices.

4. The same supposition of a normal iambic στίχος explains the statement of Dionysius of Halicarnassus (on the superiority of the elocution of Demosthenes)[32] that Demosthenes' works contain 50,000 or 60,000 στίχοι. M. Graux dismisses this statement with the words, "on voit que Denys ne tenait pas à l'exactitude absolue des chiffres." But even if we admit the estimate to be a rough one, we have a right to assume that the accurate number of στίχοι should fall *between* the assigned limits. That it does not so fall is pointed out by W. Christ in his *Attikusausgabe des Demosthenes*,[33] in which he calculates from the stichometric indications of certain manuscripts of Demosthenes that the whole number of στίχοι is not much above 42,000. The conclusion drawn by the writer (as given by M. Weil in the *Revue Critique* for Nov. 27, 1882[34])

---

29. Migne, Patrol. XVIII 657 [PG, *De engastrimytho contra Origenem* 21.11. AF].

30. [John 10.31. AF]

31. This supposition is unnecessary. Very interesting cases can be given, especially from Galen, of hexameter lines measured at over 40 letters.

32. [*De Demosthenis dictione* 57. AF]

33. [Wilhelm von Christ, *Die Attikusausgabe des Demosthenes: Ein Beitrag zur Textgeschichte des Autors* (Abhandlungen der Königlich Bayerischen Akademie der Wissenschaften, 1. Classe, 16/3; München: Verlag der K. Akademie, 1882). AF]

34. [Henri Weil, review of Christ, *Attikusausgabe*, in *Revue critique d'histoire et de littérature* 16 (1882), pp. 424-27. AF]

is that the exemplar on which the reckoning is based is one of shorter lines than is usual.

But the question immediately arises whether this case is not explicable by the hypothesis of the iambic line: increasing the estimated 42,000 στίχοι in the proportion of 7 to 9, which we have seen to be the ratio of the normal tragic verse to the heroic, we have 54,000 στίχοι, which falls nearly half-way between the limits suggested by Dionysius of Halicarnassus. We may study these stichometric indications in the important Munich MS of Demosthenes, known as Bavaricus, where the στίχοι are marked by hundreds on the margin by the letters A, B, etc. They are given by Reiske in his edition of Demosthenes,[35] and we have only to take the average στίχος from the space intervening between two successive letters.

It is necessary to show that these stichometric marks do actually refer to a line measured by the longer model. As I have not been able to obtain a copy of M. Christ's work, I have calculated the στίχος from the data given by Reiske, where the marks are given at p. xcii of the preface, with the lines to which they refer. It would be difficult to mark the stichometric intervals even if the series were perfect (which is not the case by any means), for, first, we cannot tell to what part of Reiske's line the indication applies, neither can we be sure that Reiske knew to what part of the line of the MS they applied. Thus there is a chance of error four times repeated, twice for the beginning of the stichometric interval, and twice for its close.

As an example, let us take the oration against Timocrates. Reiske gives the following references to his pages and lines for the stichometric marks: 703, 17 A; 705, 17 B; 711, pen. Γ; 715, 10 Δ; 722, 14 Z; 725, 19 H; 728, 22 Θ; 731, 26 I; 738, 18 Δ; 741, 26 M; 744, 1 N; 746, 18 Z; 752, 8 O; 755, 13 Π; 761, 22 Σ; 764, 25 T. Here the second Δ should be Λ, and the second Z should be Ξ. From these, by means of Reiske's 29-lined page, we at once get intervals 58, 185, 98, 207, 92, 90, 91, 193, 95, 62, 75, 184, 92, 183, 90 lines. Of these fifteen results, the first, fourth, tenth, and eleventh are clearly not a multiple of the stichometric interval, either because Reiske's text is not the text to which the marks can properly apply, or because the marks are wrongly placed. From the remaining results we get the value of the interval, the second being clearly the double of such an interval, and the mean of the results is 92.4 Reiske-lines. But the average Reiske-line is 40.2 letters; the stichometric interval is therefore 3714.48 letters, from which it at once appears that the marks are meant to represent the successive hundreds of hexameter lines, each line being 37 letters. This establishes the nature of the stichometry of Bavaricus.

---

35. [Johann J. Reiske (ed.), *Demosthenis quae supersunt* (9 vols.; London: Black, Young & Young, 1822–1827). AF]

1. *New Testament Autographs*

5. It is from the edict of Diocletian, *de pretiis venalium*, that M. Graux derived the statement as to the pay of the scribe by the given amount of writing. We proceed to examine the edict more closely. It is given in many exemplars, more or less complete, in the *Corpus Inscriptionum Latinarum*, Vol. III, S. 800,[36] the most important being an inscription from Stratonice. The following are the lines that affect our enquiry:

Membranario in [qua] t[r]endone pedali pergamena.	[xl denarii]
Scriptori in scriptura optima versus n° centum.	[xxv]
Se[quent]is scripturae versuum n° centum.	[xx]
Tabellanioni in scriptura libelli bel tabular[um] in versibus n° centum.	[x]

The prices are wanting in the inscription from Stratonice, but they are supplied from a Phrygian inscription marked H in the *Corpus*.[37]

The first thing to observe is the existence of two distinct types of writing, denoted respectively *optima* and *sequens*. These are, as we should say, large and small size; a study of the whole inscription gives many instances of this. Take for example the price of apples in the edict:

Mala optima Mattiana sive Saligniana	n° decem	* quattuor.
Sequentia	n° viginti	* quattuor.
Mala minora	n° quadraginta	* quattuor.

This establishes the use of the words *optimus* and *sequens* as relating to the *res venales*. Next observe that the prices of the two styles of writing are in the ratio of 25 to 20 or 5 : 4. Now the ratio of the heroic verse to the iambic is, as we have shown, very nearly 36 : 28 or 9 : 7, which is a very close approximation to the previous ratio. *The two types of writing of the Diocletian edict are therefore our two standard verses.*[38]

36. [Theodore Mommsen, *Corpus inscriptionum latinarum*, III (Berlin: G. Reimerum, 1873). AF]

37. M. Graux gives the prices differently, quoting apparently from Waddington [William H. Waddington, *Édit de Dioclétien: Établissant le maximum dans l'empire romain* (Paris: Firmin Didot, 1864. AF], and is followed by Birt (*Buchwesen*, p. 208). They write as follows:

Scriptori in scriptura optima versuum No. centum ...	
Sequentis scripturae	XL
Tabellanioni, etc.	XXV

Birt also seems to assume that "sequens" refers to quality rather than quantity: "das Monument unterscheidet hier wie überall nur zwei Sorten und bezeichnet die schlechtere als *sequens*."

38. Dr Bloomfield furnishes me with the following note: "In India, MSS are now copied and paid for by *çlokas* or *granthas*. The çloka is an iambic meter consisting of four times eight syllables, and any MS, whether prose or poetry, is now generally copied upon this basis of count. I received, myself, about a month ago two texts of the *Kāñçika-sūtra*, a

6. We observe that this table enables us to determine, to a close degree of approximation, the cost of the original transcription of the Codex Sinaiticus. Each page contains 96 iambic στίχοι, or almost the legal hundred; the cost is therefore 20 denarii a page: allowing 345½ leaves to the manuscript, the expense is 345½ × 40 denarii, or 13,820 denarii. And the date of the edict of Diocletian is so little anterior to the production of the MS that we cannot be far wrong in our estimate. But here we have only taken account of the actually existing portion of the MS, and have left out of the reckoning those portions of the Old Testament which are lost, and the 43 leaves of the Cod. Friderico-Augustanus.

Scrivener estimates the total number of leaves of the MS down to the place where Hermas breaks off at 724 at the outside: and admitting this estimate, we should have 28,960 denarii for cost of transcription.

Then comes the question of the cost of the vellum, and here again the Diocletian edict helps us to an estimate. According to the first of our quoted lines, a quaternion of four sheets or eight leaves of parchment, a foot in length, was to be sold for 40 denarii; now the Codex Sinaiticus is just over the foot in length (the Roman foot being taken to be 11.69 inches): and the vellum is of very fine quality. Allowing, then, 90 quaternions to the complete work, we put at least 3600 denarii for the material, which added to our previous reckoning gives 32,560 denarii for the complete work. If, however, we only regard the portion properly known as the Codex Sinaiticus, we have to add 1720 denarii to 13,820, giving a total of 15,540 denarii.

We conclude that the cost of a complete Bible must have been about 30,000 denarii; and Constantine's fifty Bibles for the churches of Constantinople must have been produced at an expense not very different from 1,500,000 denarii. To represent this in modern money is more difficult; perhaps we shall not be far wrong in taking the estimate of M. Waddington, that the denarius = .062 francs.

Birt (*Antike Buchwesen*, p. 209) sets the denarius down at .024 marks of modern money. This would make the scribe's pay, for 100 lines of hexameter size, .96 mark, sufficiently small to be a correct estimate of scrivener's pay; for the shorter pattern, .6 mark per hundred; while the cost of production of a complete Sinaitic Codex stands at 720 marks or thereabouts. It is not a little curious that the estimate which we have made of the cost of production of the

---

ritualistic work written in short condensed sentences, and in prose. These sentences contain mnemonic rules for the conduct of sacrifices and sacraments, and are in form and context as far removed from poetry as possible. One of the MSS was estimated at 1700 çlokas, the other at 1750. The difference in the number is due to actual differences in the text, and to the fact that the count is made in round numbers."

A similar statement will be found in Gardthausen: *Griech. Paläographie*, p. 132 [Viktor Gardthausen, *Griechische Paläographie* (Leipzig: Teubner, 1879). AF].

1. *New Testament Autographs*

books ordered by Constantine should approach so nearly to the price set by Tischendorf on the splendid edition of Sinaiticus produced by order of the Emperor Alexander II of Russia.[39]

7. There remains one line of our edict to discuss. The notary (observe the curious form *tabellanio* for *tabellio*) or writer of the small book (libellus) or of tablets, is paid at a lower rate. According to the edict, he is paid only 10 denarii per 100 verses. We cannot be far wrong in assuming his lines to be half as short as the previous type; in other words, his lines are sensibly the same as the Sinaitic line, two of which go to the iambic στίχος. Now it is not unworthy of note that we find not a few manuscripts of the New Testament written on a model very little different from the Sinaitic Codex. They are a little shorter, averaging 11 letters to the line, and indicate an original written on very narrow strips of paper. To this type belong the MSS formerly known as I, N, Γ (which are fragments of the same original); they are written in double columns, 16 lines to the page, and eleven letters to the line. Codex W is, perhaps, a little longer, 12 letters to the line, and in double columns, of 23 lines to the column.

8. The table which contains our calculation of the στίχοι for the separate books is deserving of a careful study. The first column is taken from Scrivener, p. 63 of *Introduction to N. T. Criticism*. He states that for the Gospels his figures are taken from Codd. G. S. and 27 cursives named by Scholz.[40] It will be observed that as a general rule the results of the second column exceed those of the third. But in the case of the Acts the order is nearly reversed. Probably the explanation is that the Acts is written more closely in Codex B than any other book, and so we have a smaller number of lines from which to calculate our στίχοι. The first column is at the beginning much in excess of the second and third, probably in consequence of interpolations in the Gospels followed by Codices G. S., etc., or omissions in the great uncials. For the succeeding Epistles the second and third columns give as a rule results slightly in excess of the first, except for the Hebrews, where the Sinaitic Codex has some omissions to account for, and in James and 1 John.

We may actually test the results in the case of such short compositions as Philemon and the two shorter Epistles of John. By actual reckoning then on the Second and Third Epistles of John as given in Westcott and Hort's edition,[41] we find 30 and 31 στίχοι respectively. The abbreviated forms are taken for θεοῦ, ἰησοῦ, χριστοῦ, but these abbreviations will not affect the result arrived

---

39. [Konstantin von Tischendorf (ed.), *Bibliorum Codex Sinaiticus Petropolitanus* (4 vols.; St Petersburg, 1862). AF]

40. [Johann M.A. Scholz (ed.), *Novum Testamentum graece* (2 vols.; Leipzig: Fridericus Fleischer, 1830-1836). AF]

41. [*New Testament*, I. AF]

at. For Philemon the same text gives 42 στίχοι; but if we do not abbreviate we must add nearly sixty letters; the last στίχος numbered 15 letters; and we have therefore to add about 39 letters or just over a verse, which brings the result very close to the calculation from the Sinaitic, or the estimate of M. Graux.

The result arrived at by M. Graux, and confirmed by our own researches, is in the first instance deduced from the fact that the average value of the στίχος, as calculated, fluctuates between very narrow limits. And I can imagine some one objecting that such a result would be a thing that any one might anticipate, and that we might just as well calculate the average length of a verse in the English Bible, and then draw the inference that these verses were constructed according to a pattern, which can hardly be believed in any strict sense. To reply to this objection, perhaps the simplest counter-argument would be to observe that, if there were really an average number of letters to the verse, fluctuating between limits as narrow in proportion as in the case of the number of letters to the στίχος, there ought to be an approximately uniform ratio between the number of στίχοι and the number of verses in the separate books; for if m/p is approximately constant, where m is the whole number of letters in a book, and p the number of στίχοι, and if m/q is also approximately constant, where q is the number of verses, then $p : q$ is approximately a constant ratio. We can at once test this point by taking the number of στίχοι and verses as given by Scrivener, *Introduction to N. T.*, p. 63. The result of the enquiry is as follows:

	στίχοι	Modern verses	Ratio
Matthew	2560	1071	2.390
Mark	1616	678	2.383
Luke	2740	1151	2.380
John	2024	880	2.300
Acts	2524	1007	2.506
James	242	108	2.240
1 Peter	236	105	2.247
2 Peter	154	61	2.524
1 John	274	105	2.514
2 John	36	13	2.307
3 John	32	15	2.133
Jude	68	25	2.720
Romans	920	433	2.124
1 Corinthians	870	437	1.990
2 Corinthians	590	256	2.304
Galatians	293	149	1.966
Ephesians	312	155	2.013
Philippians	208	104	2.000
Colossians	208	95	2.189
1 Thessalonians	193	89	2.168

1. *New Testament Autographs* 43

	στίχοι	*Modern verses*	*Ratio*
2 Thessalonians	106	47	2.255
1 Timothy	230	113	2.035
2 Timothy	172	83	2.072
Titus	98	46	2.130
Philemon	38	25	1.520
Hebrews	703	303	2.320
Revelation	1800	405	4.444

That is (leaving out the case of Revelation, where the number of στίχοι is obviously apocryphal), the ratio varies between 1.52 and 2.72, which is more divergent than 3 to 5. In the longer compositions the ratio tends to uniformity, as we should expect. It is clear, then, that the average of M. Graux's results is something more than a mere numerical average, and implies the existence of an underlying type.

9. It is important that we should grasp the bearing of the previous researches upon the antiquity of the texts contained in the two great uncials. Scrivener, in his collation of the Codex Sinaiticus, draws attention to the remarkable resemblance of the writing to that of the Herculanean papyri, none of which, as he ingeniously remarks, can be dated below A.D. 79. He draws a similar comparison with regard to the almost entire absence of marks of punctuation.[42] "The two manuscripts are near akin. In the Hyperides papyri are no stops at all, in the Herculanean very few."[43] With regard to the columnar arrangement his remarks are even more suggestive. "Still more striking is the likeness which Cod. Sinaiticus bears to these records of the first century in respect to its outward form and arrangement. The latter are composed of narrow slips of the papyrus, the writing on which is seldom more than 2 or 2½ inches broad, glued together in parallel columns, and kept in scrolls which were unrolled at one end for the purpose of reading, and when read rolled up at the other ... the appearance of the Sinai manuscript, with its eight narrow columns (seldom exceeding two inches in breadth), exhibited on each open leaf, suggests at once the notion that it was transcribed line for line from some primitive papyrus, whether written in Egypt or elsewhere."[44]

The main point to be noted is that the papyri from which our great manuscripts are transcribed must have been closely related, almost line for line, to the *original* papyri of the Gospels and Epistles, *or it is extremely unlikely that*

---

42. Scrivener, *Collation of Codex Sinaiticus*, p. xiv [Frederick H.A. Scrivener, *A Full Collation of the Codex Sinaiticus with the Received Text of the New Testament* (Cambridge: Deighton, Bell; London: Bell & Daldy, 1864). AF].
43. P. xxviii.
44. P. xxx.

they would end in any other way on the pages than by random distribution. And thus our investigation constitutes the proof of the important statement of Westcott and Hort, that "the ancestries of these two manuscripts diverged from a point near the autographs."[45] They might almost have said "from the autographs." But when we establish this result, we reserve the important qualification, that these MSS are not exempt from occasional errors of omission or insertion of whole sheets and lines; nor are they entirely free from that error which arises from a derangement of the order of the sheets of which the original document was composed. The latter I believe to be peculiarly the case with the Gospel of John. How far such omissions and excisions are willful, it is impossible to say; it is to such a case that the remark of Tertullian applies when he accuses Marcion of using not the pen, but the knife in his dealing with documents.[46] He probably means to imply that whole strips of papyrus had disappeared from the rolls. But I think it will be found upon a closer examination of this difficult point, that the character of Marcion has been unnecessarily blackened, and that in many respects he will turn out to be almost a champion of textual purity. It became the fashion to brand every omission from the ordinary Church MSS with the name of Marcion. We find this charge made even by so noble a spirit as Origen with regard to the concluding verses of the Epistle to the Romans.[47]

We now annex the table which gives the comparison between the number of στίχοι as quoted from early codices, and the number as calculated from the lines enumerated in tables I and II for the several books of the New Testament, on the basis of a number of lines in St John's Gospel actually measured into στίχοι. Since we find our results frequently in coincidence or near it, and seldom differing from one another more than 5 per cent, the result is confirmatory of the previous statements made as to the fixed length of the στίχος. When allowance has been made for the omissions and insertions in the MSS, we may perhaps find it useful to recalculate the figures given.

---

45. [Wescott and Hort, *New Testament*, 1.556. AF]
46. [*Praescr.* 38.9. AF
47. [*Comm. Rom.* 10.43. AF]

1. *New Testament Autographs*

Table IV

	1 V-line = 149/326 στίχοι. 1 S-line = 149/414 στίχοι. log 326 – log 149 = .3400313 log 414 – log 149 = .4438140	στίχοι from Scrivener's Introduction	στίχοι estimated for Vatican Codex	στίχοι estimated for Sinaitic Codex	στίχοι from the second hand of Sinaitic Codex	M. Graux's probable number
Matthew		2560	2442	2401		2560
Mark		1616	1492	1470		1616
Luke		2740	2629	2583		2750
John		2024	1865	1861		2024
Acts		2524	2497	2526		2556
Romans		920	944	918		920
1 Corinthians		870	886	885		870
2 Corinthians		590	608	607	612	590
Galatians		293	293	293	312	293
Ephesians		312	317	313	312	312
Philippians		208	216	210	200	208
Colossians		208	219	212	300	208
1 Thessalonians		193	205	198		193
2 Thessalonians		106	112	105	180	106
1 Timothy		230		239	250 ?	230
2 Timothy		172		174	180	199
Titus		98		100	96	97
Philemon		38		43		42
Hebrews		703		670	750	703
James		242	242	236		242
1 Peter		236	244	245		236
2 Peter		154	168	164		
1 John		274	262	263		274
2 John		30	31	31		32
3 John		32	31	31		31
Jude		68	70	71		68
Revelation		1800		1179		

C. 1. When we proceed to examine in detail the various readings and errors of the principal manuscripts in the Catholic Epistles, we come to the conclusion that there is nothing to affect our results in the two smaller Epistles of John, nor in the Epistle of James. With regard to the First Epistle of John, the only passage where we can regard the text of B as uncertain is in 4.3, where the words χριστὸν ἐν σαρκὶ ἐληλυθότα are omitted, the length of the omission being a V-line, and the passage being retained by the Sinaitic Codex; and at

4.21 there is a line omitted by B. Then we come to the question of the celebrated passage 1 John 5.7, or the "Three Heavenly Witnesses"; the text of this would occupy about five V-lines. Our method of investigation agrees with every other applied critical test in rejecting the words. The abnormal excess of the number of στίχοι noted in some early codices of St John over the number as calculated by ourselves, leads to the suspicion that there may have been Greek codices, now lost, in which the words occurred. The defenders of the passage, if there are any left, can actually count the στίχοι in the First Epistle of John and compare their results with the number as given by Scrivener. The disputed passage is a matter of 3 στίχοι.

2. The Epistle of Jude is an interesting study from our point of view. There are no various readings that are likely to affect the arrangement of the Epistle; in the 15th verse the text of the Sinaitic is perplexing, and in the 25th verse both the oldest codices agree in the addition of two V-lines to the ordinary text. But the significant feature of the examination of the text is the discovery that the scribe of the Sinaitic Codex has in v. 12 mistaken the οὗτοί εἰσιν of the verse for the same words in v. 16, and has consequently interpolated four lines from that verse before detecting his error and returning to the proper passage. His eye has, *apparently*, wandered from the top of a column nearly to the bottom in search of the words which he had either recently transcribed or was proposing to transcribe. We need scarcely say that such a supposition is extremely unlikely. When, however, we restore the pages to the S-form, as they may be easily exhibited, we see that the scribe's eye has really only wandered from the first line of the column he was transcribing to the first line of a column not very remote from it, and commencing with the very same words. And this is so thoroughly likely that it must be regarded as no slight confirmation of our theory of the subdivision of the columns.

It is not to be necessarily inferred that the Epistle was originally written on the S-page; we have already seen reason to assume the opposite type (unless, indeed, the doxology should be shown not to be genuine); but the point that we press is the fact of the reduction of smaller pages into the form given in the Sinaitic Codex. From the same enquiry another result follows: the ratio of the S-lines to the V-lines for this Epistle was abnormally high, but when we proceed to subtract the four lines inserted by the Sinaitic, and recalculate the ratio, we find 1.268 instead of 1.293.

3. We proceed to examine the text of the First Epistle of Peter, which we do more in detail in order to illustrate the methods by which we restore the text, prior to dividing it into the smaller pages.

1. New Testament Autographs

1 Peter

		Letters	Text. Rec.	ℵ	B.	W. H.	Tr.
1.22.	διὰ πνεύματος	12	+	–	–	–	–
1.23.	εἰς τὸν αἰῶνα	11	+	–	–	–	–
3.5.	ἐκόσμουν ἑαυτάς	14	+	–	+	+	
3.7.	κατὰ γνῶσιν	10	+	–	+	+	
4.5.	ἀποδώσουσιν λόγον	16	+	–	+	+	
3.16.	ὑμῶν ὡς κακοποιῶν	15	+	+	–	–	[–]
4.14.	καὶ δυνάμεως	11	–	+	–	–	–
4.14.	κατὰ μὲν αὐτοὺς βλασφημεῖται κατὰ δὲ ὑμᾶς δοξάζεται	44	+	–	–	–	–
5.2.	ἐπισκοποῦντες	13	+	–	–	–	
5.5.	ὑποτασσόμενοι	13	+	–	–	–	
5.10.	θεμελιῶσαι	10	+	+	–	–	–

In addition B omits the whole of 5.3, containing 58 letters, i.e. between 3 and 4 Vatican lines, which will certainly make the text eight Vatican columns, and 36 lines, but it does not fill the page. In the Sinaitic we have, besides the variants noted, and some smaller ones, six short columns, so that in S-pages we have 14 columns and one or two lines, which seems to indicate 56 S-pages. The letters missed or inserted look like complete Sinaitic lines, which again confirms our opinion that the original form of the document is the S-page.

When we add the missing lines to the texts and calculate afresh the ratio of the V-line to the S-line, we have 1.250.

Another remarkable confirmation of our subdivision of the Sinaitic pages is found at 2.12 of this Epistle. The scribe left his work at the beginning of the 21st S-page, where he was about to transcribe the words δοξάσωσι τὸν θεόν. These words stand at present at the second line of the page. But, in returning to his task, he opened at the Second Epistle of Peter by mistake, and here at the 11th verse of the second chapter[48] he found the key-word δόξας and began to write δόξας οὐ τρέμουσιν, thus transcribing what would be the first line of the 19th S-page in the Second Epistle of Peter. The traces of the error still remain. *And it is impossible to give a rational explanation of the aberration of the scribe unless we subdivide the pages in the manner we have indicated.*

3.[49] In the Second Epistle of Peter we rectify the text in a similar manner, the two most important phenomena being that the Sinaitic scribe has in 1.12-13, omitted 8 lines, from διὸ μελλήσω to διεγείρειν, and that the error is almost balanced by the existence of nine short columns.

---

48. [2 Pet. 2.10. AF]
49. [*Sic.* AF]

More important still is the light which the rectification of the pages throws on a very difficult passage in 3.10, where the reading adopted by Westcott and Hort is a source of immense merriment to Dr Burgon. The ordinary reading in this passage is

καὶ γῆ καὶ τὰ ἐν αὐτῇ ἔργα κατακαήσεται.

For κατακαήσεται (which is the reading of A, L, the Clementine Vulgate, the Memphitic, and some other versions) the two earliest MSS read εὑρεθήσεται, and are supported by sundry versions and by Codex K. Codex C suggests ἀφανισθήσονται.

Tregelles and Westcott and Hort import the utterly meaningless εὑρεθήσεται into the text, apparently on the ground that it is safe to follow ten times in succession a group of manuscripts which is demonstrated to be reliable in nine cases out of ten.

Burgon, on the other hand, will have the ordinary reading to be correct, and affirms the reading of Codices ℵ to B to be a rude attempt of some Western scribe to translate or transliterate the Latin word *urentur*! More strangely still, so judicious a critic as Farrar is found supporting this peculiar suggestion, and even claims the paternity of the monster. Thus he remarks: "It had occurred to me, before I saw it remarked elsewhere, that it might be some accidental confusion with the Latin *urentur*" (*Early Days of Christianity*, p. 121).[50]

We now turn to the Sinaitic Codex, and observe that exactly 24 lines beyond the disputed passage lie the words αὐτῷ εὑρεθῆ | ναι ἐν εἰρήνῃ.[51] Moreover, the passage in dispute occurs within a line of the bottom of one of the Sinaitic columns, and, in all probability, when the passage is rectified, the words are either the highest or the lowest line of an S-page. The scribe's eye, therefore, wanders laterally two columns, and hence the word εὑρεθήσεται. This explains the origin of the variant. We infer also from the discrepancy of later copies that we have here a case in which the original reading is entirely lost and the text has been restored by a conjectural emendation.

Further, since the error took place in a MS of the S-type, it follows that that type is nearer to the autograph of the Epistle than any other, which is exactly in accordance with our previous enquiry; for, otherwise, some manuscript would, doubtless, have conserved the original reading. The conjectural restoration made by the early MSS is not based upon any critical study of the text; and in order to fill the blank left by the removal of εὑρέθη, we must endeavor to determine the causes which led to the error. These are (1) the

---

50. [Frederic W. Farrar, *The Early Days of Christianity* (2 vols.; London: Cassell, Petter, Galpin, 1882). AF]

51. [2 Pet. 3.14. AF]

similarity of αὐτῇ in v. 10 to αὐτῷ in v. 14; (2) the similarity either to eye or ear of the words which have become confounded.

A reading which would satisfy both conditions would be ἐκρυηθήσεται, which Professor Gildersleeve suggests.[52] We find a similar word ἀπορρυηθήσεται in some MSS of *Barnabas* ch. 11,[53] the passage being really a quotation from the first Psalm;[54] and ἐξερύημεν is the word used for the fading leaf in Isaiah 64.5. This exactly expresses the idea of the writer.

4. We now turn to the Pauline Epistles, in which we return to our first approximation to the number of the original pages of the autographs, and examine the manner in which the results are affected by the principal errors, reserving all our conclusions for a closer scrutiny in connection with the original documents at some later time. It is extremely unfortunate that there is no critical apparatus to the New Testament except Scrivener's collation of the Sinaitic, which records the accidental omissions or repetitions of the great uncials; we are, therefore, obliged to collate for ourselves the text of every book, in order to see that no lines are dropped or repeated. And this, in spite of the compensations arising from a close study of the early arrangement of the text, is somewhat tedious and demands a great deal of time.

1 Thessalonians

		Letters	Text. Rec.	ℵ	B.	W. H.	Tr.
1.1.	ἀπὸ θεοῦ πατρὸς ἡμῶν καὶ κυρίου Ἰησοῦ Χριστοῦ	?24	+	+	−	−	−
2.16.	τὰς ἁμαρτίας	11	+	+	−	+	+
3.2.	καὶ συνεργὸν ἡμῶν	15	+	−	[+]	−	−
5.8.	καὶ ἀγάπης	9	+	−	+	−	−

These are the only three readings of any importance. The Epistle is written on the V-page to the full, and will not bear any additions; we agree with the editors in rejecting the first reading. The second reading is remarkable, as there has been a conflation by the Textus Receptus and late copies of the two simple readings καὶ διάκονον τοῦ θεοῦ and καὶ συνεργὸν ἡμῶν. Either of the alternative readings may be taken, and the length of the Epistle is not affected by our choice, provided we do not make the error of conflation and take them both.

The third reading is an omission on the part of the Sinaitic. At 2.13 the Sinaitic has repeated 10 lines by ὁμοιοτέλευτον of the letters ωντουθεου. We have thus to reduce the estimate made for the Sinaitic Codex by 11 lines, and leaves us with 11 columns and 10 lines, or very nearly 45 S-pages.

52. I see that Westcott and Hort make a similar suggestion in their introduction, and disown the very reading which they adopt.
53. [*Barn.* 11.6. AF]
54. [Ps. 1.3. AF]

50   *James Rendel Harris*

But now the question arises, why should the scribe have wandered back 10 lines in search of τοῦ θεοῦ? The interval is a very improbable one as the MS is written, but when the pages are rectified it will be found that the aberration of the scribe's eye is almost entirely lateral, and does not amount to a couple of lines vertically.

5. Second Thessalonians: Here we have both codices ending unevenly, the Sinaitic at the third line, and the Vatican at the 34th line. The text, moreover, is extremely exact. Marcion is said to have omitted in 1.8 ἐν φλογὶ πυρός, 13 letters;[55] in 2.4 the Sinaitic omits καὶ ὑπεραιρόμενος, 16 letters; and in 2.15[56] it omits ὁ ἀγαπήσας ἡμᾶς, 12 letters.[57] In 3.4 the Vatican text has inserted καὶ ἐποιήσατε, 12 letters. These seem to be all the readings of any importance.

A reference to the Codex Sinaiticus shows us the following peculiarity: it has twice made a single line of the two letters χῡ, and twice made a single line of ιῡ χῡ; the four instances are as follows:

1.2. ιῡ χῡ a fresh line, probably rendered necessary by the insertion of the word ἡμῶν.

1.8. ευαγγελι | ω του κῡ ημων ιῡ | χῡ, where the word χῡ is rejected by all the editors.

1.12. κατα την χαριν του | θῡ ημων και κῡ ιῡ | χῡ, where the word seems genuine.

2.14. περιποιησιν δο | ξης του κῡ ημων | ιῡ χῡ, where the last line is genuine.

There are one or two other very short lines. It is probably in these short lines that the explanation is to be sought of the three extra lines above pattern in the Sinaitic Codex. It will be observed that the errors of the Epistle are mainly S-errors. We conclude that the Epistle is probably represented by 24 S-pages. The result is confirmed by observing that in 3.4, B has conflated the two readings ποιεῖτε καὶ ποιήσετε, ἐποιήσατε καὶ ποιεῖτε into ἐποιήσατε καὶ ποιεῖτε καὶ ποιήσετε. It seems unlikely that this would happen if the text of B in this Epistle were modelled on the original tradition.

6. First Corinthians: The text is very good. At the beginning of ch. 13[58] the scribe of the Sinaitic has dropped 134 letters, from γέγονα χαλκός to ἀγάπην δὲ μὴ ἔχω. The error, which is almost exactly 10 S-lines, was due to the fact that a previous sentence ended also with μὴ ἔχω. Moreover, the error is facilitated, as in the case mentioned above, by the existence of the smaller pages, which bring the two similar passages into contiguity. Other errors are the

---

55. [*Sic*. AF]
56. [2 Thess. 2.16. AF]
57. [*Sic*. AF]
58. [1 Cor. 13.1-2. AF]

repetition of four lines in 1.8, the omission of four lines in 2.15, the omission of a line in 10.19; of two lines in 15.13, and of four lines in 15.26-27.

		Letters	Text. Rec.	ℵ	B.	W. H.	Tr.
1.27.	ἵνα τοὺς σοφούς ... ἐξελέξατο ὁ Θς	54	+	+	+	+	+
3.3.	καὶ διχοστασίαι	14	+	–	–	–	–
7.5.	τῇ νηστείᾳ καί	12	+	–	–	–	–
11.24.	λάβετε φάγετε	12	+	–	–	–	–

Our table must now be corrected so as to make the Epistle 206 S-pages and several lines.

7. Second Corinthians: The principal errors are as follows:

		Letters	Text. Rec.	ℵ	B.	W. H.	Tr.
8.4.	δέξασθαι ἡμᾶς	12	+	–	–	–	–
9.4.	τῆς καυχήσεως	12	+	–	–	–	–
12.7.	ἵνα μὴ ὑπεραίρωμαι	16	+	–	+	+	[–]
12.11.	καυχώμενος	10	+	–	–	–	–

Here the errors, though few, are chiefly of the S-type; from the readings given we might perhaps add 16 letters to the Sinaitic text. But this would still leave a large blank in a sheet. On the other hand, the V-pages fit exactly, only we must allow for the omission by B of a line in 1.13 and the repetition of four lines in 3.16.

8. The Epistle to the Romans does not seem to conform, as yet, very closely to any type.

Perhaps the explanation of this fact may be in the repetition by Codex B of four lines at 4.4, from ὁ μισθός to ἐργαζομένῳ. This would make the Epistle 148 V-pages.

There is a further difficulty about the concluding salutations and doxology, the consideration of which is very important, because in the first place Origen[59] distinctly charges Marcion with having excised them; secondly, we find them inserted in some codices at the end of the fourteenth chapter;[60] thirdly, some codices, notably Codex A, which can hardly ever resist an opportunity of conflation of documents, have retained the doxology in both places; fourthly, Marcion is also charged with the excision of the remainder of the Epistle from the end of the fourteenth chapter. It becomes interesting to examine the length of this portion in Vatican type. At present it does not look as if Marcion had done anything of the kind attributed to him.

---

59. Orig. Int. IV 687 [*Comm. Rom.* 10.43. AF].
60. [Rom. 14.23. AF]

The doxology starts at the top of a column, ΤΩΔΕΔΥΝΑΜΕΝΩΥΜΑΣ, and occupies in the manuscript 16 lines and 4 letters.[61] Moreover, the portion from Rom. 16.1 to the end which contains all those very doubtful salutations to people whom one can hardly believe to have been at Rome, contains very nearly 10 V-pages with the doxology; or nearly 9 V-pages without it. We may conjecture that these 9 V-pages are really a part of the subscription to another Epistle. It is not, however, a point material to our hypothesis, viz. that the Epistle to the Romans was written on the V-page.

In Romans the text is very exact.

		Letters	Text. Rec.	ℵ	B.	W. H.	Tr.
8.1.	μὴ κατὰ σάρκα ... κατὰ πνεῦμα	37	+	–	–	–	–
9.28.	ἐν δικαιοσύνῃ ... συντετμημένον	33	+	–	–	–	–
10.15.	τῶν εὐαγγ. εἰρήνην	25	+	–	–	–	–
11.6.	εἰ δὲ ἐξ ἔργων ... οὐκ ἔτι ἐστὶν ἔργον	53	+	–	[+]	–	–
12.17.	ἐνώπιον τοῦ θῦ καί	15	+	–	–	–	–
13.9.	οὐ ψευδομαρτυρήσεις	18	+	+	–	–	–
14.6.	καὶ ὁ μὴ φρονῶν ... οὐ φρονεῖ	31	+	–	–	–	–
14.21.	ἢ σκανδαλίζεται ἢ ἀσθενεῖ	22	+	–	+	–	+
15.13.	εἰς τὸ περισσεύειν ὑμᾶς	20	+	+	–	+	+
15.32.	καὶ συναναπαύσωμαι ὑμῖν	21	+	+	–	+	+
16.12.	ἀσπάσασθε Περσίδα κ. τ. λ.	49	+	+	+	+	+
16.24.	ἡ χάρις τοῦ κῦ κ. τ. λ.	39	+	–	–	–	–

The majority of these readings are of the V-type, and the text can now be easily rectified. The question of the salutations is more difficult; as already stated, we conjecture that they are a separate document, really intended as a codicil to the Ephesian Epistle; but, having been written on the V-type, a mistake easily arose in reducing the documents, and finding an Epistle of the S-type carrying final leaves of the V-pattern.

9. Galatians: The only reading of any importance is in 3.1:

	Letters	Text. Rec.	ℵ	B.	W. H.	Tr.
τῇ ἀληθείᾳ μὴ πείθεσθαι	20	+	–	–	–	–

We can, at the most, add one line to the Vatican text; but this we must not do, first, because of the consensus of authorities and editors against the reading; and, secondly, because the large writing of St Paul in the close of the Epistle

---

61. [Rom. 16.25. AF]

would run over into another page if the reading were admitted, a most improbable event. On the other hand, B has repeated a line in 1.11.

There is no reasonable conclusion other than that the Epistle to the Galatians was written on 47 V-pages. The single reading quoted seems to be of the V-type.

10. Ephesians: At first sight this Epistle seems not to be written on full sheets; or, if so, not on sheets of the V- and S-type. In one Codex, B, it occupies 16 columns and 22 lines, i.e. six lines less than 50 V-pages; and in the other it occupies 18 columns and five lines, i.e. seven lines less than 73 S-pages. We proceed to examine the codices, and to discuss those variations of the text which may affect seriously the space that it occupies.

And first of all we find that the scribe of ℵ has omitted the seventh verse of the second chapter, which has been inserted in a footnote. The reason of this error lies in the fact that both the sixth and seventh verses close with the words εν χῶ ιῦ, and probably at the same part of the Sinaitic line. The 101 letters of this verse show that it would occupy about seven or eight lines of Sinaitic type. Adding them we correct our table, which now states that Ephesians in the Sinaitic Codex occupies 73 S-pages and one line. Further, he has repeated three lines in 6.3, in the words ινα ευ σοι | γενηται και εση | μακροχρονιος | επι της γης. At 3.18 he has again repeated a line. This makes the Epistle 73 S-pages, all but three lines.

We now proceed to discuss the various readings.

		Letters	Text. Rec.	ℵ	B.	W. H.	Tr.
1.1.	ἐν ἐφέσῳ	7	+	−	[+]	[+]	+
1.3.	καὶ σωτῆρος	10	−	+	−	−	−
1.15.	τὴν ἀγάπην	9	+	−	−	−	+
3.14.	τοῦ κῦ ἡμῶν χῦ ιῦ	13	+	−	−	−	−
5.22.	ὑποτάσσεσθε	11	+	−	−	−	−
	or ὑποτασσέσθωσαν	14	−	+	−	−	+
5.30.	ἐκ τῆς σαρκὸς αὐτοῦ καὶ ἐκ τῶν ὀστέων αὐτοῦ	35	+	−	−	−	−
6.12.	τοῦ αἰῶνος	9	+	−	−	−	−
6.20.[62]	τοῦ εὐαγγελίου	13	+	+	−	[+]	+

These are the principal passages, and we see that on the most extreme methods of criticism it would be possible to add five to seven lines to the Sinaitic Codex, or in the opposite direction to remove two lines. But it is evident that there are really only two passages to discuss, the one a question of adding a line to the Sinaitic text, the other of subtracting two lines. These readings can hardly affect our result, which gives us 73 S-pages. This Epistle

---

62. [Eph. 6.19. AF]

is a good illustration of the rule that a document originally written on the V- or S-pattern will show a majority of V- or S-errors, as the case may be.

11. Philippians: Here there are only two important readings:

	Letters	Text. Rec.	ℵ	B.	W. H.	Tr.
3.16. κανόνι, τὸ αὐτὸ φρονεῖν	19	+	–	[–]	[–]	–
3.21. εἰς τὸ γενέσθαι αὐτό	17	+	–	–	–	–

Its errors are both of the V-type. The Codex B shows us 33 V-pages in the Epistle, which will not, therefore, admit of an extra line being inserted. But in noticing this apparent leaning to the V-type, we must not forget that the Epistle is only three lines short of a page in the S-type, which allows us, if we think proper, to admit one or both of the longer readings. Moreover ℵ has dropped a line at 2.18.

12. Colossians: Here we had 11 columns and 15 lines in Codex B.
12 columns and 13 lines in Sinaitic.
In either case just over the page, which is the most improbable thing that can happen.

The principal readings are:

	Letters	Text. Rec.	ℵ	B.	W. H.	Tr.
1.2. καὶ τοῦ κῡ χῡ ιῡ	9	+	+	–	–	–
1.6. καὶ αὐξανόμενον	14	–	+	+	+	+
1.14. διὰ τοῦ αἵματος αὐτοῦ	15	+	–	–	–	–
1.25. ἐγὼ Παῦλος διά	12	–	+	–	–	–
2.2. καὶ πατρὸς καὶ τοῦ	15	+	[+]	–	–	–
2.11. τῶν ἁμαρτιῶν	11	+	–	–	–	–
3.6. ἐπὶ τοὺς υἱοὺς τῆς ἀπειθείας	24	+	+	–	–	–

Of these readings 1.2 is an exact line in the Sinaitic, it is probably an addition. 1.6 is also an exact line, and has been dropped by a few codices. 1.14 is generally admitted to be an interpolation. At 1.23 and at 1.25 a line has been added by ℵ. 2.2 is very doubtful. 2.11 is probably an addition. 3.6, the passage is rejected by B only, and perhaps D; it is very likely genuine. We infer that of three places where the Sinaitic contradicts the Vatican, it is incorrect in two of them. The Epistle is now one or two lines short of 49 pages of the S-type. The errors are about evenly divided between the two types. The result is confirmed by observing that in 1.12, Cod. B has been guilty of conflation of the two readings ἱκανώσαντι and καλέσαντι, so as to make καλέσαντι καὶ ἱκανώσαντι; it seems hardly likely, then, that B contains the original type of the text of Colossians.

13. Philemon is, as already shown, 10 S-pages exactly.

14. Now let us examine the arrangement of the Gospel of Luke. Our enumeration of columns and lines gives us for the Gospel 401 V-pages or 598

S-pages. But neither of these results can be accepted, on account of the numerous and important variants which have to be considered. It is interesting to notice that the two results are very nearly in the ratio of 2 : 3. This would be exactly the case if two codices were written, one on a 12-lined page and with 14 letters to the line, and the other on a 14-lined page and with 18 letters to the line, for $12 \times 14 : 14 \times 18 = 2 : 3$. Now the two great MSS very nearly fulfil this condition; it does not, therefore, surprise us if, when one codex suggests 400 V-pages, the other suggests 600 S-pages.

Now, turning to the Gospel of Luke, we notice in the first place that the passage containing the account of the Agony in the Garden[63] has been excised from or is wanting in the chief exemplars. The Vatican Codex omits, the Sinaitic brackets it. I pointed out in my recent lectures that it was conceivable, as Epiphanius states, that the passage was excised for doctrinal reasons, and that there were probably other words, καὶ ἔκλαυσε, which had never found their way back into the text.[64] Counting the letters of the doubtful passage, and adding, if it be thought necessary, 10 letters for καὶ ἔκλαυσε, we have 155 letters, or almost exactly an S-page. Here we have a strong intimation that the Gospel was originally written on the S-page, and that the account of the Agony is an authentic part of the text, easily lost or excised.

Turning to the Sinaitic Codex we find that the passage occupies eleven lines exactly, without the words added by us, and is evidently easily detached from the main body of the text. In the plate annexed the passage is completed, and given as a specimen of the S-page.

Assuming for the present that the S-page is the original form of Luke, we examine the next important passage, bracketed by Westcott and Hort, Luke 22.19-20 from τὸ ὑπὲρ ὑμῶν διδόμενον ... to τὸ ὑπὲρ ὑμῶν ἐκχυννόμενον. At first sight it seems that the omission of this passage by the Western text might be due to ὁμοιοτέλευτον, but a closer examination shows that it contains 152 letters, or almost exactly an S-page; in the Sinaitic Codex it occupies 12 lines and 7 letters, but one of the lines is a very short one and has only three letters. It looks again as if an S-page had been either omitted or inserted; if both the passages which we have discussed were actual pages of the original document, the intervening space ought to be an exact number of S-pages, i.e. the space between the ἐκχυννόμενον of the second passage and the commencement of the account of the Agony in the Garden. Examination of the MS shows the intervening space to be a column and 33 lines, or within three lines of being 7 S-pages. It is doubtful, therefore, whether this passage be an integral part of the original document; and bearing in mind the suspicious resemblance to a passage in 1 Cor., we leave the matter in suspense until we have

---

63. [Luke 22.43-44. AF]
64. Epiph. *Ancor.* xxxi [Epiphanius, *Ancoratus*. AF].

James Rendel Harris

ΚΑΙΕΚΛΑΥΣΕ
ΩΦΘΗΔΕΑΥΤΩΑΓ
ΓΕΛΟΣΑΠΟΥΡΑΝΟΥ
ΕΝΙΣΧΥΩΝΑΥΤΟΝ
ΚΑΙΓΕΝΟΜΕΝΟΣΕ
ΝΑΓΩΝΙΑΕΚΤΕΝΕ
ΣΤΕΡΟΝΠΡΟΣΗΥ
ΧΕΤΟΚΑΙΕΓΕΝΕΤΟ
ΙΔΡΩΣΑΥΤΟΥΩΣΙ
ΘΡΟΜΒΟΙΑΙΜΑΤΟΣ
ΚΑΤΑΒΑΙΝΟΝΤΕΣ
ΕΠΙΤΗΝΓΗΝ

1. New Testament Autographs

examined the remaining variants. If we see reason to conclude that it is really a part of the text, we shall most probably find that there has been some displacement of the text in the neighborhood. Before passing we observe that the 34th verse of the 23rd chapter, which Westcott and Hort bracket, is also marked with suspicion in the Sinaitic and occupies four lines of the text.

The doubtful 12th verse of ch. 24 in the Sinaitic Codex begins a line, and occupies 8 lines all but four letters; moreover, the passage has dropped four letters from the text en route in the word μόνα after ὀθόνια.

We now proceed to examine the text in detail, much in the same way as we discussed the Gospel of John; the list of variants is very long, as the text is many times more corrupt than that of John, and we therefore content ourselves with giving approximate results, deduced from a long array of doubtful passages.

The first thing that strikes us in studying the portentous list of various readings is that the greater part of the book is marked by omissions, but when we come to the last two chapters we find a large number of suspicious additions, contradicted by the Western text. It looks painfully like as if the space lost by omissions in the early parts of the book had been utilized in the latter part for some additional matter. Examining the cases where the Sinaitic text is erroneous, or probably erroneous, we have on the whole, up to 22.25, forty-six lines to add, the criticism of the text being comparatively easy. Now the doubtful passage contained in 22.43-44 begins on the tenth line from the bottom of a column, but when the forty-six lines are added it falls at once into the proper place, the last section of a column. This would leave the Gospel, if undisturbed, to finish on the 23rd line of a column; but now the criticism becomes extremely difficult.

In 22.31. The MS is probably correct.
    22.64. The " is " "
    22.68. The " is " "
    22.62. Two lines have perhaps been added.
    23.17. Three lines must be removed.
    23.38. Correct.
    23.34. Probably four lines have been inserted, but the passage is very difficult.
    24.12. Eight lines perhaps added.
    24.31. A line lost.
    24.4. A line probably added.
    24.6. Two lines probably added.
    24.40. Four lines perhaps added.
    24.36. Two lines " "
    24.46. ⎫
       49. ⎬ Text correct.
    24.51. Text probably correct.
    24.52. Probably two lines added.
    24.53. Text probably correct.

The result being that 23 lines have been probably added, if we retain the passage 23.34 as probably authentic. That is to say, 2 S-pages, all but a line, have now to be removed. But we added previously 4 S-pages, all but a line (if we reckon καὶ ἔκλαυσε in 22.43); we have therefore on the whole added two S-pages, together with a lost page. Our original estimate was 598 S-pages, it is now 601 S-pages. Nothing can be more significant than this number of the fact that an S-page too many has crept in, and it can hardly be any other than the passage which we were in doubt about in 22.19; we therefore finally decide to remove it.

The analysis has been extremely suggestive to our own mind; we started out with the prospect of reinserting the majority of the passages usually reckoned as doubtful, but the singular predominance of additions in the closing chapters over omissions has finally led us to reject those passages, or the majority of them, in accordance with the Western text; and we have finally ended with a book of 600 pages almost exactly, which we are now prepared to print on what we believe will represent, *quam proxime*, the original sheets of uncial writing. It will be observed that the frequency of errors of the S-type in the analysis of this Gospel confirms our supposition that this is the original form of the Gospel.

15. The Acts of the Apostles is one of the books which we have indicated to ourselves as likely, from its abrupt conclusion, to be written on full sheets. When we proceed to examine the principal doubtful passages, we shall find that the majority of the errors are of the S-type. There are nearly fifty passages that have to be examined, and from these, by the use of the best critical apparatus, we proceed to correct the text of the Sinaitic Codex, in which the S-type, if it exists, is preserved.

The following are the passages requiring change:

2.9.   + καὶ ἐλαμῖται.
2.20. + καὶ ἐπιφανῆ.
2.21. A whole verse has been omitted, 4 S-lines.
2.43. A sentence has been inserted, 38 letters: ἐν Ἰερουσαλὴμ φόβος τε ἦν μέγας ἐπὶ πάντας καί.
7.60. + φωνῇ μεγάλῃ.
9.12. + ἐν ὁράματι.
13.23. + ἀπὸ τοῦ σπέρματος.
14.20-21. Two verses omitted, 66 letters, 5 S-lines.
15.32. + καὶ ἐπεστήριξαν.
21.13. + κλαίοντες καί.
21.22. − δεῖ πλῆθος συνελθεῖν.
28.27. + καὶ τῇ καρδίᾳ συνῶσιν.

This leaves us on the whole with about 14 lines to add to the Sinaitic text, which now occupies (a result by no means aimed at, and scarcely anticipated)

144 columns and 24 lines, or 578 S-pages. I do not however regard this result as more than a rough preliminary examination.

I am inclined to believe that a number of pages have been lost from the conclusion of the book. The celebrated passage 8.37 consists of about 96 letters, perhaps 8 S-lines; so it cannot be restored, on the ground of a page having been lost from the original document. It is not unworthy of note that we have seen reason to refer the Gospel of Luke to the same type and to an original document of about 600 unit sheets.

16. We shall now defer the examination of the remaining books, reserving the discussion of them, together with the important question of the closing verses of St Mark, and some other points of interest, for another occasion; and we shall conclude this present article by a brief examination of one or two early uncial texts by the light of the results already obtained, and by indicating a more general method of determining the autograph forms of any given collection of letters.

D. 1. Codex Alexandrinus is written in tolerably uniform lines, and in double columns. The number of lines to the page is normally 50, but sometimes 51, and in one or two instances we note 49. In other words, the normal size of the page copied has been affected by omissions and additions, but principally the latter. The table for this codex is as follows:

	Columns	*Lines*
Matthew begins at ch. 25.6	?	6
Mark	50	17
Luke	86	20
John	53	48
or counting the leaves lost 6.50 to 8.52	61	48
Acts	80	7
James	7	48
1 Peter	7	47
2 Peter	5	11
1 John	10	26
2 John		49
3 John		51
Jude	2	6
Romans	28	32
1 Corinthians	28	21
2 Corinthians	19	38
Galatians	9	39
Ephesians	10	39
Philippians	6	48
Colossians	6	48
1 Thessalonians	6	27
2 Thessalonians	3	23

	Columns	*Lines*
Hebrews	23	16
1 Timothy	7	31
2 Timothy	6	14
Titus	3	19
Philemon	1	18
Revelation	34	28

It will be observed that 2 John and 3 John no longer agree in the number of lines, the column on which the Second Epistle is written being wider than that on which the Third Epistle is written; this latter column has been narrowed in order to make room for a much wider column in the Epistle of Jude, which sometimes contains as many as 29 letters to the line.

In this MS the books do not begin uniformly at the top of the page, which shows that the orderly arrangement of the original matter is disappearing. Thus, 1 John does not begin at the head of a page; we have first 29 lines, then 9 columns, then 47 lines, and so we end near the foot of a column. Second Corinthians in the middle of a page; we have 21 lines, then a column of 49 lines only, then 18 more columns counting the three lost leaves, and then 18 lines. One thing, however, is very remarkable in the table, and that is the way in which the concluding lines group themselves around the numbers which are multiples of ten. It will be worth while examining this point.

Theoretically, the terminal digits of the lines 1, 2, 3, ... 0 ought to be tolerably evenly distributed, but when we examine we find

0 occurs	once.	5 occurs	not at all.
1 "	4 times.	6 "	4 times.
2 "	once.	7 "	4 times.
3 "	once.	8 "	8 times.
4 "	once.	9 "	4 times.

Now this extraordinary preference for the numbers 1, 6, 7, 8, 9 is not accidental, but is a survival of the original methods of arranging the documents.

The fact is that this document was probably originally reduced from documents of which one page is equivalent to the fifth part of the Alexandrian column; and the matter of the original documents was so arranged that the final page was more than half filled. This explains the preference for the endings which occupy the latter halves of the decades. The question arises, was this arrangement of the matter arbitrary, or are there any residual traces of the original pages?

An examination of this point will, I think, show that there was a time when the fifth of the column of Codex A was a V-page, but the traces have almost disappeared. This may be seen to be roughly the case by calculating the letters for 10 Alexandrian lines, which amount to something over 230, not far from the average letters of a V-page. And the suspicion is confirmed by remarking that the Second and Third of John, which are a column in A, are 5 V-pages. The arrangement would be suggested by the fact that the number of pages in so many of the different Epistles is a multiple of five or near it. We may detect the residual traces of the primitive form by taking some portion of an Epistle and examining its texts side by side for the two codices. Let us take the beautifully uniform writing of Codex B as our measuring line; and begin with one of the shortest Epistles, say the Second Epistle of John. By hypothesis 10 lines of A ought to be one V-page. Actually the first ten lines of A have lost two letters from the first fourteen lines of B. The scribe crowds the next line with five or six extra letters, and by the end of his 20th line is two letters ahead of the pattern. By the 30th line he is 6 or 7 letters ahead, and by the 40th line he is 12 letters ahead, thus enabling him to finish the epistle in nine more lines.

Next, let us try the First Epistle of John. The 10th line of A does not agree with the 14th of B in its ending, but we note a coincidence in ending of the

11 of A and the 14 of B

and the following successive coincidences at ending–

23 of A and the 31 of B	60 of A and the 76 of B
33 "	44 of B	62 "	79 of B
48 "	64 of B	65 "	83 of B

These give us the following and other relations between the A and B line:

$$A = {}^{14}/_{11} B$$
$$A = {}^{4}/_{3} B$$
$$A = {}^{13}/_{10} B$$
$$A = {}^{4}/_{3} B$$
$$A = {}^{3}/_{2} B$$
$$A = {}^{4}/_{3} B$$
$$\text{so } A = {}^{31}/_{23} B, \text{ and so on,}$$

the variety of which is striking; and the results vary much from our hypothesis $A = {}^{7}/_{5} B$.

The same irregularity in the text of A may be illustrated by studying the Epistle to the Galatians. The first 10 lines are exactly a V-page. The next 11 lines are a V-page and 8 letters. The next 10 lines bring us into agreement with the foot of the Vatican column all but a single letter; so that in these three V-pages Codex A has gained a line on its normal type. Or take the Gospel of John: The first 11 lines of A contain the V-page and 2 letters. The first 22 lines contain exactly the two V-pages. The next twelve lines contain a V-page and 2 letters. The next eleven lines end five lines in advance of the V-page; and finally the scribe succeeds in ending his page exactly with the 8th line of a V-page. So that A is exactly six lines behind time on its first column.

It is a wonder, when we examine the irregular writing of A, that we were able to find any trace at all of its original pattern, if indeed we have found it correctly.

2. The following table, in which, by the hypothesis, the pages of Codex A are approximately reduced to V-pages and compared with the Vatican Codex, will be useful:

	A	B
Mark	251	232
Luke	432	411
John	310	292
Acts	401	391
James	40	38
1 Peter	40	38
2 Peter	26	26 or 27
1 John	52 or 53	51
2 John	5	5
3 John	5	5
Jude	11	11
Romans	194	148
1 Corinthians	132?	139
2 Corinthians	99	95
Galatians	49	47
Ephesians	54	49
Philippians	35	33
Colossians	35	34
1 Thessalonians	33	32
2 Thessalonians	18	18

It will be seen that the type has almost disappeared except from the shorter writings. Codex A, then, is a document degenerate in type, but bearing traces of a distant genealogical relation to MSS of the pattern conserved by B.

3. If we take another instance, say Codex Augiensis, a bilingual codex collated by Scrivener, we have a tolerably even Greek text, containing 27 or 28 lines to the column, but the number of letters to the line fluctuates between wider limits than in previous cases. We may put–

	Columns	Lines
Romans	—	15
1 Corinthians	50	27
2 Corinthians	34	27
Galatians	17	15
Ephesians	18	9
Philippians	12	22
Colossians	13	6
1 Thessalonians	11	17

1. New Testament Autographs

	Columns	Lines
2 Thessalonians	5	25
1 Timothy	13	18
2 Timothy	10	2
Titus	6	6
Philemon	2	16

Here all trace of the ancient endings has disappeared, and the only thing noticeable in the endings is an accidental recurrence of multiples of 9.

E. 1. Leaving for a while the criticism of the New Testament, we now proceed to discuss and apply the general method of determining the forms of autographs of any series of letters. If there were but a single size of letter-paper in use, and a single model to intimate the breadth and number of the lines which ought normally to be found upon each separate sheet, the following phenomena would present themselves in the study of any given collection of letters:

First, there would be a very great scarcity of letters ending at the first few lines of a page; and secondly, as we move down the length of the page, we should find a greater number of letters ending at the successive places in the page. Let us call the number of epistles which occupy approximately any given space (the space itself being measured either by the lines of the paper or in any other way) the frequency for the space. Then we say that for letters occupying between n and $\overline{n+1}$ standard pages, the frequency would be a maximum somewhere near the close of the $\overline{n+1}$th page, because there is a tendency, other things being equal, to end one's epistles rather at the bottom of a page than near the top.

For convenience, we shall now change slightly our method of statement; we reserve the word *letter* for printed or written type, and use *epistle* for the document; this will save confusion; and we define as follows:

2. If x be the size of an epistle, expressed in lines of some standard length, or in actual letters, then the number of epistles in a given collection which occupy sizes between $x \pm \epsilon$ where ϵ is some small arbitrary quantity, is called the frequency for that size, and is denoted by $f(x)$. We construct the curve of frequency in the usual manner, and according to our reasoning it runs in the manner expressed by the small curve in the corner of the annexed plate.[65] The meaning of this curve is simply this, that if any length ON be taken representing the length of a given epistle, then PN represents the frequency of epistles of that size.

In our figure OA is a single page, OB two pages, and so on; and the curve intimates that the frequency is a maximum just before we reach OA, OB, OC, etc., and that the frequency diminishes precipitately when we pass the points A, B, C, etc.

65. [see p. 68. AF]

If now we assume a second size of paper and corresponding pattern, we should simply have to trace a second curve with its series of maxima over the first, and the complete system would represent the frequency. And the same would be the case if there were three, four or more patterns.

3. Conversely, if the curve were traced for us we ought to be able to determine very closely the normal sizes of the patterns of original writing. And it is to this problem that we address ourselves, since we have not a few collections of such ancient writings, and have strong evidence that the writers of those epistles used fixed models by which to write. Not to spend time in giving well-known quotations, we simply refer to Isidore, Orig. VI 12:[66] "Quaedam genera librorum certis modulis conficiebantur; breviori forma carmina atque epistulae"; and observe with Birt, *Das Antike Buchwesen*, p. 288, and Reifferscheid, that the expression of Isidore is really taken from Suetonius. We will now commence to analyse the epistles of Pliny and to determine their modulus or pattern.

4. The table which follows will express the size of the different epistles as nearly as possible in terms of the number of lines which they occupy in the Teubner edition.[67] Then from the complete tabulated results we will construct our curve, roughly to scale, and deduce the size of the normal Pliny epistle in terms of the Teubner line.

No. of Teubner Lines	Book 1	Book 2	Book 3	Book 4	Book 5	Book 6	Book 7	Book 8	Book 9	Book 10	Total
1											
2											
3											
4											
5						1		1		2	10	14
6	3	1				1	2		1	2	18	28
7						1	1	3	1	3	7	16
8				1	2			2	1	1	13	20
9					3		2	2	1	3	8	19
10		2			1		1	4	2	3	7	20
11			1		1		1	1	1	7	8	20
12	2				1	1	2		1		4	11
13	3	1			2	2	2	2			4	16
14	1				1		1	1	1	1	4	10
15							2		1	2	2	7
16				4	2		2	1			1	10
17							2	2		4		8

66. [Isidore, *Etymologiarum siue originum libri XX* 6.12.1. AF]

67. [Heinrich Keill and Theodore Mommsen (eds.), *Plini Caecili secundi Epistularum libri novem. Epistularum ad Traianum liber. Panegyricus* (Leipzig: Teubner, 1870). AF]

1. New Testament Autographs

No. of Teubner Lines	Book 1	Book 2	Book 3	Book 4	Book 5	Book 6	Book 7	Book 8	Book 9	Book 10	Total
18	1	1					1	1	2		6
19	1			2	1	1	1	1			6
20		1		1		1			2	2	8
21				2		1		1			4
22	1			1		1	1			2	6
23	3	1	1	1	1				1		8
24	1	1	2				1		1	1	7
25		1			1	1	1			1	5
26				1		1					2
27				1				1			2
28					1		1			1	3
29		1	1	2							4
30					1			2			3
31			1					1	1	1	4
32	1				2						3
33			1		1	1		1		1	5
34		1	1			1			1		4
35				1							1
36		1						2	1		4
37					1						1
38						1	1				2
39			1			1					2
40	1						1				2
41			1			1					2
42		1									1
43		1		1							2
44	1	1									2
45	1							2			3
46			1		1						2
47			2	1	2	1					6
48		1	1						1		3
49											0
50										1	1
51		1									1
52						1					1
53	1				1						2
54											0
55								1			1
56											0
57											0
58						1					1
59											0
60											0
61				1							1

No. of Teubner Lines	Book 1	Book 2	Book 3	Book 4	Book 5	Book 6	Book 7	Book 8	Book 9	Book 10	Total
62											0
63											0
64											0
65					1						1
66											0
67											0
68											0
69											0
70											0
71											0
72								1			1
73	1										1
74											0
75											0
76			1								1
77											0
78											0
79	1					1			1		3
80											0
81											0
82											0
83											0
84											0
85											0
86											0
87				1		1					2
88											0
89											0
90											0
91											0
92											0
93											0
94											0
95								1			1
96											0
97	1										1
98											0
99											0
100											0
101											0
102											0
103											0
104											0
105	1										1

1. New Testament Autographs

No. of Teubner Lines	Book 1	Book 2	Book 3	Book 4	Book 5	Book 6	Book 7	Book 8	Book 9	Book 10	Total
106											0
107											0
108											0
109											0
110											0
111											0
112											0
113											0
114											0
115											0
116											0
117											0
118										1	1
119											0
120											0
121											0
122											0
123											0
124											0
125											0
126											0
127											0
128		1									1
129											0
130											0
131									1		1
132											0
133											0
134											0
135											0
136											0
137											0
138											0
139											0
140											0
141					1						1
142											0
143											0
144											0
145											0
146			1								1

5. The curve is now approximately constructed, and is given in the annexed plate.

James Rendel Harris

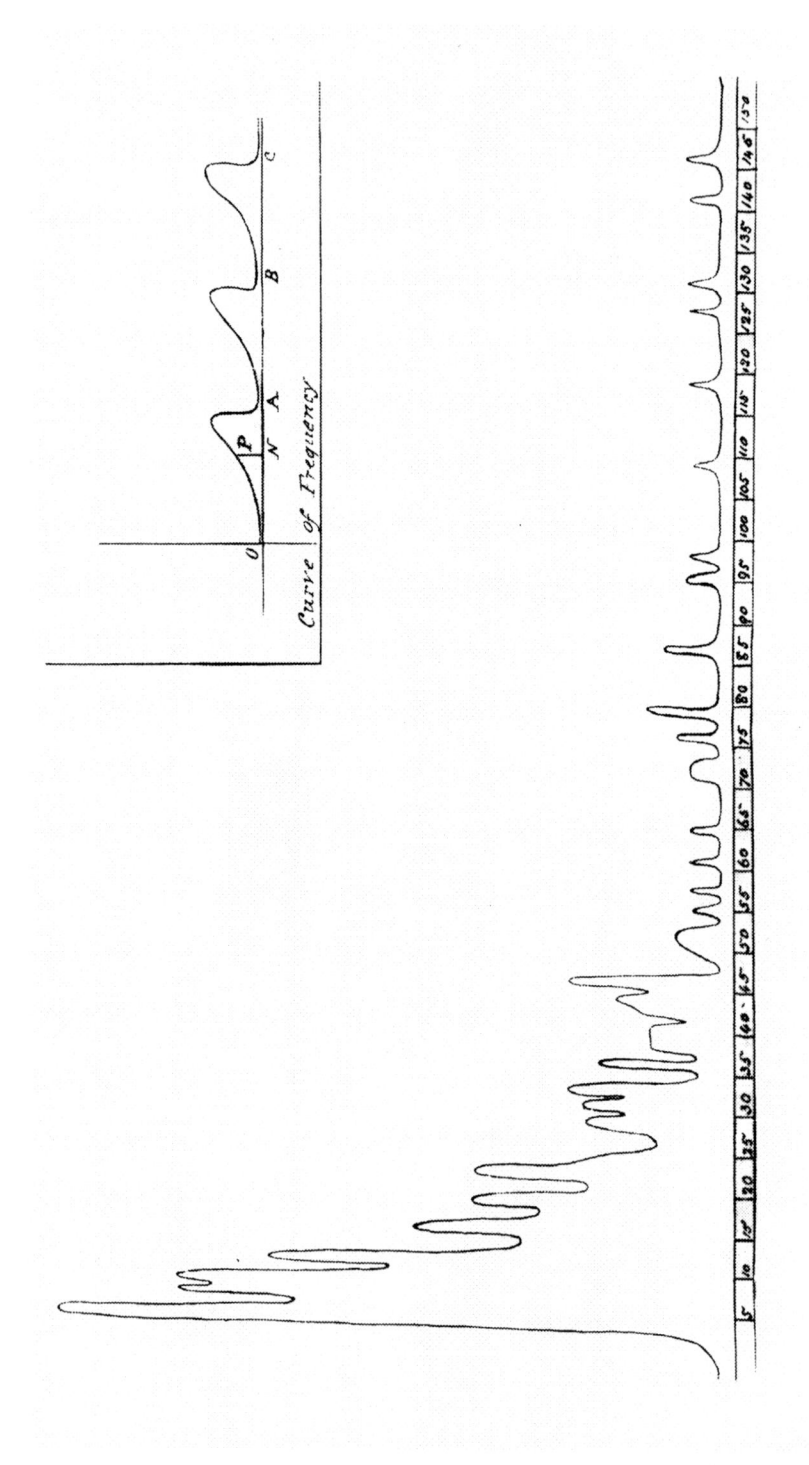

1. *New Testament Autographs*

From the arrangement of the maxim in the curve of frequency we have now to deduce the normal form. Our largest epistle is 146 lines of Teubner type; now we have Pliny's own statement that there are never more than twenty sheets to a scapus or roll, and although this statement is not strictly accurate, we have a right to assume it to be so for Pliny himself. Suppose then that this 146 lines is just under 20 sheets, this would make the single sheets just over 7.3 lines; and we should expect to find successive maxima near the points $x = 7.3$, $x = 14.6$, $x = 21.9$, $x = 29.2$, and so on; or, beginning with the figures in reverse order, we look for maxima at the points 139.7, 132.4, 125.1, 117.8, 110.5, 103.2, 95.9, 88.6, 81.3, 74, 66.7, 59.4, 52.1, 44.8 and so on. This is found to be almost exactly the case for many of the places indicated. The higher maxima above $x = 50$ are at once seen to be parts of the same system; but the lower numbers of the system seem to be a little too small.

The single sheet estimated at 7.3 Teubner lines is a little wrong in its decimal place, and probably should be 7.5 or 7.6. For it is evident that the 20th page of the letter in question (III 9) was not quite filled. He says, "Hic erit epistolae finis, re vera finis; litteram non addam."[68] Taking the latter estimate, and observing that the average Teubner line may be put at 50 letters (which is very nearly the case), we have 380 letters to the Pliny page, which is just over 10 average hexameters; in all probability, then, the majority of the Pliny epistles, especially the longer ones, are written on a 20-lined page of half-hexameters. Whether in the smaller epistles a smaller pattern is sometimes used does not at present appear; but certainly almost all the long ones are very nearly of the pattern indicated.[69]

6. We are able to apply our result to one interesting example.

In Pliny IV 11 we have an epistle of about 61 Teubner lines, in which the writer concludes by demanding an equally long reply, and threatens to count not only the pages of the answer, but the lines and syllables. "Ego non paginas tantum sed versus etiam syllabasque numerabo."[70] From the fact that the epistle is not quite 61 Teubner lines, and since $8 \times 7.6 = 60.8$, we infer that he actually finished the last sheet very closely. The allusion, then, to counting lines and syllables does not refer, as one might have at first supposed, to a superfluous page, but to his purpose not to be satisfied with an eight-paged epistle in reply unless the pages contain 20 good lines to the page, and each line of a proper length.

Birt (*Das Antike Buchwesen*, p. 161) has curiously underestimated the length of this epistle; he describes it as a long epistle, which must have

---

68. [Pliny the Younger, *Ep.* 3.9.37. AF]
69. For instance, if the normal page were 7.4 lines, there would not be more than about 3 out of the 20 longest epistles in which the concluding page was not more than half filled.
70. [*Ep.* 4.11.15. AF]

occupied over *two* pages, and infers that the desired reply is to have at least *three* pages, the third of which is to carry ten additional lines, together with a half line of ten syllables.

It may be interesting to note that the celebrated letter of Pliny to Trajan (X 96) is written on a roll of seven sheets, wanting a couple of lines or thereabouts. The answer occupies about a sheet and a half of the same style of writing.

There are traces of the use of a smaller page of 20 half-iambics, or about 5.7 Teubner lines. Perhaps it is to this model and a roll of 5 sheets that Pliny refers, when he says (III 14), about the 22nd line, "Charta adhuc superest."[71] The whole letter is not 30 lines. But it may almost as well be taken as a 4-paged letter of the larger size.

We can now print the Pliny letters from their autographs approximately.

7. It will be observed that the previous investigation enables us at once to fix a superior limit to the number of pages in the separate books to which the letters are reduced. A full page of the Teubner edition is 38 lines or 5 Pliny pages. The first book cannot therefore contain more than 105 Pliny pages. The second book gives precisely the same estimate, so does the third, and the fourth, and the fifth; the sixth gives 120 as the superior limit, the seventh 110, the eighth 105, the ninth 120, the tenth 150. *Could we have a more forcible suggestion that, in the majority of cases, the letters were actually reduced into rolls of 100 sheets apiece when they came to be edited?*

8. A precisely similar analysis applied to the Tauchnitz text of Josephus[72] enables us to determine the original form of many of the documents embedded in his writings. We have extracted between 60 and 70 letters and decrees from the *Life* and the *Antiquities*.

The results arrange themselves as follows:

Tauchnitz lines	No. of Epistles of that length	Tauchnitz lines	No. of Epistles of that length
3	1	8	5
4	7	9	2
5	0	10	1
6	1	11	5
7	6	12	5
13	1	27	1
14	2	28	1
15	2	29	0
16	1	30	2
17	3	31	0

71. [*Ep.* 3.14.5. AF]

72. ['Tauchnitz text of Josephus': Anon (ed.), *Flavii Iosephi iudaei opera omnia ad optimorum librorum fidem accurate edita* (6 vols.; Leipzig: Caroli Tauchnitii, 1850). AF]

1. New Testament Autographs

Tauchnitz lines	No. of Epistles of that length	Tauchnitz lines	No. of Epistles of that length
18	1	32	0
19	0	33	0
20	4	34	1
21	1	35	1
22	1	37	1
23	2	43	2
24	3	54	1
25	1	60	1
26	0		0

Here we are at once struck with the recurrence of the multiples of four, and examination at once shows that four lines of Tauchnitz type in Josephus are 12 half-iambics or an S-page very exactly. Similar examination will show that a page of 20 half-iambics is 6.6 Tauchnitz lines, and a page of 20 half-hexameters is 11.6 lines. From these results the majority of the writings indicated are at once reduced to their original patterns. The recurrence of the S-type simply means that Josephus has manufactured not a few of them, as letters would have been written by his own hand, for we have already determined, from the stichometry of the *Antiquities*, and confirmed the result by the examination of certain letters, that Josephus uses the iambic verse as his model.

Chapter 2

Methods of Research in Eastern Libraries

In the present lecture I shall try to point out to you, in a popular manner, some of the directions in which important research may be carried out by Patristic students in the libraries of the East, and to add a few practical hints which may be of service to the explorer. It is a time of mutual congratulation and of renewed hope amongst the students of early Christian literature when fresh matters of the highest interest are constantly being recovered; and when scarcely a year passes without being marked by some valuable restoration of lost documents, some salvage from the continual shipwreck of literature on the rocks of time. We have only to recall the titles of some of the recently recovered texts, such as the *Teaching of the Twelve Apostles*, the new Syriac and Greek texts of St Clement of Rome, Hippolytus on Daniel, Tatian's *Diatessaron*, Aristides' *Apology*, the Greek *Acts of Perpetua*, the new *Acts of the Scillitan Martyrs*, the *Gospel* and *Apocalypse of Peter*, the Greek of *Enoch*, and last but not least, my friend Mrs. Lewis' palimpsest gospels of the Syriac version, and we shall see at a glance that if anyone comes to preach to Patristic students, he does not, to use the language of the *Peter Gospel*, preach to them that are asleep: it is an offence against good sense to talk of the students of Christian origins, as though they had not yet come up out of the Hades of an assumed mediaeval ignorance and superstition. Theologians to-day do not need to find their intellectual aliment in dry bones and remainder biscuit; there are "new grapes on the vine," "new figs on the tender spray,"[1] and in common English there is new hope in the hearts of the investigators. What may be the next treasure that will come to light? We ask the question, and answer it with wishes that are the fathers of thoughts; we turn over the memoranda of Eusebius, the notes of Photius, the early stichometries, and say to ourselves of one precious lost volume after another, "Thou lost sheep of the House of Israel, I will leave my other ninety-nine volumes on the bookshelves and go into the wastes and mountains in search of thee, until I find thee; and if by good hap I shall find thee, I will call together my friends and kinsmen in other Universities and say 'Rejoice with me, for I have found my Papias which was lost'—why

---

1. [Christina Georgina Rossetti, *Passing Away*. AF]

2. *Methods of Research in Eastern Libraries* 73

not Papias? The students of the Synoptic question need him badly enough, and are hardly likely to settle their disputes without his aid, even though he were as Eusebius says, a person of rather slender understanding;[2] and I am sure the owners of landed estates would be glad of his help in the settlement of the agricultural question, and the correction of the unequal ratio between produce and rent by the production of 500 barrels of flour from a single ear of wheat, with oil and wine in the like proportion![3] What a flood of light he would throw upon the spiritualization of the Old Testament records in the preaching of the early Church, or upon the character of the school of the blessed St John at Ephesus. Do not let us despair of finding Papias. We need not be very far from the successful quest. I think we have been looking for him in the wrong direction. People have taken hold of a certain notice which seemed to imply that the works of Papias were extant in the 13th century in the library of the cloister of the Cathedral Church at Nismes, and have conjectured that we were to find the lost work in Latin in some one of the departmental libraries of France. The notice was found in a catalogue dated 1209 A.D. of the books in the library at Nismes, which catalogue was printed in the first volume of Menard's *History of Nismes* in 1750;[4] Menard's statement is:

> Quoique l'ignorance fût encore très générale dans le XIIIème siècle, il paraît que le clergé de Nismes cherchoit à s'instruire, sinon dans l'histoire profane, et dans les lettres humaines, du moins dans les études ecclésiastiques. Un inventaire que Bertrand du Pont, chanoine, nouvellement nommé à l'office de sacristain de la Cathédrale, fit faire le 11 de Janvier de l'an 1218 (1219) de tous les meubles de la sacristie, nous apprend que cette église étoit fournie de divers livres ... l'ouvrage de Papias, évêque d'Hiéraple, qui contenoit en cinq livres les explications des discours de Notre Seigneur, ouvrage qui existoit encore du temps de Trithème, abbé de Spanheim, vers la fin du XV siècle.

This inventory is printed in full by Menard: the part which concerns us is the following:

> Item inveni in claustro duo responsalia; duo officialia; et librum concatenatum ad farestol, in quo psalterium cum colletum et officiali; et librum dominicalem; librum Papiae; librum de verbis Domini; librum spissum; Matheum; passionarum qui vocatur Galazanegues etc.

The exciting sentence is as follows:

> Item inveni in claustro ... librum Papiae librum de verbis Domini.

---

2. [*Hist. eccl.* 3.39.13. AF]
3. [See Irenaeus, *Haer.* 5.33.3-4. AF]
4. [Léon Ménard, *Histoire civile, ecclésiastique et litteraire de la Ville de Nismes: Avec des notes et les preuves, suivie de dissertations historiques et critiques sur les antiquités et de diverses observations sur son histoire naturelle* (7 vols.; Paris: Chaubert, 1750–1758). AF]

If these two entries referred to the same thing, we should naturally retranslate into: Λογίων κυριακῶν ἐξήγησις which Jerome rendered as "Explanatio sermonum Domini."[5]

But I am afraid it is a mere mare's nest, and that the volume of Papias is the already printed Papias the Grammarian, who is referred to the latter part of the twelfth century and that the other work is Augustine's *Sermones de Verbis Domini*. All the light that I can get on the question tends this way, though I have not been able finally and exhaustively to prove it.

But if Papias is not to be found in a Latin translation at Nismes or in the neighbourhood of Nismes, there is another direction which is much more hopeful. Let me take a few minutes to shew the high probability that the lost work of Papias will eventually be recovered from the excavations in the Fayyûm. The way I should present the case is as follows:

We know what sort of people, ecclesiastically, lived in the Fayyûm in the third century; they were the theological followers of Papias, in holding the doctrine of the Thousand Years' reign of Christ and his saints on earth, just as Irenaeus did, and Victor of Petau and other early Fathers. There was a bishop in the Fayyûm in the third century, whose name was Nepos, of whom Eusebius tells us that he interpreted the Scripture in too Jewish a manner and that he supposed that there would be a thousand years of bodily delight on this earth. In this opinion he confirmed himself by certain passages in the Apocalypse and wrote a confutation of those Allegorists who interpreted these passages mystically. Dionysius, the famous bishop of Alexandria went down to the Fayyûm and held a long and protracted conference with the followers of Nepos, who had recently died, in which he succeded in convincing them by sweet reasonableness and arguments seasoned with charity, that they were all wrong on the subject of the Millenium. The words of Eusebius are as follows (*H.E.* VII.24):[6]

> Νέπως ἦν ἐπίσκοπος τῶν κατ' Αἴγυπτον, Ἰουδαικώτερον τὰς ἐπηγγελμένας τοῖς ἁγίοις ἐν ταῖς θείαις γραφαῖς ἐπαγγελίας ἀποδοθήσεσθαι διδάσκων, καί τινα χιλιάδα ἐτῶν τρυφῆς σωματικῆς ἐπὶ τῆς ξηρᾶς ταύτης ἔσεσθαι ὑποτιθέμενος. Δόξας γοῦν οὗτος ἐκ τῆς ἀποκαλύψεως Ἰωάννου τὴν ἰδίαν κρατύνειν ὑπόληψιν, ἔλεγχον ἀλληγοριστῶν λόγον τινὰ περὶ τούτου συντάξας ἐπέγραψε· πρὸς ὃν ὁ Διονύσιος ἐν τοῖς περὶ ἐπαγγελίων ἐνίσταται κτέ.

There is much in this that is very like the description given of the doctrine of Papias by early Church Fathers: we find Jerome (*De Virr. Ill.* 18)[7] saying of Papias that his interpretations were Jewish, and that he taught that the Lord was going to reign in the flesh with his saints: "Hic dicitur mille annorum

---

5. [*Vir. ill.* 18. AF]
6. [*Hist. eccl.* 7.24.1-3. AF]
7. [*Vir. ill.* AF]

2. Methods of Research in Eastern Libraries 75

Judaicam edidisse δευτέρωσιν quem secuti sunt Irenaeus et Apollinarius et caeteri qui post resurrectionem aiunt in carne cum sanctis Dominum regnaturum." This is very like what Eusebius says of Nepos, and the stand which Nepos made against those who allegorised the promises of the Scripture is exactly parallel to the position of Irenaeus, the follower of Papias, who maintains that it is not possible to allegorise away the promises so as to be consistent in one's interpretations. Iren. V.35.[8] "Si autem quidam tentaverint allegorisare haec quae eiusmodi sunt, neque de omnibus poterunt consonantes semetipsis inveniri." It is clear Nepos belonged to the school of Papias, and we even suspect that some of the expressions in which Eusebius describes him are borrowed from Papias.

Nepos then, is the last of the chiliastic bishops in the city of Arsenoe. It is likely that the city had from the beginning been the centre of a millennial propaganda, and perhaps the reference in the Muratorian Canon to "Arsinoi" whose books the Church did not read may be an allusion to the Arsenoite party. But whether this is the case or not, I should say that if we want to find Papias' works, we should look to the Fayyûm for them, either to the Christian tombs, or to some of the Coptic monasteries that yet remain.

You see I am not hopeless about the recovery of this valuable Father. When we find him we shall also find that his language and interpretations have coloured the books of a whole line of Patristic writers from Irenaeus down to Andreas of Cesarea. But if we are not to despair of Papias, why may we not refuse to despair of, say, Marcion? Why should he not follow the injunction of the Revised Version, which, in one of its many mistranslations has advised us to despair of no man. If there is any such thing as fitness in the nature of things, the present time when we are going through a period of speculation exactly that which worried Marcion, would seem to be a very suitable time for the recovery of the lost work on *Contradictions* in which Marcion pointed out the ethical inconsistency between the God of the Old Testament and the Father of the New. I am on the "qui vive" to turn Marcionite, and the lost *Antitheses* would probably settle me. In the last days, you will say, the sheep will be turned into wolves! Unhappily one does not know in what direction to look for works of this kind; the only thing that presents itself to my mind as possible being an excavation on the site of the Marcionite synagogue of which the ruins are said to be still extant in the transJordanic country. But here the difficulty would be that we do not know that it was the Syrian custom to bury books with the dead: we are not able to affirm that the blessed practice of supplying a book to the departed for his intellectual repose which prevailed in Egypt, and gave us our Hieratic rituals, our Greek Homer papyri, and our Peter scraps, extended to Palestine or Syria.

8. [*Haer.* 4.35.1. AF]

But whatever be the next great find, let us start with the assumption that in Christian literature the maxim of Browning applies that "the best is yet to be";[9] let us say with the Montanists "the exuberance of grace is reserved for the last days";[10] let us allegorize the Fourth Gospel, and demonstrate that big fishes are all in the last chapter. Two prejudices need to be removed; one relates to ourselves, the belief that in any given direction the mine is worked out; the other is the prejudice of the wicked world which inclines to the conviction that whenever any one finds a book, it is because he has written it, a prejudice which has been much increased by the modern criticism of the Old Testament with its unqualified depreciation of the moral character of Hilkiah the high priest.[11] However, if we can get rid of our own prejudices, we can leave those of the world to take care of themselves; for when, as we have said, every year has some notable recovery, either in classical or in Biblical literature, we have only to keep the general public properly informed of what is going on, to be sure of their sympathies after a little time has been allowed for the operation of their understanding.

And for ourselves, as I have said, we must shake off the feeling that in any direction the day of the explorer is over; that Sinai is an extinct volcano, and Nitria more than ever a desert. Need I furnish you with the classical illustration of the folly of this state of mind in the case of Dr Coxe of the Bodleian; you will find in his *Report to Her Majesty's Government on the Greek Manuscripts yet Remaining in the Libraries of the Levant* p. 7,[12] the following instructive sentence:

> My mission ended with respect to Cairo, the question arose whether I ought not to go on to Thebes and Mount Sinai. The reasons, however, why I did not consider myself justified in visiting places of such immense classical and literary interest are the following:— The object of my travel was to ascertain what was existing in places either little visited, or of which the contents were not known: but at Thebes everything as soon as discovered (and many additional Greek papyri have been lately found) is immediately made public, and offered to the highest of the many bidders always ready on the spot to avail themselves of any such opportunity, so that I should have merely added one more to the list of competitors and, under the most fortunate circumstances, could but have secured for her Majesty's Government at a great cost, what in all probability will eventually find their way to the national collectors under more favourable circumstances, or what at all events, into whosoever hands they might fall, must most assuredly be made public; whilst at Mount Sinai, after the visit of so eminent a palaeographer and critic as Dr Tischendorf to say nothing of the visits of many other literary men, there could be nothing which would justify the hope of discovering anything which has escaped their practised eyes.

9. [Robert Browning, *Rabbi Ben Ezra*. AF]
10. [*Passio Perpetuae et Felicitatis* 13. AF]
11. [2 Kgs. 22.8. AF]
12. [Henry O. Coxe, *Report to Her Majesty's Government on the Greek Manuscripts Yet Remaining in the Libraries of the Levant* (London, 1858). AF]

2. Methods of Research in Eastern Libraries 77

The date of this report is A.D. 1858; at this date there was still lying in the library a certain Codex Sinaiticus still unappropriated by the great brigand of Leipsic, to say nothing of sundry minor matters which have since come to light.

It is well to be fore-armed against the feeling that a library has been worked out by previous travellers. At Sinai few people have time to do more than nibble.

What is true of Sinai in Coxe's day is true of Sinai to-day; it is also true of almost every great library in existence East or West, from the Laura on Mount Athos to the British Museum. Now a person who is going to work in Eastern libraries must undergo a certain amount of preliminary training. He must have a few ideas about his work and the people he is to work with, a reasonable amount of currency, some knowledge of modern Greek and a superfluity of good manners. As I am usually weak on the first two heads and not a colossus in Greek, I endeavour to make up in courtesy what I want in linguistics, or in backsheesh! It is a delusion to suppose that you are going amongst a degraded set of people when you visit a Greek monastery. Dr Shaff, who visited the Sinai convent, speaks of them in one of his books as a set of dirty monks who could not read the documents which they possessed. It would probably be equally true that the party to which Dr Schaff belonged were a set of dirty tourists; certainly as regards knowledge, the monks are not to be derided, for they still take a pleasure in showing their visitor's book in which Dr Schaff has transcribed incorrectly the Nicene Creed. The great question of life is not whether we have used Pears' Soap this morning, but whether we have said our Credo rightly and whether we have washed our hands in innocency. And as for the question of knowledge my own experience is that I frequently tested the librarian at Sinai on the matter of the dates of Greek MSS and seldom found him at fault; yet he had never read any treatise on palaeography, and he could not have stolen his knowledge from Gardthausen's Catalogues of the Sinai MSS, for as he confessed to me, somewhat sadly, Prof. Gardthausen who had enjoyed the hospitality of the Convent for several months, did not send them a copy of the Catalogue.[13]

I had a lesson on the inferiority of Western manners to those of the East when I was in the convent of St John on Mt. Patmos;[14] they brought me a cutting of a New-York paper, containing a rude newspaper drawing and equally rude newspaper article on the Rvd. Paisius Ferendinus, a Patmos priest who had recently come to New-York to minister in the Greek Church. The article which I was asked to give the monks a written translation of, began something as follows: "Very many strange beasts have visited our

---

13. [Viktor Gardthausen, *Catalogus codicum graecorum sinaiticorum* (Oxford: Clarendon Press, 1886). AF]

14. [Probably in 1892. AF]

shores since the primitive savage was first disturbed from his primeval lair. But none more strange than that figure which landed last Saturday from the steamer Circassian." Then followed brilliant and epigrammatic sentences in the best journalistic style on the length of the locks of the said Paisius Ferendinus and the style of his stove-pipe bonnet. What was I to do in translating this, which the innocent Paisius, as yet unlearned in English but misled Narcissus-like, by the beauty of his own face exhibited by a rude woodcut in the midst of the tale, had forwarded to his friends on Patmos in token of the welcome which had been given him, as the representative of the holy Eastern Church. I will confess that I translated freely, paraphrastically; I usually find that the safer method, and in the case in question it was imperative; the translation ran something in this style: "The Venerable Paisius Ferendinus has recently arrived in New-York from the S.S. Circassian; he wears the dress and the hat of a Greek priest; we have not seen one like him before." I am firmly convinced that in the matter of the courtesy of life, the darker portion of the world, as the writer of the *Clementine Homilies*[15] puts it, is the West, and nothing will make one's way so much with Greek monks as studious attention to the lesser courtesies. I do not mean that one should tell lies, but if a Greek monk congratulates you, as I was congratulated on Mount Athos, on your excellent mastery of the Greek speech, by saying παντὲς οἱ λόρδοι Ἀγγλικοὶ ὁμιλοῦσιν Ἑλληνιστί, it is not necessary to inform them that you are not the first cousin of the Marquis of Salisbury; if you do that you run the risk of lowering the influence of the Marquis as well as your own. I made a mistake on this line in Patmos; I had been deploring that I had not the pleasure of bringing my wife with me into that island sanctuary, especially as I saw in the visitor's book the name of Mr. and Mrs. Theodore Bent; I demanded an explanation of this outrage upon the convent of the ἀεὶ παρθένος. The polite answer was that everything was allowed to persons of distinction (τοῖς ἐπισήμοις), I made the reply that I was afraid I was not an ἐπίσημος. This was a mistake; let another depreciate you, and not your own lips!

Often, in working in Eastern libraries, and amongst Eastern people, I have found that my success has been due to some trifling allusion to historical matters, or to hagiology, or some little witticism which they would revel over and never tire of repeating.

I believe that I won the heart of Galaktion, the Sinai librarian,[16] by the simple fact that in the calendar of the Martyrs there is mention of Galaktion and his sister Episteme; I always asked him after the health of his sister and it never failed to arouse his interest. I remember when I was working in the Lebanon at a place called Besherreh,[17] where there are two or three monasteries

15. [*Ps.-Clem., Epistula Clementis* 1.3. AF]
16. [During a visit to St Catherine's monastery in 1889. AF]
17. [In 1888. AF]

and an old church, that I owed some success to a happy turn in the conversation. Besherreh is a beautiful place, about half a day's ride from the Cedars on this side of the Anti-Libanus. Every North Syrian loves Besherreh; as I was riding along the seashore from Beyrout we got into conversation with a native, who wished to know where we were going, and when I told him Besherreh he said: "Oh! that I were a flea in your pocket, that I might go with you." We told him we were carrying freight, but no passengers! However when we came to Besherreh at night-fall, the whole village as represented by the Notables and Clergy assembled in the house of the Sheikh of the place to interview us; and I was glad of the opportunity because there were some old liturgical MSS in the church, which I coveted, not because they were my neighbour's, which would be an infringement of the Decalogue, but in the Pauline manner, because they were the best things the village possessed. We sat round on divans, and they began to put their sounding-lines down into the shallow waters of my theological and political knowledge. One of the first started was as to the locality of the garden of Eden: a difficult question; I have always had longitudinal and latitudinarian scepticism about this garden; and Prof. Ryle's book on Genesis[18] was not on hand to assist me. However, the question was put to me, and I promptly replied that it seemed to me that all the evidence pointed to its being in the neighbourhood of Besherreh. That carried the day, and it is solely to this triumph of modern criticism that I attribute the fact that next morning early they brought me two ancient Syriac liturgies from the church, to be exchanged for the modest sum of four napoleons and a backsheesh.

In Mount Athos,[19] of course, I found the monks much better informed; they were keen at theology and deep in politics. They were much interested in the Septuagint; so I used to explain to them about Hexapla readings, and shew them instances in the margins of the MSS. But what I always led up to was the reading of Symmachus in Gen. 3, to the effect that it was not good for man to be μοναχός; this observation never failed to provoke the liveliest interest, and if anyone doubted whether the narratives of Genesis had any influence on modern life, his suspicions would have been entirely dissipated.

(By the bye this usage of Symmachus has an important bearing upon the account of the ascent of the blessed Perpetua by a ladder where only one μοναχός could ascend at a time.[20])

If they found fault with my imperfect Greek pronunciation, and said that they could not understand how we western people could be so foolish as to follow the Erasmus pronunciation of the diphthongs (of which supposed

---

18. [Herbert E. Ryle, *The Early Narratives of Genesis: A Brief Introduction to the Study of Genesis I-XI* (London: MacMillan, 1892). AF]

19. [In 1891. AF]

20. [*Passio Perpetuae et Felicitatis* 5.3. AF]

crime of invention of Anglican Greek pronunciation I believe Erasmus to be innocent), I found it usually sufficient to divert the critical thunderbolt from my devoted head by the sententious remark that I believed Erasmus was dead, which tiny joke always hit the mark, and restored me to linguistic orthodoxy. The fact is, these Greek monks are delightful company; they are capital talkers, and know a good deal of what is going on in the world. When I tell you that in Patmos I read a translation of one of Prof. Drummond's recent tracts, I think it was *The Greatest Thing in the World*,[21] you will see that Patmos is not such a very out of the way place. At the Monastery of Ivéron, as we were one day discussing a banquet of snails with the chief of the fathers, the conversation became suddenly very animated; I did not at first catch what was going on, but presently I woke up to the consciousness that they were discussing materialism (for I caught the word ὑλισμός repeated several times) and in particular whether I was a materialist. They put the question at last to me definitely. I replied that, if I did not believe in a life to come, I would soon put an end to the life that was. This summary method of dealing with the convolutions of this mortal coil pleased them highly, and, with some protests on the part of one monk, who, I think, believed that I was talking evasively or at all events not theologically, I was voted a good Christian; whereupon we resumed the subject of the snails. But I hope I have said enough to satisfy you that the monks of the Greek Church are an interested and enlightened set of people, and that you will not put the snails in evidence on the other side.

And now to come to the question with which we are more especially interested, viz.: the subject of Biblical and Patristic research. The first thing that will surprise you is the facilities in the matter of catalogues, and the second the facilities in the matter of access to the MSS: on both of which points they are far ahead of Oxford and Cambridge; you will find that the major part of the libraries are not only catalogued but the catalogues are many of them printed. For example, the MSS at Smyrna were catalogued by Papadopoulos Kerameus,[22] it was his first attempt and is rather a juvenile book, but quite sufficient for purposes of reference. This catalogue will be found in one of the numbers of the Smyrna Museum. The MSS at Jerusalem are all catalogued by the same hand,[23] and most of the catalogue is printed along with part of the Anecdota of the Library. Kerameus has also catalogued the books in the Patriarchal Library at Cairo, and those in the Holy Sepulchre at Constantinople.

---

21. [Henry Drummond, *The Greatest Thing in the World: An Address* (London: Hodder & Stoughton, 1890). AF]

22. [Athanasios I. Papadopoulos-Kerameus, *Catalogue of the Manuscripts in the Smyrna Library of the Evangelical School* (Smyrna, 1877) [in Greek]. AF]

23. [Athanasios I. Papadopoulos-Kerameus, *Jerusalem Library* (5 vols.; Saint Petersburg, 1891–1915) [in Greek]. AF]

2. Methods of Research in Eastern Libraries 81

For Sinai we have Gardthausen's book,[24] which must not be taken too seriously, for it seldom gives the contents more than by approximation, and many valuable pieces are thus unnoticed. Neither does he notice the Greek fragments, nor the Oriental books. For Patmos we have a splendid catalogue by the late John Sakkelion and other Patmos monks,[25] and Sakkelion's son if I remember right is responsible for the newly issued catalogue of the University Library at Athens.[26] In the Greek islands there are also some books; for example in the island of Andros there are some good MSS of which I have an approximate catalogue, printed by a traveller of some years since. For Mt. Athos we have not only a preliminary catalogue by Lambros (and are there not some other printed catalogues of the Holy Mountain) but there are also the catalogues which our own Cambridge Press has nearly printed, containing Lambros' exhaustive treatment of all the smaller collections on Athos.[27] Unfortunately for us, Lambros has not dealt with the two great collections, viz.: the library of Vatopedi and the library of St Athanasius' Laura. Of the former of these there is a written catalogue in the monastery, a very fair product, though I do not think they will allow it to be printed; and for the Laura, where the whole of the books are being re-arranged under the care of the learned librarian Alexandros and the sub-librarian Gabriel, a catalogue is being carefully prepared. When we reflect that in Cambridge we have, if I remember aright, only three or four printed catalogues of MSS collection (such as Caius, Corpus, and the University Library) and that Trinity College has no printed handbook, nor the excellent collections at Pembroke and Peterhouse, we must admit that the East is not so far behind the times. For be it remembered, I have not counted mere *memoranda*, such as those in Coxe's report of his visit of the libraries of the Levant. Nearly all those to which I refer are *catalogues raisonnés* where the descriptions are complete, and the dates fairly exact.

Perhaps I may be allowed to quote here a few sentences which I wrote some years since in description of the Patriarchal Library at Jerusalem, which expresses what I believe would be the feeling of all persons who are custodians of valuable books:

> A catalogue, especially a detailed printed catalogue, is almost as good a protection as a fire-proof building or an iron door ... The scribe's anathema upon the alienator of books will give way to the more effectual operation of common law, and instead of invoking the malediction of the 318 Holy Nicene Fathers,

---

24. [*Catalogus*. AF]
25. [Monastery of Saint John Theologos, *Patmos Library* (Athens, 1890) [in Greek]. AF]
26. [Ioannes Sakkelion and Alkiviados I. Sakkelion, *Catalogue of the Manuscripts of the National Library of Greece* (Athens, 1892) [in Greek]. AF]
27. [Spyridon P. Lambros, *Catalogue of the Greek Manuscripts on Mount Athos* (Cambridge: Cambridge University Press, 1895–1900). AF]

we shall rely upon the protection of the civil authority who has charge of the charitable and ecclesiastical possessions.[28]

But, as I have said, the libraries are not only properly housed and catalogued, but they are accessible to persons with satisfactory credentials. Very seldom have I found any difficulty in obtaining access to the books. The only place in Athos where I found things move slowly was Vatopedi, where the librarian was an aged man who does not wish to visit the library more than once a day, nor to stay there long at a time, nor to let you have more than one book at a time in your room. But, as he comes to know you better, his rigidity relaxes, and he is really a very interesting and very intelligent person. At Athens the case was quite different. I had great difficulty here: it was a time of transition; a new keeper of the MSS was just appointed, and a new catalogue just under way. But they would not communicate the catalogue to me, apparently because there was much new matter in it and I was looked upon as a text-grabber! However, the less said on that point, perhaps, the better.

And now I will give you some rapid hints, with the aid of the map, as to the method of proceeding in Mount Athos.[29]

Perhaps I may be allowed to conclude with a few words of caution in respect to the time of the year at which it is best to visit the Athos monasteries. Athos is always delightful, but there are limitations to the happiness which it affords. Some of these limitations always exist; the absence of one sex, in man and in brute is a drawback. As a half-witted fellow said to me at one of the little farms or κελλία which I visited, you don't see any lambs here! The re-action from a state of society in which lambs can exist to one in which they are mere poetical abstractions is a very decided one: it needs to be taken gently. But besides the continual limitations of one's normal manner of life in consequence of the exaggerated monasticism of the peninsula, there are also the hardships of the greater fasts; they are severe, and not to be evaded except in a very slight degree. Lent is real business on Mount Athos, and even at Patmos, where they relax the rule a little in the case of travellers, it is hard work. But above all things, if you wish to study, do not go to the monastery of Vatopedi at the festival of the Annunciation. For this feast is a great fair, and there will be thousands of people from all parts, and great monastic welcomes, and comings and goings, and chafferings and chatterings; but for us who come from the West, it is strange to move about amongst the stalls, and see no ballads, and no one who answers to the name of Mopsa, no tawdry lace, nor pair of sweet gloves, no curds and no cream, and no one to be the queen of curds and cream.

28. ["The Library of the Convent of the Holy Sepulchre at Jerusalem," *Haverford College Studies* 1 (1889), pp. 1-17, 1-2. AF]

29. [I have not found the map. AF]

Chapter 3

THE RATE OF PROGRESS IN NEW TESTAMENT RESEARCH

The criticism of the New Testament is, in our day, one of the progressive sciences. It has history and it has outlook. In its history there are eras from which we reckon, in its prospect there are expectations which are of the colour of jocund day, in spite of the mist upon the mountain tops. Its record involves epoch-making discoveries which revolutionize the text, epoch-making minds which interpret the materials both new and old. "This was a great discovery," and "this was a great man," we say, in all the retrospect of genuine scientific life, and we can certainly say it in New Testament criticism, whether we begin our reckoning with Erasmus, or whether we end it with Hort. Listen carefully and you will hear the spirits that preside over the various sciences talking to one another and to themselves; they have been assigned the duty of ministering to those who are intellectually to inherit salvation, each having his order and his duty (as the Jews assigned angels to the separate elements and even set one to look after the wild beasts);[1] and the refrain which you will catch from their soliloquy or from their intercourse is the confession of Galileo, *E pur si muove.* This formula applies both to the matter and to the method of science, as in Galileo's own case. It was true of what he saw with his telescope, it was true of what could be seen in himself when the instrument of research was turned inward. For he could not have affirmed motion in the outward cosmos if he had not experienced motion in the inward man. There were "new lands, rivers and mountains in the spotty globe" of his own brain, as well as in the moon that he saw "from the top of Fiesole or in Valdarno." Now in every science our Master says to us "Blessed are your eyes, for they see." So we may make a calendar to suit each separate branch of knowledge out of the things seen and the people that see, out of the epoch-making events and the epoch-making men.

In the present short course of lectures I wish to say something about the text of the New Testament, considered as a field of progressive research, and to ask whether we are likely to obtain much further light in days to come, either with regard to the text or its meaning. May we say, for instance, that the text is settled; or that it is more than ever, and perhaps finally unsettled? May we

1. See Hermas. *Vis.* iv [4.2. AF].

look at the foot of the page of a critical New Testament, upon the various readings in their mounded heaps, and say complacently, as Bentley did, that it doesn't matter? Are we as sure as he was that he had a test by which to separate the precious from the vile, and that "out of a labyrinth of thirty thousand various readings that crowd the pages of our present best editions, all put upon equal credit, to the offence of many good persons, this clue so leads and extricates us, that there will be scarce two hundred out of so many thousands that can deserve the least consideration." How is that for optimism?[2] Why, there are nearly two hundred alternative readings to Matthew alone, at the foot of the pages of Westcott and Hort's New Testament[3] after a criticism that was certainly drastic, and almost as self-confident as Bentley's. "Scarce two hundred that can deserve the least consideration!" Bentley's language reminds me of an experience of my own some thirty years ago. One of the fellows of my college came into my room one day and found me poring over the various readings in Tischendorf's New Testament.[4] He asked me why I was wasting my time upon that: the question, said he, was settled thirty years before. The speaker was in the year of grace 2 B.H. (i.e. two years before Hort), and he assumed that the problem of the New Testament text had been settled in the year 32 B.H. If I had believed his warning, many things would not have happened: for example, I should not be lecturing here to-day on the rate of progress in New Testament Research. But if we must not say that the text of the New Testament is settled, what are we to say of its unsettlement? Is it true that it doesn't matter; or is the unsettlement of the text like the tremors in the seismic instruments of some volcanic observatory which tell us that Vesuvius is alive and that we are going to hear from him presently?

Dr Hort, to whom I have referred as one of the calendar men of the science, is almost as much of an optimist as Bentley, only his optimism takes a different form. He occasionally despairs of the text and suggests emendations outside the manuscript evidence; but he is quite confident that the text has never undergone heretical manipulations and that no doctrines of Christianity are affected

---

2. Equally optimistic was his reply to Collins [Anthony Collins, *A Discourse of Free-Thinking: Occasion'd by the Rise and Growth of a Sect Call'd Free-Thinkers* (London, 1713). AF] in the famous *Remarks upon a Late Discourse of Freethinking* [Phileleutherus Lipsiensis (Robert Bentley), *Remarks upon a Late Discourse of Free-Thinking in a Letter to F. H. D.D.* (London: J. Morphew, E. Curll, 1713). AF], "not frightened therefore with the present 30,000, I for my part, and (as I believe) many others would not lament, if out of the old manuscripts yet untouched 1,000 more were faithfully collected; some of which without question would render the text more beautiful, just and exact; though of no consequence to the main of religion, nay perhaps wholly synonymous in the view of common readers, and quite insensible in any modern version."

3. [*New Testament*, I. AF]

4. [Tischendorf, *Novum Testamentum*. AF]

3. The Rate of Progress in New Testament Research

by the investigations of the textual critic. To make sure that I do not misrepresent him I will transcribe some of his actual words:[5] "It will not be out of place to add here a distinct expression of our belief that even among the numerous unquestionably spurious readings of the New Testament there are no signs of deliberate falsification for dogmatic purposes." "Accusations of wilful tampering with the text are accordingly not infrequent in Christian antiquity; but with a single exception, wherever they can be verified they prove to be groundless, being in fact hasty and unjust inferences from mere diversities of inherited text." The one exception which Dr Hort allows to his rule is that of the text of Marcion, who mutilated the Gospel of Luke in the interests of his own theological system. And Dr Hort concludes with two optimistic statements: first, that "the books of the New Testament as preserved in extant documents assuredly speak to us in every important respect in language identical with that in which they spoke to those for whom they were originally written"; second, that "it would be an illusion to anticipate important changes of text from any acquisition of new evidence." A good deal has happened since those sentences were written, and much water has flowed even under the theological bridges where the currents are usually abnormally slow. It will be sufficient to say that the assumptions of textual certainty and almost final textual accuracy have not been verified, and that there is much new evidence constantly coming to light, some of which does matter not a little. Perhaps Dr Hort's misstatement under this head is due to an error, with which he and Dr Westcott started on their work that the evidence was all collected and that they had only to avail themselves of the labours of their predecessors. So far, then, we find premature optimism to prevail with regard to the outcome of New Testament criticism, and premature optimism is not one of the marks of progress.

The fact is that in spite of all the work done by great and good men upon the subject, New Testament criticism has not yet found its Newton.

That does not mean that we are not making progress, real and substantial progress. There was progress before Newton, progress after him, progress especially in him; there is progress between one Newton and the next. It is almost necessary to remind ourselves of this, because there was, and still is, especially in Cambridge circles, something like a belief that the laws of intellectual progress were suspended by Providence at the time of Dr Hort's death, and many absurd things have been said about the finality of his analysis of the grouping of the New Testament MSS, which that acute and modest scholar would have been the first to repudiate.

Now, in order to find out what has been done in this branch of science, let us look back a little; and I suggest that a good date to look back to will be the year of grace 1881. In this year there occurred three events that were, for

---

5. *Introduction* pp. 282-85 [Westcott and Hort, *New Testament*, II. AF].

Englishmen at all events, of prime importance in the history of New Testament criticism: the first was the publication of the Revised Version of the New Testament;[6] the second the almost coincident[7] publication of the Greek Text of Drs Westcott and Hort, followed by Dr Hort's *Introduction* to the same;[8] the third was the series of articles against both the Revision and the Text contributed by Dr Burgon to the pages of the *Quarterly Review*.[9] To these three great events I add one microscopic detail from my own experience. The year 1881 is the date of my own personal estrangement from mathematics, and conversion to criticism! The date explains my presence here to-day.

Now it is not my intention to discuss the rival merits of the Authorised and Revised Versions. The influence of the new version has been chiefly felt amongst the race of Bibliolaters, whom it has converted from Monolatry to Dilatry, from the cult of the A.V. to that of alternative A.V. and R.V., with a lesser subordinate divinity known as R.V. mg. The two versions have become a pair of heavenly twins to whom appeal is made alternately, much as the Romans used to swear *Mecastor* and *Edepol*. The instinctive desire of Protestant Christians for authoritative judgments from the book has expressed itself in the language of dilemma. I am not prepared to say that the desire is altogether wrong. It can be upheld on spiritual grounds. If we had nothing to discuss except a new translation of the sacred text, it would probably be sufficient to say that the Revised Version of the N.T. is a very bad translation and pass on. It is almost inconceivable to me that it can ever be accepted by the English-speaking people, whose language it so ruthlessly perverts. Dr Burgon was surely right when he denounced it as follows:

> How it happened that, with so many splendid scholars sitting round their table, they (the Revisers) should have produced a Translation which, for the most part, reads like a first-rate school-boy's crib—tasteless, unlovely, harsh, unidiomatic; servile without being really faithful—pedantic without being really learned—an unreadable Translation, in short; the result of a vast amount of labour

---

6. I.e. on May 17, 1881 [*The New Testament of Our Lord and Saviour Jesus Christ: Translated out of the Greek: Being the Version Set Forth A.D. 1611 Compared with the Most Ancient Authorities and Revised A.D. 1881* (Oxford: Oxford University Press, 1881). AF].

7. I.e. on May 10, 1881 [Westcott and Hort, *New Testament*. AF].

8. Professor Sanday (*Cont. Rev.* Dec. 1881 [William Sanday, "The Greek Text of the New Testament," *Contemporary Review* 40 (1881), pp. 985-1006. AF]) says that the publication of the Greek Text five days before the Revised Version was an undesigned coincidence: "There seems to have been no deliberate plan in such coincidence as there was." I do not find this very convincing.

9. [See John W. Burgon, *The Revision Revised: Three Articles Reprinted from the 'Quarterly Review' to Which Is Added a Reply to Bishop Ellicott's Pamphlet in Defence of the Revisers and their Greek Text of the New Testament Including a Vindication of the Traditional Reading of 1 Timothy III. 16* (London: John Murray, 1883). AF]

3. *The Rate of Progress in New Testament Research*   87

indeed, but of wondrous little skill—how all this has come about it were utterly useless at this time of day to enquire.

And I do not think that the attempts which are from time to time made to rehabilitate the Revised Version in public estimation will have any success (if indeed rehabilitation can be predicated where a position was never really occupied). The defenders of the Revised Version of the N.T. will disappear with the Revisers themselves and with those that are attached to them by what the Romans call *pietas*.[10] Dr Weymouth's *New Testament in Modern Speech*[11] will, perhaps, live longer. Why then do I refer to the Revised Version as an epoch-making event? The reason consists, not in the translation, but in the text which underlay it. Now, for the first time, the whole world of English-speaking Christians[12] was face to face with the reality and extent of the variations in the text of the New Testament. Up to the year 1881, few were aware that there were any important changes to be faced; only those who were close students, or who read independent translations like Dr Davidson's translation of the text of Tischendorf,[13] knew that the Greek text had passed into the furnace of criticism, and that it would not come out exactly the same as it went in.[14] But now on the margin of almost every page there appeared warning

---

    10. I have been struck by the way in which in certain circles the very infelicities of the Revised Version have become the object of devotion. For instance, I noted recently that a scholar of such excellent taste and judgment as Professor Burkitt quotes the Gospel in the form "If thy hand make thee to stumble" [Matt. 5.30. AF]. I also remember once taking the late Dr Schaff ("der unermüdliche Schaff" of the Germans) to call on Dr Westcott with a view to the removal of certain barbarisms from the Version upon which they had been engaged together; and when Dr Westcott asked sharply for instances of the suggested improvement and reference was made to 2 Peter 1.5 ("Supply in your faith virtue, etc."), Dr Westcott angrily replied (and it was the only occasion on which I ever saw him riding the wild horse, anger), that he would sooner cut off his right hand than alter that translation. A strange fascination for a rendering in Baboo-English of what Dr E.A. Abbot, I believe, once called Baboo-Greek.

    11. [Richard F. Weymouth, *The New Testament in Modern Speech: An Idiomatic Translation into Everyday English from the Text of "The Resultant Greek Testament"* (ed. Ernest Hampden-Cook; London: James Clarke, 2nd ed, 1903). AF]

    12. This is what differentiates the situation from that created by the publication of Mill's New Testament [John Mill (ed.), *Novum Testamentum cum lectionibus variantibus* (Oxford: e Theatro Sheldoniano, 1707). AF], and by Dr Bentley's proposals for the purifying of the Greek Text. They raised a very respectable storm, but it was in an academic teapot.

    13. [Samuel Davidson, *The New Testament: Translated from the Critical Text of von Tischendorf* (London: H.S. King, 1875). AF]

    14. Many of the rank and file read the translation of the Codex Sinaiticus which appeared as the thousandth volume of the Tauchnitz Library [*The New Testament: The Authorised English Version with Introduction, and Various Readings from the Three Most Celebrated Manuscripts of the Original Greek Text by Constantine Tischendorf* (Collection of British Authors, 1000; Leipzig: Bernhard Tauchnitz, 1869). AF]: the ministers, at

notes about what was to be read in "certain ancient MSS.," or in "some ancient authorities"; and the uncertainty produced by these references was accentuated by a suspicion that it was only the want of a two-thirds vote which kept such marginal matters out of the text itself.[15] And whatever suspicions were aroused were confirmed by the controversy which arose and the battle royal which prevailed over the merits of the Revision generally. Injudicious Revisers began to tell the secrets of their prison-house, and in a very little while the Christian Church was taking sides for or against this or that rendering. Emerson described the spiritual temper of his time as "a whole generation of gentlemen and ladies out in search of a religion"; and so here a whole generation of Christian people were out in search of a correct theory of the text of the New Testament. And when we reflect how difficult it is to get any but experts to take an interest in matters which everyone ought to know something about, I think that, if the Revisers did nothing more than to force the attention of Christian people to the origins of the Christian documents, they accomplished a great result, and so produced an epoch-making work—though not in the way that they intended. The chief value of the Revision therefore consists in the Greek text which underlies it. This is, to a very large extent, the revised text of Westcott and Hort, copies of which were confidentially placed, in advance of publication, in the hands of all the Revisers, and the merits of which could be defended and explained by the presence of the skilled editors themselves who had produced it. Thus when the Revised New Testament appeared, every Christian reader had to face such questions as to what was the real ending of Mark's Gospel, and whether Jesus really prayed for His enemies upon the Cross.

So much, in passing, with regard to the Revised Version. Our next business is with the text of Westcott and Hort and with the criticisms which it provoked from Dr Burgon. Now apart from the merits of the two sides in this

least the more thoughtful ones of my acquaintance, read Davidson's translation of the eighth edition of Tischendorf. This last has a long introductory preface, marked by extraordinary inaccuracies uttered with great air of knowledge. I remember Ezra Abbot of Harvard (the most accurate scholar I think I have ever known), pointing out to me some of Davidson's blunders. Amongst other things he tilts at Alford's Greek Text [Henry Alford (ed.), *The Greek Testament: With a Critically Revised Text, a Digest of Various Readings, Marginal References to Verbal and Idiomatic Usage, Prolegomena and a Critical and Exegetical Commentary* (4 vols.; F. & J. Rivington: London, 1849–1861). AF] because it was, by confession, a diplomatic text. Davidson did not know that "diploma" was another name for a manuscript, and that Alford's text professed to be based upon the manuscripts themselves. But the fact is, as Burgon loved to insinuate, very few of the Revisers even, who set themselves to re-construct the New Testament Text, had ever handled or collated a codex for themselves.

15. A vote of one-third of the Revisers present in favour of a reading of the Authorised Version was sufficient to secure it from disturbance.

great controversy it is matter of satisfaction that the publication and discussion of the Westcott and Hort text demonstrated that English Scholarship was to the front in the matter of textual criticism. For a time it seemed as if Germany had ceased to take an interest in the subject. Her Biblical students had moved into other fields. Tischendorf had left no successor in his native country and he had never lived to write the Prolegomena which were to justify the text of his eighth edition. No such work as Hort's *Introduction* had ever appeared in Germany, nor was there anyone in Germany who was able to bring a knowledge of Patristic quotations to bear upon the criticism of the text in the way that Burgon did, on almost every page of his *Quarterly Review* articles. For once, English scholars were leading the world; and when they fought, the rest of the world looked on and did not venture to intervene, so as to draw off attention from the main combatants. It need hardly be said that this state of things could not last. The Germans are not long outside the knowledge of any great question, and their apparent isolation was but temporary. They are now amongst the keenest of textual critics, and under the leadership of Professor Nestle, Professor Gregory, and Professor von Soden are rapidly restoring the balance of power. Here is a significant bit of evidence given me by one of my German friends. A few years since one of the most famous German Universities possessed a copy of Scrivener's edition of the Cambridge manuscript, known as the Codex Bezae,[16] which was unused and, I believe, uncut. To-day it is out of its covers from constant reference and handling. That will serve for a parable of how the tide of textual criticism is coming in again in Germany, and I think we may say that it has not altogether ebbed in England. So, if national pride be ever lawful, here is a field in which it may be indulged. Only there is a caution to be expressed with regard to our temporary primacy in this field. We did not deserve any such pre-eminence, in view of the fact that our great Universities had practically limited research in this subject to those who are not members of the Established Church by closing professorships to those who are not members of that Church. *A nation which elects to live on half its brains has no right to expect to rule the world.* And until learning is de-clericalised we cannot expect to reach or to retain the highest standards. It is surprising that no English Government sees this; or perhaps we ought to say it is surprising that the English people do not see it. We may hope that our great Universities, as is said of Wisdom generally, will be justified of their children:[17] but they do harm, by their narrowness, to the subjects that they profess to teach.

16. [Frederick H.A. Scrivener, *Bezae Codex Cantabrigiensis: Being an Exact Copy, in Ordinary Type, of the Celebrated Uncial Graeco-Latin Manuscript of the Four Gospels and Acts of the Apostles* (Cambridge: Deighton, Bell, 1864). AF]

17. [Luke 7.25. AF]

The Revised Version appeared on May 17th, 1881, and within the space of a few days was followed[18] by the Greek Text of Westcott and Hort. In the month of August appears the famous *Introduction* of Dr Hort: and in the *Quarterly Review* for October the first of the articles by Dr Burgon, afterwards incorporated in the volume entitled *The Revision Revised*. Dr Burgon tells us in the published volume that he had been working on the first of his articles all through the long summer days of 1881, and that when the October number of the *Quarterly Review* appeared he knew that the new Greek Text (and therefore the new English Version) had "received its death-blow. It might for a few years drag out a maimed existence; eagerly defended by some–timidly pleaded for by others. But such efforts could be of no avail. Its days were already numbered ..." These words were written two years after the first appearance of the Revised Version; they certainly are not destitute of self-confidence. They announce that two big birds had been killed, I will not say with one stone, but with one mitrailleuse. So it becomes proper to ask whether Burgon had really done these two things, destroyed the Greek Text of the later critics, and the English Revision which was built to a large extent, upon it. With regard to the English Revision, I should, as intimated above, make a fairly complete surrender—not on account of its underlying Greek Text so much as on account of its infelicitous renderings of any text at all. I think, too, that it should be conceded that Burgon was right in saying that none of those who had attempted to reply to him had answered his arguments. A glance over the pamphlets which were produced on the other side will show what I mean. Canon Farrar attacked Burgon in the *Contemporary Review*,[19] and assured him that "The Quarterly Reviewer can be refuted as fully as he desires as soon as any scholar has the leisure to answer him." That means that Farrar had tried to answer him and found the matter outside either his time or his capacity. He was no match for Burgon in Textual Criticism or in vituperation. Burgon calls the article a "Vulgar effusion," says that his "remarks are hysterical," assures him that "The Quarterly Reviewer can afford to wait—if the Revisers can; but they are reminded that it was no answer to one who has demolished their Master's 'Theory,' for the pupils to keep on reproducing fragments of it; and by their mistakes and exaggerations, to make both themselves and him ridiculous." You will notice the singular "him" in that last

---

18. [*Sic.* AF]

19. March, 1882 [Frederic W. Farrar, "The Revised Version and its Assailants," *Contemporary Review* 41 (1882), pp. 359-80. AF]. Farrar was astonishingly feeble, and often very loose in his statements. How does it look in the light of to-day to pen a sentence like this: "Not only has our general knowledge of the Greek language become far more accurate than it was at any previous period, but the specialities of the Hellenistic dialect have been thoroughly mastered by the labours of many successive grammarians and lexicographers." What would Deissmann, Moulton and the papyrologists say to this?

3. *The Rate of Progress in New Testament Research* 91

sentence, and the reference to the "Master"; Burgon knew well enough that it was Hort with whom he had to contend, not even Westcott and Hort. He treated the rest of them as so many buzzing flies, and went on rattling his challenge on the shield of Achilles, Achilles meanwhile keeping in his tent. It was the same with nearly all the other antagonists. They cut a sorry figure, because of their want of acquaintance with the subject; even Dr Kennedy said nothing that had any bearing on the debate,[20] and Dr Sanday barely touched the edge of the controversy.[21] An exception, however, arose when Dr Ellicott, the Chairman of the Revision, volunteered to defend with another of the Revisers, a selected position, viz.: the change of the reading in 1 Tim. 3.16 ("God was manifest in the flesh"), as well as to vindicate generally the textual theory of Dr Hort, and the consequent primacy of the Vatican Codex over all other MSS of the N.T.[22] On looking over this controversy again (and I was interested in it at the time, because I ventured to offer Dr Ellicott some MS confirmations, from my own collations, of certain of his references), it is impossible to resist the conclusion that Dr Ellicott was wholly outclassed. Burgon knew it, and told him so plainly with savage candour, and his usual skill in vituperation. How will this do for candour? "Forgive my plainness, but really you are so conspicuously unfair—and at the same time so manifestly unacquainted (except at secondhand and only in an elementary way) with the points actually under discussion—that, were it not for the adventitious importance attaching to any utterance of yours, deliberately put forth at this time as Chairman of the New Testament body of Revisers, I should have taken no notice of your pamphlet." To which piece of candid criticism may be added the following insinuations of want of competence in matters that belong to

20. Dr Kennedy's knowledge of the problem as compared with Burgon's may be seen from the following estimate of the materials for the determination of the text. *Ely Lectures on the Revised Version* [Benjamin H. Kennedy, *Ely Lectures on the Revised Version of the New Testament: With an Appendix Containing the Chief Textual Changes* (London: Bentley, 1882). AF], p. xliv. "We find also some assistance in the passages of Scripture cited by Christian writers of the earliest ages especially by those who are usually called Fathers of the Church." "Some assistance"!

21. His acquaintance with the subject at that time was not what it is to-day. Like the rest of us, I suspect, he was learning of Westcott and Hort and learning fast. He admits as much at the close of his article in the *Contemporary Review*. "As I have come forward in defence of their principles it is perhaps right that I should explain the degree of my own indebtedness to them. I am not prepared to claim (for myself at least) more than certain rough results, which a deeper knowledge may perhaps somewhat modify." A sentence marked by Sandayan indecision—and modesty. Where Sanday was decided, he was almost certainly wrong, as in the statement that we were all agreed as to the worthlessness of the Western readings.

22. [The pamphlet was published anonymously, but it was attributed to Charles J. Ellicott and Edwin Palmer: *The Revisers and the Greek Text of the New Testament: By Two Members of the New Testament Company* (London: MacMillan, 1882). AF]

the expert. "Did you ever take the trouble to collate a Sacred Manuscript? If you ever did, pray with what did you make your collation?" "From the confident style in which you deliver yourself upon such matters, and especially from your having undertaken to preside over a Revision of the Sacred Text, one would suppose that at some period of your life you must have given the subject a considerable amount of time and attention." And when Burgon had finished his bout with the Bishop, it must be admitted that he had vastly strengthened the case for the received text in 1 Tim. 3.16, for which he gathered up no less than 300 MSS witnesses, and any amount of Patristic testimony, some carried over bodily from his opponents. It is time for me to state that I believe he was entirely wrong in his conclusions, but it is impossible to ignore the vigour of his onslaught or the range of his artillery. He had spent five and a half years collating the five great ancient MSS throughout the Gospels,[23] and a man who had done that had a right to speak with conviction, even if he were not altogether right. Moreover he had accomplished the gigantic task of searching the Fathers for all the passages which they quote from the New Testament and the results of this labour are preserved in a long series of index volumes now in the British Museum. It is possible to object to many of his references and to find fault with some of the texts which he used, but I only wish that I possessed a transcript of those precious volumes. They were the magazine from which he drew his thunders in the *Quarterly Review*, to the amazement alike of his friends and enemies.

How was it then that no one answered Burgon? Well there were not more than two or three who could have done it. A person who wanted to floor Burgon would have done well to begin with his earlier book in defence of the last twelve verses of Mark.[24] Here is a case in which Burgon was undoubtedly wrong, but his defence of the conventional text was so vigorous and so adroit, that he held the position for a quarter of a century after he ought to have abandoned it. Not a few critics, such as Samuel Davidson and the like, tried to dislodge him, but theirs was mere pea-shooting. And as far as English scholarship goes, nothing really vital was said until Hort wrote the long note at the end of his *Introduction*,[25] which people at once recognised to be the counterplea to Burgon. And that note was so closely abbreviated and so inaccessible to the ordinary reader that I doubt if it made many converts. Some one should certainly have written a volume directly, as a reply to Burgon's arguments; the subject demanded and deserved a separate treatment, and it would have been a splendid training ground for one of the younger scholars of the day. Why did they not do it? Why did we not do it ourselves? Our lot might have been worse!

23. I happen to possess his copy of the Roman Edition of the Vatican Codex.
24. [Mark 16.9-20. AF]
25. He had already come forward on the question in an article in the *Academy*.

But as regards the *Quarterly Review* articles, there were not many, as I have said, who could have ventured into the arena. Dr Westcott made an attempt to galvanize the corpse of the Revised Version into fresh life, by writing a little book on its merits, which could hardly prove a reply to those who were occupied with its defects. And when he came in 1896 to re-issue the *Introduction*, after Dr Hort's death, he made the following statement with regard to the controversies which had prevailed. "No arguments have been advanced against the general principles maintained in the Introduction and illustrated in the Notes, since the publication of the first edition, which were not fully considered by Dr Hort and myself in the long course of our work and in our judgment dealt with adequately." One can scarcely call that a reply. It is only an "Ipse dixi" in the dual.[26]

There was one man, who could have held and handled Burgon, had already done it on a minor point; I mean Dr Ezra Abbot, of Harvard. I remember writing to him on the subject, and asking him whether a reply was not demanded by these articles in the *Quarterly*, and I find amongst my letters his reply to my hint dated October 22, 1883: "I agree that Burgon has not been thoroughly answered; but I have no space or time now to give my view of the matter. His book entitled the 'Revision Revised,' a reprint with some modifications of the three articles in the *Quarterly*, enlarged, with the addition of a reply to the two Revisers, was announced as on the eve of publication a month or six weeks ago, and even the number of pages in the book was given in the advertisement; but I do not know that it has yet been issued."[27] From which it appears that Ezra Abbot was too busy to take the matter up. But what, you will ask, of Achilles himself? Why did not Hort come out into the open field and settle the questions at issue, much in the same way as Bentley settled Boyle over the letters of Phalaris? I remember asking him once a question on this point; but, if I remember rightly the reasons that he gave for his silence they resolved themselves into questions of etiquette. First of all, Dr Burgon had never sent him a copy of his articles; and second, if I understood his allusion rightly, he suspected that someone had divulged to Burgon the Greek text of the N.T. which had been submitted to him in confidence as a Reviser—a proceeding which would naturally have provoked resentment, although it is difficult to

---

26. There is a precisely similar evasion of criticism on the part of Westcott in his *Lessons of the Revised Version* [Brooke F. Westcott, *Some Lessons of the Revised Version of the New Testament* (London: Hodder & Stoughton, 1897). AF], pp. 2, 3. "They [the Revisers] heard in the Jerusalem Chamber all the arguments against their conclusions which they have heard since; and I may say for myself, that no amount of restatement of old arguments has in the least degree shaken my confidence in the general results that were obtained."

27. [Three letters dated 1883 and sent by Ezra Abbot to Rendel Harris are kept in the Special Collections Department, University of Birmingham (DA21/1/2/1/2), but they do not include the letter from which the quotation comes. AF]

see how a secret of such magnitude could have been kept for so long by so many people. As far as my memory goes that is all the explanation which Dr Hort could or would give me. One is not bound, I suppose, to reply to every attack made upon himself or his positions; otherwise some of us would have a sorry life. One may elect to await the verdict of time, and let one's adversary crow in triumph over one's apparent acquiescence. Burgon, himself, quick as he was to snatch at the laurels of apparent victory, had a word from the inward monitor on the other side. In his reply to Ellicott he quotes a famous maxim from Pindar:

Ἀμέραι δ' ἐπίλοιποι μάρτυρες σοφώτατοι.[28]

That their views (i.e. those of Westcott and Hort) have been received with expressions of the greatest disapprobation, no one will deny. Indispensable to their contention is the grossly improbable hypothesis that the Peschito is to be regarded as the 'Vulgate' (i.e. the *Revised*) Syriac: Cureton's, as the 'Vetus' or original Syriac version. And yet, while I write, the Abbé Martin at Paris is giving it as the result of his labours on this subject, that Cureton's version cannot be anything of the sort. Whether Westcott and Hort's theory of a '*Syrian*' text has not received an effectual quietus, let posterity decide.

Then follows the quotation from Pindar. And what has posterity decided? The "grossly improbable hypothesis" has been confirmed in the strongest manner, by the discovery of a further old Syriac MS, and a mass of accessory evidence; the Abbé Martin's pamphlet was written when he was under intellectual aberration, and the less said about it the better; and the argument of Westcott and Hort can hardly be said to have received a quietus at all. So, as Abbot refused to reply to Burgon, and Achilles did not come out of his tent, let us keep our eyes fixed upon the remnant of the days and watch what further light is going to break on the interesting field of controversy. If you like, let us say that neither party took the laurel of victory, though one vociferously claimed it: we will leave them encamped upon the field, and see in what directions reinforcements are coming up for the conclusion of the conflict.[29]

---

28. [*Ol.* 1.33-34. AF]

29. On looking over some old letters belonging to the eighties, I find a sheaf from Dr Burgon showing the greatest interest in the work which I was doing, and giving me some of the wisest counsels as to how to concentrate my power of study and what to concentrate upon. I believe that we remained good friends to the last, and I am sure that I learned much by the direct intercourse which I had with him. It is very pleasant to remember this in the case of those whom we have sometimes remorselessly criticised.

Appendix

In the foregoing lecture I have alluded to the astonishingly optimistic statements which Dr Hort made with regard to the preservation of the New Testament from hostile and heretical influences. The only exception which he allowed was that of Marcion's readings, which consisted mainly in excisions from the text of Luke, made with a view to the removal of everything which would involve the New Testament Christian in the belief in the God of the Old Testament. Now even when Dr Hort makes the admission that Marcion mutilated the N.T. with a heretical intention, he does not seem to think that this made any difference to the evangelical tradition, but I should say that even in the matter of Marcionism Hort was too optimistic.

We know that Marcion had no Infancy Sections in his Gospel. Perhaps he had removed them because he did not wish to recognise a fulfilment of prophecy. He had no Infancy Sections because from his point of view, there was no Infancy. Christ had descended suddenly into the synagogue (everything was sudden with Marcion, says Tertullian[30]) and began His work at once. Now it stands to reason that no such opinion could be held if the Gospel of Luke, as we know it, had been held at the same time. I am not speaking of the chapters describing the Infancy, but of the passage which tells that our Lord came to Nazareth *where He had been brought up*, and went into the synagogue *according to His custom*.[31] Naturally Tertullian could at once retort upon his Marcionite antagonist and question as to how the custom arose for a person who had only just arrived. And it could only be answered by the Marcionite method of excision. Either the word *His* must be erased before custom, or the whole clause must go. If, therefore, we find the compromising words absent in a MS it raises the suspicion of Marcionite corruption. What do we actually find? One of the most famous old Latin MS (the Palatine Codex) has lost the clause about "His custom" altogether. The Codex Bezae omits the word "His," and is followed by two other Latin MSS of the first rank. Further the Codex Bezae omits the clause as to our Lord's having been brought up in Nazareth, and simply says that He came into the synagogue. Is not that sufficient to suggest Marcionism in the current texts of Luke, and ought we not to recognise it, both in Luke 4.16 and elsewhere. And will it be sufficient, on the other hand, to re-assure people and say that no harm has been done and that no one ever had a vicious intention in transcription or preparation of texts? For it will not be possible to refer all changes of this kind to Marcion himself. They are due to a school as well as to a master. And if one school can alter the text, why not another? What is true of the influence

---

30. [*Marc.* 4.11.4. AF]
31. [Luke 4.16. AF]

of the Marcionite movement upon the text is also true of the contemporary heresy of Encratism. If Marcion affected the text, are we entitled to say that Tatian never affected it? We know now that his compound Gospel, the *Diatessaron*, became for a time the standard Gospel in the Syrian Church, and that it profoundly influenced the text of the separate Gospels. Is it to be assumed that on questions like the eating of animal food, the drinking of wine, the virtue of celibacy, and the like, we are to believe that no Encratisms appear in the text? A little enquiry will soon enlighten us. We know now that Tatian along with many early believers was sorely puzzled by the presence of the locusts in the diet of that very holy man, John the Baptist.[32] One school, probably those who pass under the name of Nazarenes or Ebionites, changed the Greek name of locusts ἀκρίδες into the similarly sounding word ἐγκρίδες, "pancakes" for "locusts."[33] But Tatian was bolder than this, he removed the locusts, and gave St John a diet of "milk and honey" in place of the conventional *menu*. This meant Encratism in the text. And there must have been much more of it, for we find traces of similar corrections in the oldest Syriac MSS that are known to us. In the Lewis MS, for example, we find the "oxen and fatlings" removed from the supper of the King in Matt. 20.4:[34] and we find the period of married life of that holy woman, the prophetess Anna (Luke 2.36), reduced from seven years' felicity to a bare seven days. These instances may suffice to show how the religious movements of any time or country affect the text of that time or country. Nor can such changes be considered as unimportant or insignificant. We find the question of the re-action of Ebionite or Adoptionist views raised (or of Anti-Ebionite or Anti-Adoptionist corrections) as soon as we study the second-century textual variations in the light of the history of doctrine in the second century. Suppose, for example, we were studying Justin Martyr's *Dialogue with Trypho the Jew*, we should find Trypho expostulating with Justin over the titles that he gives to Jesus Christ. Trypho is ready, or almost ready, for the expression of some faith in Christ, but he enters a protest against Justin's way of putting it. He objects to the Virgin Birth as being comparable to the Greek legend of Perseus: Justin ought to be ashamed to say such things, and it would be much better to regard Christ as a man sprung from human origin, who on account of His law-abiding and perfect life was elected to be the Messiah (κατηξιῶσθαι ἐκλεγῆναι εἰς Χριστόν).[35] A little later Justin returned to the point, and asked Trypho with regard to his admission that, on account of his life in accordance with the law of Moses, Jesus had been *elected* to be the Messiah.[36] You can

32. [Matt. 3.4. AF]
33. [*Gospel of the Ebionites*, passage cited in Epiphanius, *Pan.* 30.13.4. AF]
34. [Matt. 22.4. AF]
35. Justin, *Dial.* 67 [67.2. AF].
36. [*Dial.* 67.4. AF]

3. *The Rate of Progress in New Testament Research*

see an Ebionite watchword protruding through the dialogue, and this means that in the second century there was a Judaeo-Christian party which called Christ, not the Son of God, but the Elect of God. Is that reflected on the text of the New Testament? An examination of the oldest witnesses will show abundantly that there has been either

(a) An unlawful insertion of the title ἐκλεκτός or ἐκλελεγμένος into the text of a number of passages; or else

(b) There has been an unlawful erasure of the same term (which is one of the pre-Christian names for the Messiah), in the interests of a progressive Christology.

This is not the place to discuss the point at length, but it may suffice to show that Dr Hort cannot be right in divesting the various readings of New Testament MSS of dogmatic significance, or in assuring us of the universal *bona fides* of the transcribers. His statement on these points must remain an astonishment to us, but perhaps enough has been said to show why we were not able to agree with his optimistic views of the textual history.

For a more balanced judgment we may compare what my friend, the late Professor Berger, wrote in regard to the text of the Latin Vulgate (*Hist. de la Vulgate*, p. viii):[37]

> La dogmatique elle-même a sans doute une grand part de responsabilité dans la corruption du texte de la Bible Latine. Les alterations dogmatiques, en effet, ne sont pas rares dans le texte de la Vulgate. Les doctrines les plus chères aux théologiens du moyen âge exercent toutes leur influence sur le texte de la Bible. Ici c'est le dogme de la Trinité, que l'on veut trouver formulé en toutes lettres dans la Bible et que l'on affirme par la fameuse interpolation du passage des trois temoins! C'est la foi en la divinité de Jesus-Christ qui s'exprime en un grand nombre de falsifications de détail, toujours au detriment de son humanité.

What is true of the Vulgate is true of the Greek texts which preceded it. But to Dr Hort the scribes were all angels, as far as theology was concerned.

---

37. [Samuel Berger, *Histoire de la Vulgate pendant les premiers siècles du moyen âge* (Paris: Hachette, 1893). AF]

Chapter 4

The Book of Testimonies

Testimonies, in the early Christian sense of the word, are, on one side, very nearly equivalent to quotations; but from another point of view, the term involves the idea of the person testifying as well as the thing witnessed; they are not only extracts from a book, they are the utterances of the person who is the author of the book. Thus the formula "it is written in the law" is impersonal and denotes strictly a quotation, but "Moses in the law saith" is a testimony, and Moses himself is the witness.

Our thesis is, that in very early times collections of such classified Testimonies were in use amongst the Christians, and that they were used polemically, either in attacking a Jewish position or in defending a Christian one; the witnesses are brought into court by the protagonists in a dispute: they are arranged in groups, and ordered in sequences; when they have said their say, it is assumed that something will have been settled. Hence arises the importance of the work of marshalling the Testimony on any particular question in debate.

From the Christian point of view they are a series of *Argumenta ad hominem*, the man being the Jew on the other side who is committed in advance by his belief in the Scriptures to the acceptance of the word of the witnesses, provided they are rightly heard and not misinterpreted. Thus the long title of such collections is that of "Testimonies against the Jews." There are, properly speaking, no Testimonies against the Gentiles, for the Gentiles and the Primitive Gentile Christians do not recognise the same court of appeal as the Jews and the Judaeo-Christians; their court of appeal is something quite different, it is the soul itself, the "naturally Christian soul" of which Tertullian speaks, which knows truth by truth's own testimony.

How, then, do we establish the existence of such collections as those which are here suggested? Three ways, at least, may be followed which lead to the result: the first consists in observing that different authors (say in the New Testament) quote the Old Testament in similar or closely-coincident sequences, and apparently without any mutual dependence upon one another for the form of the quotation. The suggestion is that they have used the same handbook.

4. *The Book of Testimonies*

The second method is by observing that from the second century onward there is a succession of actually preserved books of Biblical Testimonies, arranged under headings to prove definite points; and these collections have so much common matter that we are obliged to assume a primitive nucleus around which, and out of which, they have been evolved.

The third method turns on the occurrence in Patristic writers of Biblical quotations in such peculiar settings that one is obliged to admit that they were not taken directly from the Scriptures, but that there is some intervening link between the writers in question and the ultimate Biblical source of their citations.

I do not remember who was the first to erect the hypothesis of a Book of Testimonies. Looking at the matter from the standpoint of acquired knowledge, it would seem most natural that existing books of prophecies and Testimonies should have suggested a common early original. As a matter of fact, I believe the first hint came from the study of the quotations in the New Testament, and was made by Dr Hatch of Oxford; and his suggestions were at a later date endorsed by Dr Drummond of Oxford. It will be interesting to see how they stated the matter.

In Dr Hatch's *Essays on Biblical Greek*[1] we have the following statement:

> It may naturally be supposed that a race which laid stress on moral progress, whose religious services had variable elements of both prayer and praise, and which was carrying on an *active propaganda*, would have, among other books, *manuals* of morals, of devotion and of *controversy*. It may also be supposed, if we take into consideration the contemporary habit of making collections of *excerpta*, and the special authority which the Jews attached to their sacred books, that some of these manuals would consist of extracts from the Old Testament. The existence of composite quotations in the New Testament, and in some of the early Fathers, suggests the hypothesis that we have in these relics of such manuals.

Here it will be seen that the observed fact from which Dr Hatch proceeded was the existence of composite quotations; while the words which we have italicised show that he suspected these quotations to have been used for controversial and missionary purposes.

What is peculiar in Hatch's hypothesis is that he imagined the collections of extracts made for the propaganda of Judaism. It is difficult, on this hypothesis, to see how they could have been immediately converted into Christian books of Testimonies against the Jews. The ancestry of "against" is hardly to be found in arguments "for"; "pro" does not easily beget "con." Where Hatch went wrong was in not recognising the use which the Christians made of their collections: but as regards his observations of the existence of composite

---

1. P. 203 [Edwin Hatch, *Essays in Biblical Greek* (Oxford: Clarendon Press, 1889). AF].

quotations, recurring here and there in early Christian writings, the key to the discovery was in his hand. Dr Drummond in his book on the *Character and Authorship of the Fourth Gospel*[2] followed somewhat on the lines of Hatch: he made the link between Jewish and Christian propaganda in the common matter of Messianic preaching and Scriptural proofs of Messianic doctrines. In this way he thought to explain some peculiarities in the citations from the Old Testament in the Gospel of John. He expresses himself as follows:[3]

> It may have become a matter of common knowledge among those who cared for the Scriptures, that certain passages required emendation. The Christians would naturally turn their attention to Messianic quotations: and it is conceivable that there may have grown up, whether in writing or not, an anthology of passages useful in controversy, which differed more or less from the current Greek translation. This is, of course, only conjecture; but I think it affords a possible explanation of the phenomenon of the Johannine quotations.

Here the anthology for controversial purposes is the same thing as Hatch's manuals of controversy. Drummond's difficulty with the Johannine quotations, and his solution of the same, does not necessarily involve us in resorting to Jewish manuals, if we allow sufficient antiquity to the undoubtedly existing Christian manuals. And it seems that this is the direction in which Dr Drummond was looking, and in which the investigation was taking him.[4]

My own researches on this line began many years since, and if I remember rightly the starting-point was a curious coincidence which I observed in the writings of Justin Martyr and in those of Irenaeus.

Let us transcribe a sentence from the fourth book of Irenaeus' *Against Heresies*;[5] Irenaeus is explaining how certain utterances of the Hebrew prophets were fulfilled in the life and work of Jesus Christ; and he makes the following statement,—

> Now those who say that at his coming the lame man shall leap as an hart, and the tongue of the dumb shall be smooth, and the eyes of the blind shall be opened and the ears of the deaf shall hear, and the relaxed hands and feeble knees shall be strengthened; and the dead men that are in the tombs shall arise, and he himself shall take our infirmities and bear our sicknesses, they, I say, announced the cures which were being accomplished by him (the Christ).

---

2. [James Drummond, *An Inquiry into the Character and Authorship of the Fourth Gospel* (London: Williams & Norgate, 1903). AF]

3. L.c. p. 365.

4. For the actual discussion of the composite quotations to which reference is made, we may consult Hatch and Drummond, as cited.

5. Lib. iv. 55. 2: ed. Massuet 273 [*Haer.* 4.33.11. René Massuet (ed.), *Sancti Irenaei episcopi lugdunensis et martyris detectionis et eversionis falso cognominatae agnitionis seu contra haereses libri quinque* (Paris: Joannes Baptista Coignard, 1710; repr. in PG 7.1). AF].

4. The Book of Testimonies

I want you to notice the structure of this passage; it is a series of prophecies, strung together from Isaiah 35, Isaiah 26, and Isaiah 53.[6] The passages from the thirty-fifth of Isaiah are introduced by the added words "At his coming"; these words are due to what precedes in the chapter, "Your God shall come with a recompence ... He shall come and save you."[7] And they are a summary of what precedes, answering in anticipation the question which might have been asked, if the quotation had been made in the exact language of the prophet, "*Then* shall the eyes of the blind be opened," "*then* shall the lame man leap as an hart." For if anyone asked "When," on the hearing of "then," the right reply would be from the Scripture, "When God comes." Keep your attention fixed for a while on the introductory formula which has here been added to the prophecies quoted. And now let us go back from Irenaeus' time, some thirty or forty years, and examine the writings of Justin Martyr. Justin presents an Apology on behalf of the Christians to the Roman Emperor and to the Roman senate; and in the course of his defence makes great use of the Argument from prophecy. Here is a specimen.[8]

> And that our Christ was foretold as one who should heal all diseases and raise the dead, listen to the things that were said: they are as follows. "*At his coming* the lame man shall leap as an hart, and the tongue of the stammerers shall be smooth; blind men shall recover sight and lepers shall be cleansed, and dead men shall arise and walk about."

Here we find again a series of prophecies, loosely joined together; and the first of them is the passage from Isaiah, ch. 35,[9] with the very same introductory words. We have to explain to ourselves the coincidence in the manner of quotation. One way would be to say that Irenaeus had been imitating Justin, with whose writings he was acquainted. But this will not satisfy us, for the quotations show too much independence to allow that one writer borrowed a passage from the other. Moreover, there is no reason why Irenaeus, when wishing to quote the Old Testament, should have run off in search of Justin Martyr's writings, simply because he remembered that Justin had somewhere employed the same passage. The motive for an obscure reference of this kind appears to be altogether wanting.

The alternative suggestion, then, is that both Irenaeus and Justin have been using some other authority, not the Scriptures, but a handbook of prophecies taken from the Scriptures and furnished with such necessary glosses, expansions and introductions as the subject might require.

---

6. [Isa. 35.5-6, 3; 26.19; 53.4. AF]
7. [Isa. 35.4. AF]
8. Justin. *1 Ap.*, 48 [*1 Apol.* 48.1-2. AF].
9. [Isa. 35.6, 5. AF]

Now it does not demand a very lively exercise of the imagination to affirm that such a book as we here suggest must have been arranged with the prophecies grouped under headings. The particular group to which our attention has been drawn is introduced by Justin in such a way that we can detect the heading of the section: it must have been very nearly like this;

That Christ should heal diseases and raise the dead.[10]

That will be sufficient to start the hypothesis; we do not need to give the passages in Greek; the argument is just the same, if we use English translations. Now, if this is a just hypothesis, it will be confirmed by similar phenomena elsewhere, either in Justin and Irenaeus, or in some other writers of the early Church. Here is a very striking, an almost romantic confirmation which came under my notice. When the two Oxford Scholars, Grenfell and Hunt, brought out their third volume of papyri[11] which they had disinterred from the sands of Oxyrhynchus, they gave a series of broken fragments from an unknown Christian writer, which were of peculiar interest because they judged them from the handwriting to be perhaps as old as the second century. These fragments came under the notice of Dr Armitage Robinson, the Dean of Westminster, who recognised that they were bits of a passage in the third book of Irenaeus,[12] and succeeded in piecing the fragments together into an almost complete whole. I will try to restore a part of the same fragments in English, instead of the original Greek of Irenaeus.

> *of whom also the S*
> tar Balaam *thus pro*
> phesied: There shall *rise a*
> star out of Jacob.

It is impossible to represent the Greek letters by corresponding English letters, but this will give the idea of what resulted when the pieces of papyrus were arranged together, by the aid of the already known Latin text of Irenaeus. Something like this, only of course done in Greek letters, was the restoration of the Dean of Westminster. To this, however, I took exception, on the ground that two of the best copies of Irenaeus did not read *Balaam* but *Ysaias*; and I said we must edit this reading in Irenaeus, and not leave it to a footnote, as the editors of Irenaeus had done. It looked unlikely, you will say, to credit

---

10. Irenaeus, as we said, has arranged the matter somewhat differently, but his extracts also are described in the same words: he has the raising of the dead with a different proof-text.

11. [Bernard P. Grenfell and Arthur S. Hunt (eds.), *The Oxyrhynchus Papyri*, III (London: Egypt Exploration Fund, 1903), pp. 10-12. The fragments belong to papyrus 405. AF]

12. [*Haer.* 3.9.2. AF]

4. *The Book of Testimonies*   103

Irenaeus (for the newly recovered scraps of papyrus were almost contemporary with him), with a mistake that a schoolboy ought not to have been guilty of, in referring a famous prophecy of Balaam in the book of Numbers[13] to Isaiah.

My position was justified by the following consideration. On turning to Justin's *Apology*[14] the following passage can be read:

> And Isaiah also, another prophet, prophesying to the same effect by other expressions, said: "There shall rise up a star out of Jacob and a flower shall ascend out of the root of Jesse."

Now this is extremely interesting: first of all, we have again the reference of the prophecy in Numbers to Isaiah; that confirms my hypothesis that it is not a mere error of the scribes of Irenaeus. Second, we see why Isaiah came in, for there is a famous prophecy of Isaiah about the root of Jesse[15] immediately following: so it is a case of composite quotation in which the authorship has been wrongly defined. But if this is the explanation of the error, we have an extraordinary confirmation of our previous hypothesis. Here we have Irenaeus and Justin both making a similar mistake: but no one can maintain that Irenaeus was quoting Justin in the passage that we have pieced together: he is evidently composing on his own account. So we are obliged to admit that both he and Justin have been using the same book of prophetical quotations, and that the error into which they have both fallen was already made in the book referred to. Nor is it difficult to see how the error could have arisen. We may, if we please, imagine the quotations written down in order, and the author's name attached to each quotation on the margin. In that case, it only needs that one reference should have been missed, or a single word moved a little up the margin, in order to mislead any one who copied without sufficient attention.

And I think we can now restore a fragment of the lost book that we have begun to bring to light: it must have been something like this:

> *Moses*: "A star shall rise out of Jacob."
> *Isaiah*: "A flower shall spring out of the root of Jesse."

Here you will check me, and ask why I put Moses on the margin, instead of Balaam, or instead of a reference to Numbers.

Well, I will justify that in two or three ways. Observe, however, the point that we have reached. We detect Justin in the employment of a collection of Messianic references. If we turn to the writings of Lactantius, at the beginning of the fourth century, we shall find the same Messianic reference, in the following terms:

---

13. [Num. 24.17. AF]
14. Justin: *1 Ap.* 32 [*1 Apol.* 32.12. AF].
15. [Isa. 11.1. AF]

> But Moses also, in Numbers, thus speaks, "There shall arise a star out of Jacob, and a man shall spring forth from Israel" (Num. 24.17).[16]

Here Lactantius has definitely referred the Star-prophecy to Moses. Was that an error of his own, or did he find it already made? Let us see: while Lactantius was writing his *Divine Institutes*, Athanasius in Alexandria was composing his famous treatise on the *Incarnation of the Word*. In the course of this work, he occupies several chapters (chs. 33-40) in refuting Jewish unbelief by means of passages taken from the prophets. Quite at the beginning of the argument, he brings forward the famous Star-passage from Numbers to which we have been referring: the passage is introduced as follows:

> And Moses, who was really great and was accredited amongst the Jews as a true man, esteemed what was said of the Incarnation of the Saviour as of great weight, and having recognised its truth, he set it down, saying, "There shall arise a star out of Jacob, and a man out of Israel, and he shall break the princes of Moab."[17]

Here, again, we see the same ascription of authorship as in Lactantius, and as there is no possibility of one writer in Rome having influenced his contemporary in Alexandria, we are led to conclude that they have both been using the same prophetical handbook. They do not make the mistake, which Justin and Irenaeus do, of referring the prophecy to Isaiah, but that is explained by their following a text into which the error had not crept. Taking the evidence together, we see reason to believe that the original *Book of Testimonies* had its passages grouped in this way:

> *Moses*: "There shall arise a star out of Jacob."
> *Isaiah*: "There shall spring up a flower from the root of Jesse."

But now, having gone so far, we cannot stop at this point: for we have put the little book not only on the shelf of Justin and Irenaeus, but also into the libraries of Athanasius and Lactantius. And we must examine further into the common matter which these writers have borrowed from the original prophetical collection. Here is another very interesting line of investigation which immediately opens up before us. We notice that Justin, when making his reference to the Star out of Jacob, was working from a sequence of prophecies: for he says,—

> Isaiah also, another prophet,

so we turn back to see what prophet has preceded. When we examine the context we find that he has been quoting the famous Messianic passage, in

---

16. Lactantius: *De Div. Inst.* [*Inst.* 4.13.10. AF].
17. [*Inc.* 33.4. AF]

Genesis,[18] about the coming of Shiloh: "There shall not fail a ruler from Judah, nor a governor from his loins etc." But how does he introduce the matter? Let us look at Justin's language—"And Moses also, who was the first of the prophets, says expressly as follows: 'A ruler shall not fail from Judah etc.'"[19]

Here the prophecy of the dying Jacob is expressly put into the mouth of Moses, just as the prophecy of Balaam was in a previous case. Is this one of Justin's own blunders? or does it occur elsewhere, in such a way as to suggest that some one had made the mistake before him?

In the first place we can see that if it was a blunder of Justin, it was a deliberate one; for if we read the passage a little further we find him saying,

> It is your part, then, to examine accurately and to learn until whom the Jews had a ruler and King of their own: it was until the Manifestation of Jesus Christ, our teacher and the interpreter of the recognised prophecies, as was said aforetime of the holy and divine prophetical spirit *through Moses*.[20]

So it is clear that Justin was speaking deliberately when he put the famous Messianic prophecy in the mouth of Moses. Now let us, in the next place, see whether we can find other people making the same mistake. Suppose we turn once more to Irenaeus, and we shall find that he has a whole chapter in which he shows that Moses foretold the advent of Christ.[21] In the course of the argument he says that "Moses had already foretold his advent, saying, 'A ruler shall not fail from Judah etc.,'" and ends up, in language very like that of Justin, by saying, "Let those look into the matter who are said to investigate everything and let them tell us etc." Clearly Irenaeus has made the same mistake as Justin, and had the matter in somewhat similar setting.

Returning again to Justin, we find him discussing the matter at a later point of his *Apology*,[22] as follows:

> Moses, then, the prophet, as we said before, was senior to all the chroniclers, and by him, as we previously intimated, the following prophecy was uttered, "A ruler shall not fail from Judah etc."[23]

If now we were to turn to a later work of Justin, his *Dialogue with Trypho the Jew*, we should find him again quoting the famous oracle from the Blessing

---

18. [Gen. 49.10. AF]
19. [*1 Apol.* 32.1. AF]
20. [*1 Apol.* 32.2. AF]
21. Irenaeus. lib. iv ch. 20 [*Haer.* 4.10.2. AF].
22. Justin *1 Ap.* ch. 34 [*1 Apol.* 54.5. AF].
23. He continues a little lower to refer again to the "prophecy of Moses" [*1 Apol.* 54.7. AF].

of Jacob,[24] but now he has corrected his mistake, but not so as altogether to obliterate the original error, as the following passages will show.[25]

> By Jacob the patriarch it was foretold that there should be two advents of Christ,[26]

after which he quotes freely from the Blessing of Jacob.

> That which was recorded by Moses, but prophesied by the patriarch Jacob etc.

> Concerning whose blood also Moses spake figuratively that he should wash his robe in the blood of the grape etc.

> And as to what Moses said that he should wash his robe in the blood of the grape, is not just what I said to you over and over again about his having secretly prophecied to you etc.

So here again we have abundant evidence that Justin really believed, at all events for a length of time, that Moses was the prophet to whom the famous oracle was to be referred. You can see him trying to correct his blunder.

That this tradition that Moses was the author of the great Messianic prophecy about the ruler who should not fail from Judah until he should come whose right it was, may be seen in another unexpected corner. For here also we have the evidence of Athanasius in his treatise *On the Incarnation*, as follows:

> *And Moses prophesies*, saying that the Kingdom of the Jews should stand till his (Christ's) day, saying, "A ruler shall not fail from Judah, etc."[27]

So here again we have the concurrence of Justin, Irenaeus and Athanasius in a curious error of quotation; and, as before, it is reasonable to refer the mistake to the use of a common document.

At this point we may control the accuracy of our inductions by a test. Let us see whether Athanasius, who is supposed to be using the *Book of Testimonies*, has any knowledge of the passage from Isaiah 35, with which we began our investigation, and of the added introductory words "At his coming." In ch. 38[28] Athanasius quotes against the Jews the words of Isaiah, beginning with "Be strong, ye relaxed hands and paralysed knees," and continues to the words "the tongue of the stammerers shall be smooth." Here there is no sign of the introductory words: but as we read on, we have the following comment:

---

24. [Gen. 49.10. AF]
25. Justin: *Dial.* chs. 52, 54, 63, 76 [*Dial.* 52.2; 54.1; 63.2; 76.2. AF].
26. [*Dial.* 52.1. AF]
27. Athanasius l.c. ch. 40 [*Inc.* 40.3. AF]. I give the reading of the Bodleian MS: other copies have altered it from Moses to Jacob.
28. [*Inc.* 38.3. AF]

4. *The Book of Testimonies*

> What then can the Jews say even on this point, and how can they dare even to face this statement? For the prophecy intimates the *arrival of God*, and makes known the signs and the time of *His coming*: for they say that *when the divine coming takes place* the blind will see etc.[29]

Here we can see the added words lurking, even though they are absent from the direct quotation. And our judgment is confirmed that Athanasius is using the *Book of Testimonies*.

This, then, was the way in which I was led to the belief in the existence of an early book of Testimonies against the Jews. The argument is cumulative, and there is much more to be said on the same line. It is, however, already sufficient to establish the hypothesis. We can now go on to enquire into the age of production of the little book in its first form. So far, nothing has appeared in the argument requiring us to go to the extreme length with Dr Hatch, and refer the book to an original Jewish hand; on the contrary, almost everything that has been brought forward is anti-Jewish, and the treatment of the subject by Justin and Athanasius, is expressly directed against the Jews. It is not Trypho who is quoting texts to prove the character and time and place of appearing of the Messiah: it is Justin, who is hurling them, as fast as he can control his artillery, at the head of Trypho and his companions. We may, for the present at all events, limit ourselves to the Christian use of Testimonies, and ask how soon they took the form of a definite and orderly collection.

The first rough answer is that a book, which was used independently as an authority by Justin and Irenaeus must have had a respectable ancestry. It is on the borders of contemporaneity with the New Testament, to say the least. May we say more than that? The way to answer that question will be to examine whether any traces of the same kind of quotations and the same kind of mistakes as we noticed in other writers can be remarked in any of the books of the New Testament. Composite quotations were the thing that arrested Dr Hatch's attention: and our analysis has shown that with such composite quotations the scribes have a tendency to go wrong (as in *Isaiah* for *Balaam* or *Moses*, where only the latter part was really Isaiah). The moment we make the suggestion of composite quotations whose ascription has become confused, we are reminded of the textual difficulty in the opening verses of Mark.[30] Ought we to read,

> As it is written in the prophets:
> "Behold! I send my messenger before thy face,
> Who shall prepare thy way:
> The voice of one crying in the wilderness,
> Prepare the way of the Lord,
> Make his paths straight";

29. [*Inc.* 38.4. AF]
30. [Mark 1.2-3. AF]

or should it be,

> As it is written in the prophet Isaiah, "Behold! etc."

The textual critics insist rightly that "Isaiah" is the true reading, whether it makes Mark look inaccurate or not. Suppose, then, for a moment that Mark had taken this proof of Christ's coming out of a prophetical Testimony book; such a book ought to have had on the margin the two names

> *Malachi*: "Behold I send etc."
> *Isaiah*:   "The voice of one crying etc."

We have shown, in an exactly parallel case, how easy it is for one title to be neglected, and for the other to govern the whole of a composite quotation.

The suggestion is a startling one, and will need confirmation; for Mark is our earliest Gospel, and to put the *Book of Testimonies* behind all the Gospels is a bold step. Perhaps some one will object at once and say that Mark is not the evangelist who bases his argument on the fulfilment of prophecy, which is rather the characteristic of the Gospel according to Matthew. No doubt there is some force in the objection: but I should like to draw attention to a chapter in which Mark affirms the argument from prophecy. If we turn to the close of Mark's seventh chapter, in which the miracle of the Ephphatha healing is recorded, the incident is summed up in the words, "He has done all things well: he makes both the deaf to hear and the dumb to speak."[31] Here the word "well" means "appropriately," "as he should have done," "in accordance with prophecy."[32]

Thus the people recognise, in Mark, the fulfilment of prophecy: and Mark, himself, under such circumstances, could not miss it. What was the prophecy that they recognised as fulfilled? The answer is, the 35th chapter of Isaiah; and that Mark has this very chapter in mind is betrayed by the fact he calls the subject of the miracle κωφός and μογιλάλος, "deaf" and "speaking with difficulty."[33] The rare word μογιλάλος is, in itself, sufficient to show that Isaiah 35 is in the mind of the evangelist, even if that passage had not been intimated by the closing words of the section about the making of deaf people to hear and speechless folk to talk. But this passage of Isaiah is, as we have seen, a leading proof-text in the *Book of Testimonies*. We may almost say that Mark wrote his seventh chapter to be read along with the *Book of Testimonies*. And certainly his interest in the verification of prophecy by Christ is betrayed in the chapter to which we have referred. There is no difficulty in making Mark into a student of prophecy.

---

31. [Mark 7.37. AF]
32. Cf. Mark 7.6 ("Well did Isaiah prophecy") and the similar language in Acts 28.25.
33. [Mark 7.32. AF]

4. *The Book of Testimonies*

But if this is correct, we shall expect verification of our hypothesis, from other parts of the New Testament. Suppose we ask the question whether there are any other places in the Gospels in which the suggestion of a misplaced title for a prophecy would be at home. We at once think of that much disputed passage in Matthew (Matt. 27.9),[34] concerning the purchase of the potter's field: here we read—

> Then was fulfilled that which was spoken by Jeremy the prophet, saying "And I took the thirty pieces of silver, the price of the valued one whom they priced of the children of Israel, and I gave them for the potter's field, as the Lord commanded me."

You know the trouble over this passage: the quotation is from Zechariah 11.13: but the textual critics (those at least who deal in honest wares), will not allow you to alter "Jeremy the prophet." On the other hand the coincidence with Zechariah is far from being exact. My suggestion is that Matthew has used a Testimony book in which a quotation from Zechariah was preceded or followed by one from Jeremiah, and that he has not accurately defined the limits of his quotations.[35] For instance if we turn to Gregory of Nyssa's collection of *Testimonies against the Jews*, we shall find under the proof-texts for the Passion of Jesus,[36] the following sequence:

> *Jeremiah*: "But I as an innocent lamb was led to the slaughter; I did not know," and again: "Come and let us put wood on his bread and let us erase his name from the living, and let his name be remembered no more."
> *Zecharias*: "And they took the thirty pieces of silver, the price of the valued one, whom they priced of the children of Israel, and they gave them for the field of the potter, as the Lord commanded me."[37]

Here the passage from Zechariah is quoted just as in Matthew, but I do not think it has been emended from the canonised Gospel. It looks as if it were the original from which Matthew worked: and in any case the sequence of Nyssen's quotations suggests directly the blunder in the reference to Jeremiah.

Some such explanation, arising out of a collection of proof-texts of the kind indicated, would clear up the difficulty which has long been perplexing the students of the Gospel.

---

34. [Matt. 27.9-10. AF]

35. See what I have said in confirmation of this opinion in *Expositor* for September, 1905 ["Spoken by Jeremy the Prophet," *Expositor*, 6th series, 12 (1905), pp. 161-71; repr. in *Testimonies*, 1.53-60. AF].

36. Zacagni p. 309 [Lorenzo A. Zacagni, "Gregorii Nysseni de Judaeis," in *Collectanea monumentorum veterum ecclesiae graecae ac latinae* (Rome: Typis Sacrae Congregationis de Propaganda fide, 1698; repr. in PG 46.194-234. Citation from *Jud.* 6.3. AF].

37. [Jer. 11.19 and Zech. 11.13. AF]

I admit, however, that this is not such a good instance as the previous one, and it is wanting in completeness of proof: for I have not cleared up the variation of the text of Zechariah as quoted, when compared with the original prophecy.

Next let us examine a case of composite quotations, such as those to which Dr Hatch drew attention.

We have a striking combination in 1 Pet. 2.6-8,

> Behold! I lay in Zion an elect corner-stone,
> A precious stone;
> And he that believeth on Him shall not be confounded ...
> The stone which the builders rejected is become the head of the corner, and a stone of stumbling and a rock of offence.

Here we have quotations from Isa. 28.16; Ps. 118.22 and Isa. 8.14, the connecting link for the composite passage being the idea that Christ is a stone.

Now suppose we turn to Romans 9.32-33, we have the statement made concerning the Jews that

> They stumbled at the stumbling-stone, as it is written: "Behold! I lay in Zion a stone of stumbling and a rock of offence, and he that believeth on Him shall not be confounded."

Here the same two passages from Isaiah appear again, interwoven into a single reference. If now we could show that the early books of Testimonies actually had a section in which Christ was treated as the Stone spoken of by the prophets, it will become quite clear why Peter and Paul both make the same extracts from Isaiah.

Fortunately this can be at once established. For when we turn to Cyprian's collection of *Testimonies against the Jews*, we find a whole section headed by the words,

> That the same [Christ] is called a stone,

and the next section is

> That the same stone should become a mountain and fill the earth;[38]

and other passages to the same effect may be cited from Justin and elsewhere. Cyprian begins with two of the quotations which we have been discussing, after which he goes stone-hunting all over the Old Testament. This is the way in which he commences:

> Cyp. *Test.* ii.16. That Christ is also called a stone in Isaiah: "Thus saith the Lord, behold I place on the foundations of Sion a precious stone, elect, chief, a corner stone, honourable; and he who trusteth in Him shall not be confounded."

---

38. [*Test.* 2.16 and 2.17. AF]

4. *The Book of Testimonies*   111

Also in the 117th [118th] Psalm: "The stone which the builders rejected, the same is become the head of the corner. This is done by the Lord, and it is wonderful in our eyes. This is the day etc."[39]

Accordingly I claim that both Peter and Paul have had access to a collection of prophetical Testimonies: putting this with what has gone before, and with what might easily be expanded from other parts of the New Testament, we frame the hypothesis that the early Christian Church used collections of prophetical Testimonies, especially in their controversies with the Jews, and that these can be traced back as far as the very beginning of the canonical Christian literature.

It is interesting to note that in Prof. Gwatkin's recently published *Church History*,[40] the antiquity of the collected Testimonies is practically conceded, and they are inferred to be at least earlier than the Gospel of Matthew. The passage to which I refer runs as follows:

If they [the early Christian writers] were all borrowing from some very early manual of proof-texts [Rendel Harris and Burkitt have this theory] which must be at least earlier than the first Gospel, we may safely say that few books have so influenced Christian thought.

And now what prospect have we of recovering the lost book? In its original form there is, perhaps, but a slight probability of our ever laying hands upon it, although a handbook which was probably in use wherever the Church and the Synagogue were debating with one another must have been widely diffused and may turn up somewhere someday. But if we cannot recover the original form, we can often restore it from its descendants; and it is really surprising on how many lines its tradition has been preserved to us. For example, of actual books of Testimonies there are quite a number. We have the first two books of Cyprian's *Testimonies*, which certainly are modelled on an earlier form; we have the book of *Testimonies* ascribed to Gregory of Nyssa, and published by the Vatican Librarian Zacagni in his *Collectanea*; we have also a most instructive treatise by the great Syriac Father Bar Salibi, which I detected in an unpublished work of his against Moslems, Jews and Heretics. The part relating to the Jews, is a collection of Testimonies, translated for the most part, from a very early base.[41] No doubt additions can be

---

39. [Isa. 28.16 and Ps. 118.22. AF]

40. Vol i. p. 199 [Henry M. Gwatkin, *Early Church History to A.D. 313* (2 vols.; London: MacMillan, 1909). AF].

41. This has been published in Syriac by my former pupil Mr. J. de Zwaan [Johannes de Zwaan (ed.), *The Treatise of Dionysius Bar Ṣalibhi against the Jews: Part I, the Syriac Text Edited from a Mesopotamian Ms (Cod. Syr. Harris 83)* (Leiden: Brill, 1906). Part II, the translation, was never published. A handwritten and typewritten translation by de Zwaan, the latter with notes by Rendel Harris, is in DA21/1/1/8, Special Collections, University of Birmingham. The Bar Ṣalibhi manuscript is in Harvard. AF].

made to these. Then, beyond the actual collections, there are whole regions of Patristic literature which the work in question has affected. We have seen one or two instances in what precedes; especially we may note the works of Justin and Irenaeus. From these various sources, it ought to be possible to re-edit the lost book with some approximation to accuracy. The difficulty will arise, however, that a polemical work like this was constantly being altered and amended. In the original draft there were proof-texts that turned out to be apocryphal, and arguments that would not stand criticism. The first generations of Christians were by no means infallible, whatever their successors may have become; sometimes they corrected their mistakes; and sometimes they held on to them: sometimes they attached the most important theological conclusions to mistranslations and misquotations. A single instance may be given, which is the most striking that I know. The doctrine of Christ's nature, and especially his pre-existence was proved to the Jews by a passage from the 110th Psalm; in the Hebrew which is itself perhaps corrupt, the prince who is addressed in the Psalm is said to have "the beauty of holiness from the womb of the morning"; and to have "the dew of his youth"; this unintelligible matter is given by the Septuagint in the form,

From the womb before the day-star I begat thee;[42]

and this was seized on by some Christian controversialists as a conclusive proof of Christ's pre-existence.

One would suppose such an argument would have been brushed away at once, at least by an appeal to the Hebrew. On the contrary all the Fathers, from Justin onward, use it: and it was one of the weapons with which Athanasius demolished Arius at the Council of Nicaea.

Primitive Christianity, on the Dogmatic side, must not always be taken seriously. They would have done better to content themselves with the prologue to St John's Gospel and to have left alone these prophetical Testimonies.

Before leaving this question, I should like to draw attention to another which has been raised by the discussion of the hypothesis of the *Testimony Book*.

A reference to Prof. Gwatkin's new *Church History* will show, in a footnote on p. ,[43] the statement that Rendel Harris and Prof. Burkitt believe there was a primitive collection of Biblical Testimonies, and that Prof. Burkitt is disposed to identify this collection with the famous lost book on which Papias commented. It will be remembered how much controversy has raged round

42. [Ps. 110.3. AF]

43. [Rendel Harris did not give the page number. He refers to the 1912 ("new") edition of Gwatkin, *Early Church*, 1.199, where the note has been expanded in comparison to the first edition. Clearly, Rendel Harris added to his 1910 Haskell Lecture a new section beginning with the preceding sentence. AF]

4. *The Book of Testimonies* 113

the lost work of Papias on the *Dominical Oracles*, a lost commentary on a lost book: and the question as to the nature of these lost oracles is still far from a solution. It has been commonly held that the five books of Papias were a commentary upon the lost Sayings of Jesus; but objection to this has been made, that *Sayings* (λόγοι) are not the same thing as *Oracles* (λόγια), and that the word Oracles belongs rather to the Old Testament than to the collected words of Christ. It is not, therefore, surprising that Prof. Burkitt should have suggested that our *Book of Testimonies* from the Old Testament is the real work upon which Papias made his comments.

Here is a new argument which brings some support to Burkitt's hypothesis.

It will be remembered that in his treatise *On the Incarnation*, Athanasius devotes a number of chapters to the refutation of the Jews, and that in those chapters we detected the use of the *Testimony Book*. Well, in the beginning of ch. 38 Athanasius expresses himself as follows:

> If they do not think the preceding arguments sufficient, let them be persuaded by further oracles (λόγια) from those which they have in their possession.[44]

Then he goes on to quote passages from Isaiah, which belonged to the *Testimony Book*. So here we see Athanasius actually describing his Biblical extracts by the name of Oracles (λόγια).

This is suggestive, but not finally decisive. For when we turn to Justin's *Apology* (ch. 49)[45] where Justin is going to quote the very same passage that Athanasius had used against the Jews (Isa. 65.1-3), he calls the passage "Sayings" (λόγοι) and not "Oracles"; ("these sayings were spoken as if in the person of Christ"). So the same collection might be described either way. And this rather inclines us to believe that the terms "Oracles" and "Sayings" were more nearly synonymous than we might have at first supposed. If this were so, we could not affirm that Papias' book was a comment on Old Testament passages. It might have been, but the matter would require further investigation.[46]

---

44. [*Inc.* 38.1. AF]
45. [*1 Apol.* 49.1. AF]
46. We shall find the same ambiguity in Justin, *Dial.* 15 [*Dial.* 15.7. AF], where he has a chapter which was probably taken from the *Testimony Book*, and concludes his quotation by saying, "Circumcise then the uncircumcision of your hearts, as the Sayings (λόγοι) of God throughout all these Sayings (λόγοι) demand." Here the Testimonies seem to be called Sayings of God, which is not very far removed from the *Dominical Oracles* of Papias; and if we read a little further, observing that Justin has been quoting *Sayings of Jesus* as well as *Testimonies from the Prophets*, we find him (ch. 18 [*Dial.* 18.1. AF]) remarking as follows: "Since you, Trypho, have admitted that you have read the teachings of that Saviour of ours, I don't think I shall be doing anything out of place in reminding you of some brief Oracles of his in addition to those taken from the prophets." Here the

It is possible that, in trying to clear up difficulties, especially where the matter of the writings discussed overlap the record of the New Testament, that we may raise more problems than we solve. I can quite understand that people do not like to be told that there may be primitive errors in the Gospels, and some people will not like to be told that there were earlier books from which the Gospels may have derived them. Also it is possible that the method of exploring for minute peculiarities in the texts of early Fathers, like Justin and Irenaeus, may seem to be unduly subtle. We may, however, be sure that in work of this kind it pays to take pains: and it is absolutely necessary to be conscientious. Painstaking comparison of Gospel texts, along with determined honesty has convinced all sound scholars that we must read *Isaiah* in the opening of Mark and not *the prophets*:[47] and that we must read *Jeremy the prophet* in Matthew's account of the betrayal.[48] If then, by close and careful comparison of the common quotations in early Patristic writers, we can make the hypothesis reasonable of their borrowing from a common source, and confirm its accuracy in a multitude of ways, we have in our hands the instrument for the correcting of the errors which may seem to have been imported into the text of the Gospels: we know how they arose, we are a step further in the problem of their composition, and we are in closer touch than we were before with the mind and the method of the early Christian Church. All of this is genuine progress; and each step taken prepares the way for a further step and for a wider vision.[49]

---

term λόγια is used both of the Testimonies from the Prophets and of the Sayings of Jesus. In the very next chapter (ch. 19 *ad fin.* [*Dial.* 19.6. AF]) we have a passage from Ezekiel quoted as ὁ λόγος αὐτοῦ. From these passages it seems right to infer that we are not justified in restricting the term Oracles to the Old Testament, or Sayings to the New or literature bordering on the New.

47. [Mark 1.2. AF]
48. [Matt. 27.9. AF]
49. In reference to the explanation by means of the shifting of carelessly transcribed or marginally arranged titles, I see that Zacagni, the librarian of the Vatican, who edited for us the *Testimonies* of Gregory of Nyssa, had ingeniously detected the error in question in one passage, and almost gave the explanation. As it is important to collect these instances, which are far more numerous than one would suppose, I will translate (transcribe) the passage in question [*Jud.* 4. AF], along with Zacagni's note. It runs as follows:

Concerning the miracles which the Lord was to show forth after his incarnation.
Jeremiah: "Behold! I have set thee for a covenant of the race, for a light of the Gentiles, that thou mayest establish the earth and possess the inheritance of the desert, saying to those who are in bonds, Go forth; and to those who are in darkness, be enlightened."
And that these things cannot be said by a mere man concerning himself is clear, since it was the same one who said:

4. The Book of Testimonies 115

Before leaving this brief statement of an admittedly imperfect investigation, it may be worth while to ask the question what the net result of the enquiry is upon the general subject of the correct statement and proper defence of Christian doctrine. It is quite evident that the results of the examination into the mode of composition and transmission of prophetical Testimonies is inconsistent with the ordinary belief in a verbally inspired Gospel canon. For a large part of the argument turns upon an observed coincidence in blunders of transmission, and we were not able to limit these errors to persons belonging to the sub-apostolic or sub-evangelic Age. So that an enquiry of this kind is barred in advance for those who insist on an infallible text of the Scriptures as a preliminary to the enquiry. Not only is the argument one which is, of necessity, fallacious from their point of view, but in order to maintain the position in which they are entrenched, they have to surrender to impossible textual criticism (as by reading "the prophets" for "Isaiah" in the opening of Mark), or to equally impossible exegesis (as in explaining away "Jeremy the prophet" from the text of Matthew).

On the other hand, so soon as we admit the possibility of errors in transmission, we are in the great position of advantage of seeing how a number of such errors have arisen and of reflecting upon the very small importance that attaches to them historically.

But then there is another advantage that is gained by this method of enquiry. We are often challenged as to the validity of the Christian Gospels, considered as historical documents, in view of the generally accepted conclusion that they were not composed until nearly a quarter of a century after the events which they record. That empty space between the date of the Ascension and the beginning of the Christian literature, is one of the difficulties that have to be met. Even when we allow the Pauline and other letters to be adduced in evidence of the beliefs of the early Church, we are still far from being adequately supplied with material for historical interpretation: nor does it seem to me that we can fairly meet the difficulty by talking as positively as some do, about the Oral tradition and the existence of the order of Catechists, who are assumed to have the tradition by heart from the first Apostolic utterances onward, and never to have made serious errors of memory in the transmission

> [*Baruch*] "This is our God and there shall not be reckoned another beside Him."
> *Isaiah*: "Be strong, ye relaxed hands and feeble knees etc."

Here the first extract is not from Jeremiah, but from Isaiah (49.6, 8 [49.6, 8-9. AF]). Zacagni explains the matter thus: Nyssen took it for a passage of Jeremiah, because he subjoins a testimony from Baruch (Bar. 3.36 [Bar. 3.35. AF]), who is often quoted under the name of Jeremiah. He meant it, therefore, to be referred to Jeremiah. It only remains, then, to add that the error must be earlier than Nyssen; and that it arose from the wandering of the eye of a scribe from the correct Isaiah to the Jeremiah (Baruch) which followed.

of the tradition. Now it is in just such directions as we have been occupied that the void which perplexes us begins to be filled up. *There are lost books of the Early Church*, and some of them have been employed in the composition of our existing Gospels. Of this family one leading member was the *Book of Testimonies*; a second, to which we shall refer presently in another lecture, was the lost *Book of Sayings of Jesus*.[50] And I have little doubt that, if our critical eyes were keener, and especially if we could recover some more fragments of early Christian literature, we should be able to affirm the existence of quite a little library of early Christian books. In this way much would become clear that is now somewhat obscure in the Evangelic history. We should not only have the original Mark, of which the critics talk (if there was an Ur-Marcus), and the companion document which they call Q which has been employed by both Matthew and Luke, but we should have two or three other leading Christian documents, belonging to the very space that was perplexing us by its vacancy. And it is easy to imagine that the vacancy (which is only due to the carelessness of the Church over its records) might wholly disappear. For we do not forget what Luke tells us about many who had tried to compose a Gospel History and who were certainly not Oral traditionalists or Catechists![51]

Our enquiry, then, is a real alleviation of the difficulty of the situation, and the first step, perhaps, towards its complete removal.

On the other hand it may be urged that in emphasising the use of the Old Testament in early Christian times, we are making things worse for the exegete and the believer: for if the primitive Christians appealed so freely to prophecies of all kinds, they must often have made wrong appeals which were discredited almost as soon as made, or which are certainly not to be credited amongst ourselves.

This part of the problem, however, is not new: we shall have to settle for ourselves, quite apart from the *Book of Testimonies*, whether Matthew was right in his interpretation of the calling of the Son out of Egypt.[52] If he was the victim of an incorrect exegesis, this may have been, on our hypothesis, some one else's mistake and not his own. We shall still have to decide this and other matters with the best light we can get. And the real advantage of our method lies in this very direction, that it is an increase of light and an extension of knowledge. And I do not think the central figure of Christianity or its central doctrines are likely to be obscured by a careful restoration of the broken and almost lost fabric of its earliest literature.

---

50. [This is Haskell Lecture 2, which I have not been able to find. AF]
51. [Luke 1.1. AF]
52. [Matt. 2.15. AF]

Chapter 5

THE ORIGIN OF THE PROLOGUE TO ST JOHN'S GOSPEL

Preface

In the following pages I have gathered together and made some additions to a series of articles which I recently published in the pages of the *Expositor*.[1] If I am right in the results here reached, we must recognise that a fresh chapter has been added to the *History of Christian Dogma*, and one that stands very near to the beginning of the book. A nearer approach to the origin of the Christology of the Church means a closer approximation to the position of those who first tried to answer the question "Who do men say that I am?"; and to be nearer the Apostles is to be nearer, also, to Christ Himself. It is not easy to say how much of the argument is really new; as far as I know, British theologians have hardly touched the question; they are always more at home in the fourth century than in the first! The best account of the subject that I have come across is Lebreton's *Origines du dogme de la Trinité*,[2] which combines Catholic doctrine with a good deal of sound reasoning as to the evolution of that doctrine. I should have quoted it several times if I had read it before my brief essay was written. As it is, I can only refer to it here, without suggesting that my commendations should be reckoned along with the

---

1. ["The Origin of the Prologue to St John's Gospel," *Expositor*, 8th series, 12 (1916), pp. 147-60, 161-70, 314-20, 388-400, 415-26. There are numerous handwritten additions in Rendel Harris's personal copy of the book, which is kept in the Rendel Harris Room, Woodbrooke. Some of them are clearly intended for a second edition. I transcribe all of them in footnotes between square brackets. When he adds a footnote, I introduce it as "HCF"; what looks like new material to be inserted into the body of the text as "HCB"; comments apparently intended for personal reference as "HCC"; if the addition is on one or more flyleaves, the number of the flyleaf is reported within square brackets. In this case, I place the footnote reference at the last word of the page in the original edition, to which the flyleaf/flyleaves is/are attached; furthermore, I report the number and the first words of the page so that the reader might understand what are the limits of the page itself. I have not edited Rendel Harris's notes. This is why there are, for instance, missing diacritical signs. AF]
2. [Jules Lebreton, *Histoire du dogme de la Trinité des origines à Saint Augustin* (2 vols.; Paris: Beauchesne, 3rd edn, 1910). AF]

imprimatur under which it appears. They are appreciations rather than endorsements. It is certainly a book from which very much can be learned by students of every school of thought. While these pages are passing through the press I have had the pleasure of examining Prof. Hans Windisch's essay on *Die göttliche Weisheit der Juden und die paulinische Christologie*,[3] in which a number of the conclusions in this book are either adumbrated, or definitely stated. It would have been easy for Prof. Windisch to carry his argument further, if he had known the bearing of the early *Testimony Book* upon the Christological problem.

In theology generally we seem to be at a standstill from which we can only be moved by the discovery of fresh facts, or the opening up of fresh lines of enquiry. It will certainly be to many a discovery that Jesus was known in the first century as the Wisdom of God; with equal certainty the application of this new fact to the existing Christian tradition will be productive of not a little motion amongst its dry bones.

My thanks are due to the Editor of the *Expositor*, from whose pages much of the following volume is reproduced, and to my friend Vacher Burch, who has assisted me greatly in the composition and correction of the volume.

Rendel Harris.
October, 1916.

I

In a recent number of the *Commonwealth*, Professor Scott Holland writes with enthusiasm in praise of the Poet Laureate's new book *The Spirit of Man*.[4] But he says that he has one real regret and one only. He regrets that Dr Bridges was persuaded to give the opening passage of St John's Gospel as "In the beginning was mind."[5] The criticism here made, which I quote from that excellent little paper, entitled *Public Opinion* (as I have no access to the *Commonwealth*), raises once more in our minds the question as to the real meaning and the actual genesis of the Prologue to the Fourth Gospel. Are we nearer to the actual sense of the words when we say with the Poet Laureate that "in the beginning was Mind," or, as some would say, "in the beginning was Thought," or are we to say with Professor Scott Holland that *Mind* is an

---

3. [Hans Windisch, "Die göttliche Weisheit der Juden und die paulinische Christologie," in *Neutestamentliche Studien für Georg Heinrici zu seinem 70. Geburtstag (14. März 1914) dargebracht von Fachgenossen, Freunden und Schülern* (ed. Adolf Deissmann and Hans Windisch; Leipzig: Hinrichs, 1914), pp. 220-34. AF]
4. [Robert S. Bridges, *The Spirit of Man: An Anthology in English and French from the Philosophers and Poets* (London: Longmans, 1916). AF]
5. [John 1.1. AF]

5. *The Origin of the Prologue to St John's Gospel*   119

inadequate term, and that the idea must have included "speech, expression, the rational word"?

It seems evident that there must be other questions to be resolved before we come to the hermeneutical and exegetical problems over which the Professor and the Poet are in danger of a collision. For instance, we want to know more about this Prologue, which is attributed commonly to St John, and which, in any case, contains theological statements of the highest importance, deserving, if any such statements necessarily deserve, an apostolical authority. Is this Prologue an intellectual Athena bursting forth suddenly from the brain of a mystical Zeus? or is it, like so many other surprising statements of poets, sages and saints which seem to defy evolution and to be as independent of ancestry as Melchizedek, a statement which carries about it, upon close examination, marks of an ancestry in stages and by steps, like most of the religious, intellectual and physical products with which we are acquainted?

To put it another way. The Church is firmly persuaded, and not without strong supporting reasons, that these opening sentences of the Fourth Gospel are among the most inspired words in the whole of the Christian records. It is not merely that they have resonance, and apparent novelty, and depth of meaning, and unexpected views of the world *sub specie aeternitatis*. They are so unlike any other evangelical prologues: their *Beginning* is not the "Genesis of Jesus Christ" in Matthew,[6] nor the "Beginning of the Gospel" in Mark;[7] their glory of the Son of God is not the abrupt formula with which Mark opens, and which he uses his pictorial records to attest: the artistic fashion of them does not appear to be made on the lines of some previously successful literary artist, like the elegant Greek of the first verses of St Luke. Is it any wonder that direct and immediate inspiration has been claimed for these majestic sentences? Thus Jerome, in his prologue to Matthew,[8] speaks of St John as *saturatus revelatione* when he wrote his opening words: and it is possible that the same sense of constraint is involved in the terms in which Jerome describes St John as setting pen to paper;

    in illud proemium caelo veniens eructavit In principio erat verbum:

but this ought not to be unduly pressed, since Jerome's *eructavit* is really borrowed from the opening of Psalm 45:[9]

    Eructavit cor meum *verbum* bonum,

where the language is taken to express the emission of the doctrine of the Logos by St John, and goes back to the Septuagint, ἐξηρεύξατο ἡ καρδία μου

    6.   [Matt. 1.1. AF]
    7.   [Mark 1.1. AF]
    8.   [*Comm. Matt.* Praefatio. AF]
    9.   [Ps. 45.1. AF]

λόγον ἀγαθόν. However that may be, it is certain that the Prologue of St John is the high-water mark of inspiration for those who read the Scriptures reverently.

It is just at this point that the enquiring mind puts in a protest and asks whether it is not possible that, conceding the inspiration of the words, we might legitimately question the immediateness of the inspiration. Suppose then we go in search of any prior stages of thought that may underlie the famous Prologue. To begin with, there is the description of Christ as the Logos. Was that reached immediately, as soon as Philosophy and Religion looked one another fairly in the face in Ephesus or Palestine, or Alexandria? How soon did the term "Word of God" acquire a metaphysical sense? The question is, perhaps, easier asked than answered. In the Synoptic Gospels the term "Word of God" is always used of the utterance divine or the record of that utterance. It is that which the sower sows, that which the traditionalist makes void by his tradition, that which the multitudes throng round Jesus to hear. And the curious thing is that in the Fourth Gospel there is a similar usage, after one passes away from the Prologue and the doctrine of the Incarnation. Jesus Himself speaks of the readers of a certain Psalm as those to whom the Word of God came, and of His own message (rather than Himself) as the Word of the Father which He has communicated to His disciples. "I have given them thy word."[10] The suggestion is natural that we should regard the philosophical use of Logos as the latest deposit upon the surface of the narration, a verbal usage which has displaced an earlier meaning and sense. It is the more curious that the evangelist never reverts to the Logos with which he opens his narrative, in view of the fact that Christ speaks as "Light" and "Life" in various parts of the Gospel, and so identifies Himself (or is identified) with the metaphysic of the Prologue.

Is it possible, we ask next, that the Logos may have displaced an earlier metaphysical title as well as that employment of the word which we usually indicate by not writing it in capitals?

All through the rest of the New Testament the Word of God means the Evangelic message, except in one passage in the Apocalypse,[11] where it is a title of the Messiah, and a doubtful place in Hebrews where the "quick and powerful"[12] word of God appears to be explicable by Philonean parallels in a metaphysical sense.

We find, however, that there is occasionally another title given to Jesus Christ. He is called "*the Wisdom of God* and the Power of God,"[13] and is said

---

10. John 17.14, where the sense of λόγος is fixed by the alternative ῥήματα of v. 8.
11. [Rev. 19.13. AF]
12. [Heb. 4.12. AF]
13. [1 Cor. 1.24. AF]

5. *The Origin of the Prologue to St John's Gospel*   121

to become the *Wisdom of His people.* "He has become to us Wisdom."[14] So the question arises whether Sophia may not be an alternative title to Logos and perhaps prior to it.

For instance, in the Gospel of Luke (11.49) the Wisdom of God is personified and speaks of sending prophets and wise men to be rejected by the scribes and Pharisees. Apparently this is not meant for a Biblical quotation, and in that sense is not the Word of God; the "Wisdom" that speaks is not the title nor the contents of a book. In the corresponding passage of Matthew (I suppose we must refer the origin to the lost document Q) we have simply "Therefore, behold! I send unto you, etc."[15] So when Tatian made his Harmony, he naturally produced the sentence, "Behold! I, the Wisdom of God, send unto you, etc.," which brings out clearly the involved, personified Wisdom-Christ; and inasmuch as God is personified and speaks through Sophia, when He sends His processional array of prophets and wise men, we have what in Greek looks like a feminine form of the Johannine Logos. The suggestion arises (at present in the form of a pure hypothesis) that *the way to Logos is through Sophia and that the latter is the ancestress of the former.* Now let us try if we can re-write the Johannine Prologue, substituting the word Sophia for the word Logos. It now runs as follows—

> In the beginning was the Divine Wisdom,
> and Wisdom was with God,
> and Wisdom was God.
> The same was in the beginning with God:
> All things were made by her, and without her was nothing made that was made.

As soon as we have written down the sentences we are at once struck by their resemblance to the Old Testament: we could almost say that we were transcribing a famous passage in Proverbs:

> Prov. 8.22-30: The Lord possessed me (Sophia) *in the beginning* of His way, before His works of old. I was set up from everlasting, *from the beginning* ... when He prepared the heavens *I was there*: when He set a compass upon the face of the deep ... then *I was by Him.*

It seems clear that we have found the stratum of the Old Testament upon which the Prologue reposes. This is practically admitted by almost all persons who find Old Testament references in the New: they simply cannot ignore the eighth chapter of Proverbs. If this be so, and if the Logos is quoted as being

---

14. First Corinthians 1.30, where the use of the conjunctions makes it clear that the emphasis is on Wisdom, which should have a capital letter, and be explained by "righteousness, sanctification and redemption." See Moffatt in loc. [James Moffatt, *The New Testament: A New Translation in Modern Speech, Based upon the Greek Text by von Soden* (London: Hodder & Stoughton, 1913). AF].

15. [Matt. 23.34. AF]

and doing just what Sophia is said to be and to do in the Book of Proverbs, then the equation between Logos and Sophia is justified, and we may speak of Christ in the metaphysical sense as the Wisdom of God, and may write out the first draft of the doctrine of the Logos in the form which we have suggested above. In other words, we have in the Prologue not an immediate oracle, but a mediated one, in which separate stages can be marked out, and an original ground-form postulated. Now let us examine the Greek of the Prologue and compare it with the Greek of the Septuagint in Proverbs. We readily see the principal parallels consist in the collocation of—

$$\begin{cases} \text{ἐν ἀρχῇ ἦν ὁ λόγος and} \\ \text{κύριος ἔκτισέν με ἀρχὴν ὁδῶν αὐτοῦ... πρὸ τοῦ αἰῶνος ἐθεμελίωσέν με} \quad (8.22)^{16} \\ \text{ἐν ἀρχῇ} \end{cases}$$

$$\begin{cases} \text{ὁ λόγος ἦν πρὸς τὸν θεόν and} \\ \text{ἤμην παρ' αὐτῷ} \quad (8.30) \end{cases}$$

$$\begin{cases} \text{οὗτος ἦν ἐν ἀρχῇ πρὸς τὸν θεόν and} \\ \text{ἡνίκα ἡτοίμαζεν τὸν οὐρανόν, συμπαρήμην αὐτῷ} \quad (8.27) \\ \text{cf. also ὁ θεὸς τῇ σοφίᾳ ἐθεμελίωσεν τὴν γῆν} \quad (3.19) \end{cases}$$

$$\begin{cases} \text{ἐν αὐτῷ ζωὴ ἦν and} \\ \text{αἱ γὰρ ἔξοδοί μου ἔξοδοι ζωῆς} \quad (8.35) \\ \text{ξύλον ζωῆς ἐστι πᾶσι τοῖς ἀντεχομένοις αὐτῆς} \quad (3.18) \end{cases}$$

It is clear from the collocation that John uses πρὸς τὸν θεόν for παρὰ τῷ θεῷ, a usage which recurs in the First Epistle in the expression παράκλητον ἔχομεν πρὸς τὸν πατέρα.[17]

This is not to be explained in a mystical manner, as though πρὸς τόν conveyed some deeper sense than παρὰ τῷ, it means "with God," as commonly translated: the change in grammatical form is due to the writer's or the translator's Greek, or if we prefer it, want of Greek,[18] coupled with the fact of the relative paucity of the prepositions in Semitic, which causes the pleonastic representation of a Semitic pronoun by a variety of Greek pronouns, and to

16. [Prov. 8.22-23. AF]
17. [1 John 2.1. AF]
18. Accordingly Euthymius Zigabenus says, πρὸς τὸν θεόν, ἤγουν παρὰ τῷ πατρί, ἵνα τε παραστήσῃ τὸ ἰδιάζον τῶν ὑποστάσεων καὶ ὅτι ἀχώριστοι πατὴρ καὶ υἱός [*Commentarium in Joannem* (PG 129.1109CD). AF]. On the other hand Liddon, *Bampton Lectures* (p. 231) [Henry P. Liddon, *The Divinity of Our Lord and Saviour Jesus Christ: Eight Lectures Preached before the University of Oxford in 1866, on the Foundation of the Late Rev. John Bampton* (London: Rivingtons, 1867). AF], says: "He was not merely παρὰ τῷ θεῷ but πρὸς τὸν θεόν. This last preposition expresses beyond the fact of co-existence or immanence the more significant fact of perpetuated intercommunion. The Face of the Everlasting Word, if we dare so to express ourselves, was ever *directed towards* the Face of the Everlasting Father." [HCC: Note that Eusebius H.E. i.2 [*Hist. eccl.* 1.2.3. AF] has ἐν ἀρχῇ, παρὰ τῷ Πατρὶ τυγχάνοντα Θεὸν Λόγον.]

some extent the variations of the pronouns *inter se* for persons who do not know much Greek. It is not necessary to assume an actual reference back to the original Hebrew of Proverbs: the Septuagint text will probably be sufficient to explain the form of the Prologue. The restoration of Sophia into the place occupied by the Logos in the Prologue will help us to understand better the course of the argument. For example, the statement that "all things were made by her" is a summary of the verses in Proverbs describing Wisdom's activity at the Creation; while the repetition "and without her nothing was made,"[19] shows that we have in the verse a reflection from another passage, where we are told that "in wisdom (or by wisdom) He hath made them *all*" (Ps. 104.24).

The next step will be to see whether the proposed scheme of evolution for the Johannine Prologue will throw light on the remaining clauses of the argument contained in it. Perhaps, however, this will be sufficient for a first statement. So we will merely recapitulate our hypothesis, which is, that the Logos in the Prologue to John is a substitute for Sophia in a previously existing composition, and the language of the Prologue to the Gospel depends ultimately upon the eighth chapter of the Book of Proverbs.

If we are right, then Dr Bridges was right, at least as far as the basal document is concerned, in saying that "in the beginning was *Mind*": for it is *Mind* that is the proper substitute for *Sophia*, and not any particular expression of the rational word, as suggested by Scott Holland in the passage to which we referred at the beginning of this paper.[20]

* * * * *

Our hypothesis that the Logos of the Fourth Gospel is a substitute for a previously existing Sophia involves (or almost involves) the consequence that the Prologue is a hymn in honour of Sophia, and that it need not be in that sense due to the same authorship as the Gospel itself. The best way to test the hypothesis is to see where it will take us, and what further light it will shed upon the primitive Christian doctrine. Let us then retrace our steps for awhile and see whether the foundations of the argument are secure.

The first thing that needs to be emphasised is that we are obliged to take a different view of the Greek of the Fourth Gospel from that which is commonly taken by New Testament exegetes. They are in the habit of describing the Greek of the Gospel as simple, but correct, and of contrasting it in that respect with the Greek of the Apocalypse. Our position is that the very first

19. [John 1.3. AF]
20. [HCF: (1) I see that in the Notes at the end of his book Dr Bridges who has printed the Chant in Proverbs and the Prologue to John adjacent to one another, admits that in translating *Logos* by *Mind*, misunderstanding may be caused: but he urges that the rendering sets a plain man on the right track.]

verse of the Gospel ought to have undeceived them as to the linguistic accuracy of the writer, and to have marked him as a "barbarian" in the Greek sense. In other words, ἦν πρὸς τὸν θεόν is not Greek at all: and a Greek scholar ought to have felt this at the very first reading. The various subtleties which are read into the expression are self-condemned, in that they can neither be justified by the theological thought of the time when the book was composed, nor can they be made to harmonise with the assumed simplicity of the writer's diction. When Mr F.A. Paley,[21] with the dew of Æschylean studies upon him, and in that sense very far removed from the possibility of understanding Hellenistic Greek, began to translate the oracular opening of the Gospel, he said:

> In the beginning was the Logos, and the Logos was *in relation to God*, and the Logos was God,

and then added a note that "the usual translation 'the Word was with God' (from the Latin Vulgate) conveys no clearly intelligible idea." One wonders what was the clearly intelligible idea that was conveyed by the words "The Logos was in relation to God"!

If Jerome gave us the rendering "apud Deum," he was in any case following the primitive Latin tradition; when the Old Latin version was revised, the original "sermo" was changed to "verbum," but apparently no one thought of changing "apud" into some other preposition. What other word ought they to have used if the passage was to remain simple and intelligible? It will not do to lay the burden of unintelligible translation upon the Latin: for even if we assume that the Latin is obscure, we have in the Syriac the rendering—

ܐܠܗܐ ܠܘܬ (=l_ewath Alaha)

which was, as any Syriac scholar will admit, the only possible rendering of πρὸς τὸν θεόν, and in itself capable of equation with *apud Deum*. It is this Syriac rendering that is the key to the understanding of the passage, for (i) it is the equivalent either of πρὸς τὸν θεόν or of παρὰ τῷ θεῷ, and (ii) if we take it in the second of the two senses, we have the exact parallel to the language of the Proverbs, where Wisdom is described as being "with God," in the sense of being seated by God and in attendance upon Him. If the language of the Gospel is to be taken as unintelligible, the language of the Book of Proverbs must be taken as unintelligible also.

Let us, then, leave Mr Paley, who in these matters counts for very little, and let us turn to Dr Westcott, who counts for a very great deal.[22]

---

21. [Frederick A. Paley, *The Gospel of St John: A Verbatim Translation from the Vatican MS. with the Notable Variations of the Sinaitic and Beza MS., and Brief Explanatory Comments* (London: S. Sonnenschein, Lowrey, 1887). AF]

22. [Brooke F. Westcott, *The Gospel according to St John: The Authorised Version* (London: John Murray, 1882. AF]

The first thing that Westcott says is that "the phrase (ἦν πρός, Vulgate *erat apud*) is remarkable. It is found also in Matthew 13.56; Mark 6.3; Mark 9.19; Mark 14.49; Luke 9.41; 1 John 1.2. The idea conveyed by it is not that of simple coexistence, as of two persons contemplated separately in company (εἶναι μετά, 3.26, etc.) or united under a common conception (εἶναι σύν, Luke 22.56) or (so to speak) in local relation (εἶναι παρά, 17.5), but of being (in some sense) *directed towards* and regulated by that with which the relation is fixed (5.19)."

The passage quoted is characteristically obscure, but we may try to unravel its meaning. Westcott wants to translate πρὸς τὸν θεόν as "in the direction of God"; so much was due to his pedagogic tradition; but this does not satisfy him, so he prefixes a parenthetic "in some sense" before the words "directed towards," and leaves us to find out as best we may what the sense was in which the Logos was polarised *towards* God. When we come to examine the parallel passages by which the remarkable usage of πρός is to be justified, we notice that Matthew and Luke ought not to be quoted. Matthew 13.56 is from Mark 6.3; and Luke 9.41 is a repetition of Mark 9.19. The usage is clearly Marcan; and we have therefore to enquire what Mark meant by saying:

> His sisters are with us,

or

> How long shall I be with you?

or

> I was daily with you in the Temple:[23]

surely the sense of these passages is clear enough: we should not improve the rendering by saying:

> His sisters are (in some sense) directed towards us and regulated by that which fixes the relation between them and us.

The fact that the language is Marcan, taken with the known result of criticism, that Mark's language is, in part at least, Aramaic, encourages us to see how the texts look in the Old Syriac. The Syriac scholar will know without looking that the equivalent is ܠܘܬܢ (=l_ewathan) for πρὸς ἡμᾶς and ܠܘܬܟܘܢ (=l_ewathkōn) for πρὸς ὑμᾶς. The Greek then of Mark has carried over a mistranslation of the Syriac ܠܘܬ (l_ewath) exactly similar to what occurs in the Prologue to John.[24] We are dealing with what is called "Translation Greek" or "Semitic Greek." The Marcan and Johannine uses are one and the same.

---

23. [Respectively, Mark 6.3, 9.19, 14.49. AF]

24. [HCC: Perhaps there is another case of the same confusion in Matt. 26[18] πρὸς σὲ ποιῶ τὸ πάσχα = ܠܘܬܟ]

This does not mean that they were incapable of translating the Syriac preposition. St John has the correct παρὰ σεαυτῷ and παρὰ σοί in 17.5, where the Syriac reader will note the occurrence of ܠܘܬܟ (l_ewathak) in the Peshito for both expressions (though the older Syriac has a rather cumbrous paraphrase).

[Before leaving the linguistic alley into which we have wandered it will not be waste of time or space to remind readers of New Testament Greek to be on the look-out for usages and misunderstandings similar to the series to which we have been drawing attention. For example, the Aramaic idiom for "he went away" is

ܐܙܠ ܠܗ (ezal leh),

answering very nearly to the Old English "he went *him* away"; the second pronoun in the English and the expletive ܠܗ (= leh, him *or* to him) in Syriac being without an equivalent and untranslatable in modern English. The early translators of the New Testament documents, however, were at pains to find nothing untranslatable and to leave nothing untranslated. For example, in the interpolated passage Luke 24.12, we are told that Peter went away from the tomb in amazement at what had occurred; in Greek it is

ἀπῆλθεν πρὸς αὐτόν
or πρὸς ἑαυτόν,

which evidently stands for a simple Aramaic statement that "Peter went away," and in the first rendering was

ἀπῆλθεν [πρὸς αὐτόν],

where we add brackets to show the redundancy of the translator.

Now we see what happens. The Greek passage goes back into Syriac; the translator does not see that it is a case of his conventional idiom, and laboriously replaces the redundant word by ܠܘܬܗ (l_ewatheh), and so loses the idiom altogether. As we have pointed out, the words πρὸς αὐτόν ought not to have been translated in the first instance, in turning Aramaic discourse into Greek, nor rendered again in the second, in turning a Greek sentence into Syriac.

The whole incident is either derived from the Fourth Gospel (John 20.3-10) or from some closely related document. In the Fourth Gospel, however, we have two disciples visiting the tomb, and not merely Peter: but whether the original story was told of one person or two, it ends up significantly in John with the remark that the two disciples went away πρὸς αὐτούς. This time the Lewis Syriac restores the idiom correctly, ܐܙܠܘ ܠܗܘܢ (ezālu l_ehōn), "they went them away." The Peshito, however, tries to bring more out of the Greek than is really in it, and presents us with "they went away to their 'own' places."]

5. *The Origin of the Prologue to St John's Gospel*

Now let us return to Sophia. Our supposition that the Logos of the Gospel is a substitute for a primitive Sophia will be confirmed if we can show

(i) that there is any literature, devotional or otherwise, connected with the praises of Sophia:

(ii) if we find that Jesus, who is equated with the Logos, is also equated with the Wisdom of God:

(iii) if the praises of Sophia are as notably derived from the Book of Proverbs, as we have seen the Prologue of the Gospel to be; and

(iv) if the conjunction of Logos and Sophia is intellectually sufficiently close to allow one of them to be interchanged with the other.

With regard to the first and third points, we hardly need to remind ourselves that there is a whole series of Sapiential books, of which the principal representatives, the so-called Wisdom of Solomon, and the Wisdom of Jesus the Son of Sirach, are seen by a very superficial criticism to be pendants to the great hymn in the eighth chapter of Proverbs. If, for example, the Book of Proverbs represents Wisdom as saying,

> I was by Him as one brought up with Him,[25]

this Attendant-Wisdom or Assessor-Wisdom appears in the prayer of Solomon "Give me Wisdom that sits by Thy throne" (Wis. 9.4) and is said to have been:

> With Thee and aware of Thy works, and present with Thee at the world's making (Wis. 9.9);

and a further prayer as follows:

> Despatch her from the Holy Heaven,
> Send her from the Throne of Thy Glory (Wis. 9.10);

in all of which passages Wisdom is conceived, as we said before, as the Co-Assessor and Attendant of the Creator. The motive for all these rhythms is in the eighth chapter of Proverbs. The ninth chapter of the Wisdom of Solomon is, in fact, a pendant to the eighth of the Proverbs of Solomon: it occupies an intermediate position between Proverbs and John. More than this, it furnishes the transition from Logos to Sophia, by using parallel language for the two personifications. The chapter opens thus:

> O God of our fathers and Lord of Thy mercy,
> Who hast made all things *by Thy Word*,
> And hast ordained man *by Thy Wisdom*.[26]

Here the parallel is made between creative word and creative wisdom: the Word and the Wisdom are almost equivalent: the earlier concept, Wisdom, in

---

25. [Prov. 8.30. AF]
26. [Wis. 9.1-2. AF]

the Book of Proverbs, by whom all things were made, has attached to it a second concept, the Logos, and what was said of the former is now said of the latter: we have passed from

> Without her was nothing made,

to

> Without Him was nothing made.

We have crossed from Proverbs to John; the bridge upon which we crossed is the ninth chapter of the Wisdom of Solomon: so the praises of Sophia become the praises of the Logos.

The chapter closes with another suggestive parallelism between Sophia and the Holy Spirit, as follows:

> Who knoweth Thy counsel
> Unless Thou givest Wisdom
> And sendest Thy Holy Spirit from on high?[27]

When we pass from the so-called Wisdom of Solomon to the Wisdom of Jesus the Son of Sirach, we are confronted with similar phenomena to those which we have already adumbrated. Again we see that the underlying text is the Great Chant in Proverbs, and that these so-called Sapiential books are variations of the same theme, that Wisdom is with God, that She is before all things, and that She is involved in the creation of all the works of God.

We are to set over against Proverbs 8.22

> The Lord created me in the beginning of His way,
> Before His works of old,

the passage

> Wisdom has been created before all things,
> Intelligence and understanding from Eternity (Sir. 1.4);

and

> The Lord created her Himself
> ****
> And shed her forth over all His works (Sir. 1.9).

But when we have made these obvious parallels we cannot detach them from the language of the Prologue:

> In the beginning was the Word
> ****
> All things were made by Him.[28]

27. [Wis. 9.17. AF]
28. [John 1.1 and 1.3. AF]

5. The Origin of the Prologue to St John's Gospel

The dependence of Sirach in its Sophia-doctrine upon Proverbs will be conceded readily enough: whole sentences are, in fact, transferred bodily, e.g.:

Prov.	9.10.	ἀρχὴ σοφίας φόβος Κυρίου.
Sir.	1.14.	ἀρχὴ σοφίας φοβεῖσθαι τὸν θεόν.
Prov.	8.17.	οἱ δὲ ἐμὲ ζητοῦντες εὑρήσουσιν.
Sir.	4.11.	ἡ σοφία ... ἐπιλαμβάνεται τῶν ζητούντων αὐτήν.
Prov.	8.36.	οἱ μισοῦντές με ἀγαπῶσιν θάνατον.
Sir.	4.12.	ὁ ἀγαπῶν αὐτὴν ἀγαπᾷ ζωήν.

And so on.

It will not, perhaps, be so readily conceded that the language of the Johannine Prologue is a case of similar dependence; the practical difficulty arises from our insufficient familiarity with the language of the Sapiential books, and from the lack of the clue furnished by the inter-relation of σοφία and λόγος, to which we have drawn attention above.

Jesus, then, is identified with the Wisdom of God and the Word of God successively: first with the Wisdom because the Logos-doctrine is originally a Wisdom-doctrine, and after that with the Word, because the Wisdom becomes the Word.

It cannot, indeed, be unreasonable to suggest a stage in which Jesus was identified with Wisdom, when, as we have shown, He is called the Wisdom of God by St Paul, who does not present us with the Logos-doctrine, although he does predicate of Christ all that the Fourth Gospel predicates of the Logos. And, as we have shown, the Gospels themselves are in evidence, and perhaps one of the leading Gospel sources (Q) for identifying Christ with the Wisdom of God. The fact is that Logos and Sophia were originally very near together, almost a pair, although under Gnostic speculation they were moved far apart. The substitution of Logos for Sophia in the primitive Christology was little more than the replacing of a feminine expression by a masculine one in Greek-speaking circles, and the transition was very easy. It appears, then, that we can justify the evolution of the Johannine Prologue from the eighth chapter of Proverbs, and we can show the line of the evolution to have passed through the Sapiential books.

If this be so, we do not need to imitate modern exegetes who speak of the influence of the teaching of Heraclitus upon the Ephesian philosophers or upon the early Ephesian Church. It is doubtful whether there is any need to introduce Heraclitus at all. Certainly we can explain further points in the primitive Christology, without turning aside from the path we have already been taking. A Sapiential student, if we may so describe a person who makes himself acquainted, from the Sapiential books, with the virtues and potencies and privileges of the personified Wisdom of God, will tell us, for example, that Wisdom is a *Holy Spirit* and an *Only-Begotten Spirit* (cf. Wis. 7.22, ἔστιν γὰρ ἐν αὐτῇ πνεῦμα νοερόν, ἅγιον, μονογενές), where, in the first instance, the meaning of the word μονογενής was simply that She was the only one of her kind; a little lower down this expands itself into the statement that "because She is One, She can All" (μία δὲ οὖσα πάντα δύναται [7.27]).

Thus behind the Only-Begotten Son of God to whom John introduces us, we see the Unique Daughter of God, who is His Wisdom, and we ought to understand the Only-Begotten Logos-Son as an evolution from the Only-Begotten Sophia-daughter.

Let us take another instance from the early Christology, not exactly coincident with the Johannine doctrine, but running parallel to it; I mean the Christology of the Epistle to the Hebrews. In the very lofty opening sentences of this Epistle, we find the statement that the Son of God is the heir of all things, and that by Him the ages (or worlds) were made, and that He is the Radiance of the Divine Glory, and the Reflexion of the Divine Being.[29] Now recall what we said of the identification of Jesus with the Wisdom of God, and see what is said in the Wisdom of Solomon of the Divine Wisdom, that she is the

> Radiance[30] of the Eternal Light (7.26),

and the

> Spotless Mirror of the Divine Activity,

and the

> Image of His goodness.

The statements from the Epistle to the Hebrews can be deduced at once from the Sapiential books: for it was the Wisdom of God that made the worlds, Wisdom that is the Radiance of God (ἀπαύγασμα) and Wisdom that is the imprint of God (χαρακτήρ in Hebrews, εἰκών and ἔσοπτρον in the Wisdom of Solomon).

Thus we can see the doctrine that Jesus is the Divine Wisdom underlying the Christology of Hebrews.

* * * * *

Now let us come to consider some of the difficulties in the supposed dependence of Logos on Sophia, and of the Johannine Prologue upon Proverbs.

Up to the present point, the enquiry can be expressed in the simplest terms. The "barbarism" in the opening Greek sentence of the Prologue can almost

---

29. [Heb. 1.2-3. AF]
30. Or perhaps *Reflexion* (ἀπαύγασμα).

5. *The Origin of the Prologue to St John's Gospel*   131

be made intelligible in English, with Westcott's commentary[31] to help us: and when the peculiar language is corrected, the dependence of the Prologue upon the Book of Proverbs can be established by an English-Bible student, without any outside help. The Bible, however, cannot be read satisfactorily apart from the Church History (old Church and new Church) in which it is embedded: and the question at once arises as to whether there is corroborative evidence on the side of the Church History and Literature for the assumed transition from Sophia to Logos: if there is an evolution of the one from the other, why are there no more traces of the change in the Biblical and semi-Biblical literature, and in the writings of the Early Fathers? For it must be admitted that the evidence for Sophia in the New Testament is not overwhelming. So we will address ourselves to this point: we want more evidence that Jesus is the Sophia of God, and more evidence that the eighth chapter of Proverbs has been a factor in the production of a primitive Christology.

The earliest Christian books, of which we recover traces as having been current in the period that elapsed between the death of the Founder of the Faith and the circulation of the canonical Christian Gospels, are mainly two in number; there was a book called the *Sayings* or *Words of Jesus*, of which fragments occasionally come to light in early papyri or in the citations of early Patristic and other writers; and there was over against this another volume or collection, which comprised *Quotations*, or as they were called *Testimonies*, or with a more explicit title, *Testimonies against the Jews*, the object of which collection of passages from the Jewish writings was to prove to the Jews from the Old Testament those Christian claims which constitute the doctrine of the New Testament. There need be no doubt as to the antiquity of this anti-Judaic quotation book, for it has survived in a number of more or less modified forms, and its influence may even be detected in the New Testament itself. Amongst the forms in which it has come down to us, one of the most interesting is the three books of *Testimonia adversus Judaeos* which are bound up with the writings of Cyprian: of these the first two are easily seen to be the adaptation by Cyprian of an earlier text-book, which he modifies from time to time, and to which he adds matter which can often be confidently credited to himself. The original arrangement can clearly be made out: the matter is arranged under headings which are almost always primitive, and the selected proof-texts are those which can be traced in the web of not a few early Patristic works.

Now let us look at the second book of Cyprian's *Testimonia*, which contains the Christology, and see how the matter is arranged for the early Jewish objector or enquirer. The book opens with a capitulation as follows:

---

31. [*Gospel.* AF]

1. *Christum primogenitum esse et ipsum esse sapientiam Dei,* per quem omnia facta sunt.
2. *Quod Sapientia Dei Christus,* et de sacramento concarnationis eius et passionis et calicis et altaris et Apostolorum,[32] qui missi praedicaverunt.
3. Quod Christus idem sit *et sermo Dei.*
4. Quod Christus idem manus et brachium Dei.

And so on.

There is no need to transcribe the rest of the headings under which the citations are grouped. The first two headings appear to stand for a single primitive capitulation, according to which Christ is declared to be the *Wisdom of God*, or, perhaps, the First-born Wisdom of God: and this is followed by a third heading which tells us that the same Christ is the *Logos of God* (*sermo* being the primitive translation of λόγος).

We may say with confidence that the order of appeal made by the early Christian controversialist to the unconverted Jew proceeded from an article which equated Christ with the Wisdom of God, and continued with a proof that the same Christ is the Word of God. The order of the proof is naturally the order of evolution of the Christology. Now let us see how the teaching is presented from the Scriptures of the Old Testament.[33] It opens with Proverbs 8.23-31.

> Dominus condidit me initium viarum suarum ...
> cum laetaretur orbe perfecto.

Then follows a passage from the Wisdom of Jesus the Son of Sirach, which is introduced as being "from the same Solomon in Ecclesiasticus," the writer having confused the Wisdom of Ben Sira with the so-called Wisdom of Solomon: the passage quoted is 24.3-16.19, and runs as follows (it is necessary to quote the passage in full for there are important consequences that will result from it).

> Ego ex ore Altissimi prodivi ante omnem creaturam.
> Ego in caelis feci ut oriretur lumen indeficiens,
> et nebula texi omnem terram.
> Ego in altis habitavi et thronus meus in columna nubis.
> Gyrum caeli circumivi et in profundum abyssi penetravi,
> et in fluctibus maris ambulavi et in omni terra steti
> et in omni populo et in omni gente primatum habui
> et omnia excellentium et humilium corda virtute calcavi.
> Spes omnis in me vitae et virtutis.
> Transite ad me, omnes qui concupiscitis me.

---

32. The genitives are governed by περί in an original Greek, περί μυστηρίου κτέ. [HCC: 1. de calice et altari; et de Apostolis.]
33. [*Test.* 2.1. AF]

The speaker is the Divine Sophia, and the passage in Ben Sira is described as the *Praise of Wisdom* and opens with the statement that "Wisdom will praise herself."

The passage as it stands in the *Testimonies* shows striking variations from the Septuagint and from the Vulgate: for example, the opening words in the Greek LXX are

> ἐγὼ ἀπὸ στόματος Ὑψίστου ἐξῆλθον,[34]

and there is nothing to answer to

> ante omnem creaturam.

The Vulgate, however, says definitely

> primogenita ante omnem creaturam.

The word *primogenita* is necessary to the argument of the *Testimonies*, which tell us that Christ is the First-born and the Wisdom of God. And it is still more evident when we notice the coincidence with the language of the Epistle to the Colossians, that "Christ is the First-born of every creature,"[35] which passage is actually quoted a little lower down by the *Testimony Book*. It is not necessary to assume, nor is it likely, that the first draft of the *Testimony Book* quoted New Testament writings at all. The point is that Colossians is itself, in part, a book of Testimonies, and that St Paul is quoting from Sirach. He has transferred the "First-born of every creature" from Sophia to Christ. We shall see this more clearly presently. Meanwhile observe that the difficulty as to the non-occurrence of the Sophia-doctrine in the New Testament is going to be met. It underlies the Pauline Christology as well as the Johannine, and is necessary to its evolution.

The twenty-fourth chapter of Sirach is now seen to be a typical member of a series of *Praises of Wisdom*: but it is equally clear that it is a pendant to the eighth chapter of Proverbs. There can be no doubt as to the origin of the following sentence, when spoken by Sophia:

> πρὸ τοῦ αἰῶνος ἀπ' ἀρχῆς ἔκτισέν με. Sir. 24.9 (14).[36]

Returning to the *Testimony Book*, we note that the second section of the proof that Christ is the Wisdom of God is taken again from Solomon in Proverbs; it is the opening of the ninth chapter of Proverbs: "Wisdom hath built her

---

34. [Sir. 24.3. AF]
35. [Col. 1.15. AF]
36. [HCC: Cf. Sir. 43[21] [42.21. AF] τὰ μεγαλεῖα τῆς σοφίας αὐτοῦ ἐκόσμησεν καὶ ὡς ἔστιν πρὸ τοῦ αἰῶνος καὶ εἰς τὸν αἰῶνα.]

house,"[37] and is treated as predictive of the Sacraments; but this is a deduction from the equation between Christ and Sophia.

The section which follows is the proof that Christ is the Word of God. The chief point is to notice that it opens with

> Eructavit cor meum verbum bonum (Ps. 45.1);

and its appearance in the *Testimony Book* is a sufficient verification of our previous remark that Jerome was not the first to use the Psalm for Christological ends.

Assuming then that the equation between Christ and Sophia was fundamental in the *Book of Testimonies*, it will be interesting to take a later form of the same collection, that namely which is attributed to Gregory of Nyssa, and which will be found in the *Collectanea* of Zacagni.

Here we shall find many of the Cyprianic *Testimonies*, but the order of the argument is changed. We begin with the Trinity and with the proof-texts from the Old Testament that Christ is the Word of God. At first sight it looks as if Sophia had disappeared: but as we read on, we suddenly stumble on the expression of 1 Corinthians 1.24, that Christ is the Power of God and the Wisdom of God. And then follows abruptly something which appears to have been broken away from another setting:

> (It says) *in the person of Wisdom, that is to say, of the Son*, when He prepared the Heaven I was there by Him, and I was the One in whom He delighted; every day was I joying before His face.[38]

It is the very passage with which Cyprian opens the second book of his *Testimonies* to which we referred above.

It is becoming increasingly clear that the eighth chapter of Proverbs, and those associated chapters of the Apocryphal Wisdom-books, are fundamental for the primitive Christology, as it was presented in the proof-texts against Judaism. The *Book of Testimonies*, then, shows clearly that the doctrine that

> Christ is the Word of God

reposes on an earlier doctrine that

> Christ is the Wisdom of God.

The Prologue to the Fourth Gospel is constructed out of the material furnished by the *Praises of Wisdom*, and the very same material is seen to underlie the great Christological passage in the Epistle to the Colossians. In both of these great passages we have to translate the language back into an earlier and

---

37. [Prov. 9.1. AF]
38. [*Jud.* 1.4. AF]

5. The Origin of the Prologue to St John's Gospel

intermediate form. For instance, it will have struck the reader of the *Praise of Wisdom* in the twenty-fourth chapter of Sirach that the expression

In every people and in every race I had the primacy (*primatum habui*)[39]

is something like the expression in Colossians, "that in all things He might have the pre-eminence";[40] and Cyprian (or one of his forbears) thought so too, for he follows his identification of the First-born Wisdom with "Christ the First-born of every creature" (Col. 1.15), and adds the remark: "Item illic: primogenitus a mortuis ut fieret in omnibus ipse primatum tenens."[41]

In the Greek the identification is not quite so easy: the text of Sirach is often faulty: as commonly edited we have the sentence

ἐν παντὶ λαῷ καὶ ἔθνει ἐκτησάμεν (Sir. 24.6)

which has probably to be corrected to ἡγησάμην; for this there is MS authority, which would answer exactly to *primatum habui*, and we may then discuss whether this is not also a proper equivalent of πρωτεύων in the Epistle to the Colossians.

In any case, we have to go over the Christological passage in Colossians,[42] and underline as probably Sapiential such terms as

εἰκὼν τοῦ Θεοῦ τοῦ ἀοράτου·
πρωτότοκος πάσης κτίσεως·
ἐν αὐτῷ ἐκτίσθη τὰ πάντα·
τὰ πάντα δι' αὐτοῦ ... ἔκτισται·
ὅς ἐστιν ἀρχή·
and ἐν πᾶσιν αὐτὸς πρωτεύων.[43]

II

In the previous section we examined the primitive books of *Testimonies against the Jews*, in order to see whether they showed any traces of an evolution of the Logos-Christology out of a previous Sophia-Christology. The results were significant, and we were able to take the further step of affirming that the great Christological passage in the Epistle to the Colossians was like

39. [Sir. 24.6. AF]
40. [Col. 1.18. AF]
41. [*Test.* 2.1. AF]
42. [HCF: (1) We may compare Moule, *Colossian Studies* p. 80 [Handley C.G. Moule, *Colossians Studies: Lessons in Faith and Holiness from St Paul's Epistles to the Colossians and Philemon* (London: Hodder & Stoughton, 1898). AF] "The Son is revealed to us as Cause, Head and God of the Created Universe" to which the note is added, "To a degree unexampled even in St Paul's Epistles. John I and Heb. are the only adequate parallels."]
43. [Col. 1.15-18 *passim*. AF. HCF: to which we may add τὰ πάντα ἐν αὐτῷ συνέστηκεν [Col. 1.17. AF] for which the parallel is Sir. 43[26] καὶ ἐν λόγῳ αὐτοῦ συνκεῖται πάντα.]

the Prologue to the Fourth Gospel in its ultimate dependence upon the eighth chapter of Proverbs. The next step would seem to be an enquiry as to whether these results are confirmed by Patristic study. Do the early Christian Fathers show, by survival or reminiscence, or in any other way, any traces of (*a*) the equation between Christ and Sophia, or (*b*) any signs that the famous statement that "the Lord created me the beginning of His way, before His works of old,"[44] has been a factor that can be recognised in the development of the doctrine of the Person of Christ. To these points we may now address ourselves. In so doing, we may occasionally be repeating the evidence of the previous section, for the reason that the earliest Patristic literature is coloured by the conventional Testimonies that were employed by Christian propagandists; but this overlapping is inevitable, and we need not discount the evidence of Irenaeus or Justin because it contains elements that run parallel to the *Book of Testimonies*: if they are saying the same things twice over, in any case, they say them from a different point of view, and by the mouth of fresh witnesses. Justin Martyr, for example, uses the method of prophetic Testimony beyond any other Christian writer; but his evidence runs far beyond the small pocket edition of Quotations used by a primitive controversialist. Let us leave the hypothetical *Book of Testimonies*, and if we please, the actual Cyprianic collection, and ask the question whether Justin ever calls Christ Sophia, and whether he argues from the Sapiential books when he develops his Christology.

Here is a striking passage from the *Dialogue with Trypho* (ch. 139), where Justin has been deducing plurality in the Godhead from the book of Genesis ("Behold, the man has become one of us"[45] and similar well-known passages), and where he goes on to quote Proverbs, under the title of Sophia, as though the real Wisdom of Solomon was the Book of Proverbs itself. So he says:

> In Sophia it is said: If I announce to you everyday occurrences I can also recall matters out of eternity. The Lord created me the beginning of His ways ... Before the hills He begat me.[46]

After quoting the famous speech of Sophia from the Book of Sophia, he turns to his listeners and says that the thing which is here said to be begotten is declared by the Word of God to have been begotten before all created things, and every one will admit that there is a numerical distinction between that which begets and that which is begotten.[47] We see that Justin uses the word Logos, not for Christ but for the Scripture; the Heavenly Birth is not the Logos but the Divine Wisdom, which he identifies with Christ. In a previous chapter (ch. 126) he definitely calls Christ the Wisdom of God, after the

---

44. [Prov. 8.22. AF]
45. [Gen. 3.22. AF]
46. [*Dial.* 129.3. AF]
47. [*Dial.* 129.4. AF]

5. The Origin of the Prologue to St John's Gospel

manner of the *Book of Testimonies*, to which he may even be referring, and he says: "Who can this be who is sometimes called the Angel of the Great Counsel, and by Ezekiel is called a man, and by Daniel like a Son of Man, and by Isaiah a child, and Christ and God worshipful by David, and Christ and a Stone by many writers, and *Sophia by Solomon*, etc., etc."[48]

In the sixty-first chapter of the same dialogue, Justin goes over the same ground, and introduces the matter as follows:

> I am now going to give you, my friends, another Testimony from the Scriptures that God before all His other creatures begat as the Beginning a certain spiritual Power, which is also called Glory by the Holy Spirit, and sometimes Son, *and sometimes Sophia*, and sometimes Angel, and sometimes God, and *sometimes Lord and Word*, and sometimes calls Himself Commander-in-Chief, etc.[49]

He then continues that "The Word of Wisdom will attest what I say, being itself God begotten from the Father of the Universe, and being *Word and Wisdom* and the Glory of its Sire, as Solomon affirms": after which we are again treated to Proverbs 8.21-36.[50] It is clear that this speech of Sophia in the eighth of Proverbs occupied a large space in the accumulated material for Justin's Christology.

Now let us turn to the writings of Theophilus of Antioch whose three books addressed to Autolycus are dated in A.D. 168. We shall find in Theophilus the two streams of Christology flowing into one another, and we can actually see the absorption of the doctrine that

> Christ is the Wisdom of God,

by the doctrine that

> Christ is the Logos of God.

For awhile they flow side by side, but it needs no commentator to point out which of the two is to absorb the other. For instance, when Theophilus talks of the Creation of the world, he tells us:

> Ps. 33.6: God by His Word and His Wisdom made all things: for by His Word were the Heavens established; and all their host by His Spirit. Very excellent is His Wisdom.

> Prov. 3.19: By Wisdom God founded the earth, and He prepared the Heavens by understanding. Theoph. *ad Autol.* i. 7.[51]

---

48. [*Dial.* 126.1. AF]
49. [*Dial.* 61.1. AF]
50. [*Dial.* 61.3-5. AF]
51. [*Autol.* 1.7.3. AF]

He returns to the theme at a later point where his language will require careful consideration.

> Ps. 45.1: God having within Himself His own inherent Word, begat Him with His own Wisdom, having emitted Him before the Universe.[52]

This passage is, for our purpose, important, (1) for the co-existence of the Word of God and the Wisdom of God,[53] (2) because the word *emitted* (ἐξερευξάμενος) is due to the finding of the "good word" in Ps. 45 (My heart is emitting a good word): this identification of the Logos with the language of the Psalm we have shown to be very early, and to have been current in the primitive *Book of Testimonies*. Theophilus goes on: "This Word He had as His assistant in the things that were made by Him, and it was through Him that He made all things. This "Word" is called beginning (ἀρχή) because He is ruler (ἄρχει) and lord of all things that have been created by Him. It was He, who, being the Spirit of God, and the Beginning and the Wisdom and Power of the Most High, descended on the prophets and through them discoursed of the Creation of the World and all other matters. Not that the prophets were themselves at the Creation of the World; but what was present was the Wisdom of God that was in it (the World?) and the Holy Word of His that was always with Him."[54]

Here we see that the reference to the Logos as Beginning (ἀρχή) leads at once to the introduction of the Sophia who is the Archē of the O.T. The writer says as much: the Logos is Archē and Wisdom. When he states the co-existence of the Word and the Wisdom in Creation, he uses of the Logos the expression "always present with Him" (ἀεὶ συμπαρὼν αὐτῷ)[55] which we recognise at once as borrowed from the description of Wisdom in the eighth chapter of Proverbs. And lest we should miss the reference, and the consequent equivalence of Word and Wisdom, Theophilus explains:

> This is why He speaks as follows through Solomon: When He prepared the heavens I was by Him (συμπαρήμην αὐτῷ), etc. Theoph. *ad Autol.* ii. 10.[56]

The Logos-doctrine of Theophilus, then, although earlier than himself (as is clear not only from his well-known references to the opening verses of John,

---

52. [*Autol.* 2.10.2. AF]
53. Athanasius frequently restates this equation, which is a commonplace with him: e.g. ἐν ταύτῃ γὰρ καὶ τὰ πάντα γέγονεν, ὡς ψάλλει Δαβίδ, Πάντα ἐν Σοφίᾳ ἐποίησας. καὶ Σολομῶν φησιν Ὁ Θεὸς τῇ Σοφίᾳ ἐθεμελίωσε τὴν γῆν, ἡτοίμασε δὲ οὐρανοὺς ἐν φρονήσει. Αὐτὴ δὲ ἡ Σοφία ἐστιν ὁ Λόγος, καὶ δι' αὐτοῦ, ὡς Ἰωάννης φησίν, Ἐγένετο τὰ πάντα κτέ. *Orat.* I. *contra Arianos* 19 [*C. Ar.* 1.19.8-9. AF].
Note the connection with the Prologue.
54. [*Autol.* 2.10.4-6. AF]
55. [*Autol.* 2.10.6. AF]
56. [*Autol.* 2.10.6. AF]

5. The Origin of the Prologue to St John's Gospel

but also from the use of Ps. 45), is based upon a still earlier Wisdom-doctrine, which it is gradually displacing.[57]

Sophia does not, however, wholly disappear; Theophilus goes on to talk of the creation of Light and the Luminaries, and explains that "the three days which elapsed before the creation of the Luminaries, are a type of the Trinity, i.e. of God, and *His Word and His Wisdom.*"[58] This is the first mention of the Trinity in theological literature, in express terms (τριάς), and Theophilus arrives at it by a bifurcation of the original Wisdom into Word and Wisdom, the τριάς being thus an evolution of a previous δυάς: if we prefer to put it so, we may say that Theophilus identified the Wisdom-Christ, now detached from the Logos-Christ, with the Holy Spirit. It will be seen from the foregoing that theologians will have to make a new study of the doctrine of Christ the Wisdom of God, and that incidentally, the often quoted passages in Theophilus will obtain a fresh illumination. For it is no casual remark that Theophilus has dropped; it expresses his fundamental position: he returns to it later, when he has to explain the plurality of the language in Genesis ("Let us make man");

> To no one else did He say, Let us make man, but to *His own Logos and His own Sophia* (2.18);[59]

and again, when he has to explain how God could appear in a garden and converse with man, he says:

> It was *His Word*, by whom He made all things, *which was His Power and His Wisdom* that assumed the Person of the Father and Lord of the Universe, and so came into the garden, etc. (2.22).[60]

The foregoing passages will suffice to show the direction in which Christian thought was moving and what it was moving into.

Next let us turn to Irenaeus. We shall find that the matter is now complicated by the Gnostic theories about the aeon Sophia, who has gone astray, and is not the Redeemer, but the lost one to be redeemed.

In the following passage, Irenaeus undertakes to prove the Eternal Sonship by a quotation; he says, "We have abundantly shown that the Logos, that is, the Son, was always with the Father, and He says through Solomon, that Sophia also, who is the Spirit, was with Him before any created thing. For

---

57. [HCF: **We get the same connection of ideas, and the same displacement of Sophia by Logos in Marcellus of Ancyra: ἐπεὶ οὖν ἀδύνατον ἦν χωρὶς λόγου καὶ τῆς προσούσης τῷ λόγῳ σοφίας ἐννοῆσαι περὶ τῆς τοῦ οὐρανοῦ κατασκευῆς τὸν Θεόν, εἰκότως ἔφη· ἡνίκα ἡτοίμαζε τὸν οὐρανὸν συμπαρήμην αὐτῷ Euseb. *c. Marcell.* i. p. 40 [*Marc.* 2.2.32. AF]. Cf. also p. 41 αὐτὸς ὁ Λόγος ὁ συμπαρών τε καὶ συμπλάττων, πρὸς ὃν ὁ Πατὴρ "ποιήσωμεν ἄνθρωπον" ἔφη "κατ' εἰκόνα ἡμετέραν καὶ ὁμοίωσιν" [*Marc.* 2.2.37. AF].]
58. [*Autol.* 2.15.4. AF]
59. [*Autol.* 2.18.2. AF]
60. [*Autol.* 2.22.2. AF]

'the Lord by Wisdom established the Earth, by understanding He created the Heaven. By His knowledge the depths were broken up, and the clouds drop down dew' (Prov. 3.19-20). And again, 'the Lord created me the beginning of His way,'" and so on, Proverbs 8.22-25. Here we see Irenaeus (lib. iv. ch. 34, § 2, p. 253 Massuet)[61] using the very same passage from the speech of Wisdom concerning herself, and applying it to the Holy Spirit. It is clear that the Sophia-doctrine is one of the oldest pieces of Christology that we can detect, and that it precedes and underlies the doctrine of the Christ and the doctrine of the Holy Spirit.

When Irenaeus has finished his quotation from Proverbs, he continues:

> So there is one God, who *by His Word and His Wisdom* has made all things;[62]

in which we again see the collocation of Sophia and Logos, and infer the replacement of one of them by the other, in accordance with our hypothesis.

Nor should it escape our notice, in view of what we detected in the Cyprianic *Testimonies* of the transfer of the Pre-eminence of Sophia to the Pre-eminence of Christ, that the very same thing is said by Irenaeus which was disclosed by Cyprian. In the chapter which precedes the one from which we were just quoting, we find the following sequence:

> Omnia Verbo fecit et Sapientia adornavit, accipiens omnium potestatem, quando Verbum caro factum est, ut quemadmodum in caelis principatum habuit Verbum Dei, sic et in terra haberet principatum ... principatum autem habeat eorum quae sunt sub terra, ipse primogenitus mortuorum factus.[63]

Here again we see that the passage in Colossians (1.18) depends upon the twenty-fourth chapter of Sirach, which is used in the *Testimonies* to prove that Christ is the Wisdom of God.[64] The groundwork of Irenaeus' argument is that "Wisdom has made the world and holds the primacy in it"; but this he expands by coupling Logos with Sophia in the opening sentence, and by substituting Logos for Sophia in the language borrowed from Sirach. The evolution of the Christology can be made out with sufficient clearness. The Logos is first substituted for Sophia, and then in the Wisdom passages the Word and the Wisdom appear together.

III

The same enquiry can be made in other writers of the same period, Tertullian, for example. In writing against Praxeas, whose Sabellianism was to be

---

61. [*Haer.* 4.20.3. Massuet, *Sancti Irenaei.* AF]
62. [*Haer.* 4.20.4. AF]
63. [*Haer.* 4.20.2. AF]
64. [*Test.* 2.1. AF]

confuted, it became necessary for Tertullian to re-state the doctrine of the Trinity in such a way as to preclude the "Crucifixion of the Father."

He tells us to listen to Sophia as a second created person. Then follows the famous passage in Proverbs, "The Lord created me the Beginning,"[65] and he explains that Sophia is a constituent of Logos. He then points out it is the Son in His own person who *under the name of Sophia* confesses the Father. For though in the passage quoted it might seem as if Sophia were herself created by the Lord for His works and His ways, *yet we must remember that elsewhere it is said that all things were made by the Logos, and nothing made without Him.* Tertullian accordingly replaces Sophia by Logos in the passage from the eighth of Proverbs, and this proves that the Logos is not the Father.[66] It is easy to infer that the displacing Logos is itself a derivative from that which it displaces. At all events, Tertullian saw clearly the interdependence of the Wisdom passage and the Prologue. They cannot be kept apart.

Much more is said by Tertullian on the relation of the Divine Wisdom to the Divine Word in his tract against Hermogenes, who would have the universe created out of previously existing matter. Tertullian denies the existence of this uncreated matter: "the apostles and prophets did not thus explain the creation of the world by the mere appearance of God and His approach to existing matter; they never mention matter at all, but *first of all they say that Sophia was created the Beginning of His ways for His works*, as in the eighth chapter of Proverbs; and *after that came the emitted Word* by whom all things were made and nothing made without Him."[67]

Here we see the same collocation of the Sophia story and the Logos Prologue, and that Sophia has a certain priority to the Logos.

It is not necessary to deal with the matter at greater length in this connection. All students of Theology and of Church History know that the Wisdom passages in Proverbs became the standard proof-texts for the doctrine of the Eternal Sonship, and that around the words "The Lord created me, etc.,"[68] raged the battle with the Arians, who, like their antagonists, regarded the Greek text with its ἔκτισεν for ἐκτήσατο as sacrosanct. All that we have to do is to note the theological interdependence of the eighth of Proverbs and the Johannine Prologue, and to emphasise that one of them is, by admitted consanguinity, derived from the other.

It may be interesting to find out whether Origen has anything to say on the collocations which we have made and the inferences which we have drawn. We shall find that, like the earlier Fathers and the authors of the Testimony

---

65. [Prov. 8.22. AF]
66. [*Prax.* 6-7.4. AF]
67. [*Herm.* 45.1. AF]
68. [Prov. 8.22. AF]

books, he identifies the Logos with the *Eructatio* of the forty-fourth Psalm,[69] and then finds himself in the difficulty that the Psalm continues with *Audi filia*.[70] How could the Logos be addressed in the feminine? His explanation is that such changes of persons are common; we have to remember that the Logos was in the Beginning, but it is conceded from the Testimonies in the Proverbs that Sophia is the Beginning, for "the Lord created me the Beginning, etc."; and this makes Sophia a prior concept to Logos which expresses it. Hence the evangelist does not merely say that the Logos was with God, but that the Logos was in the Beginning (sc. in Sophia) with God.[71]

There is much more of the same in the Commentary of Origen upon John, but this will suffice to show that Origen also has clearly before him the connection between the Prologue and Proverbs, and that he holds, in a certain sense, the subordination of Logos to Sophia. (See Origen *in Joann.* lib. I. chs. 34, 39, etc.)[72]

The chain of Patristic interpretation which deduces Logos from Sophia is practically unbroken: the finding of the investigation may be summed up in the *Prophetic Eclogues* of Eusebius (pp. 98 sqq.),[73] who tells that the whole of the Book of Proverbs appears to be written in the person of Wisdom, who sometimes lays down ethical principles, and sometimes takes to herself the words of others: at one time offering us riddles, and at another teaching us concerning herself and instructing us as to her own Divine dignity. From these we may select whereby to learn that Wisdom is indeed a Divine creature and altogether to be praised in her nature, being the same as the second cause of the Universe after the prime Deity, and as the Word-God who was in the beginning with God, and as the Providence of God which regulates and orders all things, and penetrates to matters terrestrial, which Wisdom was created before every other Being and Substance, being the Beginning of the Ways of the whole creation. And what she, Sophia, says herself is on this wise: Then follows Proverbs 8.12: This, then, is the teaching of Wisdom concerning herself; and who she is the holy Apostle teaches us, saying:

Christ the power of God and the Wisdom of God (1 Cor. 1.24).

---

69. [Ps. 45.1. AF]
70. [Ps. 45.10. AF]
71. [*Comm. Jo.* 1.39.287-290. AF].
72. Πάλιν δὲ ἀρχὴ καὶ τέλος ὁ αὐτός· ἀλλ' οὐ κατὰ τὰς ἐπινοίας ὁ αὐτός. ἀρχὴ γάρ, ὡς ἐν ταῖς παροιμίαις μεμαθήκαμεν, καθὸ σοφία τυγχάνει, ἐστί· γέγραπται γοῦν Ὁ Θεὸς ἔκτισέ με ἀρχὴν ὁδῶν αὐτοῦ εἰς τὰ ἔργα αὐτοῦ· καθὸ δὲ λόγος ἐστὶν, οὐκ ἔστιν ἀρχή. ἐν ἀρχῇ γὰρ ἦν ὁ λόγος [*Comm. Jo.* 1.31.222. AF].
73. [Thomas Gaisford (ed.), *Eusebii Pamphili episcopi Caesariensis eclogae propheticae* (Oxford: e Typographeo Academico, 1842), 98-100. AF]

And again

> Who of God is made unto us Wisdom (1 Cor. 1.30).

It is Christ, then, who is the speaker in the passage from Proverbs. Wisdom is also the Word of God, by whom all things are made. For "In the beginning was the Word and the Word was with God, and the Word was God. All things were made by Him," and

> By Him were all things created, whether in Heaven or on Earth, whether visible or invisible, as the Apostle says (Col. 1.16).

And just as in one aspect He is called the Word of God, and in another Life and Truth and True Light, and whatever other names the Scriptures give Him, *so also He is entitled Sophia*, the Handmaid of the Father for the Providence and Regulation of the Universe.

In these words Eusebius hands on the ecclesiastical traditions which we have been considering, identifying Sophia and Logos, and explaining the Prologue in John and the Christological passage in Colossians by the help of the eighth chapter of Proverbs, from which they are thus admitted to have been derived.

It is not for the sake of multiplying references that we cite one Father after another, but with the object of showing the continuity and consistency of the Patristic tradition, which appears to have been inadequately treated by leading commentators of our day, who did not see the meaning of the constant reference to Christ as the Wisdom of God, nor recognise the close connection between these early Patristic commentaries and the primitive collections of Testimonies. To illustrate the matter once more from a fresh point of view, suppose we go back to the opening capitulations of the second book of Cyprian's *Testimonies*, the book that contains the prophecies concerning Jesus Christ. We pointed out that these opening summaries of the sections that are to follow bore evidence of having been somewhat modified; for example, that the theme of the first chapter was originally the identification of Christ with the Wisdom of God, and that this Wisdom was the First-born (primogenita), the adjective being applied to Sophia in the first instance. Now if we were to turn to Eusebius, *Evangelical Demonstration*, we should find the very same theme before us, the collection of prophetic arguments for Christological purposes; and it would be quite easy to show that Eusebius, while working with great freedom, is not independent of the approved Testimonies which have come down from the early days of the Church.

The first chapter of the fifth book of the *Demonstratio Evangelica* has for its heading the statement that "among the Hebrews the most wise Solomon was aware of a certain *first-born* (πρωτότοκος) Power of God, which he also entitles His Wisdom and His Offspring, with the same honour that we ourselves also bestow." Compare that with the First-born Wisdom of the

Testimonies, and then note how the writer plunges at once into Proverbs 8, and after enumerating the praises of Wisdom, remarks that Wisdom is the Divine and all-virtuous Substance that precedes all created things, the intellectual (νοερός) and first-born (πρωτότοκος) Image (εἰκών) of the Unbegotten Nature, the true-born and only-born (μονογενής) Son of the God of all.

Here Christ is declared to be the Wisdom of God, in *the terms in which Wisdom is described in Proverbs and the other Sapiential books* (see especially Wis. 7.22 sqq.). And, just as in the early Testimonies, Eusebius goes on to quote Colossians (1.15, 17) and complete the proof that Christ is the First-born of every Creature; for Christ, he says, was speaking in His own person when Wisdom (apparently) spoke in hers.[74] The equation between Christ and the Wisdom of God covers the whole of the argument. Reviewing the course of the enquiry, we see that the commentators upon the great Christological passages in the New Testament, the Prologue to St John, and the parallel passage in Colossians, have failed to set these passages in the true line of their historical evolution. We have tried to restate the texts upon which the accepted Christology is based, first by correcting a grammatical error in the first verse of St John's Gospel, which ought to have been obvious to an unsophisticated reader; second, by showing that the theology of the Church is best seen in the first days of its making by a careful consideration of the primitive books of Testimonies; it follows from these corrections and identifications that the key to the language of the Johannine Prologue and to St Paul's language in the Epistle to the Colossians lies in the Sapiential tradition, and not in the reaction from Plato or Philo or Heraclitus.

It is not pretended that this point of view is altogether new. Many critics and interpreters have occasionally come near to it; few have altogether ignored it; but it is not sufficient to put a stray marginal reference to Proverbs or Sirach in the New Testament; we must examine those occasional references and disclose the system to which they belong. It will perhaps surprise some students to know that it was Alford[75] who came nearest to what we believe to be the right solution: at least, the following sentences from his commentary are significant for the identification of the Word of God and the Wisdom of God:

> We are now to enquire how it came that St John found this *word λόγος so ready made to his hands, as to require no explanation.* The answer to this will be found by tracing the *gradual personification* of the *Word* or *Wisdom of God*, in the Old Testament ... As the *Word* of God was the constant idea for his revelations *relatively to man*, so was the *Wisdom* of God for those which related to *His own essence* and attributes. That this was a later form of expression than the simple recognition of the Divine Word in the Mosaic and early

---

74. [*Dem. ev.* 5.1.1-4 and 5.1.7. AF]
75. [Alford, *Greek Testament*. AF]

5. The Origin of the Prologue to St John's Gospel

historical books, would naturally be the case ... In Sap. Sir. i. 1 Wisdom is said to be

παρὰ Κυρίου καὶ μετ' αὐτοῦ εἰς τὸν αἰῶνα.

Then in c. xxiv. 9, 21, the same strain is continued,

πρὸ τοῦ αἰῶνος ἀπ' ἀρχῆς ἔκτισέν με.

... In the Book of the Wisdom of Solomon ... we find a similar personification and eulogy of Wisdom. In this remarkable passage we have Wisdom called

πάρεδρος τῶν σῶν θρόνων (c. ix. 4),

and said to have been

παροῦσα ὅτε ἐποίεις τὸν κόσμον,[76]

and parallelised with

ὁ λόγος σου (c. ix. 12,[77] c. xvi. 12).

The foregoing passages indicate the right way to approach the subject, and are only in error in the assumption that the Sophia of the Old Testament is a later development of the Logos.

If we are substantially right in the foregoing investigation, the next step will be to see how much further elucidation of St John's Prologue will result from the restoration of Sophia to its right place in the theme. This further enquiry will involve important considerations.

Before, however, we turn to this part of the enquiry it will be interesting to show that the suggestion of hymns in honour of Sophia, produced in the time that is adjacent to that in which the Fourth Gospel was written, is not a hypothesis destitute of illustration outside of the Scriptures. We actually have a Sophia-hymn of the kind that we have described in the *Odes of Solomon*.

The twenty-third Ode of this collection, after a somewhat obscure opening, in which Divine Grace appears to be speaking in the Person of Christ, goes on to tell of a Perfect Virgin, who stands and cries to men:

> There stood a perfect Virgin, who was proclaiming and calling and saying, O ye sons of men, return ye; O ye daughters, come ye: and forsake the ways of that corruption and draw near unto me, and I will enter into you and will bring you forth from perdition, and make you wise in the ways of truth: that you be not destroyed nor perish: hear ye me, and be redeemed. For the Grace of God I am telling among you, and by my means you shall be redeemed and become blessed. I am your judge; and they who have put me on shall not be injured; but they shall possess immortality in the new world: my chosen ones, walk ye

---

76. [Wis. 9.9. AF]
77. [Wis. 9.1? AF]

in me, and my ways will I make known to them that seek me, and I will make them trust in my name.[78]

One has only to recall the language of the Book of Proverbs in the beginning of the eighth chapter,

> Doth not Wisdom cry?
> And Understanding put forth her voice?
> ****
> Unto you, O men, I call;
> And my voice is to the sons of men.[79]

It is clear that the Virgin speaker is *Sophia* and we are to illustrate the Ode in question by Proverbs 8, upon which it is based. It will be easy to adduce fresh parallels to the language, but what is really important for us to note is that the Sophia who speaks exchanged personality with the Christ. "I will make them trust in my name";[80] and the "Grace who stands on a lofty summit"[81] (at the beginning of the Ode) and cries from one end of the earth to the other, is, perhaps, only a modification of the figure of Wisdom in Proverbs 8.2, who "standeth on the top of high places."

Thus we have actually found a Sophia-Christ-Ode in the early Christian Church, quite unconnected with the Sophia that we discovered in the *Testimony Book*. Note in passing that she describes herself as a Preacher of Divine Grace.

In the preceding series of arguments we have attempted to show that St John in his Prologue was working from existing materials, which comprise the *Praises of Sophia* in the Sapiential books, and perhaps from some Sophia-songs that are no longer extant. There are foundations apparent underneath his edifice; and it is only reasonable to ask whether we can go further in the detection of the sources, and whether we can thereby throw any further light upon the language of the Prologue.

For example, we have in the seventh chapter of the book of Wisdom, a description of Wisdom as the Radiance of the Eternal Light,[82] and it is natural to compare this with the Johannine doctrine that Christ is the Light,[83] and the doctrine of the Epistle to the Hebrews that Christ is the Radiance of the Father's Glory.[84] When we read a little further we find (Wis. 7.29) that Sophia is "more illustrious than the Sun and brighter than the positions of all stars,"

78. [*Odes* 33.5-11. AF]
79. [Prov. 8.1 and 8.4. AF]
80. [*Odes* 33.11. AF]
81. [*Odes* 33.3. AF]
82. [Wis. 7.26. AF]
83. [John 1.4-5, 7-9. AF]
84. [Heb. 1.3. AF]

5. *The Origin of the Prologue to St John's Gospel*   147

and that compared with all "created" Light (*or* with "day"-light) she is found to be anterior;

φωτὶ συγκρινομένη εὑρίσκεται προτέρα:

this answers very well to the statement in the Fourth Gospel that "in Him was Life and the Life was the Light of men";[85] we may imagine, if we please, an earlier form that

> In her was *Life*, and the *Life* was the *Light* of men:

or

> In her was *Light* and the *Light* was the *Life* of men;

but now see what follows: the writer goes on to argue for the priority and the permanence of the Light in these words:

> Night, indeed, follows on created Light.
> *But no evil overpowers Wisdom.*[86]

Here we evidently have the origin of the phrase in the Johannine Prologue, which is commonly rendered,

> and the darkness comprehended it not:

but which is better expressed in Moffatt's translation,[87]

> Amid the darkness the Light shone,
> *But the darkness did not master it.*

There can hardly be a reasonable doubt that the explanation of the phrase in John is to be found in the passage of the Wisdom of Solomon. It does not require any philosophical reference to dualistic conflicts between Good and Evil, and Light and Darkness, *except as such conflicts are assumed in the language of the Wisdom of Solomon*. The darkness which masters the light is the darkness which comes on at the end of the day, existing potentially throughout the day but operating triumphantly when the end of the day comes. We are to take κατέλαβεν in John 1.5 as the equivalent of ἀντισχύει in Wis. 7.30, and to say that Wisdom, being the Radiance of the Everlasting Light, has no ending to the day which it produces. Thus the chapter which furnished us with the explanation of the Johannine *Only-Begotten*, the *Radiance* of Hebrews, and the *Image* in Colossians,[88] furnishes us also with the clue to the argument in John 1.5, and with the right way to translate the words.

---

85. [John 1.4. AF]
86. The corresponding sentence in Proverbs appears to be 3.15, οὐκ ἀντιτάξεται αὐτῇ (sc. σοφία) οὐδὲν πονηρόν [the passage is from Wis. 7.30. AF].
87. [Moffatt, *New Testament*. AF]
88. [John 1.18; Heb. 1.3; Col. 1.15. AF]

Our next instance shall be the great Incarnation verse (John 1.14), which tells us that

> The Word became flesh and dwelt among us:

where there is much discussion as to the meaning of the word ἐσκήνωσεν, which is connected by etymology with the word σκηνή (a tabernacle or tent) and so with the Hebrew word *Shekinah*. Moffatt, indeed, discards this explanation, perhaps as being too subtle and mystical, and tells us to translate,

> So the Logos became flesh and tarried among us:

and the first impulse of an educated theologian would be to annotate the rendering as inadequate. Yet Alford says "*sojourned* or *tabernacled* ... the word is one technically used in Scripture to import the *dwelling of God among men*": and there is not much difference between "sojourned" of Alford and "tarried" of Moffatt. Since, however, we are arguing from the hypothesis that the Logos has been evolved from Sophia, the first thing to be done is to ask whether σκηνόω or its equivalent κατασκενόω is one of the Sapiential words, and in what sense it is used in the *Praises of Wisdom*. The answer is that it occurs over and over again in the Αἴνεσις Σοφίας in the twenty-fourth chapter of Sirach: for example:

Sir. 24.4:	I dwelt (κατεσκήνωσα) on high
****	
Sir. 24.8:[89]	He that created me pitched *my tent* (σκηνήν),
	And said, *Dwell thou* in Jacob (κατασκήνωσον).
	Let thy inheritance be in Israel:
(= Prov. 8.22):	Before the world from the Beginning He created me,
	(And said) unto the end of the world I will not forsake thee.
	In the Holy Tabernacle (σκηνῇ) before Him I ministered,
	And thus was I established in Zion:
	In the beloved City likewise He made me to rest,
	And in Jerusalem was my authority:
	I took root among the honoured people;
	In the Lord's portion of His inheritance.

Reading these rhythms carefully we see they are founded on the eighth chapter of Proverbs, and that they essay to prove that Wisdom has made her dwelling among the Jews, and especially in Jerusalem. He says this over and over in eight different ways[90] and he uses the etymology of σκηνόω from

---

89. [Sir. 24.8-12. AF]
90. [HCC p. 32, "Hebrews, and the ...": [1] p. 32 "The voice of Christ, like the voice which Moses heard, may be called the voice of God, and it may be said that the wisdom of God (i.e. wisdom more than human) took upon itself in Christ human nature, and that Christ was the way of salvation.

5. The Origin of the Prologue to St John's Gospel   149

σκηνή and suggests that we may have to employ the awkward word *Tabernacle* instead of *dwelling* or *tarriance* if we are to bring out the force of his words. It results, moreover, from these Sapiential passages, which lead up to the *Dwelling* or *Tabernacling* of the Logos, that we ought to understand in John 1.14 that the Logos made His dwelling among the Jews, and in this case we must look back a sentence or two, and understand the words: "He came to His own, and His own received Him not," in the sense that "He came to the Jews," and here we shall be again surprised to find Alford saying: "τὰ ἴδια cannot well mean *the world*, or οἱ ἴδιοι *mankind in general*: it would be difficult to point out any Scripture usage to justify such a meaning. But abundance of passages bear out the meaning which makes τὰ ἴδια his own inheritance or possession, i.e. Judaea; and οἱ ἴδιοι the Jews: compare especially the parable Matthew xxi. 33 ff. and Sirach xxiv. 7 ff."[91] Here Alford actually quotes from the *Praises of Wisdom*, only beginning at an earlier point with the words,

> With all this I sought for rest,
> And in whose inheritance *shall I make my dwelling?*[92]

Nor is it less interesting that Westcott makes the very same explanation and quotes the very same passage: what they both appear to miss is that the references (which are more to the point than they imagined) carry with them the sense of ἐσκήνωσεν in John 1.14, and that, therefore, if, as Westcott supposes, ἐσκήνωσεν ἐν ἡμῖν refers to the indwelling of Christ in believers, and not to anything of a racial character, it can only carry this meaning as an antithesis to the known dwelling of Sophia amongst the Jews in Jerusalem. It is, however, doubtful if we ought to resort to antithesis. The first draft of the argument appears to have been of the type that

> In Jewry God is known;

and the first persons who received the Messiah are of the group described as οἱ ἴδιοι, i.e. of the Jews. Naturally we go on to refer to such believing Jews the words,

> The Sophia-Logos dwelt among us.

It will now be clear that this investigation divides itself into two parts, (1) the discovery of those Johannine and Colossian terms which belong to the Sapiential tradition; (2) the enquiry whether in either John or Colossians an

---

I must at this juncture declare that those doctrines which certain churches put forward concerning Christ I neither affirm nor deny, for I freely confess that I do not understand them." Spinoza. *Tract. Theol. Pol.* t. 1. p. 19 (ed. Bolen [the word is unclear. AF]).]
  91. [*Greek Testament*. AF]
  92. [Sir. 24.7. AF]

additional Sapiential document should be assumed to underlie the Christian teaching. A good deal has been done in the way of defining which terms are really Sapiential: we can underline ἀρχή and ἀπαύγασμα and εἰκών and ἐσκήνωσεν and πρωτότοκος and μονογενής, as well as certain sentences in which the action of the Divine Wisdom is intimated. Some of these sentences do not require a special bridge to be built for them from the Sapiential books to the New Testament: the statements

πάντα δι' αὐτοῦ ἐγένετο (John 1.3),

and

ἐν αὐτῷ ἐκτίσθη τὰ πάντα (Col. 1.16),

are equivalents to the language of Proverbs, which are capable of immediate deduction, so soon as we have agreed that Jesus is the Wisdom of God. So also the doctrine that

αὐτός ἐστιν πρὸ πάντων (Col. 1.17)

is an immediate consequence of the existence of Sophia πρὸ τοῦ αἰῶνος,[93] and similarly for other obvious deductions. It is not so easy, however, to infer the immediate derivation of such terms as Μονογενής or Πρωτότοκος. No doubt Monogenēs is a Sapiential term, but it is as unique in use as it is in meaning. When we come to the Gospel we find that it is one of the current words of the New Testament religion, and it is difficult to believe that it acquired currency so immediately, as to become, by one stroke, from an obscure adjective, one of the leading terms of theology. We seem to need an intermediate document, but do not quite see how to prove that it is absolutely required. To suspect is not enough.

Meanwhile, it is interesting to observe that Colossians does not exactly agree with St John in its treatment of the Logos-theme. In Colossians 1.18 Jesus is the ἀρχή in agreement with Proverbs,[94]

ἀρχὴν ἔκτισέν με.

But in John this is somewhat obscured, and the language of Proverbs is interpreted to mean ἐν ἀρχῇ; the source is the same, the treatment is different. In Colossians, Jesus is the First-born who has the First Rank, even among the dead. We have shown reason to suspect that this is an interpretation of a primitive ἡγήσατο, used of the First-born taking the lead; but in the Gospel we have what looks like a variant of the same theme, viz., "Μονογενής ... ἐκεῖνος ἐξηγήσατο,"[95] where the difficulty of interpreting ἡγήσατο has been partly got

93. [Prov. 8.23. AF]
94. [Prov. 8.22. AF]
95. [John 1.18. AF]

5. The Origin of the Prologue to St John's Gospel

over by the substitution of a compound verb for the simple form. Yet it is not really got rid of, for ἐξηγέομαι can also mean "to take the lead," "to have the front place," and does not necessarily mean anything different from the πρωτεύειν of Paul.[96]

Both writers, then, are working on the same theme, and working independently, but John is working more freely than Paul. The passage in Colossians resembles a list of the titles and offices of Christ; the Prologue in John is more like a poem, and in so far as it is poetic, is nearer to the Sapiential origins, even though in detail it may be more remote from them.

Consequently, if there is a Sophia-document missing, it underlies John rather than Paul; or if it underlies both of them, John is nearer to the form of the document.

As we have learnt a good deal by comparing the Colossian doctrine of the Logos with the Johannine, we make a further observation, and we notice that both writers have the doctrine of the Pleroma, which in later days, i.e. in Gnostic circles, acquired such prominence.

The Gospel has it in the form that "we have all received of the Pleroma of Jesus and grace for grace."[97] The Epistle tells us that "according to the good pleasure of the Father all the Pleroma dwelt in the Son."[98] After what we have already seen of the relation of the Gospel and Epistle *inter se*, it is not too much to say that they are working here from a common vocabulary. On the other hand, there does not seem to be any trace of the use of this word in the Sapiential books upon which we have been working; and the word itself is so striking when used as expressing a communication of Divine Attributes, that we have a right to say that it has been found in some document intermediate between the Sapiential books and the New Testament. It may have been a hymn in praise of Sophia.

That it is Sophia who possesses the Pleroma may be seen in another way. The language of the Gospel is:

> and we have all received of His Pleroma, grace piled on grace; for the law was given by Moses, Grace and Truth came by Jesus Christ.[99]

The antithesis is recognised as being one between Law and Grace, the latter of which displaces the former. If, then, the writer is modifying a previous document and replacing Sophia by Jesus, we ought to have a sentence connecting Law and Truth with Sophia. The missing sentence is found in Proverbs 3.16:

---

96. [Col. 1.18. AF]
97. [John 1.16. AF]
98. [Col. 1.19. AF]
99. [John 1.16-17. AF]

Out of her mouth goeth forth Righteousness,
Law and Mercy she bears on her tongue.
ἐκ τοῦ στόματος αὐτῆς ἐκπορεύεται δικαιοσύνη,
νόμον δὲ καὶ ἔλεον ἐπὶ γλώσσης φορεῖ.

The bridge between Proverbs (Law and Mercy) and the Gospel (Grace and Truth) will be found in Wis. 3.9 (and 4.15), *Grace and Mercy* to His elect.

οἱ πεποιθότες ἐπ' αὐτῷ συνήσουσιν ἀλήθειαν·

****

ὅτι χάρις καὶ ἔλεος τοῖς ἐκλεκτοῖς αὐτοῦ (Wis. 3.9).

The suggestion to replace Law by Grace, so natural to the primitive Christian, had already been made in part by the Wisdom of Solomon. We can see the passages growing from one form to another before our eyes. But this will require that the Pleroma also should be a transfer from Sophia to Jesus. And I think that we may find the origin of the Pleroma: it was a Pleroma of Law. That was the way in which Wisdom was to find expression. In order to see this, we may take two related passages of Sirach, as follows:

> They that fear the Lord will seek out His good pleasure (εὐδοκίαν)
> And they that love Him will be filled with the Law (ἐμπλησθήσονται τοῦ νόμου). Sir. 2.16.

> He that fears the Lord will accept chastening,
> And they that rise early will find His good pleasure (εὐδοκίαν);
> He that seeks Law will be filled with it (ἐμπλησθήσεται). Sir. 35.14-15.[100]

The two passages are, as we have said, cognate: they imply a Pleroma of Law, and this is what pleases God; the Law is the Good Pleasure.

Now let us turn to Colossians and see how the Pleroma is introduced: we are told that "it was the Father's good pleasure that all the Pleroma should make its residence in the Son,"

ἐν αὐτῷ εὐδόκησεν πᾶν τὸ πλήρωμα κατοικῆσαι,[101]

where we have again the connection between the εὐδοκία and the πλήρωμα.

The displacement of the Sophia that is interpreted as Law by the Sophia that is interpreted as Grace, may be illustrated from an actual equation made by the Jewish Fathers between Thorah and Wisdom, as represented in the eighth chapter of Proverbs: thus in *Pirqe Aboth* (vi. 10) we learn that the Holy One has five possessions in the world; of these, Thorah is one possession ... Thorah, whence? because it is written, *the Lord possessed me in the beginning of His way, before His works of old* (Prov. 8.22). Here Sophia is clearly equated with Thorah.

100. [Sir. 32.14-15. AF]
101. [Col. 1.19. AF]

5. *The Origin of the Prologue to St John's Gospel*

Other cases of the same equation will be found in Taylor (*Sayings of the Jewish Fathers*, ed. 2, p. 173);[102] e.g., *Bereshith Rabbah* begins with Proverbs 8.30, "Then was I by him as one brought up with him ... and I was daily his delight as one brought up with him." Thorah is here identified with Wisdom, and is also made to say with reference to Proverbs l.c., "I was the instrument by which he created the world." See *Aboth* iii. 23. "Beloved are Israel that there was given to them the instrument with which the world was created."

We have assumed in the foregoing that the πλήρωμα is an experimental knowledge of the Law, in accordance with the statements of Sirach

> They that love Him *will be filled* with the Law (2.16),
> He that seeks Law *will be filled* with it (35.15).[103]

In these passages we are almost bound to take the Law as an equivalent of *Wisdom*, just as in the *Sayings* of the Jewish Fathers, the Wisdom passage, Proverbs 8.22, is made to apply directly to the Thorah, which is one of the Divine possessions, because "the Lord possessed me (Wisdom) in the beginning."

We thus see that there is a line of development of thought open, in which Christ will be announced not merely as Σοφία but also as Νόμος. It can be shown that this subordinate equation between Christ and Law was actually made, sometimes with the reservation that Christ is the *New* Law.[104] Thus Clement of[105] Alexandria quotes the *Preaching of Peter* to prove that Christ is Νόμος and Λόγος:

> Νόμος καὶ Λόγος, αὐτὸς ὁ Σωτὴρ λέγεται, ὡς Πέτρος ἐν κηρύγματι. *Eclogae in Script. Proph.* ii. 1004 (Potter).[106]

---

102. [Charles Taylor, *Sayings of the Jewish Fathers: Comprising Pirqe Aboth and Pereq R. Meir in Hebrew and English* (Cambridge: Cambridge University Press, 2nd edn, 1897). AF]

103. [Sir. 32.15. AF]

104. B.W. Bacon in the *Story of St Paul*, p. 317 [Benjamin W. Bacon, *The Story of St Paul: A Comparison of Acts and Epistles* (London: Hodder & Stoughton, 1905). AF] makes the mistake of supposing Thorah to be anterior to Wisdom, whereas the evolution is evidently in the opposite direction. He says, 'Baruch (iii. 29-37) simply substitutes for the word *Torah* in Deuteronomy (xxx. 12-14) the philosophic term *Wisdom*, and Paul takes the next step and proceeds to identify this Wisdom in the heaven above and the abyss beneath with Christ'. It need hardly be pointed out that it was not Paul who identified Christ with Wisdom. It was a part of the regular and official apostolic teaching, and had nothing to do with Deuteronomy in the first instance.

105. [HCC pp. 36-37, "we ought to have a sentence ...": [1] Pleroma, as an actual title of Christ, will be found in Eusebius: *De eccl. theol. contra Marcellum* iii. 2 [*Eccl. theol.* 3.2.16-17. AF], λόγον ὄντα καὶ σοφίαν καὶ ζωήν, παντός τε καλοῦ καὶ ἀγαθοῦ πλήρωμα, ὡς δι' αὐτοῦ κυβερνᾶσθαι καὶ διασώζεσθαι τὰ σύμπαντα.]

106. [*Eclogae propheticae* 58. The reference is to John Potter (ed.), *Clementis alexandrini opera quae extant* (2 vols.; Oxford: e Theatro Sheldoniano, 1715). AF]

The same thing occurs in a fragment of Hippolytus on *Luke* as follows:

> Luke 2.22. Ἱππολύτου· ὅτε αὐτὸν ἀνήγαγον εἰς τὸ ἱερὸν παραστῆναι τῷ Κυρίῳ, τὰς καθαρσίους ἐπιτελοῦντες ἀναφοράς· εἰ γὰρ τὰ καθάρσια δῶρα κατὰ τὸν νόμον ὑπὲρ αὐτοῦ προσφέρετο ταύτῃ καὶ ὑπὸ τὸν νόμον γέγονεν· οὔτε δὲ ὁ Λόγος ὑπέκειτο τῷ νόμῳ, καθάπερ οἱ συκοφάνται δοξάζουσιν, αὐτὸς ὢν ὁ Νόμος. (P.G. 10. 701 A)[107]

There is another direction in which the idea of *Pleroma* might have been reached by the student of the Old Testament who was in search of Christ in its pages. It is, in fact, said of the Holy Spirit that it fills the whole world:

> πνεῦμα Κυρίου πεπλήρωκεν τὴν οἰκουμένην (Wis. 1.7),

and this passage is one of Gregory of Nyssa's proof-texts for the Holy Spirit.[108] It is, however, clear as we have shown by a variety of illustrations that the Holy Spirit came into the Christian Theology, through the bifurcation of the doctrine of the Divine Wisdom, which, on the one side, became the Logos, and on the other the Holy Ghost. It is Wisdom which is, in this passage, denoted by the Holy Spirit.

It appears to be quite natural that the Law should turn up in the praises of Sophia, when Sophia is interpreted in a pre-Christian sense, and that it should be spoken of depreciatingly, when Sophia is interpreted in a Christian sense.

From the foregoing considerations it follows that there is an anti-Judaic element in the Fourth Gospel, from its very first page. The Law is antagonised and the people to whom the Law came.

When we make that statement and follow Alford and Westcott in what is certainly the right explanation of "His own who did not receive Him," we are again treading on the heels of the first composers of books of Testimonies against the Jews; for a scrutiny of Cyprian's *First Book of Testimonies* shows conclusively the very same rejection of the Jews on the ground that they have rejected the Lord.

Let us turn to the third chapter of the book in question. It is headed as follows:

> That it was foretold that they (i.e. the Jews) would neither recognise the Lord nor understand *nor receive Him*.

Then follow the proofs, and we readily anticipate the opening verses of Isaiah, with its appeal to a sinful nation, Israel that doth not know, my people that doth not understand.[109] But a little lower down we come upon a reference to Proverbs 1.28ff. as follows:

---

107. [PG 10.700D-701A. AF]
108. [*Jud.* 22. AF]
109. [Isa. 1.2-4 in *Test.* 1.3. AF]

> Item apud Solomonem: Quaerent me mali et non inuenient. Oderunt enim *Sapientiam, sermonem* autem *Domini non receperunt.*

Here we have the Logos and Sophia side by side in the same verse, and the statement that the Wisdom has been hated and the Word not received. The parallel with John 1.11 is obvious. That verse is of the nature of an anti-Judaic Testimony. It is an adaptation of the LXX of Proverbs 1.29

> ἐμίσησαν γὰρ σοφίαν, τὸν δὲ λόγον τοῦ Κυρίου οὐ προσείλαντο.

The transition from σοφία to λόγος is natural and easy, and a primitive statement that Wisdom came to the Jews and the Jews did not receive her, would readily be re-written in terms of the Logos, who

> Came to His own, and His own did not receive Him.

The two statements are in part equivalent; and Alford's interpretation was right as far as it went.

In this connection belongs a curious chapter in the *Book of Enoch*, which Dr Charles had actually suggested to be parallel with the Prologue of John.[110]

The forty-second chapter of *Enoch* opens as follows:

> Wisdom found no place where she might dwell;
> Then a dwelling place was assigned her in the heavens.
> Wisdom came to make her dwelling among the children of men,
> And found no dwelling place,
> Then Wisdom returned to her place,
> And took her seat among the angels.[111]

The parallels with the Logos who dwelt among us, and who had not been received by His own, are striking. And we are confirmed in our belief that the Prologue to the Gospel can be turned back from a Logos-Hymn to a Sophia-Hymn.

One more illustration may be given of the derivation of the language of the Prologue from the Sapiential sources which preceded it.[112]

---

110. [Robert H. Charles (ed.), *The Book of Enoch: Translated from Professor Dillmann's Ethiopic Text, Emended and Revised in Accordance with Hitherto Uncollated Ethiopic Mss. and with the Gizeh and Other Greek and Latin Fragments Which Are Here Published in Full* (Oxford: Clarendon Press, 1893). AF]

111. [*1 En.* 42.1-2. AF]

112. [HCB pp. 38-39, "Alexandria quotes the *Preaching of Peter* ..." [The flyleaves seem to have been misplaced and to refer to the second quotation on p. 173. AF]: [1] It is common for the Fathers to explain the Wisdom of God and the Power of God in i Cor 1[24] by a reference to Prov 8. Thus Cyril of Alexandria says that 'the Son is the Wisdom and Power of the God and Father, by which (δι' ἧς) all things are brought to birth and when made are preserved (Cramer, *Cat.* in loc. [John A. Cramer (ed.), *Catenæ in Sancti Pauli Epistolas ad Corinthios* (Oxford: e Typographeo Academico, 1841). AF].

The Gospel, after reciting the unresponsiveness of the Jewish people generally to the Logos who had come among them, goes on to explain that there were some who did receive the Logos, and that, in consequence of this reception, they became *children of God*, and experienced a spiritual birth; "to as many as received Him, to them gave He power to become the children of God, owing their birth not to carnal generation nor human impulse, but to the Divine Will."[113] It may be asked whether this striking passage has any counterpart in the Sophia literature upon which we have been drawing.

The connection is clearly with Proverbs, as is shown by the use of the feminine relative pronoun, but it is made almost in the language of the Prologue to John ('all things were made by Him' [John 1.3. AF], i.e. the Logos). There were, however, some Christian readers who rejected the cross-reference to Proverbs. Severianus regards it as improper to speak of the 'foolishness of God,' which is wiser than man, 'the weakness of God,' which is stronger than man, in the sense of the Logos; he says it means the preaching that is the weak wise thing and not the person who is Preached: God's weakness is the Cross and not the Crucified, the word of the Cross and not the Word. The great Theodore objects to the reference to Proverbs on another ground: he saw the advantage [2] which the Arians had in handling the verse 'The Lord created me Beginning of his way', and so he boldly says that in i Cor 1^{24} we are not to take the Sophia and Power of God as representing the Divinity of the Only Begotten, but to refer the words to the Preaching of the Cross. In this way one can confute the Arians and Eunomians who are always trying to show that Logos is Sophia, and from the language of Proverbs to deduce their blasphemy (see Cramer *Cat.* in loc.).

[3] The identification of Jesus with the Sophia-Logos was the thing that Paul of Samosata contested. For, said he, 'the Logos was greater than Christ. It was through the Sophia (=Logos) that Christ became great. Let us not destroy the dignity of the Divine Wisdom': (Routh. *Rell.* ii. 300) and in another passage he says, 'Jesus Christ is one thing, the Word is another'; (ibid [*Acta de Paulo Samosatensi in Antiocheno concilio* 2 and 3, in *Reliquiae sacrae* (ed. Martin J. Routh; 5 vols.; Oxford: e Typographeo Academico, 2nd ed, 1846–1848), 3.300 and 301. AF]).

[4] The persistence of the belief that Christ is the Wisdom of God may be illustrated from the inscription which Dante puts over the door of the Inferno.

> Giustizia mosse il mio alto fattore,
> Fecemi la divina potestate,
> La somma sapienza e il primo amore.

Here the commentators point out that the inscription contains a reference to the Trinity, the Father being Power, the Son Wisdom and the Holy Spirit Love. A reference to Dante's *Convito* ii.6 shows the correctness of the interpretation: "Puotesi contemplare la potenza somma del Padre ... la somma Sapienza del Figliuolo ... e la somma e ferventissima carità dello Spirito Santo."

[5] It should be noticed that Aquinas deduces the doctrine that Christ is the Wisdom of God from the seventh chapter of the Wisdom of Solomon (more exactly, the first verse of the eight chapter) as follows. "Sed contra est quod Christus, qui est Dei Sapientia, suaviter et convenienter disponit omnia, ut dicitur Sap. 8".]

113. If we follow the very early reading ὃς ... ἐγεννήθη, the latter part of the sentence

5. The Origin of the Prologue to St John's Gospel

The answer is that to this beautiful description of the appearance of the Life of the Spirit as given in the Gospel, there is a parallel, shorter indeed, but almost as beautiful, in the seventh chapter of the Wisdom of Solomon, from which we have already taken so many illustrations. "In all ages Wisdom entering into holy souls, makes them *Friends of God* and prophets."[114]

It is this work of Sophia in the making of "Friends of God" (φίλους Θεοῦ) that has prompted the "Children of God" (τέκνα Θεοῦ)[115] who result from the reception of the Logos.[116]

In explaining ἐξηγήσατο of John 1.18 as being the equivalent of ἡγησάμην in Sirach 24.6, we have found the reason for the little inserted testimony of John the Baptist in John 1.15, which is also occupied with the doctrine of the priority and primacy of Jesus. It may, however, be urged that in thus changing the interpretation of ἐξηγήσατο, we have broken sequence with the statement that precedes it as to the "invisibility of God," whom it is the business of the Unique-born Logos to *expound* to men.

The sentence as to the invisibility of God is another Sapiential loan: it is parallel to Colossians 1.15

ὅς ἐστιν εἰκὼν τοῦ θεοῦ τοῦ ἀοράτου,

where it is followed by

πρωτότοκος πάσης κτίσεως

just as the passage in John is followed by the reference to the *Monogenēs*: both sequences are Sapiential, and are suggestive of a common document and a common sequence of thought. In such a document ἡγησάμην must be interpreted in the sense that Sophia had the first rank, after God, in the order of being. Note carefully that neither in Sirach nor in John is there any object attached to ἡγέομαι: it is therefore, to be taken intransitively. The case of ἐκδιηγήσομαι in Sirach 42.15, 44.31 is, therefore, not an objection to the intransitive interpretation, for here the object is expressed.

Was there anything in the underlying document that corresponded to the statement that "the Word became flesh"? Will the critical reagent bring it up?

Suppose we turn to Methodius, the *Banquet of the Ten Virgins* (iii. 4; P.G. ix. 18. 65),[117] we shall find a very curious passage, whose obscurity has baffled both translators and interpreters. The writer has been explaining the difficulties which arise from the Pauline language when the Apostle compares Christ and

---

relates to the Logos, and goes back to ὁ κύριος ... γεννᾷ με of Proverbs 8.25 [the reference is to John 1.12-13. AF].

114. [Wis. 7.27. AF]
115. [John 1.12. AF]
116. Hence, perhaps, the masculine οἵ in John 1.13.
117. [*Conv.*, Oratio 3.3-4 (PG 18.63B-68A). AF]

the Church mystically with Adam and Eve in the Book of Genesis. How could the comparison have been made between the pure and the impure? we might as well compare odd and even. No wonder that persons have taken exception to the comparison between the First Adam and the Second. Methodius explains that it was the Wisdom of God that was joined to the First Adam, and became incarnate: and this Wisdom was Christ. His language is very peculiar, and needs closer examination.

It was appropriate, says Methodius, that Wisdom (the First-born, the First Offshoot, the Only-born of God) should be united with the First and First-born Man (Adam) by an incarnation. We notice the array of Sapiential terms with which we have become familiar.

The result of this incarnation was Christ, "a man filled with the pure and perfect Godhead, and God received into man." In other words, *Christ is the Incarnate Wisdom of God*. Thus there lies behind the phrase

ὁ λόγος σὰρξ ἐγένετο,[118]

the expression

ἡ σοφία σὰρξ ἐγένετο.

If Christ is First-born, and Only-born, He has derived these appellations from Sophia.

Methodius continues the explanation: "it was most suitable that the oldest of the aeons and the first of the Archangels (viz. Sophia), when about to hold communion with men, should dwell[119] in the oldest and the first of men, even

---

118. [John 1.14. AF]
119. [HCB pp. 40-41, "The Gospel, after reciting ..." [The flyleaves seem to have been misplaced. AF]:
[1] *Wisdom and the Pre-existence of Jesus.*
A good example of the way in which the early church taught, from Proverbs viii, the pre-existence of Jesus, by identifying him with the Eternal Wisdom, may be seen in Eusebius. Eusebius (H.E. iii.27 [*Hist. eccl.* 3.27.3. AF]) is discussing the beliefs and disbeliefs of the so-called Ebionites in Palestine; some of them, he says, agree with us that the Lord was born of the Holy Spirit and the Virgin Mary, but they do not confess *his pre-existence as being the Divine Word (Θεὸν λόγον) and Wisdom*. In other words, they had not taken the forward step, by means of the Wisdom passage in Proverbs, which the rest of the church had taken.
[2] Gregory Thaumaturgus, *Credo* (Caspari, *Alte und Neue Quellen zur Geschichte des Taufsymbols und der Glaubensregel*, 1879, 10 [Carl P. Caspari, *Alte und Neue Quellen zur Geschichte des Taufsymbols und der Glaubensregel* (Christiania, 1879). AF]) = *Expositio Fidei*, P.G. 10 985 A.
εἷς κύριος μόνος ἐκ μόνου, θεὸς ἐκ θεοῦ, χαρακτὴρ καὶ εἰκὼν τῆς θεότητος[(1)], λόγος ἐνεργός, σοφία[(2)] τῆς τῶν ὅλων συστάσεως περιεκτικὴ καὶ δύναμις τῆς ὅλης κτίσεως ποιητική, υἱὸς ἀληθινὸς ἀληθινοῦ πατρός, ἀόρατος ἀοράτου καὶ ἄφθαρτος ἀφθάρτου καὶ ἀθάνατος ἀθανάτου καὶ ἀΐδιος ἀϊδίου.

5. *The Origin of the Prologue to St John's Gospel*   159

in Adam." The passage suggests for Sophia a description almost identical with the Johannine language, that "the Word became Flesh"; for "the Word" restore "Wisdom."

It is interesting to note further that Methodius has elsewhere identified Christ with the Wisdom of God, by a combination of the language of Proverbs with that of St John's Gospel. In his discourse on the Resurrection, he tells us that "Wisdom, the First-born of God, the parent and artificer of all things, brings forth everything into the world ... whom the ancients called Nature and Providence, because she, with constant provision and care, gives to all things birth and growth. For, *says the Wisdom of God,* 'my Father worketh still, and I work'" (John 5.17).[120] We note the identification of Jesus with the Wisdom of God, and compare the way in which the passage from John is introduced with the similar feature which we observed in the Gospel of Luke (11.49).

Rufinus trans—Unus Dominus, solus ex solo Deo, figura et imago deitatis, verbum penetrans, sapientia comprehendens omnia et virtus, qua tota creatura fieri potuit, filius veri et invisibilis ex invisibili et incorruptibilis ex incorruptibili et immortalis ex immortali et sempiternus ex sempiterno [Caspari, *Quellen*, 15. AF].

Old unnamed trans: Et unus Dominus ex uno, deus de deo, figura substantiae patris, imago Dei, deus verbum vividum et totius substantiae opifex, sapientia continens omnia, qua existunt, et virtus totius creaturae creatrix, Filius verus de Patre vero, invisibilis de invisibili, incorruptibilis de incorruptibili, immortalis de immortali et sempiternus de sempiterno [Caspari, *Quellen*, 16. AF].

(1). Caspari refers: Origen, *in Joann.* xiii.36.
(2). Or. *in Joann.*, i.22;

Gennadius of Massilia, *de fide disputans*, (pg: 30 [unreadable sign. AF] Caspari)
Filius ergo dei, qui dicitur verbum dei et sapientia dei, carnem adsumpsit ex virgine Maria.

---

[3] For the Holy Spirit as the mother of Jesus we may compare a lovely statue in the Leiden Ethnographic Museum of Prajnaparanita de volnaskte wÿsheid, de moeder van Adi-Buddha. The statue came from Java.

[4] A good instance of the identification of Christ with the Wisdom of God will be found in Eusebius's treatise on Ecclesiastical Theology against Marcellus, as follows:

καὶ σοφίαν δὲ αὐτὸν ὀνομάζει Σολόμων ἐπὶ παροιμίαις λέγων· ἡ σοφία ᾠκοδόμησεν ἑαυτῇ οἶκον, καὶ ὑπήρεισε στύλους ἑπτὰ κτέ. καὶ ὅτι προκόσμιος ἦν ἡ σοφία ζῶσα καὶ ὑφεστῶσα αὐτὸς ἐδίδασκεν ἐκ προσώπου αὐτῆς ταύτας προέμενος τὰς φωνάς· ἐγὼ ἡ σοφία κατεσκήνωσα βουλήν, καὶ γνῶσιν, καὶ ἔννοιαν ἐπεκαλεσάμην· εἶθ᾽ ἑξῆς ἐπιλέγων, δι᾽ ἐμοῦ βασιλεύουσι βασιλεῖς κτέ.
Euseb. *De Eccl. Theol* i.22. [*Eccl. theol.* 1.20.81. AF]

120. [*Res.* 15 (PG 18.288C). Between "world" and "whom" there should not be ellipsis points. AF]

An even more remarkable equation between Christ and the Wisdom of God will be found in the fragments of Methodius on *Created Things*, which are preserved for us in the *Bibliotheca* of Photius. Here the equivalence of the opening verses of the Prologue with the eighth chapter of Proverbs is insisted upon:

> Methodius says, of the words "In the Beginning God created the Heavens and the earth," that one will not err who says that the Beginning is Wisdom. For Wisdom is said by one of the Divine Band to speak in this manner concerning herself: "The Lord created me the Beginning of His ways for His works; from eternity He laid my foundation." It was fitting and more seemly that all things which came into existence should be more recent than Wisdom, since they existed through her. Now, consider whether this saying "In the beginning was the Word, and the Word was with God and the Word was God,"—whether these statements be not in agreement with those. (Photius, *Bibliotheca*, Cod. 235.)[121]

The doctrine of Methodius appears to have been that Sophia became incarnate in the First Adam and also in the Second. In the eighth chapter of the *Banquet* he sums up the results of his mystical investigations as follows:

> It has been already established by no contemptible arguments from Scripture, that the first man may probably be referred to Christ Himself, and is no longer a type and representation and image of the Only-Begotten, but has actually become Wisdom and Word.[122]

There is still a good deal of obscurity in the statements of Methodius, but it is quite clear that the Incarnation of which he speaks is the Incarnation of Wisdom. Whether it is Christ or Adam or both that are the subject of the Incarnation is not quite clear.

Now let us try to restore the Prologue to something like its intermediate form. It should run as follows:[123]

Prov. 8.22 ff.:	The Beginning was Wisdom,
	Wisdom was with God,
Wis. 9.4:	Wisdom was the assessor of God.
	All things were made by her;
	Apart from her nothing that was made came to be.
Wis. 6[7].26:	With her was Light, and the Light was the Life of men.
	That Light shone in the Darkness,
Wis. 6[7].29:	And the Darkness did not overmaster it.
	For no evil overmasters Wisdom.
	Wisdom was in the World,
	In the World which she had made;

---

121. [*Bibliotheca* 235.304a. AF]
122. [*Conv.*, Oratio 3.8. AF]
123. [Between square brackets the corrections penned by Rendel Harris in his personal copy. AF]

5. *The Origin of the Prologue to St John's Gospel* 161

Prov. 1.28:	The world did not recognise her.
Sir. 34.13ff.: Enoch 41.1ff.:[124]	} She came to the Jews, and the Jews did not receive her.
Wis. 7.27:	Those that did receive her became Friends of God and prophets.
Sir. 34.6: Wis. 7.25:	} She tabernacled with us, and we saw her splendour, the splendour of the Father's Only Child,
Wis. 3.9:	Full of Grace and Truth.
Ode Sol. 33:	(She declared the Grace of God among us).
Sir. 35.15:[125]	From her pleroma[126] we have received Grace instead of Law, For Law came by Moses,
Wis. 3.19[9]:	Grace and Mercy came by Sophia;
Wis. 9.26:[127]	She is the Image of the Invisible God;
Wis. 6.22: Sir. 34.6:	} She is the only Child of God, in the bosom of the Father,[128] and has the primacy.

Christ As the Hand of God

When we study the surviving texts of that very early Christian book, known as the *Testimonies against the Jews*, we find that one of the things which has to be established against the Jews is that *Christ is the Hand of God*; one does not at first see the reason for this statement nor for the emphasis laid upon it: yet it is clear that it occupies an early and an important position amongst the theses which the primitive Christian nailed on the doors of the Synagogue. In the second book of Cyprian's *Testimonies*, for example (that section which contains the Christology—it is important to remember that primitive Christian propaganda *is* primitive Christology), we find that the fourth place in the list of propositions to be discussed and defended is the statement that

> *The same Christ is the hand and the arm of God.*[129]

124. [Probably *1 En.* 42.1-3. AF]
125. [Sir. 32.15. AF]
126. [HCF: (1) So Spenser, *Hymne of Heavenly Beautie*.

> "Both heaven and earth obey unto her will,
> And all the creatures which they both containe;
> For of her fullnesse which the world doth fill
> They all partake:]

127. [Wis. 7.26. AF]
128. [HCF: (2) Our sage and serious Spenser understood this:

> "There in his bosome Sapience doth sit,
> The sovereign darling of the Deity,
> Clad like a Queene in royal robes, most fit
> For so great powre and pearlesse majesty."
> Hymne of Heavenly Beautie]

129. [*Test.* 2.4. AF]

The preceding theses are concerned with the proof that Christ is the Wisdom of God, and the Word of God.[130] Why should these high-level statements in theology drop down to such an unexpected piece of exegetical poverty as that Christ is the Hand of God?

The first thing that suggests itself is that the author of the theses is following the way of escape, which Jewish theologians of a progressive type had found, out of the temptations to anthropomorphism in the O.T. We may imagine the situation as it would occur to an Alexandrian of the school of Philo, or to a Palestinian thinker, who has to explain away the speech of God, and the walk of God, and the form of God, and the eyes, hands, organs and dimensions of God. He has to be rid of all these without getting rid at the same time of God and of the activity of God. This can only be done by the introduction of a subordinate being, who shall bear the name of God, and possess in a sufficient degree His attributes, or by the philosophical hypostasis and personification of the attributes themselves, either simply or in combination; that is, an angelic or archangelic person, or a supra-sensual idea. Then, if the Jewish world has already, in the person of its leading thinkers, attained to such a theological reconstruction as may secure them, when they revile the Olympians, from a counter-revilement, it will be easy for the Christian polemist to explain to the Jews that they have in reality discovered the Christ; have, in fact, in running away from the dread spectre of a pursuing anthropomorphism, run into his very arms, the arms of God; the everlasting ones of that species of representation being the arms of Christ!

Such a method of expounding the nature of the first Christian propaganda cannot be altogether wide of the mark: but it is always as well, in reconstructing a lost, or studying a nascent theology, to let the documents talk first, and say all that they have to say on the subject, before we ascend the rostrum ourselves.

We need to consider, for example, the continuity of the theses discussed, and the light thrown on them by contemporary or subsequent literature. Why does the doctrine of the Hand follow so closely on the doctrine of the Wisdom and the doctrine of the Word? The answer is a curious one: the fourth thesis of the second book of *Testimonies against the Jews* is based upon an earlier form in which it was said,

> That the same Wisdom is the Hand of God.

We establish this thesis, which takes us to a somewhat different point of view (but not altogether diverse), in the following way. In the *Clementine Homilies* (which contain so much early controversial matter by way of survival), we have in the sixteenth Homily a dispute between Peter and Simon Magus over

---

130. [*Test.* 2.2 and 2.3. AF]

5. The Origin of the Prologue to St John's Gospel

the Divine Unity. Simon challenges the consistency of the doctrine of the Unity with the language of Genesis (1.26) "Let us make man, etc.," and Peter replies as follows:

> He who said to His Wisdom, Let us make, is one. And His Wisdom is that with which He always joyed as though it were His own spirit: for She is united as Soul to God: *and is stretched out by Him as a Hand for the creation of the world.*
>
> καὶ ὁ Πέτρος ἀπεκρίνατο· εἷς ἐστὶν ὁ τῇ αὐτοῦ Σοφίᾳ εἰπών· ποιήσωμεν ἄνθρωπον· ἡ δὲ Σοφία, ᾗ ὥσπερ ἰδίῳ πνεύματι αὐτὸς ἀεὶ συνέχαιρεν (Prov. 8.30). ἥνωται γὰρ ὡς ψυχὴ τῷ Θεῷ· ἐκτείνεται δὲ ὑπ' αὐτοῦ, ὡς χείρ, δημιουργοῦσα τὸν κόσμον. *Clem. Hom.* XVI. 12.[131]

If Wisdom is the Hand of God, and the Creative Instrument, we see why the statement to that effect occupies the position that it does in the *Testimony Book*. The whole of the passage quoted is of interest, and is redolent of antiquity. The great stumbling-block for monotheists in the first chapter of Genesis, is explained by a duality in God, rather than a Trinity. Simon says, "Let us make" implies two or more. *There are, says he, evidently two who created.*[132] Peter accepts it and identifies the second Creator with the Sophia of the eighth chapter of Proverbs. There is the Begotten God and the Unbegotten; the latter makes the World by the former.

When we turn to examine the actual Testimonies quoted in Cyprian we have first a passage from Isa. 59.1, "Is the Lord's hand shortened, etc.," and it is clear from the context that this passage is quoted rather to show the sinfulness of the Jews than the nature of the Divine Hand. "Your iniquities have separated between you and God, etc."[133]

Then follows a reference to the "arm of the Lord, etc." in Isa. 58.1, evidently brought in for the sake of the "arm" and contributing nothing immediate to its explanation.

After that we come to Isa. 66.1ff., which leads up to the enquiry

> Hath not my hand made all these things?[134]

viz.: Heaven and Earth.

---

131. [*Ps.-Clem., Hom.* 16.12.1. AF]
132. [*Ps.-Clem., Hom.* 16.11.1-2. AF]
133. [HCC pp. 44-45, "theses which the primitive Christian ...": [1] Acts of Sharbil [in William Cureton (ed.), *Ancient Christian Documents Relative to the Earliest Establishment of Christianity in Edessa and Neighbouring Countries, from the Year after Our Lord's Ascension to the Beginning of the Fourth Century* (London: Williams and Norgate, 1864). AF]) p. 43 "He also has existed with his Father from eternity and for ever, his arm, and his right hand, and his power, and his wisdom, and his might, and the living Spirit, which is from him."]
134. [Isa. 66.2. AF]

This is the creative Hand again. Lower down we have a long passage from Isa. 41.15ff., ending up with

The Hand of the Lord hath made all these things:[135]

here again we are concerned with creative and redemptive acts attributed to the Hand of God; and for this Divine Hand we have given the primary explanation; it is the Divine Wisdom.

It will be interesting to see how this interpretation that the Hand of God is His Wisdom, by which He instrumentally made the world, can be reconciled with correct theology. The interpretation is clearly ancient, and it labours under a difficulty, in that it represents God as a Duality, and not as a Trinity. In the dispute between Peter and Simon Magus in the Clementine story, this is conceded on both sides. It is, however, clear that it will have to be modified, or there will be theological friction. The way of escape is to say that *God has two hands* or creative instruments, viz.: (i) His Wisdom, (ii) His Word, or, comprehending them under a single formula, His Word and His Wisdom.

If we want to see the formulae in process of evolution, we may turn to the pages of Irenaeus. We are told (see Iren. p. 218 Mass.)[136] that Adam was made of Virgin earth, and was "fashioned by the *Hand of God*, i.e. *by the Word of God*," according to the saying of John that all things were made by Him.[137] Here the Word has been substituted for the Wisdom in the definition of the Hand.

Somewhat later (p. 228), Irenaeus repeats the statement that man was formed in the similitude of God, and was fashioned *by His hands*, viz., *by the Son and the Spirit*, those to whom He was speaking when He said, Let us make man.[138] Here the Son has replaced the Logos, and the Spirit stands for Sophia. Both of the Creative Hands are in operation. Further on (p. 253), we come to the statement that the angels could not be responsible for the creation of man, since *God had His own Hands*. "He had always by Him the Word *and the Wisdom, the Son and the Spirit* through whom and in whom of His own free will He made all things, and whom He addresses when He says, Let us make man in our own image and likeness."[139]

Here we find the Son and Spirit side by side with the Word and Wisdom with whom they have been equated.[140] The same interpretation of "Let us

---

135. [Isa. 41.20. AF]
136. [Massuet, *Sancti Irenaei*. AF]
137. [*Haer.* 3.21.10. AF]
138. [*Haer.* 4. Praefatio 4. AF]
139. [*Haer.* 4.20.1. AF]
140. The Son and the Spirit as the Hands of God will be found again in Iraeneus (p. 327) as follows: "Et propter hoc in omni tempore, plasmatus initio homo per manus Dei, id est, Filii et Spiritus, fit secundum imaginem et similitudinem Dei" [*Haer.* 5.28.4. AF]. Here

5. The Origin of the Prologue to St John's Gospel

make" is found elsewhere in the Fathers; sometimes it is explained of the co-operation of the Logos, and sometimes of Logos and Sophia. For example, in Theophilus *ad Autolycum* (ch. 18), the two Hands of God are implied, and they are the Word and the Wisdom:

> He considers the creation of man alone worthy His own hands. Nay, further, as if needing assistance, we find God saying, "Let us make man in our image and likeness": but He said "Let us make" *to none, other than His own Logos and Sophia.*[141]

The same tradition re-appears in Procopius of Gaza,[142] "the Hands of God are the Son and the Holy Spirit," where we have clearly an evolution from the earlier statement as to Logos and Sophia.

In Clement of Alexandria the doctrine of one hand is commonly involved, for he interprets ποιήσωμεν in Gen. 1.26 as addressed to the Logos.[143]

The transition from "one hand" to "two hands" in the description of the instruments by which Creation was effected, may be seen very clearly in Tertullian's *Treatise against Hermogenes*: after contesting the belief of Hermogenes as to the eternity of matter on philosophical grounds, he turns to the evidence of the Scriptures and the teaching of the prophets:

> They did not mention matter but said that *Wisdom* was *first* set up, the beginning of His ways for His works (Prov. 8.22); *then* that *the Word* was produced through whom all things were made, and without whom nothing was made (John 1.3) ... He (the Word) is the *Lord's right hand, indeed His two hands,* by which He worked and fashioned. For, says He, the Heavens are the works *of thine hands* (Ps. 102.25) wherewith He hath meted out the Heaven, *and the earth with a span* (Isa. 40.12, 48.13). Adv. Hermogenem, ch. 45.[144]

The reasoning borders on the Rabbinical method, but it is not to be condemned on that account as non-primitive; the course of the argument clearly shows the stages by which Wisdom was replaced by the Word, and the Hand of God (His Wisdom or His Word) was replaced by His two Hands, which were His Wisdom and His Word.

We shall find that the same theology prevails in the writings of Athanasius and Augustine, both of whom identify Christ with the Wisdom of God by

---

again the reference to the creation of man shows that the first stage of the doctrine which Irenaeus presents was a reflection upon the words "Let us make man," according to which it was explained that God spoke to His Wisdom, which was His Hand, i.e. to the Word and the Wisdom which were His Hands, i.e. to the Son and the Spirit. The growth of the successive statements is clearly made out.

141. [*Autol.* 2.18.1-2. AF]
142. P.G. 87. 134 A [*Commentarii in Genesin* (PG 87/1.133A). AF].
143. [*Paed.* 1.12.2-3. AF]
144. [*Herm.* 45.1-2. AF]

whom the worlds were made, and both of whom apply the title "Hand of God" to Christ.

For instance, Athanasius tells us[145] that we may learn from the Scriptures themselves that Christ "is the Word of God and the Wisdom, and the Image, *and the Hand* and the Power." He quotes the appropriate Scriptures, and when he comes to the first three verses of John, tells us that John composed his Gospel, because he knew that "the Word is the Wisdom and *the Hand* of God." And Augustine says expressly that "The Hand of the Father is the Son."[146]

These references may easily be multiplied: they show us clearly that the doctrine that Christ is the Word of God does not arise, in the first instance, from a sentiment adverse to anthropomorphic representations of God; for, as we have abundantly made clear, we start from the position that Christ is the Wisdom of God, an earlier position than the hypostatising of a supposed Memra; and indeed, the Memra in the sense of the Targums does not appear in our investigations. Neither do we start from Creation, as Creation is described in the first chapter of Genesis. Our point of departure is the Book of Proverbs, especially the eighth chapter, with an occasional divergence into the Psalter; Genesis comes later in the argument; when we explain "Let us make man," Wisdom is introduced, already identified with the Creative Instrument from Proverbs. This Wisdom is either the Divine Conjugate or the Divine Offspring; it is not quite clear which. If the former, the Logos is her Son; if the latter, the Logos is her brother. The former position leads on to the curious Word of Christ in the *Gospel of the Hebrews*, "My Mother the Holy Ghost,"[147] the latter to the twinship of Jesus and the Holy Spirit, as we find it in the *Pistis Sophia*. When the Logos becomes also an Assessor Dei, we have the Christian Trinity: but behind this there is the earlier stratum of a Christian Duality (the Holy Spirit being not yet come, in a theological sense, because the Divine Wisdom has not been divided into Logos and Pneuma).

We now begin to see that the controversy between Arius and Athanasius is not a mere struggle of an orthodox Church with an aggressive and cancerous heresy: the heretic is the orthodox conservative, and the supposed orthodox champion is the real progressive. The conflict is one between two imperfectly harmonised strata of belief. Arius and Athanasius do not stand at opposite poles: they are really next-door neighbours. This appears, *inter alia*, from the fact that they practically use the same traditional Scripture proofs; we have

---

145. *De Secretis Nicaenae Synodi*, §17 ff. [*De decretis Nicaenae synodi* 17.3-7. Correction in Rendel Harris's personal copy. AF].

146. *In Joann.* xlviii. 7. *Enarr. in Ps.* cxviii. *Serm.* 23, 5 and 143, 14 [*Tract. Ev. Jo.* 124.48.7; *Enarrat. Ps.* 118.18.1. AF].

147. [Origen, *Comm. Jo.* 2.12; *Hom. Jer.* 15.4. AF]

5. The Origin of the Prologue to St John's Gospel

shown elsewhere[148] how painfully faithful Athanasius is to the body of conventional Christian Testimonies. It is not, however, that Arius is at heart a Jew, and must be struck down with the weapons proper to anti-Judaic struggle. Arius is as much anti-Judaic as Athanasius; only his collection of Testimonies has not been completed as to the text, and still less as to the interpretation. Both of the great protagonists begin by saying the same words,

> The Lord created me the Beginning,

both of them explain that Christ is here speaking in the person of Wisdom. Neither of them doubts that ἔκτισέν με (the Lord created me) is applicable to Christ, though it was a false rendering of the Septuagint: they differ when they come to harmonise the Divine Creation with the other statement that Wisdom was older than the worlds and was the First-born of God. Athanasius[149] explains that the Christ is a creature, but *not as one of the creatures*; he saves his proof-text at the expense of its natural meaning: Arius explains away the eternity of the Divine Wisdom, by saying that Wisdom is eternal relatively to the Creation, but not eternal relatively to God.[150]

Now if we bear in mind the facts which we have established, that the Nicene conflict is concerned with two different strata of the traditional proof-texts for primitive Church doctrine, we shall find it very much easier to see our way through the smoke of the conflict into the real meaning of the battle. That Athanasius himself is in possession of the whole story, and the evolution of the doctrine of the Trinity, will be clear now to the readers of his *Orations against the Arians*, which run over with the matters which the Church had discussed in the centuries that preceded him. In order to illustrate this point we take a single passage from Athanasius and hold it up in the light of the discoveries which we have made as to the origin and growth of the Christian tradition.

In his second *Oration against the Arians* Athanasius says as follows:

> All things that were made, were made by the Hand, and the Wisdom of God, for God Himself says:
>
> "My Hand hath made all these things" (Isa. 66.2 ff.)
>
> and David sings:

---

148. ["Athanasius and the Book of Testimonies." *Expositor*, 7th series, 9 (1910), pp. 530-37; repr. in *Testimonies*, 1.87-93. AF]

149. [HCC: ? is not this Arius. Or rather Eusebius of Nicomedia? See Athan. *De Synod.* 16 [*Synod.* 16.2. AF] κτίσμα τοῦ Θεοῦ τέλειον ἀλλ' οὐχ ὡς ἓν τῶν κτισμάτων and cf. *c. Arianos* ii.16 (on Prov. 8^{22})].

150. Hence I was wrong in saying in *Testimonia* [i.e. in *Testimonies*, 1.87-93. AF] that it was not inept for Athanasius to have felled Arius to the ground with a missile borrowed from *Testimonies against the Jews*. Both of the combatants were anti-Judaic.

"Thou Lord in the beginning hast laid the foundations of the earth and the Heavens are the work of Thy hands" (Ps. 101.26).[151]

And again in the 142nd Psalm:[152]

"I remembered the days of old,
I meditated on all thy works:
On the works of thy hands did I meditate."

So then the things made were wrought by the Hand of God, for it is written that

"All things were made by the Word
And without Him was nothing made" (John 1.3).

And again, there is

"One Lord Jesus, by whom all things are made" (1 Cor. 8.6),

and

"In Him all things exist" (Col. 1.17).

So it must be obvious that the Son cannot be a work of God, but is Himself *the Hand of God and the Wisdom.*
The martyrs of Babylon understood this, Ananias, Azarias and Misael, and they confute the impiety of the Arians, for they say

"O all ye works of the Lord, bless ye the Lord."[153]

They did not say "Bless the Lord, Logos, and praise Him, Sophia"; in order to show that all the rest that praise are God's works, but the Logos is not the work of God nor of the company that praise, but is with the Father the object of praise and worship, and is reckoned Divine (θεολογούμενος), *being the Word and His Wisdom,* and the Artificer of His works. The same thing is expressed by the Spirit in the Psalms with an excellent distinction between the Word and the Works.

"*The Word of* the Lord is right,
And *all His works* are in faith."

Just as it says elsewhere,

"O Lord, how great are *Thy works*
Thou hast made them all *in Wisdom.*"[154]

Here we have gathered together in a single statement as to the origin of the Creation the doctrine that Christ is (*a*) the Wisdom of God; (*b*) the Word of

---

151. [Ps. 102.25. AF]
152. [Ps. 143.5. AF]
153. [Dan. 3.57. AF]
154. [*C. Ar.* 2.71.28-36. AF]

5. The Origin of the Prologue to St John's Gospel

God, (c) the Hand of God; and that the two Hands of God are, in fact, His Word and His Wisdom.

The difference between Arius and Athanasius is a question whether the Hand of God is co-eternal with God Himself; did God make the Hand by which He made the world?

As we have several times indicated, the Christian statements which we find in the Fourth Gospel are not derived immediately from Philo and his speculative Logos. The two evolutions of doctrine are very nearly independent of one another. It is interesting to see that Philo has the same problem before him, of the relation of the hypostatised Wisdom to God, and to observe how differently the problem of the Persons is worked out. In one passage Philo makes Wisdom the Divine conjugate, and the Divine Son is the Cosmos. Thus we have the following Trinity:

God = Sophia
|
The only-begotten Son, who is the world.

That Sophia is really here the Mother will appear from a study of the passage which we transcribe:

> We shall affirm that the Mother of the created thing is *Understanding*, with whom God had intercourse (not in a mundane sense) and begat creation (ἔσπειρε γένεσιν). She it was who received the Divine seed, and by a perfect child-bearing (τελεσφόροις ὠδῖσι) brought forth the Only Son, the Beloved, the Perceptible One (αἰσθητόν), the World.[155]

And by one of the Choir of Heavenly Singers Wisdom is introduced as speaking of herself on this wise:

> The Lord *possessed* me the foremost (πρωτίστην) of His works, and before eternity He founded me. For of necessity all those things which came into being are younger than the One who is the Mother and the nurse of the Universe (τῶν ὅλων). Philo, *De Ebrietate* i. 362.[156]

Here we see Philo wrestling with a similar problem to that of the early Christian thinkers; he agrees with them in reference to the relation of Wisdom to the Divine Nature, and differs from them altogether with reference to the Divine Son: and, as has often been pointed out by recent theologians, the differences between Philo and St John (or St Paul) are more conspicuous than the agreements.

---

155. [*Ebr.* 30. AF]
156. [*Ebr.* 31. AF]

On the Ascription of Sapiential Titles to Christ

We have shown in what precedes that the recognition of Christ as the Wisdom of God led to the ascription to Him of all those titles and qualities attached to Wisdom in the Sapiential books, and that the primitive Christology was largely made up out of such ascriptions. Some of these titles were easily recognised from their employment in the Epistle to the Colossians or the Epistle to the Hebrews: but there were others that were not so clearly identified. Take for example, the statement that "Wisdom is the unsullied mirror of the Divine activity";[157] it was not quite easy to establish the equation between Christ and the Mirror of God in the New Testament; but at this point the *Odes of Solomon* came to our aid and we found the 13th Ode opening with the statement

> Behold! the Lord is our mirror![158]

In commenting upon this[159] I drew attention to the occurrence of the identification that we are trying to establish in the pseudo-Cyprianic tract *De montibus Sina et Sion.* I transcribe portions of the comment referred to.

> We may also in this connection refer to a remarkable passage, which is found in a tract falsely ascribed to Cyprian, and known as *De montibus Sina et Sion.*[160] We are reminded in this passage first that Christ is the Unspotted Mirror of the Father, as is said of Wisdom in the book called the Wisdom of Solomon (Sap. Sol. vii. 26). Hence the Father and the Son see one another by reflexion. The writer then continues as follows: "And even we who believe in Him see Christ in us as in a mirror, as He Himself instructs and advises us in the Epistle of His disciple John to the people: 'See me in yourselves, in the same way as any one of you sees himself in water or in a mirror'; and so He confirmed the saying of Solomon about Himself, that 'He is the unspotted mirror of the Father.'"

When I wrote this comment I had hardly noticed the underlying identification of Christ with Sophia, and certainly did not recognise that the "mirror" was a part of the identification. Now that the Sophia Christology has come to light, we can understand the language of the Ode and of the author of *De montibus* a great deal better.[161] So much concerning Christ as the Spotless Mirror. Now let us try a more difficult case. The same chapter of the Wisdom of Solomon describes Wisdom as a breath (*or* vapour) of the power of God: ἀτμὶς τῆς τοῦ

---

157. [Wis. 7.26. AF]
158. [*Odes* 13.1. AF]
159. [*Odes and Psalms of Solomon* (1909), p. 107. AF]
160. [*De montibus Sina et Sion* 13. AF]
161. Incidentally we may note that Ephrem had no right to alter the 13th Ode in the interests of Baptism and read it as "The water is our mirror."

5. The Origin of the Prologue to St John's Gospel

θεοῦ δυνάμεως.[162] The question arises naturally enough whether this term ἀτμίς has been taken up into Christology, and applied to Christ. It hardly seems likely at the first glance: if anything has been transferred from this expression it would be the simple "Power of God" and not anything so doubtful of meaning as "Vapour of the Power of God." Christ the *Power of God* and the Wisdom of God may very well have been derived from this; but where shall we find Christ described as ἀτμίς?

We do find it.

If we turn to a fragment of Theognostus of Alexandria (one of the heads of the famous catechetical school) preserved for us in the epistle of Athanasius *De Decretis Nicenae Synodi*[163] we shall find Theognostus speaking of the nature of the Son of God as follows:

> He was born of the substance of the Father, as the ἀπαύγασμα from the light, *and as the* ἀτμίς *from the water*; the ἀτμίς is not the water; nor is the ἀπαύγασμα the Sun itself, though not of another nature to it. Christ is an ἀπόρροια from the substance of the Father.

So here is ἀτμίς coupled with two other Sapiential terms from the same connection:

> ἀτμὶς γάρ ἐστιν τῆς τοῦ θεοῦ δυνάμεως,
> καὶ *ἀπόρροια* τῆς τοῦ παντοκράτορος δόξης εἰλικρινής·
> *ἀπαύγασμα* γάρ ἐστιν φωτὸς ἀιδίου (Wis. 7.25-26).

There can be no doubt that Theognostus is interpreting the seventh chapter of Wisdom and that he equates ἀτμίς with Christ, as well as ἀπαύγασμα and ἀπόρροια.[164]

The same interpretation occurs in Dionysius of Alexandria:

> φωτὸς μὲν οὖν ὄντος τοῦ Θεοῦ, ὁ Χριστός ἐστιν ἀπαύγασμα, πνεύματος δὲ ὄντος (πνεῦμα γάρ, φησίν, ὁ Θεός), ἀναλόγως πάλιν ὁ Χριστὸς ἀτμὶς λέγεται Ἀτμὶς γάρ, φησίν, ἐστὶ τῆς τοῦ Θεοῦ δυνάμεως. (Athan. *Ep. de sent. Dionys.* xv.:[165] in Routh, *Rell.* iii. 391.[166])

It is interesting in view of the proved use of Sapiential language by the author of the *Odes of Solomon* to which we adverted above, to note that Gressmann

---

162. [Wis. 7.25. AF]
163. Routh, *Rell.* iii., 411 [Routh, *Reliquiae sacrae*. AF].
164. [HCB pp. 52-53, "Here we see Philo …": *For* σοφία *in the Creed*
In the Creed of Gregory Thaumaturgus (Caspari: *Alte und Neue Quellen des Taufsymbol* p. 10) we have the following description of the Son: εἷς κύριος, μόνος ἐκ μόνου, θεὸς ἐκ θεοῦ, χαρακτὴρ καὶ εἰκὼν τῆς θεότητος, λόγος ἐνεργός, σοφία τῆς τῶν ὅλων συστάσεως περιεκτικὴ καὶ δύναμις τῆς ὅλης κτίσεως ποιητική, υἱὸς ἀληθινὸς ἀληθινοῦ πατρός, ἀόρατος ἀοράτου καὶ ἄφθαρτος ἀφθάρτου καὶ ἀθάνατος ἀθανάτου καὶ ἀΐδιος ἀϊδίου.]
165. [*Dion.* 15.5-6. AF]
166. [Routh, *Reliquiae sacrae*. AF]

thinks he has found the ἀτμίς also in the *Odes*. The immediately preceding Ode, the twelfth, is concerned with the powers and qualities of Christ as the Logos, and some of its expressions are almost certainly Sapiential. We have in v. 5 the following sequence:

> For the swiftness of the Word is inexpressible;
> And like its expression (!) is its swiftness and its sharpness.

The first line of this is a versification of Wis. 7.24 ("Wisdom is more mobile than any motion"); and in the next line Gressmann suggests that we read ܪܘܚܐ for ܪܘܩܐ, "and like an ἀτμίς is its swiftness, etc.," by a very slight change in the Syriac; this emendation makes parallelism with Wis. 7.25.

No doubt the proposed emendation will be estimated in the forthcoming facsimile edition of the *Odes*. At present we merely draw attention to it. There seems no doubt that Ode xii of the Solomonic collection is working over the seventh chapter of Wisdom and kindred matters. The "sharpness" of the Word, to which allusion is made above, is taken from Wis. 7.22, where the Spirit of Wisdom is described as

> σαφές, ἀπήμαντον, φιλάγαθον, ὀξύ.

The foregoing enquiry brings out clearly that ἀπαύγασμα and ἀτμίς are Christological terms, and attaches to them the ἀπόρροια. It is probable that this term also, which occupies such an important position in the *Odes of Solomon*, is originally Sapiential in origin, and is a term for the Sophia-Christ.

We noted in the earlier pages of this work that there was one passage in Hebrews which was usually explained by Philonean parallels, the passage which speaks of the Word as "quick and powerful and sharper than a sword with two edges, and penetrating to the division of soul and spirit" (Heb. 4.12). It has been suggested to me[167] that we should abandon the references to Philo, and derive the language directly from the *Book of Wisdom*. The comparison would have to be made between

Heb.	Wis.
ἐνεργής	ἐνεργητικόν (?)
τομώτερος	ὀξύ
διϊκνούμενος κτε.	διήκει καὶ χωρεῖ κτε.[168]

The matter certainly deserves a careful consideration, in view of the obvious loans from Wisdom in the first chapter of Hebrews. Our conclusion that all these Sapiential terms, the ἀπαύγασμα, the ἀπόρροια, the ἀτμίς, the εἰκών and the rest have been transferred to Christ in the earliest period of the crystallisation of Christian Theology may be confirmed by the following passage from

---

167. By my friend, C.A. Phillips.
168. [Wis. 7.22-24. AF]

5. The Origin of the Prologue to St John's Gospel

Origen *De Principiis*: we shall find that Origen tries to show that the Sapiential titles were to be recognised indeed as titles of Christ, but that the derivation was in the opposite-order; they were hers (Wisdom's) because they were His.

> Ait apostolus Paulus unigenitum filium imaginem esse Dei invisibilis, et primogenitum eum esse totius creaturae: ad Hebraeos vero scribens dicit de eo, quia sit splendor gloriae et figura expressa substantiae eius. Invenimus nihilominus etiam in Sapientia quae dicitur Salomonis, descriptionem de Dei sapientia hoc modo scriptam: vapor est enim, inquit, virtutis Dei, et ἀπόρροια gloriae omnipotentis purissima: ideo ergo in eam nihil commaculatum incidere potest. Splendor enim est lucis aeternae et speculum immaculatum operationis Dei, et imago bonitatis ejus. Sapientiam vero dicimus, sicut superius diximus, subsistentiam habentem non alibi nisi in eo qui est initium omnium; ex quo et nata est quaeque sapientia, quia ipse est qui solus natura filius, idcirco et unigenitus dicitur (*De Principiis* i. 2. 5).

So runs the passage in Ruffinus' translation, who would have done better in translating Μονογενής in the last sentence, to render it *unigenita*, for it is clearly a title of Wisdom. The translator was bewitched by the author to regard Christ as the original *Only-Begotten*. The argument is resumed as follows: after quoting Wis. 7.25 with its statement that Wisdom is the ἀτμίς of the Divine Power, etc.:

> Quae ergo hic de Deo definit, ex singulis quibusque certo quaedam inesse Sapientiae Dei designat: virtutem namque Dei nominat, et gloriam et lucem aeternam, et inoperationem et bonitatem. Ait autem Sapientiam vaporem esse non gloriae omnipotentis, neque aeternae lucis, nec inspirationis patris, nec bonitatis eius: neque enim conveniens erat alicui horum adscribi vaporem; sed eum omni proprietate ait virtutis Dei vaporem esse Sapientiam ...
>
> Secundum Apostolum vero dicentem, quia Christus Dei virtus est (1 Cor. 1.24); jam non solum vapor virtutis Dei, sed virtus ex virtute dicenda (*Ibid.* i. 2. 9).

This is a very interesting passage; it shows that when the Sapiential term ἀτμίς was applied to Christ, it was taken as we suggested above, in the sense of ἀτμὶς δυνάμεως. It is also evident that Origen is still arguing that Christ is Sophia because Sophia is Christ; He is derived from her because she is derived from Him: for that reason if Wisdom is Power, she might more correctly be spoken of as "Power of Power." If Origen had taken the argument a little further, he might have reduced it even more clearly *ad absurdum*: for since Sophia is the ἀρχή since "the Lord created me the ἀρχή, etc.";[169] and Christ is also the ἀρχή of the Creation of God, according to the Apostle, it follows that Wisdom is the Beginning because Christ is the Beginning, and

---

169. [Prov. 8.22. AF]

might, therefore, be described as ἀρχὴ ἐξ ἀρχῆς, a Beginning derived from a Beginning!

We have shown again in the course of the discussion that ἀτμίς is a true term for Christ, though it is veiled in the Pauline Epistles by the use of the term "Power of God";[170] and that ἀτμίς, ἀπόρροια and the rest are all terms that are involved in the primitive theology of the Church.

Here is a further piece of evidence that Jesus was familiarly known as the *Wisdom of God* in certain early Christian circles.

We have referred from time to time in this investigation to the *Dialogues between Christians and Jews*, of which the earliest example is the *Dialogue between Jason and Papiscus* by Ariston of Pella, which is lost, though no doubt it survives in a number of more or less modified descendants: amongst these one of the most interesting is the *Dialogue between Athanasius and Zacchaeus* published some years since by Mr. F. C. Conybeare.[171] In this *Dialogue* the points of the *Testimony Book* turn up to such an extent, that the *Dialogue* may be treated as a literary recast of the other anti-Judaic document. In the course of the argument Zacchaeus challenges the statement of Athanasius that Christ is spoken of in the prophets as the Λίθος. "Do you mean to say," he interjects, "that the *Wisdom of God* is a Stone?" Athanasius has to explain the sense in which these typical terms are used and to give him illustrations.

When Athanasius demonstrates from the Old Testament the Divine Nature of Jesus, there is again an interruption on the part of the other member of the debate. "Do you mean to say that the *Wisdom of God* is another God?"[172] It is very curious to remark that the equation between Christ and Wisdom is accepted by Zacchaeus. The whole passage is interesting, on account of its parallelism with certain clauses in the Nicene Creed.[173]

Ζακχαῖος εἶπε· θέλεις εἰπεῖν ὅτι ἄλλος θεός ἐστιν ἡ σοφία τοῦ θεοῦ; Ἀθανάσιος εἶπε· ἄλλος θεὸς ἐκτὸς τοῦ Θεοῦ οὐκ ἔστιν· ὥσπερ οὐδὲ ἄλλο φῶς τὸ ἀπαύγασμα τοῦ φωτός (Wis. 7.25)·[174] ἀλλὰ φῶς μὲν τὸ φῶς καὶ τὸ ἀπαύγασμα φῶς· ἀλλ' οὐχὶ ἄλλο καὶ ἄλλο φῶς· οὕτως καὶ ἡ Σοφία τοῦ Θεοῦ.[175]

The question as to the nature of the Divine Sophia is raised by Zacchaeus, and answered in terms of the Wisdom of Solomon; that is very significant; for though the final conclusion is that Christ is φῶς ἐκ φωτός as in the Nicene

---

170. [1 Cor. 1.24. AF]
171. [Frederick C. Conybeare (ed.), *The Dialogue of Athanasius and Zaccheus and of Timothy and Aquila* (Anecdota Oxoniensia; Oxford: Clarendon Press, 1898). AF]
172. [This and the previous quotation are from *Dial. Ath.* 113. AF]
173. [HCC: Justin. *Dial* 11 [11.1. AF] οὔτε ἔσται ποτὲ ἄλλος θεός, ὦ Τρύφων, οὔτε ἦν ἀπ' αἰῶνος ... πλὴν τοῦ ποιήσαντος καὶ διατάξαντος τόδε τὸ πᾶν.]
174. [Wis. 7.26. AF]
175. [*Dial. Ath.* 9. AF]

formula, He is also again seen to be Sophia, for He is the ἀπαύγασμα which Wisdom is declared to be.

If we could find out how much of this dialogue is derived from the previous *Jason and Papiscus* we should be able to tell whether the foregoing identifications and their Nicene consequences were trans-Jordanic in their ultimate origin; for the first of the Dialogues in question comes from Pella.

Did Jesus Call Himself Sophia?

As soon as we have decided that behind the Logos-doctrine there lies a more Jewish and less metaphysical Sophia-doctrine, and that the early Christian preaching about Jesus proclaimed Him as the Wisdom of God, we cannot avoid the enquiry whether Jesus identified Himself with the Wisdom of God and announced Himself as such.

The first impulse of response to such an enquiry is to negative the suggestion on the ground (*a*) that it is inherently improbable, (*b*) that there is no evidence in support of such an idea either on the Biblical or on the Patristic side. Both of these objections, however, are too *à priori*. We do not really know without careful enquiry what is likely to have occurred, nor can we tell superficially what is implied in the Biblical and Patristic evidence. We might equally have affirmed that there was no Biblical or Patristic evidence for the substitution of Logos in the place of Sophia, and that it was inherently unlikely that Jesus had been the subject of such a change of title.[176]

Whatever be our views with regard to the nature of the personality of the Lord Jesus, we cannot altogether de-orientalize Him; nor, it might be added, ought we to hyper-philosophize Him. In quite recent times we have had the phenomenon before us of the rise of a new Oriental religion and in the Bâb-movement have been able to detect remarkable analogies to the early Christian history. Probably nothing surprised us more, at the first presentation of the cult to our notice, than the amazing titles given to the leaders of the movement; who would have thought that the end of the nineteenth century could have produced a teacher whose name is *Ṣubḥ-i-ezel* or *Dawn-of-Eternity*? And as to the adoption of this title by the person himself to whom it was attached, the following note by Professor Browne in his *Episode of the Bâb* (p. 95)[177] may be of interest:

---

176. [HCC p. 57, "that the equation ...": [1] *Martyrium St Pauli et Julianae* PG. 115. Column. 585 [*Martyrium Sancti Pauli et Julianae* 22 (PG 115.585C). AF] "Ipse igitur Deus, Verbum Dei ac Patris Filius, ante saecula omnia est sapientia ipsius, et potentia et dextera."]

177. [Edward G. Browne, *Traveller's Narrative Written to Illustrate the Episode of the Báb: Edited in the Original Persian, and Translated into English* (2 vols.; Cambridge: Cambridge University Press, 1891). AF]

> The name alluded to is of course that of *Ezel* (the Eternal) bestowed on Mirza Yaḥya by the Bâb. Gobineau calls him *Ḥazrat-i-Ezel* (L'Altesse Eternelle), but his correct designation, that which he himself adopts, and that whereby he is everywhere known, is *Ṣubḥ-i-Ezel* (the Morning of Eternity).[178]

Reasoning from analogy, we may fairly argue that *à priori* objections ought not to settle the question whether Jesus was or was not the *Wisdom of God*: if He was such, there is nothing to prohibit Him from announcing Himself as such; and if, on the other hand, He was merely a teacher who provoked admiring appellations from His followers, as in the case of the leaders of the Bâb movement, or who suggested such appellations to His admiring followers, still there is no *à priori* objection to such a phenomenon amongst the early Christian teachers and leaders. We can, therefore, approach the question whether Jesus called Himself the *Wisdom of God* without the hindrance of antecedent improbability.

One thing seems quite clear: *Jesus did not announce Himself as the Word of God.* That title came from His followers and not from the first generation of them: but since we have shown reason to believe that *Word of God* is a substitute for *Wisdom of God*, it is not unlikely that this latter title, admitted to be antecedent to the second generation of discipleship, may go back to Jesus Himself, for it certainly belongs to the first generation of His followers; and therefore either they gave it to Him or He gave it to Himself. The two things are, in any case, not very far apart chronologically.

Another way in which we approach the subject, without wandering off into comparative religion, is to notice how readily we ourselves recover the title when we are speaking in an elevated strain of His Being and Perfections: for example, amongst modern religious writers, one of the illuminated of the last generation was certainly T. T. Lynch, both as Preacher and Poet; he says somewhere of Jesus:

> He is the new and ancient Word,
> All Wisdom man hath ever heard
> Hath been both His and He:
> He is the very life of truth.
> In Him it hath eternal youth
> And constant victory.

Here the writer has taken his flight from St Augustine's "Beauty, Ancient and yet new,"[179] to the Logos, who is also the Eternal Wisdom and the Eternal Truth.[180] And Augustine might be quoted in the very same strain; for he also

---

178. [HCF: (1) An even better illustration might be taken from the other leader of the Babi movement, whose name is *Beha Ullah* or *Splendour of God*.]

179. [*Conf.* 10.27.38. AF]

180. It is noteworthy that the same identification occurs in a letter of George Fox to the daughter of Oliver Cromwell: "Then thou wilt feel the power of God, which will bring

5. The Origin of the Prologue to St John's Gospel

accepted Wisdom as an Eternal Divine Hypostasis. We may recall that great passage from the conversation at Ostia:

> We came to our own minds and passed beyond them, that we might arrive at that region of never-failing plenty, where thou feedest Israel for ever with the food of truth, and where Life is the Wisdom by whom all these things were made, both what have been and what shall be, and she herself is not made, but is as she hath been, and so shall be for ever; yea, rather, to have been and hereafter to be are not in her, but only to be, seeing she is eternal.[181]

Evidently St Augustine would have found no difficulty in a statement that "Wisdom was with God and that Wisdom was God": and it was as easy for him as it is possible for us, to recover the lost title "Wisdom of God" for Jesus.

Such a title is almost involved in "the Truth and the Life,"[182] which Jesus in the Fourth Gospel affirms Himself to be: but we naturally desire more direct evidence and if possible Synoptic evidence as to the use of the term by Jesus of Himself. The passages which Tatian harmonised from Matthew and Luke[183] into the form "therefore, behold! I, the Wisdom of God, send unto you prophets and wise men and scribes," would be decisive if we could be sure that Tatian had recovered the original meaning or given the original sense to the passage of Q which Matthew and Luke are quoting. It is not an easy point to settle. It is, however, much more likely that Jesus spoke in the person of the Divine Wisdom, than that the passage is a reference to Scripture either extant or non-extant; and I therefore incline to believe that Tatian has given the sense of the passage. It may be asked why we do not quote the passage in which Jesus declares Himself to be greater, in respect to Wisdom, than Solomon. The answer is that whatever indication may be taken out of these words from Q is negatived by the accompanying statement that Jesus is greater than Jonah. If the queen of the south who came to hear the Wisdom of Solomon (Matt. 12.42, Luke 11.31) had stood in a text by herself, without the addition of Jonah and the Ninevites, we might have argued that the Wisdom of Jesus, which He affirmed to be superior to that of Solomon, was the Wisdom of God, and so have looked towards the missing formula that we are in search of. It is not safe to lean upon such uncertain evidence.

That this Wisdom of Jesus was one of the things that most impressed His contemporaries is evident from the Synoptic tradition,

---

nature into its course, and give thee to see the glory of the first body. There the Wisdom of God will be received, which is Christ, by which all things were made and created, and thou wilt thereby be preserved and ordered to God's glory."

So also C. Wesley in a hymn which is headed Prov. 3.13, 18: "Wisdom and Christ and Heaven are one".

181. [*Conf.* 9.10.24. AF]
182. [John 14.6. AF]
183. [Matt. 23.34 and Luke 11.49. AF]

Whence hath this man this Wisdom? (Matt. 13.54, Mark 6.2).

According to Luke He was from His earliest years filled with Wisdom and advancing in the same: but this does not necessarily involve the doctrine that Sophia has descended to dwell amongst us (Luke 2.40, 52).

St Paul, it should be observed, not only identifies Jesus with the Wisdom and Power of God, but also affirms Him to be the repository of *"all the treasures of Wisdom and Knowledge"* (Col. 2.3).

The tradition of His Wisdom is conserved for us in a curious Syriac fragment referred to Mara, the son of Serapion, where we are asked "what advantage the Jews derived from the death of *their wise king*, seeing from that time their kingdom was taken away?" (Cureton, *Spicilegium*, p. 72).[184]

No doubt it was by His Wisdom that Jesus impressed His own and succeeding generations.

This, however, is insufficient evidence for our purpose. Another direction suggests itself, by which we can infer that Jesus identified Himself with the Sophia of the Old Testament. It has been from time to time affirmed that the explanation of many of His sayings is to be found in parallel utterances in the Sapiential books; as for instance, that the verses in Matt. 11.28-30 are to be traced back to Sirach 24.19, where Sophia says,

> *Come, unto me all ye* that desire me,
> Fill yourselves with my fruits;
> For my memorial is sweeter than honey,
> My inheritance than the honey-comb,

with Sirach 51.26,

> *Put your neck under her yoke* etc.

Similarly it is suggested that the Words of Jesus that

> He that cometh to me shall never hunger,
> He that believeth on me shall never thirst (John 6.35)

are an antithesis to the language of Sophia in Sirach 24.21,

> They that eat me shall hunger again,
> They that drink shall thirst again.

If we could be sure that we had traced these sayings of Jesus to their proximate original, it would be easy to infer that He had borrowed the language of Sophia and was speaking in her person. This would very nearly settle the question that we are investigating. Jesus would be Sophia because His invitations would be those of Sophia.

---

184. [William Cureton (ed.), *Spicilegium syriacum: Containing Remains of Bardesan, Meliton, Ambrose and Mara Bar Serapion* (London: F. & J. Rivington, 1855). AF]

5. The Origin of the Prologue to St John's Gospel

In this direction it is possible that further illumination may be forthcoming. Meanwhile we have got far enough in the enquiry to see how completely off the mark was Dr Plummer in his commentary on Luke in the passages under discussion.[185] He tells us:

> Nowhere does he style himself "The Wisdom of God," nor does any evangelist give him this title, nor does θεοῦ σοφίαν or σοφία ἀπὸ θεοῦ (1 Cor. i. 24, 30) warrant us in asserting that this was a common designation among the first Christians so that tradition might have substituted this name for ἐγώ used by Jesus ... Rather it is of the Divine Providence (Prov. viii. 22-31) sending Prophets to the Jewish Church and Apostles to the Christian Church, that Jesus here speaks, "God in his wisdom said."

In view of the preceding investigations which we have made into the origin of the Logos-Doctrine, it appears that we might contradict almost every one of the statements here made: or at least we might say, in imitation of the language of Ignatius, πρόκειται, "that is the very point at issue": and if it is conceded that it was Wisdom of the eighth chapter of Proverbs that is responsible for sending prophets and Apostles, we have given abundant reason for believing that Jesus was, by the first generation of His followers, identified with this very Wisdom. In that case, ἐγώ and Σοφία are interchangeable, at least in the mind of His adherents, and perhaps in His own.

St John and the Divine Wisdom

It has been shown in many ways that the identification of Christ with the Wisdom of God is fundamental in the primitive collection of Testimonies employed in the propaganda of the first Christian teachers. It was the first article of the Christian theology, so far as that theology is involved in the archetype of the collection of Testimonies made by Cyprian, and it can be shown to be equally involved in a variety of Christian writings. In a previous chapter we have pointed out that the Cyprianic chapter that "Christ is the hand and arm of God" has behind it the doctrine that "Sophia is the hand of God." There can be no doubt that in the primitive *Testimony Book* Christ was equated with *Sophia*.

If, then, we can show that the Fourth Gospel betrays a direct dependence upon the Apostolic collection of Testimonies, we shall then be entitled to affirm that the writer was acquainted with the Sophia-Christ equation and that he made his Logos-Christ equation in view of the previous identification, which he must consequently have modified. This is what we have to prove. It

---

185. [Alfred Plummer, *A Critical and Exegetical Commentary on the Gospel according to S. Luke* (ICC; Edinburgh: T. & T. Clark, 1896). In the following quotation Rendel Harris has left out the words "of Christ" after "designation." AF]

is *à priori* probable that the case was as we suggest, for if the *Testimony Book* antedates the Pauline Epistles, it antedates the Fourth Gospel; and as it was certainly an apostolic document, it would not be surprising for the author of the Fourth Gospel to be acquainted with it.

An actual proof that this was the case may be obtained by studying the sequence and argument of John 12.37-40. The writer has been recording the increasing alienation between Jesus and the Jews, until he comes to the point where Jesus is obliged to go into hiding to escape the hostility of the unbelieving Jews. At this point he stops his narration in order to point out, that it had been predicted that they would not believe in Him, for had it not been written by Isaiah as follows:

> Who hath believed our report,
> And to whom hath the arm of the Lord been revealed? (Isa. 53.1).

And the Jewish unbelief was inevitable, for had not Isaiah also said,

> He hath blinded their eyes (Isa. 6.9-10)?

So the question arises naturally, whether these anti-Judaic verses belong to a primitive collection of *Testimonia adversus Judaeos*.

In order to answer this question we turn in the first instance to Cyprian.

He quotes Isa. 53.1 twice over in the *Testimonia*, once to prove that *Christ is the arm of the Lord* ("to whom is the arm of the Lord revealed?"),[186] and once to prove that *Christ is lowly in His first advent*,[187] where Cyprian goes on to prove that Jesus is the root out of a dry ground, etc. In neither of these passages, however, is there an immediate reference to the unbelief of the Jews. We should have expected the quotation to occur in the first book of the *Testimonia* under some such heading as that

> it had been foretold that they would not know the Lord nor understand.

And we think it must actually have stood there, for in that very section stands the second Johannine reference, as follows:

> Vade et dic populo isto: aure audietis et non intellegetis et uidentes uidebitis et non uidebitis. incrassauit enim cor populi eius, et auribus grauiter audierunt, et oculos suos concluserunt, ne forte uideant oculis et auribus audiant et corde intellegant et curem illos (Cyp. *Test*. i. 3).

Both of the Johannine quotations are, then, in the *Testimony Book* according to Cyprian, and one of them is in its right place. We may, therefore, say that John 12.38-40 has all the appearance of being taken from a collection of

---

186. [*Test*. 2.4. AF]
187. [*Test*. 2.13. AF]

5. The Origin of the Prologue to St John's Gospel 181

Testimonies. Very good! but then we are face to face with the fact that the extract given above from Cyprian does not agree with

τετύφλωκεν αὐτῶν τοὺς ὀφθαλμοὺς,
καὶ ἐπώρωσεν αὐτῶν τὴν καρδίαν,
ἵνα μὴ ἴδωσιν τοῖς ὀφθαλμοῖς,
καὶ νοήσωσιν τῇ καρδίᾳ καὶ στραφῶσιν,
καὶ ἰάσομαι αὐτούς·

while it does agree almost exactly with the LXX and with the Greek of Matt. 13.14-15 and of the Acts 28.26-27, in both of which cases in the N.T. the passage is employed in an anti-Judaic sense.

Nor is this variation of John from the LXX the only thing to be noted in the history of this famous quotation. It occurs in Justin Martyr, to whom we must now turn. In two strongly anti-Judaic passages in his *Dialogue with Trypho* Justin tells his Jewish audience as follows:

(a) *Dial*. ch. 12[188] τὰ ὦτα ὑμῶν πέφρακται,
οἱ ὀφθαλμοὶ ὑμῶν πεπήρωνται,
καὶ πεπάχυνται ἡ καρδία.

(b) *Dial*. ch. 33[189] τὰ δὲ ὦτα ὑμῶν πέφρακται,
καὶ αἱ καρδίαι πεπήρωνται.

The two passages are fragments of the same tradition, the second of the two having got into confusion through dropping a clause.

We have now three forms of the passage from Isaiah before us, one of which is the plain Septuagint text; the other two may be taken, following Papias' suggestion, as independent modifications of a primitive Aramaic. If this be the correct explanation, we must be right in saying that John knew and used the *Book of Testimonies*; and he could hardly have done this without knowing its leading proposition that Jesus is the Wisdom of God.[190]

---

188. [*Dial*. 12.2. AF]
189. [*Dial*. 33.1. AF]
190. There is still something queer about the two Justinian forms (a) and (b). If we read πεπώρωνται in (b) we are much nearer to the Johannine form. But then what becomes of form (a)? Shall we read

τὰ ὦτα ὑμῶν πέφρακται,
οἱ ὀφθαλμοὶ ὑμῶν πεπήρωνται,
καὶ πεπώρωται ἡ καρδία,

and treat πεπάχυνται as introduced from the LXX?
The variations in the text of Isaiah as quoted are a sufficient evidence of the wide diffusion of the *Testimony*.
On the other hand, the evidence of the Oxyrhynchus *Fragments of Sayings of Jesus* ("They are blind in their heart") is in favour of attaching πεπήρωται to καρδία [Papyrus Oxyrhychus 1.11-21. AF.

The point reached by our investigation appears to mark an advance in the following sense. Two fresh facts (hitherto unnoticed or almost unobserved) have come to light: first that the tradition of the *Testimony Book* is earlier than the New Testament, antedates the Gospels, is Apostolic in origin, and the common property of all schools of Christian thought. Second, in accordance with the tradition of the *Testimony Book*, as well as from several other lines of enquiry, it is clear that the first and foremost article of Christian belief is that *Jesus is the Wisdom of God*, personified, incarnate, and equated with every form of personification of Wisdom that could be derived from or suggested by the Scriptures of the Old Testament. Upon the recognition and right evaluation of these two facts our reconstruction of the theology of the first age of the Church will depend. Here is a simple instance, to conclude with, to show the re-action of the argument upon the interpretation of the Epistles.

The recognition of the Sapiential origin of the appellation of Christ in the first chapter of Colossians will help us to the understanding of a passage in Romans, where we are told that believers are fore-ordained to a conformity to the image (εἰκών) of the Son of God, so that He may be the First-born (πρωτότοκος) among many brethren.[191] Here the apparatus of the reader of the New Testament naturally suggests for the "First-born," a reference to Colossians: but since in Colossians 1.15-16, we have the sequence:

Image (εἰκών) of the invisible God;
First-born (πρωτότοκος) of all creation;

it is natural to suggest that in Romans 1.29[192] we have a similar transition. That is to say, we must put a comma after εἰκόνος and read τοῦ υἱοῦ αὐτοῦ in apposition to it:

that we may be conformed to *the Image*,
    i.e. to His Son,
that the Son may be *the First-born*,
    i.e. among many brethren.[193]

---

191. [Rom. 8.29. AF]
192. [Rom. 8.29. AF]
193. [HCB: It is interesting to note that the Geneva translators of the Bible annotated on their margin the equation between Sophia and Christ, and made the connection with the Prologue to John: e.g. in Prov. viii.

v. 22 "He declareth hereby the divinitie and eternitie of this wisdome, which he magnifieth and prayseth through this booke: meaning thereby the eternall Sonne of God Iesus Christ our Saviour, whom S. Iohn calleth the Word which was in the beginning."

v. 27 "He declareth the eternitie of the Sonne of God, which is meant by this word Wisedome, who was before all time, and ever present with the Father."

v. 30. "Some reade a chiefe worke: signifying that the Wisedome, even Christ Iesus was equall with God his Father, and created, preserveth, and still worketh with him, as Ioh. 5.17."

5. *The Origin of the Prologue to St John's Gospel* 183

Note. Origen and the Sapiential Christ

The doctrine that Christ is the ἀπόρροια of God appears again in Origen in the following form: *Comm. in ep. ad Romanos*.[194]

> vii. 13. Unus autem uterque est Deus, quia non est aliud Filio divinitatis initium quam Pater; sed ipsius unius Paterni fontis (sicut Sapientia dicit) purissima est manatio Filius. Est ergo Christus *Deus super omnia.* Quae omnia? Illa sine dubio quae et paulo ante diximus, Eph. 1.21. Qui autem super omnia est, super se neminem habet. Non enim post Patrem est ipse, sed de Patre. Hoc idem autem Sapientia Dei etiam de Spiritu Sancto intelligi dedit, ubi dicit: Spiritus Domini, etc. (Wis. 1.7).

Here it is clear that Origen is finding Christ in the Wisdom of Solomon, and that one of his identifications is that Christ is the ἀπόρροια or *manatio*. This identification is important for its theological value and for its literary interest. The Fathers commonly take it to mean an outflow of light from a source of light, which leads us to the Nicene formula; but in the literature of the early Church it appears as an irresistible flow of water, as in the sixth Ode of Solomon; where, by the way, the Gnostic author of the *Pistis Sophia* changes the explanation to an emanation of light.[195]

---

v. 31. "By earth he meaneth man, which is the worke of God in whom wisedome tooke pleasure: in so much as for man's sake the Divine Wisdome tooke man's nature and dwelt among us, and filled us with unspeakable treasures, and this is that solace and pastime whereof is here spoken."]

194. [*Comm. Rom.* AF]

195. [HCC [this material is gathered together and is not attached to any page]: [1] D.B. Macdonald in the *Moslem World* (Jan. 1916), vol. VI. p. 26 "There remain two usages, the full meaning of which lay in the future. In Psalm ii,7 Jehovah says to a king on his enthroning [unreadable word], "Thou art my son; this day have I begotten thee". The "begetting" was the enthroning as anointed king over the people of Israel, and so its outlook was to the final anointed one, the King Messiah. In this thought the verse is quoted twice in the Epistle to the Hebrews (i.5 and v.5). The second is in Proverbs viii.24,25. There we have personified as the teacher of men the primeval Wisdom by which Jehovah in the beginning created the word, a Wisdom which was not created but born, and that before all things. "When there were no depths I was brought forth ... before the hills was I brought forth." This is the Logos (reason) that was in the beginning with God; "all things were made through him". There is kinship more than merely verbal or of coincidence between the passage in Proverbs and the Prologue to John's Gospel. And so the King Messiah and the eternal creative Word are the last expression of the realities dimly felt by the ancient Semites—in truth, mysteries hid from the foundation of the world.

[2] Orig. *c. Cels.* V.40 [*Cels.* 5.39. AF] shows the reason for the transition from σοφία to λόγος. "We must not, on account of their feminine name and nature, regard wisdom and righteousness as females: for these things are in our view the Son of God, as His genuine

disciple has shown, when he said of Him, "Who of God is made to us wisdom and righteousness ec".

[3] For God as Wisdom, Love and Power see Irenaeus. adv. h. lib. V.17.1 (p. 313) [*Haer.* in Massuet, *Sancti Irenaei.* AF]: ἔστι δὲ οὗτος ὁ δημιουργός, ὁ κατὰ μὲν τὴν ἀγάπην πατήρ, κατὰ δὲ τὴν δύναμιν κύριος, κατὰ δὲ τὴν σοφίαν ποιήτης καὶ πλάστης ἡμῶν.

[4] *Golden Legend* (Caxton [Jacobus de Voragine, *Legenda aurea* (trans. William Caxton; 1483). AF])
Life of S. Demetrius.

> "He ever endoctrined and taught the others how the divine Sapience was descended in the earth, who by his own blood had quickened or raised from death the man, which by his sin was put to death."

? not in the *Legenda Aurea* of de Voragine.

[5] *Verbum = Sophia*
The equivalence of *Word* and *Wisdom* was so well known in the time of Irenaeus that the one is used for the other without a comment. In c. II. lib. V.c.24 (Mass 321 [*Haer.* 5.24.1. Massuet, *Sancti Irenaei.* AF]) we have the following argument: "Non enim ipse [sc. diabolus] determinavit hujus saeculi regna, sed Deus: *Regis enim cor in manu Dei.* Et per Salomonem autem ait Verbum: Per me reges regnant et potentes tenent justitiam." (Prov 8[15]). Here we have two equivalences: (i). Verbum and Deus; (ii). Verbum and Sophia; for it is God that ordains kings and Sophia that speaks of the same ordination in Proverbs.

[6] [Faded text. AF]

[7] Origen, *Frag: in Ep: ad Hebraeos:* [*Fr. Heb.* (PG 14.1307D-1308D. AF]:

> Cum autem discutitur hoc quod dictum est de Filio Dei, quod sit splendor gloriae, necessaris videtur simul disserendum et illud quod dictum est, non solum quod splendor est lucis aeternae, sed et quod huic simile in Sapientia Salomonis refertur, in qua seipsam Sapientia describit dicens: *Vapor enim est virtutis Dei, et aporrhaea gloriae Omnipotentis purissima* (Sap 7.[25]).
>
> (Et post aliquanta)
>
> Oportet autem scire nos quia per ineffabilia quaedam, et secreta, ac recondita quemdam modum, sibi faciens Scriptura sancta conatur hominibus indicare, et intellectum suggerere subtilem. Vaporis enim nomen inducens hoc ideo de rebus corporalibus assumpsit, ut vel ex parte aliqua intelligere possimus quomodo Christus qui est Sapientia, secundum similitudinem ejus vaporis qui de substantia aliqua corporea procedit, sic etiam ipse ut quidam vapor exoritur de virtute ipsius Dei: sic et Sapientia ex eo procedens ex ipsa Dei substantia generatur. Sic nihilominus et secundum similitudinem corporalis Aporrhaeae, est dicitur aporrhaea gloriae Omnipotentis pura quaedam et sincera. Quae utraeque similitudines manifestissime ostendunt communionem substantiae esse Filio cum Patre. Aporrhaea enim ὁμοούσιος videtur, id est, unius substantiae cum illo corpore ex quo est vel aporrhaea, vel vapor. [A few unreadable words follow separated from the above text by a long line. AF]

Chapter 6

THE FIRST TATIAN READING IN THE GREEK NEW TESTAMENT

It is thirty-five years since I published in the *Journal of Biblical Literature and Exegesis*[1] an account of a MS of the New Testament, containing a reading of which I could find no trace anywhere else, but which later discoveries show to have stood in the text of Tatian the Harmonist, in the latter part of the second century. As the matter is an important one and yet seems to have been overlooked, I am going to make a brief summary of the evidence which I then brought forward and of the subsequent literature bearing upon the supposed extract from the Tatian Harmony.

The MS to which I refer was originally described by Scrivener as Cod. Ev. 561, and by me with the longer title of Codex Algerinae Peckover, after the owner of the MS, who had derived it by inheritance from her brother, Mr. Jonathan Peckover, of Wisbech. He, on his part, obtained it by purchase from Quaritch, the London bookseller. By the grace of the owner, it has now passed into my own possession, so that I have had the opportunity of examining it *de novo*, and of verifying or correcting my former impressions. It will always be associated with Miss Peckover's name, whatever its ultimate destiny may be in the matter of ownership.[2]

When I first examined the MS I assigned it to the eleventh century; the date was challenged by Gregory in his *Prolegomena to Tischendorf*.[3] He said that it is of the twelfth or even the thirteenth. On looking at my first statement in the *Journal*, I see that I described its date in the following terms:— "The handwriting may be referred to the eleventh century, *or a little later*."

It appears, therefore, that Dr Gregory's correction was already latent in my first description; I do not think that the MS should be regarded as a thirteenth-century product. My first description is, I think, nearly accurate. On referring to my first notes, I see that I had said twelfth or thirteenth century, and added a

---

1. For December, 1886, pp. 79-89 ["Cod. Ev. 561.–Codex Algerinae Peckover," *Journal of the Society of Biblical Literature and Exegesis* 6 (1886), pp. 79-89. AF]. But I see that I had also described it in the Philadelphia *Sunday School Times* for Nov. 6, 1886.
2. [The manuscript is now kept at the University of Birmingham. AF]
3. [Caspar R. Gregory, *Prolegomena* (vol. 3 of Tischendorf, *Novum Testamentum*). AF]

query. Gregory also noted that the MS, according to a suggestion of Quaritch, had formerly been at Athens; but this observation is quite useless, as I showed from internal evidence on the margins that it was a Constantinople MS, probably in use at an early date in St Sophia. Gregory saw the MS in 1883. I think this gives him the priority in the description of the MS for my first notes are dated in 1884. But both of us had been anticipated by Dean Burgon in 1882. It was he who in a letter to Scrivener (the fifth of a series published in the *Guardian* in 1882) announced the existence and location of the MS and gave it a number amongst the catalogued MSS of the New Testament. The only thing that Burgon says about the text of the MS is that "the codex contains the troubling of the pool, but is without the *pericope*" (sc. *de adultera*).[4]

So it appears that neither Burgon nor Gregory knew of the unique reading which the MS contains, or they would certainly have drawn attention to it. It is surprising that Gregory, who refers to my article on the MS in the *American Journal*, does not allude to the reading, but only to the possible connection of the MS with what is known as the Ferrar group.

Before leaving this question (a very stupid one) of the order in which scholars have examined Miss Peckover's MS, I may note that there seems to be a mistake in another direction in Kenyon's *Handbook to New Testament Criticism*,[5] where I am credited with having examined the MS as far back as 1877; his statement is as follows:—

> Evan. 561 [Greg. 713]: eleventh to twelfth century; in the possession of Miss A. Peckover, of Wisbech. Identified in 1877 by Mr. Rendel Harris as akin to the Ferrar Group; but in his recent study of the group he makes no mention of it.

I am afraid this is an impossible date; I do not think that I had begun my studies in the New Testament text by that year; and certainly I could not at that time have known anything of Ferrar and his group of texts. However, I collated the text twice as soon as I found out that it contained a jewel of the first water; first, by comparison with the received text, and next, in order to see if it really was a Ferrar MS with the text of that group as edited by Ferrar and Abbott.[6]

The next stage in the study of the text was, I suppose, when a young German scholar, named Pott, came to England to investigate under Prof. v. Soden's scheme for a new edition of the text of the Greek New Testament.[7]

---

4. [John 5.4 and 7.53-8.11. AF]

5. [Frederic G. Kenyon, *Handbook to the Textual Criticism of the New Testament* (London: MacMillan, 1901). AF]

6. [William H. Ferrar, *A Collation of Four Important Manuscripts of the Gospels: With a View to Prove their Common Origin and to Restore the Text of their Archetype* (ed. Thomas K. Abbott; Dublin: Hodges, Foster, and Figgis; London: MacMillan, 1877). AF]

7. [Hermann von Soden (ed.), *Die Schriften des Neuen Testaments in ihrer ältesten*

6. *The First Tatian Reading in the Greek New Testament* 187

Prof. v. Soden's ambassador was very glad to have the loan of one of my collations, and on his return to Germany he made a careful study of the text for his doctor's dissertation,[8] with the object of showing that where the MS diverged from the common tradition, it was under Syriac influence, and might be compared with the Syriac text as published by Cureton.[9] Prof. v. Soden in his textual apparatus added the Tatian reading to his notes; but, although he was bent on proving that most of the variation in the text of the New Testament was due to Tatian, he does not seem to have given any special attention to the reading; of course, as in other cases, he added to our existing confusion by giving the MS a new name; it was now denoted by the sign ε 351.

Returning now to the precious MS itself and its unique reading it will be interesting to recall briefly the steps by which we arrived at the conclusion that we had discovered a genuine Tatianism, the first that had really been recognisable in Greek. The passage in Matthew 17 runs as follows:—

> 25. Of whom do the kings of the earth take custom or tribute? Of their own children or of the aliens?
> 26. Peter saith to him: Of the aliens. Jesus said to him: *Then are the children free? Simon said: Yea. Jesus saith: Then do thou also give, as being an alien to them.*
> 27. But that we do not offend them, go to the sea and cast a hook, etc.

The peculiar features of the Greek text are (i) the turning of the remark of our Lord about the freedom of the children into a question, and (ii) the necessary addition of Peter's reply, accompanied by Christ's rejoinder, in the words:—

> ἄραγε ἐλεύθεροί εἰσιν οἱ υἱοί; ἔφη Σίμων· ναί. λέγει ὁ Ἰησοῦς. δὸς οὖν καὶ σύ, ὡς ἀλλότριος αὐτῶν.

All that I was able to say, at the first publication of this passage was, that there were some signs of agreement with the Curetonian Syriac (e.g., in the introduction of the name *Simon* for Peter, etc.); but I contented myself with the observation that "the passage, if a gloss, is one of the most remarkable I have ever seen; and it deserves very careful consideration." How then does one attach the name of Tatian to the words which here appear under the suspicion of a gloss? It is evident that I was not familiar in 1886 with the Armenian commentary of Ephrem upon the text of Tatian, to which I shall refer presently as containing the famous reading; and the Arabic text of the *Harmony of Tatian* did not appear until the year 1888, when it was brought

---

erreichbaren Textgestalt: Hergestellt auf Grund ihrer Textgeschichte (3 vols.; Berlin: Glaue, 1902–1913). AF]

8. [August Pott, *Der griechisch-syrische Text des Matthäus: E 351 im Verhältnis zu Tatian ssc Ferrar* (Leipzig: Teubner, 1912). AF]

9. [William Cureton, *Remains of a Very Ancient Recension of the Gospels in Syriac Hitherto Unknown in Europe* (London: John Murray, 1858). AF]

out by Ciasca, with a Latin translation, in honour of the Pope's Jubilee.[10] When, however, I examined the Arabic text in question, I found the desiderated gloss; and two years later I published a preliminary dissertation upon the Tatian Harmony (an early piece of work, long since out of print)[11] in which I drew attention to the existence of the passage answering to our Greek text as follows:—"Matthew 17.25,[12] 'Simon saith to him: From aliens. Jesus said to him: Then the children are free. *Simon saith to him, Yea. Jesus said to him: Then do thou also give to them as being an alien.* But lest they should be offended, go to the sea, and cast a hook, and, having opened the mouth of the first fish that comes up, thou shalt find a stater."

On comparing this Arabic text with that of the Peckover MS it was clear that they had a common origin. Accordingly I said,[13] "That which is eccentric in the modern Harmony must certainly be taken from the primitive Harmony, the Arabic from the early Syriac: that which is eccentric in the Greek looks as if it had a Syriac origin; the abrupt change from Peter to Simon is sufficient to suggest this"; and I drew the conclusion, with proper caution and due modesty, that "it is within the bounds of possibility that the Peckover Codex has been affected by the text of a Diatessaron, possibly a Syriac Diatessaron." No one will think that an over-statement. But now we come to the verification furnished by Ephrem's *Commentary on the Diatessaron*, in which successive passages from the *Harmony* were transcribed in their Syriac text, and accompanied by a Syriac commentary. To get at this Syriac text and comments we have to work from an Armenian translation; the editor does the whole for us into Latin (as being the working language of scholars), and indicates by spaced type which is the text and which is commentary.[14] We shall find our singular reading already in print, but it has been mistaken for commentary and consequently not spaced out as belonging to the text. Here is the whole passage done into English.[15] We shall see the importance of it in a little while:—

> And that it saith, *That thou set not a stumblingblock before them*, that is, that thou appear not vile unto them, since thou makest manifest that they wish to contrive occasions of contention; *Go thou to the sea and cast there the net*; because they thought me a stranger, the sea shall teach them that I am not only a priest but also a king: so then go, *give thou also as one of the strangers.*

---

10. [Agostino Ciasca (ed.), *Tatiani evangeliorum harmoniae arabice* (Rome: Ex Typographia Polyglotta, 1888). AF]

11. [*The Diatessaron of Tatian: A Preliminary Study* (London: Clay, 1890). AF]

12. [Matt. 17.26. AF]

13. *Diatessaron*, p. 43.

14. [Georg Moesinger (ed.), *Evangelii concordantis expositio facta a Sancto Ephraemo doctore syro* (Venice: Libraria PP. Mechitaristarum in Monasterium S. Lazari, 1876). AF]

15. With the assistance of Dr Armitage Robinson [*Comm. Diat.* 14.17. AF].

6. *The First Tatian Reading in the Greek New Testament* 189

It is quite clear that the words which we are studying were a part of Ephrem's text, and not of his own commentary upon the text. It is a mere lapse on the part of a transcriber or editor that they have not been recognised as Biblical matter. So, if any doubt remained in our minds as to the propriety of referring to Tatian something in Ciasca's Arabic which does not correspond with the Syriac Vulgate, our hesitation is finally overruled, and we are obliged to register our gloss, if it be a gloss, as Tatian's own text.

But this raises another question, nay! several questions. Did the text occur in the copies of the Gospel that he was harmonising, i.e., in Tatian's copy of Matthew, since there is no Synoptic parallel? Are there any possible traces of the reading or of comments upon it elsewhere? And, in any case, Tatian or pre-Tatian, what does it all mean? Why should an expansion have occurred, or an omission have been made?

The comment of Ephrem upon the question addressed to Peter as to our Lord's payment of tribute is not easy to disentangle. It is not evident, on the surface, whether the tribute is temple-tax (supposed to be involved in the term *didrachma*), or general tribute and custom (such as kings levy on subjects and especially on foreigners). Whichever is the right explanation, Ephrem thinks that a trap was being laid for our Lord by way of dilemma. Does He pay or not pay? If He does not pay, He is a rebel, that is, if the payment is to king or Caesar. Or perhaps He does not pay to the temple; then He claims to be either priest or Levite or superior to both, or else He is no true Israelite. But suppose He does pay: then we have His own admission that He is *alienus* and not *filius*. Ephrem seems to have a royal tax in his mind, for he explains that the king did not tax the priesthood. On that supposition our Lord would be held to have claimed priestly rank. As we have said, the argument is not very lucid. From this point it changes from the tax-collector's question to our Lord's explanation. Jesus has introduced into the dialogue a curious word; He speaks of the sons of the king (i.e., his subjects proper) as distinct from the alien or ἀλλότριος. They think, says the Lord, that I am an alien; the sea shall teach them that I am both priest and king; I need not pay tribute or tax; the sea will own my priesthood and my lordship and pay it for me. And you also, Simon, shall be one of the royal and priestly caste, though, like me, you pay as an alien. The fishes of the sea shall bear testimony to my rank, for one of them will come up with a stater in its mouth, which is a sign of lordship, and has the king's head upon it.

Ephrem then makes a general statement that all created things had recognised the advent of the great High Priest, and had come to pay him their tribute, angels, prophets, magi and the like; and had it not been foretold that the obedience of the sea should be turned towards that just alien?[16]

---

16. Apparently a reference to Isaiah 40.5, with a misprint of *obedientia* for *abundantia* [*Comm. Diat.* 14.16-17. AF].

The concurrence of the two terms, *just* and *alien*, shows that Ephrem has his eye on the Marcionites, whom his soul hates; and he is taking the opportunity of proving that the *Stranger*, with whom Marcion identified Jesus as the emissary of the unknown God, is at the same time the Demiurge, or Creator, whom Marcion admitted to be just, for do not all created things obey him and do him homage?

At this point it is possible that Ephrem's discourse, in spite of its obscurity, may throw a light upon the fortunes of the text itself. For here we have the very word which the Marcionites desiderated used by our Lord of Himself and His disciples. He admits, the Marcionites will say, that he is the *Stranger*, who has come to rescue men from their allegiance and servitude to the Creator; he is the Good One, who will pluck us out of the toils of the Just One.

If then the text, as we read it in an expanded form, had existed before Marcion, or if, at a later date, it had been accessible to Marcion's followers, they would have been tempted to use it against their Catholic opponents; and then the Catholic party might have resorted to excision of the passage in self-defence. This argument is not invalidated by the fact that Marcion and his followers accept Luke's Gospel only; for Marcion himself sometimes borrowed from other Gospels, and his followers need not have hesitated to borrow a shaft from them also. Thus we see that it is not necessary to assume that the gloss is Tatian's own composition; we have proved it to be a part of his text, but it might have had a previous history. On the other hand it can hardly have been a Marcionite invention; for it is well known that Marcion does not invent; in his own Gospel of Luke he subtracts, but does not add; the expansions are practically *nil*; he used the sponge but not the stylus.

Then we must leave it an open question whether the gloss is a gloss at all. It may be a bit of true text which Tatian preserved, and which zealous anti-Marcionites have removed. This possible explanation must be reserved; but whether it be correct or not, we remark in passing that the sudden elevation of a twelfth century reading to second century rank should be carefully noted; for it shows that the readings in the Gospels which seem to be the earliest may sometimes be challenged from what looks, at first sight, to be a much later source.

We have been obliged to admit, from Ephrem's own language, that the *Stranger* is the *Just One*, whom all created things obey; Ephrem tells us that Christ is the Creator, and that Marcion's description of the Creator as the Just One may be accepted. This is quite in the manner of Tertullian; but it has conceded to the Marcionites that ἀλλότριος, the *Alien* or *Stranger*, is a proper title of Christ.

Now for the other alternative; let us say that the gloss is Tatian's own. Against this the argument does not hold that Tatian makes no additions, in the way that it holds for Marcion. Tatian is not free from a tendency and a

6. *The First Tatian Reading in the Greek New Testament*   191

willingness to expand. Moreover, he is a very acute mind, and would naturally have asked why Christ's concession to the demands of the tribute-collector should have involved Peter, as in the injunction to give them the stater for "thee and me."

This involves Peter in the same inquisition for taxes as well as our Lord Himself; and it is not impossible that Tatian might have noticed this, and that our gloss is his added explanation. On the whole this seems to be the more likely solution of the problem. Why should we go beyond Tatian, when, by a reference to him and to his *Harmony*, we can explain all the textual phenomena?

From the secure vantage-ground of a proved Tatianism, we can now return to the study of our precious MS and begin, with Dr Pott's assistance, a search for any further influences coming from the same quarter. As a general rule, the Peckover text is of the usual Byzantine type; but there are some divergences which look like Syriasms or Tatianisms, which must be carefully collected, and referred, tentatively, to the *Harmony*. In conclusion we remark that the enquiry upon which we have been engaged, in which the first Greek reading from Tatian's lost work has been brought to light, must not be taken as a proof that the *Harmony* itself ever existed in Greek. We have shown that this gloss, if it be a gloss, is probably Syriac in origin; if so, it is the Syriac of Tatian, and not a hypothetical Greek. If any one should persist that it is not a gloss at all, the reply would be that in that case, neither is it Tatian's handiwork. We must not, however, press further at the present time into the debateable regions of New Testament criticism.

Chapter 7

Josephus and his Testimony

The controversy over the authenticity of the passage in the eighteenth book of the *Antiquities* (or *Archaeologia*) of Josephus concerning Jesus Christ[1] is one of the longest debated of all the disputes in the history of criticism. It is not necessary to recapitulate the points that were said to be conceded by the Jewish historian. They were important for the Christian world as constituting the first evidence of the existence of Christ and the Christian Faith outside the Christian documents properly so called. What strikes the student who goes over the records of the controversy, say from its great revival in the eighteenth century down to the present time, is the singular change which comes over the minds of the critics as they express from time to time the results of their enquiry, and after having positively affirmed that the passage in the *Antiquities* cannot be genuine, because it is too Christian for a Jew to have written, then turn upon themselves and say the very opposite, affirming on the ground of internal evidence and closer scrutiny of words, that it is certainly the language of Josephus, and not the product of a later age nor of a Christian hand. One of the most interesting of these critical repentances was the case of the French scholar Daubuz,[2] who, having in the eighteenth century convinced himself and done his best to persuade others that Josephus cannot have been the author, reconsidered his opinion and made a splendid defence of its authenticity; many of his arguments will be found to reappear in recent times, when the genuineness of the Flavian Testimony has been re-affirmed by Harnack, by Professor Burkitt, and by his colleague Professor Emery Barnes.[3] It is an unusual phenomenon to find what is something like a stampede on the part of the critics from one opinion to the opposite, especially when the first opinion was so naturally attractive that it could hardly be resisted except by those who are supposed to be subject to hereditary prejudice.

1. [*A.J.* 18.63.3. AF]
2. The treatise of Daubuz was published in 1706 [Charles Daubuz, *Pro testimonio Flavii Josephi de Jesu Christo libri duo* (London: R. Sare, 1706). AF], and re-published as a supplement at the end of Havercamp's edition of Josephus [Sigebert Haverkamp (ed.), *Flavii Josephi quae reperiri potuerunt* (2 vols.; Amsterdam: R. & G. Wetstenius, 1726), 2.187-232. AF].
3. Dr Eisler calls Barnes an Oxford theologian! in his recent work on Jesus Christ.

7. *Josephus and his Testimony*

In all such matters we expect a change of opinion, if opinion has to be changed, to arise either from closer reasoning or from the accumulation of further evidence. It is under the second of these heads rather than the former that an acute situation has recently been produced; fresh documentary evidence was said to be forthcoming, had in fact actually been produced, which affects the whole of the controversy and may, perhaps, lead to a final decision. This fresh evidence is the discovery of a Russian version of the *Jewish War* of Josephus, which contains the disputed passage in a new form different from what is commonly edited,[4] as well as a good deal of fresh matter bearing on primitive Christianity, and on the relations of John the Baptist to Jesus and conversely. Thus the *Testimonium* has turned up not only in a new language, but also in what is an earlier document, for while the *Jewish War* was produced almost immediately after the fall of Jerusalem, the *Antiquities* belong to near the close of the first century, when Josephus had been for many years domiciled in Rome, under distinguished patronage and in close touch with the Imperial Household. Did the *Testimonium* really belong to the earlier document, or does it form a part of the narration in the *Antiquities*, and has it been lifted from the latter work into the former by Russian translators or scribes; or perhaps it may have belonged to both?

The new evidence was at once acclaimed as genuine Josephus by Dr Robert Eisler[5] and by Vacher Burch,[6] who followed the first publication of the text in Germany by Berendts and Grass[7] by treatises upon it. In the first instance an attempt was made to show that the ancestry of the Russian text ran back into an Aramaic version of the *Jewish War*, which Josephus tells us that he had made for his compatriots in Northern Mesopotamia, but it soon became evident that the thesis of direct derivation of the Russian text from a lost Aramaic Josephus could not be sustained, and that the Russian text was descended from a Greek original. This original text varied much from what we may call the canonical Josephus. Were its variants trustworthy? Did they go back to Josephus himself? Dr Eisler studied the whole question afresh in a

---

4. [Addition between *B.J.* 2.174 and 175. English translation in Josephus, *The Jewish War, Books IV-VII* (trans. Henry St.J. Thackeray; vol. 3 of *Josephus*; trans. Henry St.J. Thackeray *et al.*; LCL; Cambridge, MA: Harvard University Press, 1928), pp. 648-50. AF]

5. [Robert Eisler, "Jésus d'après la version slave de Joséphe," *RHR* 93 (1926), pp. 9-21; "The Newly Rediscovered Witness of Josephus to Jesus," *The Quest* 17 (1926), pp. 1-15; "The Present Position of the Slavic Josephus," *The Quest* 20 (1928), pp. 1-19. AF]

6. [Henry V. Burch, *Jesus Christ and his Revelation: Fresh Evidence from Christian Sources and Josephus* (London: Chapman & Hall, 1927). AF]

7. [Alexander Berendts and Karl K. Grass (eds.), *Flavius Josephus. Vom jüdischen Kriege Buch I-IV: Nach der slavischen Übersetzung deutsch herausgegeben und mit dem griechischen Text verglichen* (Dorpat: C. Mattiesen, 1924–27). AF]

volume of nearly 1500 pages of astonishing erudition,[8] in which the story of Jesus, now conceded to be historical, was re-written in a manner that was startling indeed to the Christian historians, however grateful the latter might be for Eisler's assistance in disposing, perhaps finally, of the theorists who had talked of a mythological Christ. If they had escaped from Scylla, it looked as if they were going to be plunged into Charybdis; for the recovered Jesus was one of a series of unsuccessful revolters against Roman rule, who operated from a pacifist foundation, and finding it untenable, led his followers into an armed rising, which was promptly quelled by the combined forces of the Jewish priesthood and the Roman governor. Eisler found at first a strong supporter, and loyal friend, in our greatest Josephus scholar, St John Thackeray, the editor of Josephus in the texts and translations of the Loeb Library. "You have convinced me," he is reported to have said, "but against my will." From this almost absolute surrender he seems to have receded into a position of suspense of judgment, if we may judge from the Loeb volumes, and from a splendid series of lectures which he delivered in New York before his lamented removal from amongst us. These lectures contain his last and best work.[9] The *Antiquities* are shown to have been reduced to the form in which we have them by the aid of a number of learned Greek amanuenses, one of whom can be detected by his imitations of the style of Thucydides, and another, more poet than historian or philosopher, borrows turns of speech from Sophocles and Euripides, including under the latter head a loan from Euripides' lost play, the *Ino*.

It is easy to see what a loss has befallen the world of classical and Biblical learning by the migration of this great scholar, whose final opinion upon some of the points at issue would almost have been of the nature of a verdict.

Now let us return for a moment or two to Dr Eisler's treatment of the current text of the Flavian Testimony. It was necessary for Eisler to show that if the Testimony was authentic it had been through Christian hands to make it presentable. The first step in this direction had already been taken, many years

---

8. [Robert Eisler, *IHCOYC BACIΛEYC OY BACIΛEYCAC: Die messianische Unabhängigkeitsbewegung vom Auftreten Johannes des Täufers bis zum Untergang Jakobs des Gerechten, nach der neuerschlossenen Eroberung vom Jerusalem des Flavius Josephus und den christlichen Quellen* (2 vols.; Religionswissenschaftliche Bibliothek, 9; Heidelberg: C. Winter, 1929–1930). English translation by Rendel Harris's friend, Alexander H. Krappe, *The Messiah Jesus and John the Baptist according to Flavius Josephus' Recently Rediscovered 'Capture of Jerusalem' and the Other Jewish and Christian Sources* (London: Methuen, 1931). AF]

9. The title is *Josephus: The Man and the Historian*; and they are published at New York by the Jewish Institute for Religion Press [Henry St.J. Thackeray, *Josephus: The Man and the Historian* (The Hilda Stich Stroock Lectures at the Jewish Institute of Religion; New York: Jewish Institute of Religion Press, 1929). AF].

since, by Heinichen in his edition of Eusebius[10] where Josephus is quoted. The current text tells us that Jesus was a teacher of those who receive the truth with gladness, διδάσκαλος ἀνθρώπων τῶν ἡδονῇ τἀληθῆ δεχομένων, in which Heinichen detected that ἀληθῆ was a correction of ἀήθη, a favourite term in Josephus for the *disorders* of his time, so that a text was suggested which changed "people who receive the truth with gladness" to "people who gladly take up with innovations." The inference is that a Christian hand has deleted the fondness for disorder and replaced it by a love of truth. It would only mean a change of a single letter.[11] From this point Eisler proceeds to amend the current text so as to bring it into a form which would consist with a Josephan authorship. He found that the author of the Apocryphal *Acts of Pilate* had made use of the *Testimonium*, and proceeded to restore several missing lines which he thought could have been preserved in that quarter. I do not think that he strengthened his case by his interpolations. Apart from the new discovery of the Russian text, he seems to have made too many changes to secure conviction, and most students will feel that he has handled his text too roughly in turning it back from an almost Christian statement of doctrine into the record of a Jewish historian. If Christian changes have been made, they must surely have been slight, like the one which Heinichen suggested. It may, however, be conceded that Eisler went to work in the right way, apart from any new textual finds, to recover a possible Jewish form which might have been subject to Christian manipulation; for the analysis of the language in the current text certainly suggests Josephus. Let us see if we can assist him in his reconstructions.

We are sketching very rapidly the opening section of Eisler's work, because we have important additions to make to his argument, which take us away from conventional rivalry. We draw fresh attention to Heinichen's emendation of the text of Josephus, because it gives us the key to Eisler's first arguments, and will equally, in our judgment, supply the necessary clue to the understanding of Josephus himself. If Heinichen is right, Jesus, in Josephus' point of view, takes his place in a series of innovators and revolutionaries whom Josephus wishes to denounce and on whom he lays the blame for all the troubles that befell the Jews in their relations with Rome: it was not only natural for Josephus to take up such an anti-zealot or anti-reform position when writing what was to be read in Rome; he was, as a Pharisee, hostile to the movements among his excitable compatriots which could not be kept within bounds or made to harmonise with the ideas of settled government. That Jesus should be classified with Theudas and Judas and the mad

---

10. [Friedrich A.H. Heinichen (ed.), *Eusebii Pamphili Historiae ecclesiasticae libri* (3 vols.; Leipzig: C.G. Kayser, 1827–1828). AF]

11. Eisler gives from Thackeray five instances of the use of ἀήθης and its compounds by Josephus.

Egyptian, apart from chronological sequence, was natural enough for a historian who was also a champion of public order. "He stirreth up our nation," according to the charge against Jesus in the Gospel,[12] was a sufficient reprobation, apart from the question whether that included a "forbidding to give tribute to Caesar."[13] The emendation, then, of Heinichen, which Eisler rightly adopts, is fundamental to the understanding of the subject, quite apart from the discovery of a Russian Josephus. Jesus was one of the "disorderly"; that is a long step towards the vindication of the authenticity of the great passage. It was what Josephus ought to have said and did say. So much by way of preliminary. We have laid emphasis on the most important word in the current text.

Our next direction of enquiry relates to the Russian text of the *Testimonium*, from which we propose in the first instance to take a single clause, which we shall tentatively add to the canonical text, reserving the rest of the Russian document for future study. If there is anything in that new evidence that is genuine Josephus, it must be the statement that "I will not call him an angel," which falls naturally into sequence with the existing statement "if one must call him a man" or "if indeed it is right to call him a man." The statement as generally interpreted is taken to be Josephus' admission that Jesus was more than a man, or else to be a Christian interpolation qualifying the statement that Jesus was a wise man. The hypothesis that the words "I will not call him an angel" follow on from the previous statement as to calling Jesus a man, excludes the idea of a Christian interpolation. Whatever it means it is Josephan, with a slight margin for Christian modification, but no room for deliberate glossation by an added clause. Josephus says, "I will call him a man but I cannot call him an angel." The origin of this statement, whatever be its primitive form, is what we have to go in search of. In order to make the quest successfully, we must now leave on one side both Eisler and the Russian text, and take a path which at first will appear to be outside the area of regular criticism and to lead nowhere, as far as the question of the Flavian *Testimonium* is concerned.

Dr Plooij has been emphasising the importance of what I have called the *Testimony Book* (an early Christian collection of Messianic and other prophecies), for the understanding of the origin and evolution of Christian doctrines and beliefs.[14] I hope that the multiplicity of the illustrations which he gives will not obscure the emphasis which he is desirous of expressing. He carries on the arguments by which I had maintained the antiquity of the earliest

12. [Luke 23.5. AF]
13. [Matt. 22.15-22; Mark 12.13-17; Luke 20.20-26. AF]
14. [Daniel Plooij, *Studies in the Testimony Book* (Verhandelingen der Koninklijke Akademie van Wetenschappen te Amsterdam. Afdeeling Letterkunde, NS, 32/2; Amsterdam: N.V. Noord-Hollandsche, Uitgevers-Maatschappij, 1932). AF]

collection of Old Testament prophecies concerning Christ, and the evident absorption of certain Testimonies and groups of Testimonies by New Testament writers. It is surprising that this should ever have been doubted, it is regrettable that it has in some quarters been grudgingly conceded. Dr Plooij shows more than I had imagined to be the case with the primitive *Testimony Book*; he proves that it was *Palestinian in origin, Aramaic in diction, and that it has connecting links with the Targums on the Old Testament*. In some ways this is more important than my own suggestions that Paul was using the Testimonies against the Jews in the ninth and tenth chapters of the Epistle to the Romans, or that the Epistle to the Hebrews was using it from the first verses onwards. I do not think, as far as I remember, that it had occurred to me to assume or define closely an Aramaic original beyond an occasional suggestion; from such an Aramaic original the priority of the collection of Testimonies to the rest of the New Testament follows almost of necessity; the local origin accentuates the antiquity. We are on Palestinian or Syrian soil for certain. Not only so, but with the proof of Targumic influence before us we are either actually in the Synagogues where Christianity had its origin, or not so far from the doors of the Synagogue that we cannot hear them disputing inside over the meaning and applicability of certain Old Testament passages. The disputes naturally resulted in the transition to the Dialogue form, in which representative leaders on either side discussed the statements contained in the challenging Testimonies; for it is certain that the extant Dialogues between Jew and Christian go back to a very much earlier date than is commonly supposed, even if we do not possess them in Aramaic but only in Greek or Latin. We are indebted to Dr Plooij for having brought so much fresh evidence to bear upon the question. The headings of the separate sections under which Testimonies are grouped are shown to be as early as the texts that are actually quoted, and although some changes are made both in the texts and their headlines by the time we come to the age of Cyprian, we are surprised to observe how few are the changes that have actually been made.

Now let us return to Josephus and the Russian version: the statement "for I cannot call him an angel" implies two things; first, that someone has been calling him an angel; second, that he has been called something else, a statement which is the proper antecedent to what we have quoted. This suggests at once a complete statement something like this: "I will call him a man, but I really cannot call him an angel." Where shall we find or to whom shall we refer the statement that Christ was Man and Angel? The answer to this is that it stood so in the *Testimony Book*. We can see this in two ways: first of all Cyprian in his *Testimonies* has a section headed, "that Christ is Angel and God,"[15] which is an obvious modification by a Christian hand of an earlier

---

15. [*Test.* 2.5. AF]

statement that "Christ is Angel and Man." Next we find the very combination "Man and Angel" in Justin Martyr's *Dialogue with Trypho* (ch. 128): the language of Justin is as follows:

> Christ (or "the Messiah") being Lord and existing as God the Son of God, appeared aforetime in power as Man and Angel: καὶ ὅτι κύριος ὢν ὁ χριστός, καὶ θεὸς θεοῦ υἱὸς ὑπάρχων καὶ δυνάμει φαινόμενος πρότερον ὡς ἀνὴρ καὶ ἄγγελος κτέ.[16]

The πρότερον ("aforetime") refers to the Old Testament from which the evidence comes for the identification of the Messiah under either head. The language of Justin with regard to *Man and Angel* is, then, Testimony language. We have recovered the same Testimony heading as we suspected to underlie the language of Cyprian.[17]

This being established, since we have the same combination involved in the language of Josephus, we may say that Josephus has before him a Testimony Book, or an extract from the same, with which he is partly in accord and partly in disagreement. As a Jew he had no objection to Christ being called *Man* (whether the statement be buttressed from the Old Testament or not), but he declines to call him *Angel* on any terms.

We may say that in the statement, "A man but not an angel," Josephus is tilting at the Testimonies. We can easily reinforce the separate statements for Christ as Man and Christ as Angel; indeed Dr Plooij has gone far with the proof of both; but without expanding the argument, and perhaps throwing it out of focus, let us observe that Dr Eisler had come to a similar conclusion with ourselves;[18] he had also detected the origin of Josephus' Testimony in a group of other testimonies but without perceiving that there was an actual Testimony heading extant by implication in his text; but here is his very language; we quote it at length, on account of its importance, both as regards Josephus and as regards the *Book of Testimonies*, which are now seen to reinforce one another, the genuineness of one being conceded along with the antiquity of the other:

> The appeal to the fulfilled predictions of the prophets in the mouth of Josephus is not only unprejudiced (*einwandfrei*), but constitutes in fact a Testimony of the first importance for the fact that to him the Christian statements with regard to the Life, Death and Resurrection of Jesus were known in a form which laid the greatest weight on the fact that every peculiarity in the narration presents

---

16. [*Dial.* 128.1. AF]

17. So in *Dial.* 34 [34.2. AF] Christ is ἄγγελος καὶ ἄνθρωπος. Christ as "angel" occurs many times in Justin.

18. Thackeray endorses the judgment of Eisler in the following terms. "In Palestine the followers of Jesus possessed [in A.D. 64] no written records beyond perhaps a collection of sayings of their Master, and another collection of Old Testament prophecies with corresponding fulfilments in the events of his earthly life," p. 127 [*Josephus*. AF].

itself as the fulfilment of some sort or other of Messianically implied prophecy of the Scripture. To put it somewhat differently, he is tilting (*polemisiert*) against the very same collection of prophetical Testimonies, at which already in the time of Claudius, in the year A.D. 62,[19] the Samaritan chronicler Thallus had been dealing blows—the very same collection in fact to which Papias bore witness, which had been recognised by Gregory, Burkitt, Selwyn and Rendel Harris as a series of *Oracles*, which were the Matthaean *Logia* of the life of Jesus.[20]

This is a great concession, a great discovery we may say, on his part and on ours, for, as we have seen, we came at it independently; it establishes finally, as one may reasonably suppose, the authenticity of Josephus' *Testimonium* and the antiquity of the collection of Oracles which are implied in the *Testimonium*, to which the writer refers. According to Eisler, and here again he seems to be quite correct, this collection is earlier than the year A.D. 62 (more correctly A.D. 52) when it provoked the criticism of a learned Samaritan, who had migrated, as literary men were wont to do, to Rome, but who was, of course, perfectly familiar with the Testimonies even if they should be written in Aramaic or glossed from the Targum. We are in possession, then, through the evidence of Josephus, as rightly interpreted by Eisler, of a series of statements concerning Christian beliefs at least as early (may we not say?) as the middle of the first century.

To Josephus also it must be conceded that he was dealing with a real person; when he said *Man* he meant man, and when he said *Angel* or anything else, he meant *Man*. His Messiah of whom the Christians affected to speak in language borrowed from the prophets, was a real person. The prophets expressly said *Man*.

It is interesting to note in this connection that when Josephus begins by saying that Jesus was "a wise man" (σοφὸς ἀνήρ), in which connection the question of "man or angel" arose, he is giving the first place to the idea of Wisdom as the Testimonies do, which begin with the heading that "Christ is the Wisdom of God," a term with which we are familiar in St Paul.[21] We hesitate to correct this as Eisler does to σοφιστὴς ἀνήρ "a Sophist man"; σοφιστής is not an adjective, and could be written without an explanatory ἀνήρ (man): but as we have seen the "Man" is necessary to the argument. Indeed it does not seem that very many changes are necessary to carry back the canonical Josephus to its original form. The mighty works (παράδοξα) must stand, and the prophets who foretold everything cannot be dismissed. A very little change will put the whole text right. We will return later to define

---

19. Should not this be 52?

20. Eisler, Vol. i. p. 79 [*IHCOYC*. AF]; the statement is repeated in Vol. ii. p. 142, with date corrected.

21. [1 Cor. 1.24. AF]

more closely what changes are necessary. Meanwhile we reserve the question of the σοφιστής.

We have now reached conclusions of the first importance in which, quite independently of Dr Eisler, but concurrently with him, we have vindicated the genuineness of the Testimony of Josephus, with a certain modification by Christian hands, and have shown that Josephus himself has in his eye, with doubtful friendliness, an earlier document which we call the *Testimony Book*. This book is the credential of a real person, who is held to have been the Messiah. *It is unthinkable that Josephus recorded his opinions about a myth or a spectre.* He allows him to be "a man" but denies that he is rightly described as "an angel." So now we must assist him in his scrutiny of the document and see what can be said further about the *Testimony Book* considered as an original source of history, composed in the first instance in Aramaic and circulated in its first form in Palestine. We have established Josephus in the witness box, and we have accepted the Slavonic text of his *Jewish War*, so far as to take its most striking statement about Jesus and to annex it, in its proper place, to the canonical *Testimonium Flavianum*. It is not to be thought that this is all that the Slavonic text has to say; it has many confusions, but cannot be treated as altogether outside history.

Our real concern, in pursuing the investigation from Josephus to the Christian Messianic texts to which he refers, is to see whether we can turn the *Testimonia adversus Judaeos* back into history.

The statement that Christ is both *Man* and *Angel* has been shown to be a primitive combination, attested in part by Cyprian and in completeness by Justin Martyr. It is parallel in its duality to many other statements in the *Testimony Book* and in the New Testament, as for instance in the case which Dr Plooij threw so much light on, that Christ is the "Angel and High Priest," or that passage in Hebrews where Christ is called the "Apostle and High Priest."[22] It is evident, however, that even if the duality of a pair of associated titles is conceded to be early, the separate members of the dual combination must be earlier still. People must have said, *He is the Man* and *He is the Angel* before they could say *He is Man and Angel*. What then did they mean by calling him either the one or the other? Dr Plooij has shown that the *Angel* comes from a passage in Exodus (23.20) treated Messianically. The other half of the Testimony is more difficult. Where shall we find in the Old Testament an Oracle, or Pseudo-Oracle connecting Jesus as "Man" with the Messiah?

The answer is that when we call him *The Man* we can find him in one of the most strongly accentuated Messianic Oracles in the Prophets. In Zechariah (6)[23] we have the story of the fortunes of Joshua the son of Jozedek the High

---

22. [Heb. 3.1. AF]
23. [Zech. 6.10-15. AF]

Priest. To the early Christians and first followers, this Joshua is Jesus. Concerning him the Lord of Hosts declares, "Behold the man whose name is Branch; it is he who shall build the temple of the Lord."[24] On this great oracle the Targum explains: "This Man, Messiah is his name."[25] In Hebrew this oracle opens with:

הנה־איש ("Behold the Man"),

in the Aramaic Targum as commonly edited, it is

ܗܐ ܓܒܪܐ ܕܡܫܝܚܐ ܫܡܗ

where we must clearly read ܗܐ for ܗܘ i.e., "Behold the Man (gabra = ἀνήρ) whose name is Messiah."

Here then is the *Man* whom the Testimonies matched with the *Angel* (the *Apostle* of Hebrews 3.1).

The importance of this identification lies in the fact that we have recovered a Messianic slogan of the time of Jesus Himself: and this is true whether we read the Targum as "He is the Man" or as "Behold the Man."[26] That the latter is the preferable explanation is clear from the fact that it throws light on an obscure passage in the Fourth Gospel, and in the exact Biblical form.

It will be remembered (the Gospel in Art will remind us if we have forgotten it) that Pilate brings Jesus out of the Praetorium to the mob and appeals to them with the words

Ecce Homo.[27]

It is difficult, in the ordinary exegesis, to explain what Pilate meant. Was he thinking to move the compassion of the crowd? Would he be likely to do so? Suppose, however, that he had simply repeated the slogan of the followers of Jesus, which we have shown to be itself derived from the prophet Zechariah, we can understand that it was an appeal, away from the priests to the people, something like the suggestion "Your King! Shall I crucify your king?" by which Pilate thought to provoke a reaction on the part of the multitude against the Jewish officials. "Ecce Homo" was, from this point of view, entirely sympathetic. Even the traditional exegesis assumes that; it becomes adroit as well as sympathetic when we know what it meant in the ears of the people.

At this point we may have to move cautiously; we are not only trying to interpret an expression in the *Testimony Book* by putting it against a historical background, but we are bound to ask whether this background can be trusted. The Fourth Gospel is commonly held to be, in parts at least, of an

---

24. [Zech. 6.12. AF]
25. [*Tg. Heb.* AF]
26. We may for a parallel usage compare the German "Der Tag," of pre-war time.
27. [John 19.5. AF]

unhistorical character. In the case before us Christ crowned with thorns is Synoptic: it has a parallel in Zechariah where a crown is set on the head of Joshua the High Priest; but there is no reference to the *Ecce Homo* incident in Mark. All that we can say is that the Johannine incident becomes luminous enough, if we read it as parallel to the appeal "Shall I crucify your king?" Pilate is speaking in either case sympathetically, not ironically. The Gospels are clear as to the general statement that Pilate was on the side of Jesus. The Slavonic Josephus with its suggestion that Pilate had received thirty Talents to make away with the agitator, appears to be out of court and to be derived from, or connected with, the thirty pieces of silver for which Judas sold his Master. We shall assume then tentatively, that we have recovered a popular slogan of the Messianic party, which they applied to Jesus. It must have been applied to Jesus, for it was derived from the Oracle about Jesus the High Priest in Zechariah.

We shall see the importance of this, and may be sure that we are writing history, if we reflect that a similar title was applied to John the Baptist. If Testimonies about Christ and slogans based on Testimonies were current, to some extent at least, in our Lord's lifetime, it is highly probable that similar Messianic proofs were extant concerning John the Baptist. Jesus was not the only possible Messiah, whose marks of identification had to be tested. There was a competitor. "All men mused in their hearts of John whether he were the Messiah or not."[28] One of the things that were disputed concerned this very title of *Angel*. To the followers of Christ this title is his, by virtue of an Oracle in Exodus.[29] One is surprised to find, that what seems an easier prooftext in Malachi ("my Angel") was not applied to Christ.[30] It was, perhaps, so applied. If so, it passed, by Christian concession, to John the Baptist. Either of them, however, was Messianically identified with the "Angel." The same thing appears to have been true of the "Man." Eisler is probably right in this respect also in suggesting that the Baptist, as well as Jesus, had been identified with the *Son of Man* (= *the Man*) in the Vision of Daniel.[31] In the Fourth Gospel we have the Baptist as "a man sent from God."[32] If this could be clearly made out, the competition between Jesus and the Baptist over the titles *Man* and *Angel* would stand out on the first page of their history with fresh suggestiveness. It is reasonable to believe that if the Testimonies on behalf of Jesus go back in part at least to his own lifetime, or to the time immediately subsequent to his death, there were similar and rival Testimonies in circulation with regard to the Baptist. After all, as Dr Plooij clearly brings

28. [Luke 3.15. AF]
29. [Exod. 23.20. AF]
30. [Mal. 3.1 in Matt. 11.10 par. Luke 7.27 and in Mark 1.2. AF]
31. [Dan. 7.13. AF]
32. [John 1.6. AF]

7. *Josephus and his Testimony*

out, they had nothing except the Old Testament out of which to develop history, or by which to illustrate it, until the actual Gospels arrived; and, as we have shown elsewhere,[33] these were supported on the Testimonies as their foundation. How far these Testimonies will disclose actual historical details in the life of Christ requires further and closer study. Some of them may reduce to mere illustrations. In the same way the Slavonic expansions to the text of Josephus require further and closer study: some of them may turn out to be mere romance, but this can hardly be the complete explanation. The conflict, for instance, between John the Baptist and Simon the Essene has every appearance of being genuine history.[34] Less certain is the story that Jesus had healed Pilate's wife. On all these points we must wait for further illumination. Meanwhile, we have gone a long way with Josephus, and some distance with Dr Eisler. The whole situation has been changed by the intrusion of the *Book of Testimonies*.

Note on Christ Not Called Angel

Mr H. G. Wood has drawn my attention to the fact that in the Epistle to the Hebrews there seems to be a definite avoidance of the term *Angel* as applied to Christ. It is said that "he taketh not on him the nature of angels, but he taketh on him the seed of Abraham."[35] So here we have another writer from an opposite view saying "I will not call him Angel, but I will call him man." It has, however, been clearly proved from many aspects that the Epistle to the Hebrews is following the line of the *Testimony Book*. If he has dropped the Angel from his text, the natural explanation is that a Docetic use has been made of the term. That Hebrews is an anti-Docetic document may be seen from its reference to the "strong crying and tears"[36] of the Redeemer when anticipating his suffering and rejection.

It may also be remembered that in another passage of the Epistle, Christ is spoken of as "a little lower than the angels";[37] a passage on which stress could hardly be laid if the writer wished to say that Jesus was the Angel of Jahweh.

On a Supposed Florilegium Employed by St Paul

In the foregoing enquiry we made our point of departure from the hypothesis of a primitive Christian book of anti-Judaic Testimonies, which hypothesis

---

33. [*Testimonies*. AF]
34. [The addition on John the Baptist is between *B.J.* 2.110 and 3. English translation in Josephus, *Jewish War*, 644-5. AF]
35. [Heb. 2.16. AF]
36. [Heb. 5.7. AF]
37. [Heb. 2.7. AF]

had received recently remarkable confirmation from researches of Dr Plooij, who showed that the nucleus of such a collection of Old Testament prooftexts was of Palestinian origin, of Aramaic diction, and earlier in date than the canonical Christian Literature. Anticipating the complete statement and publication of Dr Plooij's important results, we went on to show that the much-debated Testimony of Josephus concerning Jesus Christ had just such a collection in view, and was antagonising the same, at least in part, though the statement of Josephus had undergone some slight modification by Christian hands, before it reached the form in which it has come down to us.

In connection with the foregoing assumption and its important extension and verification by Dr Plooij, a ray of further illumination has recently been cast over the whole question of Judaean and Christian controversies in a paper published by Professor Cerfaux of the University of Louvain. The title of this paper is, *Vestiges d'un Florilège dans I Cor. I.18-3.21*, to which the writer modestly attaches an unnecessary note of interrogation.[38] The origin of this paper and the suggested *Florilegium* is as follows: M. Cerfaux found in the course of his public lectures on the First Epistle to the Corinthians that the Biblical passages cited by St Paul had an internal nexus which suggested that they were taken from a collection of texts grouped and classified together with the intention of showing the fallaciousness of human wisdom. Such a collection would, according to M. Cerfaux, constitute a broadside of the orthodox Rabbinic school against the importation and the seductions of Greek learning. A protest of this kind, amounting almost to an official denunciation, could hardly be credited to Alexandria, and found its natural home in Jerusalem. The subject of the protest was necessarily early in date, and the protest itself referable to the time when Wisdom and Anti-Wisdom were matters of practical politics. So M. Cerfaux concluded that his supposed *Florilegium* was of Palestinian origin and earlier in date than St Paul and his letter to the Corinthians. I hope I am summarising his conclusions rightly, and with a due regard to the modesty of his note of interrogation.

The student who will now turn to the marginal references of his New Testament will be able to pick up some, at least, of the threads which M. Cerfaux was spinning into a *Florilegium*. For instance, he will at once detect that in 1 Cor. 1.18-19[39] there was a profusion of Old Testament matter. Isaiah 29.14 was quoted for the destruction of the Wisdom of the Wise, and a composite reference followed to Job 12.17, Isaiah 19.12 and 33.18. Such composite references are the safest guides one can have for the detection of a *Florilegium*. The references might easily be expanded, and M. Cerfaux makes a careful linguistic study of them, and shows that to some extent his *Florilegium* is

38. See *Revue d'Histoire Ecclésiastique*, xxvii. 3 (1931) [Lucien Cerfaux, "Vestiges d'un florilège dans I Cor., I, 18–III, 23?," *RHE* 27 (1931), pp. 521-34. AF].
39. [1 Cor. 1.18-20. AF]

independent of the translation of the LXX. The suggestion was natural that we had recovered a fragment of a tract, which might be entitled *Testimonia adversus Sapientes*. At this point I turned to my marginal notes, and found that I had already staked out a claim for the use by St Paul of some of these passages of primitive Christian *Testimonia adversus Judaeos*. First of all it was noted that Justin Martyr in his *Dialogue with Trypho* (ch. 78) had actually quoted Isaiah 29.14 in an anti-Judaic sense, having previously quoted Isaiah 29.13, a passage used by Our Lord Himself, as we learn from Mark 7.6[40] in denunciation of the Jews.

Many references may be given to Justin to show that he is using the anti-sophist texts of Isaiah and elsewhere in an anti-Judaic sense.

The actual text of ch. 78 is as follows:—

> This grace (the Divine grace) has been transferred to us (the Christians), as Isaiah says, speaking on this wise: This people draws nigh to me with their lips, but their heart is far from me; and in vain do they worship, teaching the ordinances and teachings of men. And therefore I will further add to remove *this people*, and I will remove them, and will destroy the wisdom of *their* wise, and the intelligence of the men of understanding I will reject.[41]

Concerning which extract from Justin I note further that it is not only anti-Judaic in every respect, but that in the last clause the word αὐτῶν ("*their* intelligent men") has dropt from the text. That it belongs there may be seen from the parallel usage of the text in Tertullian, as follows:

> auferam, inquit, sapientiam sapientum *illorum*, et prudentiam prudentium *eorum* abscondam ... Sapientibus *eorum*, id est scribis, et prudentibus *eorum*, id est, pharisaeis—Tert. *adv. Marc.* iii. 6.

It is needless to repeat that these references are conclusive as to the use of the passages quoted by M. Cerfaux.[42] His *Florilegium* is the same as our *Liber Testimoniorum*. If further confirmation were desired, it could be found in the fact that when Bar Ṣalibi produced in Syriac a volume of definite Testimonies against the Jews, the crucial passage from Isaiah finds its place among the rest (see Bar Ṣalibi *adv. Judaeos*, in the edition of de Zwaan, 7, 10).[43] We shall conclude, then, provisionally and with every appreciation of M. Cerfaux' work, in the equivalence of the supposed *Florilegium* and the *Book of the Testimonies*. Indeed there was no need to burden St Paul, who uses the *Book of Testimonies* so freely elsewhere, as in Romans 9, for example, by sending

---

40. [Mark 7.6-7. AF]
41. [*Dial.* 78.11. AF]
42. We shall get the inserted αὐτῶν once in Justin, *Dial.* 23 [32.5. AF], where again in the same passage the anti-Judaic reference is clear.
43. [De Zwaan, *Treatise*. AF]

him down the ages with a Testimony Book under one arm and a *Florilegium anti-Hellenisticum* under the other.

There is no finality in the problems that we have been discussing. The reader will already have been saying to himself the question, whether the supposed antiquity, Aramaic origin and Palestinian location of the nucleus of the Testimonies does not involve the Master Himself in their authorship, especially when we have the definite employment of such passages as the one quoted by Mark, and the oracle of the Rejected Stone,[44] etc. We have long had our attention fixed on such a possibility. If it could be verified, it would give us a new direction for the quest of the *Gospel according to Jesus*.

John the Baptist

When we examine the story of John the Baptist in the Russian text of the *Jewish War*, we find ourselves in some difficulty. We have now three accounts of the ministry of the Baptist; one is the evangelist's, which is familiar enough; the second is that of Josephus himself[45] who has a good deal to say on John and on the public opinion of him, as well as of his untimely end; and then, last of all, we have the Slavonic story in which the Baptist appears as a wild man clad in skins, a sort of Indian fakir or fanatic, fearing the faces of none, whether of prince or priesthood, denouncing sin in high places, and calling for individual and national righteousness and repentance. This last account differs much from what we find in the canonical Gospels or in the canonical Josephus. It has one striking expansion, which describes a public quarrel between the Baptist and an Essene leader named Simon. The story is so vivid that it must be genuine history. No motive can be assigned for its fabrication. Then there are curious divergences from, and convergences with, the text of the Gospels. For example, the Synoptic statement that, at the preaching of John, "there went out to him all Judea and the country round about Jerusalem,"[46] is repeated almost verbatim in the Russian text; this coincidence is held to be a contamination of the Russian text from the Gospels. But then the same account gives a different story both of the dress and the diet of the Baptist from what we find in the Gospels. In the latter we have a coat of camel's hair and a leathern belt,[47] in the former we have a curious statement that the wild man had covered the non-hairy part of his body with skins of beasts.

Similar divergence may be noted in the matter of the Baptist's diet. The Gospel tells us that it was "locusts and wild honey": the Russian text makes

---

44. [Matt. 21.42. AF]
45. [*A.J.* 18.5.2. AF]
46. [Matt. 3.5. AF]
47. [Matt. 3.4; Mark 1.6. AF]

the Baptist say that "I live on cane (? sugar cane) and roots and fruits of the tree." A further notice says that he would not eat bread; and that he would not allow wine or strong drink to be brought nigh him, and that he abhorred animal food, and that the fruits of trees served him for his needs. Here again we have what looks like a reference to the Gospel of Luke with regard to the Baptist's abstinence from intoxicating liquors.[48] The divergence of the account from the Gospel should be noted as well as the occasional agreement. The Russian diet seems more likely than that in St Mark; but how are we to explain these curious variations?

It is possible that the divergence of the accounts is due to two separate attempts made to write up a history of which the nucleus is common to both. In that case the nucleus must be the hairy integument of the prophet, whether natural or artificial. That takes us at once to the account in the first chapter of the Second Book of Kings, where Elijah the prophet sends to the King of Israel to denounce his disloyalty to the God of Israel and to announce his death. "What kind of a man?" the King asks. The reply was that "he was a hairy man, and girt with a girdle of leather about his loins." The Hebrew text is ambiguous, it says "A lord (Baal) of hair."[49] What does this mean?[50] The Authorised Version suggests that the hair is the characteristic of the man; but the Revised Version has an alternative rendering "a man with a garment of hair," which is not quite the same thing. Just as the modern divines varied in their explanation of the "lord of hair," so it seems did early interpreters. The Gospel explains by means of hair from a particular quarter, to wit, the camel; the Russian text has two interpretations involved in it, one that the man was hairy, at least in part; the other that he was covered in skins of beasts, where not already covered by his own hairy skin. All these explanations go back to the Old Testament and are bent on clearing an obscure text. *Their underlying object is to show that John the Baptist is Elijah.* It has been observed that St Mark begins his Gospel on this very note,[51] with a string of Testimonies, from which we infer that the involved *Testimony Book* had a section especially devoted to John the Baptist and his relation to the Elijah of the Old Testament.

We have shown then that the confusion in the Slavonic account is due to an attempt to combine two explanations of the "Lord of Hair" in the Old Testament. We may further note that since there is no reference anywhere in the Old Testament account to a camel's hair garment, that the story in the Gospel

---

48. [Luke 1.15. AF]
49. [2 Kgs. 1.7-8. AF]
50. We may compare the description of Joseph as a dreamer (Gen. 37.10), "master of dreams" or "the bird of the air" as a winged creature (Prov. 1.17), "lord of wing."
51. [Mark 1.2-3. AF]

is probably correct in this respect, there being no motive for the intrusion of the camel. The reference to the "locusts and wild honey" is also, as far as we can see, without a definite suggestion in the ancient text. The real reason for such an impossible diet is obscure: and if we are to make intelligibility our criterion, the Russian text has the right of way.

Enough has been said to advise caution in the use of these early narratives, and certainly the Russian story must not be relegated *en bloc* to the synagogues of the Middle Ages.

The Christian Alterations in the Testimonium Flavianum

Assuming, as I think we now may, the substantial accuracy of Thackeray's defence of the Flavian Testimony, we must still ask what further changes are due to a Christian hand, as well as examine further the form which the Testimony takes in the Russian text. For it is clear that even Thackeray's concessions with regard to the actual authorship do not land us in a final text of what Josephus meant to say: and it is further becoming more and more clear that there are some elements in the Russian text which come from an Aramaic original. In the latter case we must allow for the possibility that there is a *Testimonium Flavianum* in the *Jewish War* as well as in the *Antiquities*. It is the Russian text, moreover, which gives us the clue to the changes which Christian hands have made in the text of the *Antiquities*. First of all, we have the description of Jesus, without a name, as the *Wonder-worker*. This is evidently the Greek θαυματουργός, and it involves the favourite Jewish description of Christ's works as due to jugglery or magic. If this word had stood in Josephus' text, no Christian reviser would have tolerated it; he would have replaced it, to avoid the suspicion of magic, by some such term as ποιητής παραδόξων ἔργων, which we actually find in the *Antiquities*, and which is so unlike the speech of Josephus, for whom ποιητής is always "a poet," that Eisler deletes the word from the text and connects the παραδόξων ἔργων with the following διδάσκαλος. But this will not do: the Russian text shows that θαυματουργός is necessary. We must delete the whole expression and not merely the first word. It is the regular title of Christ and must be allowed to stand. The "*doer* of marvellous works" is a Christian emendation.

Further than this, the Russian text shows that the marvellous works were the cause of the hesitation of Josephus, in debating whether to use the term "Man" or "Angel." Was it right to call him a man, whose works were superhuman? At all events, says Josephus, I will not call him an Angel.

It is necessary, then, to retain in the *Antiquities* the reference to the "doer of marvellous works" and not to delete, as Eisler does, the word ποιητής as being offensive to a Josephan vocabulary; the whole of the expression must be linked up with the hesitation about calling him a man, who did such deeds. We notice in passing that Josephus has no doubt about the miracles, whatever hesitation he may have had concerning the worker.

7. *Josephus and his Testimony*

We come, now, to a more difficult point. We have already touched on the use which Eisler has made of a passage in the *Acts of Pilate* in which another Josephus (he of Arimathea) addresses Jesus as "most astonishing of men, if indeed one ought to call thee a man who didst such marvels as never man hath wrought"; εἰ χρὴ μέν καὶ ἄνθρωπον ὀνομάζειν σε, τὸν οἷα οὐδέποτε πεποίηκεν ἄνθρωπος θαύματα ἐργασάμενον (Tischendorf: *Acta Pilati*, B. 314).[52]

Now if we assume with Eisler that this is under the influence of Josephus, we must recognise in the language the traces of the θαυματουργός disguised as ἐργασάμενος and also the ποιήτης of the Christian corrector in πεποίηκεν. We restore these words as stated above to the text of the Testimony, without transferring *en bloc* the parallel which Eisler detected in the *Acts of Pilate*.

And now we find ourselves in a serious difficulty. For in the farewell discourse of Jesus in the fifteenth chapter of John, we find as follows: "If I had not *done* among them *the works which none other did*, they would not have had sin" (John 15.14); εἰ τὰ ἔργα μὴ ἐποίησα ἐν αὐτοῖς ἃ οὐδεὶς ἄλλος ἐποίησεν ...

The language differs from that in the *Acta Pilati*, but the sense is the same: cf. the *Acta Pilati* as quoted above, τὸν οἷα οὐδέποτε ἐπεποίηκει ἄνθρωπος θαύματα ἐργασάμενον, and the suspicion arises that both these passages depend upon the Flavian Testimony. In that case the Johannine discourse is artificial, and has made Jesus quote Josephus.

The whole section in the Gospel where these words occur is anti-Judaic in character, and supports its statements by means of Testimonies. We escaped from Scylla in company with Dr Eisler, and now find ourselves in the grip of Charybdis. Perhaps we have made too many changes in the text of the *Testimonium*. We shall see.

For the rest of the passage the text is fairly sound. We restore λεγόμενος before "Christos," the *so-called* Messiah, for this is the correct usage of Josephus elsewhere, and it would be natural for Christian readers to delete the word. It does not appear to have been deleted in the time of Origen, who is careful to state that Josephus did not believe Jesus to be the Messiah. On the whole, as we have said, the Christian changes in the text of the Testimony are slight; Josephus is almost a believer, as it used to be said of him, and he remains a credible historian, so far as his Testimony is concerned. Other matters reported in the Russian text are a problem of another colour.

---

52. [Konstantin von Tischendorf, *Evangelia apocrypha* (Leipzig: H. Mendelssohn, 2nd edn, 1876). AF]

A Further Note on John the Baptist

Before leaving this question of the diet and drink of the Baptist, on which there is certainly room for further research and discovery, we may draw attention to one curious expression in the Russian document.

We are told that John was such a sound and ardent Prohibitionist that he would not allow wine and spirits *to be brought near him*. Now this is certainly queer language. It does not express a natural situation. Who wanted to bring them near him in the woods or wastes that he frequented? It is hardly English or sense to talk that way. What one expects in the connection of the chronicle of John's habits and way of life, is a statement that he himself would not allow himself to touch wine nor spirits. His maxim with regard to them would be "touch not, taste not." When we state the case like that, the Syriac scholar will see at a glance what has happened. The Aramaic root $q\ r\ b$ means "to come near, to approach, to touch." In the passive form it is "to be brought near, to approach, to touch." So the suggestion arises that, after all, there is an Aramaic element somewhere behind the Russian text; and it is surprising that we should be able to detect it, after the original has passed successively through the media of translations into Greek, Slavonic, and English. Certainly we must be careful not to conclude hastily that the theory of an Aramaic Josephus can be definitely discarded: on that note of caution we may, for the present, suspend our enquiries as to the Russian story of the Baptist, with the usual petition for more light and further study: for it does not seem that the reference to drinking wine or strong drink came from the Gospel of Luke.

Now let us return to the Flavian Testimony about Christ and the changes which it has undergone.

A Semitic Element in the Flavian Testimony

There is still one curious expression in the Testimony of Josephus as contained in the *Antiquities*, which seems to point to an Aramaic original. We refer to the statement near the close that the divine prophets had spoken all these and *ten thousand other marvellous things* concerning him. It is the exaggeration of the statement that attracts our attention. Josephus can hardly be held responsible for an exaggeration of a statement which he had an interest in reducing to modest dimensions. Was he, then, reporting the extravagance of Christians' beliefs that they could find all about their Master in the prophets? Even in that case the "ten thousand other things" could hardly have been gathered from the pages of the *Testimony Book*. It may, conceivably, be scornful, but the explanation does not seem to be adequate. If, however, we say "many other marvels" instead of "ten thousand other marvels," we have a case similar to that which we unearthed in an article which I wrote some years since on a *Midrash on the Blessing of Isaac*.[53] The paper referred to was an explanation of the story which Papias puts into the mouth of Jesus with regard to the fertility of the earth in the World to Come. Ten thousand branches to the vine, ten thousand twigs to the branch, ten thousand clusters to the twig, ten thousand grapes to the cluster: similar abundance in the ripened grain. We were able to show that this was a Midrash on the "abundance of corn and wine" which Isaac promised prophetically to his son Jacob, the Hebrew word *rōb* (abundance) being read as *ribbu* (ten thousand). It is customary to ridicule Papias for telling this tale, because it makes Jesus ridiculous, but as the midrash has since turned up in the *Book of Enoch*, the ridicule is misplaced. The story is part of the millennial currency.[54]

If such an explanation cleared up the meaning of an otherwise rather childish story, may it not be that a similar explanation will bring the Flavian Testimony within the bounds of reasonable speech, whether for himself or for the Christians whose opinion he is quoting? That is to say, Josephus may have meant to say "very many" and been erroneously transcribed as "ten thousand." This would require us to admit that the Testimony in the *Antiquities* goes back, as does the Russian story of the Baptist, to an Aramaic original, viz., to the book which Josephus wrote for his compatriots in Northern Mesopotamia. The argument, however, is not as convincing as in the Russian case, where we were obliged to concede Aramaic elements in the story, quite against our first impressions. So we will leave the "ten thousand" prophetical Testimonies in a measure of uncertainty.

Justin Martyr and Josephus

We now propose to show that Justin Martyr was acquainted with the Flavian Testimony in the form in which Josephus wrote it, and before it had undergone the slight transformation at Christian hands which gave us a canonical text. We have shown that the principal changes were, (i) to get rid of the offensive θαυματουργός or "Magician"; (ii) the deletion of the word λεγόμενος before the name of Christ, although it must be remembered that this is for certain Josephus' term, being attested elsewhere by his reference to James, the brother of the *so-called* Christ; (iii) we may imagine that before the string of prophetical Testimonies from the prophets, there stood some such words as, "and they say, etc." Now let us turn to Justin Martyr and try to realise the situation in which he found himself, when he proposed to address the Senate of Rome and the Imperial Household on the question of the Christian Faith. It will be remembered that, ever since the war with the Jews, Josephus had

---

53. ["A New Patristic Fragment," *Expositor* 5th series, 1 (1895), pp. 448-55. AF]
54. See *Enoch*, ch. x, 19 [*1 En.* AF].

found his works officially canonised in the State Library at the Capitol, where they could, of course, be referred to as authoritative. Now Justin Martyr coming to Rome with his *Book of Testimonies*, which he means to throw at the heads of the Roman State, has always had something of an irrational or fanatical appearance, but perhaps he was not quite the fool that some people have taken him to be. Before he took up his parable in dead earnest, to show that the Divine Prophets had foretold the Divine Christ, he asked himself the question what kind of missile was likely to be thrown at him in return. Let us then see how he safeguards himself in his *Apology* and how he unmasks the fire of his battery of Biblical quotations. The matter is so important for the restoration of the environment of the courageous missionary that we must quote one passage at length.

> In case any one should oppose us and say "What is to hinder the belief that our so-called Christ (τὸν παρ' ἡμῖν λεγόμενον χριστόν) being a man sprung from the human race, wrought by magic art the mighty works of which you speak, and on that account appeared to be Son of God?" We will now make our demonstration, not putting our faith in people who are mere talkers, but being persuaded of necessity by those who prophesy of events before they happen, etc.—*Apol.*, i. 30.

Now here we are struck both by the language and by the course of the argument. Jesus is a man who works by magic, whom deeds of power reveal to be Son of God, so they say; but we prefer to follow the prophets who spoke of things before they occurred. This prepares the way for the introduction of the Testimonies. The supposed objector refers to the *so-called* Christ; that is the language of Josephus, uncorrected as yet. He was a man, whose magical powers made them think him to be divine; that is the opening statement of Josephus about the man who was a thaumaturge or wonder-worker, who led people to a false opinion about him; that is the Josephan doctrine uncorrected, as we have seen, which makes the Christ a Magician. Finally, we have the challenge to refer disputed matters to the prophets. It is natural to assume that this section of Justin has its motive in the *Testimonium Flavianum*, which follows that manner of presenting the subject; Justin must have known that the statements of Josephus were officially recognised in Rome as historical verity, just as his account of the Jewish War was accepted. He would have to face Josephus, and does it by the simple method of writing a short section, expressing the thought that "perhaps some one will say," the some one in that case being Josephus himself. The statements about Man, Magic, the so-called Messiah and the prophetical Testimonies are all alluded to, as they occur in Josephus, and show that a Christian hand had not meddled with the historian's statements. Justin goes on to explain to the Senate who these "prophets of God" were, who told things in advance. His eye is on the "divine prophets" of Josephus.

This, however, is not all that we learn as to Justin's knowledge of Josephus. It will be remembered that Eisler, against the judgment of almost all critics, restored to his Josephan text the form σοφιστής "a Sophist" instead of σοφὸς ἀνήρ, "a wise man." I must admit that this at first seemed to be a wanton and unnecessary alteration; it was, however, defended by Eisler as a term which Josephus uses elsewhere of people who seem to be wise, and are thought to be so on account of their much speaking. Now it will be remembered (for the passage has often been quoted in debate between the Synoptics and the defenders of the Fourth Gospel), that Justin actually protests against this description of Jesus as a Sophist. "Short and concise," he says, "were all his discourses; *for he was not a Sophist*, but his discourse was the Power of God" (*Apol.*, i. 14).[55]

We take it that Justin was here replying to the opening word of the statement of Josephus about Christ, just in the same way as elsewhere he protests against the explanation of the works of Christ by making him a Magician.

On this account we withdraw any objection which we might have felt at first to the alteration which Eisler makes in the canonical text of Josephus. The reference in Justin, taken along with the rest of the objections which he refutes, implies that *Sophist* stood in the original Josephan text.

The Testimony of Josephus to Jesus Christ
(Thackeray's Translation)

> Now about this time arises Jesus, a wise man [*read*, a man, a sophist], if indeed he should be called a man. For he was a doer of marvellous deeds [*read*, a thaumaturge], a teacher of men who receive the truth [*read*, who take up disorders] with pleasure, and he won over to himself many Jews and many also of the Greek (nation). He was the [*add*, so-called] Christ. And when, on indictment of the principal men among us, Pilate had sentenced him to the Cross, those who had loved (or perhaps rather "been content with") him at the first, did not cease, for [they say that] he appeared to them on the third day alive again, the divine prophets having (fore) told these and ten thousand [*read*, many] other wonderful things concerning him. And even now the tribe of Christians, named after him, is not extinct.

The authenticity of the passage, or at least of its nucleus, is strongly supported by the consideration of style to which Thackeray has given such close attention. The argument from style is two-fold.

First of all there is the verification from the other parts of Josephus' writings that almost every word belongs to that writer's vocabulary. In this Thackeray has the advantage over other critics that he had made for himself a Concordance to Josephus, and so was able to illustrate words and turns of speech as they recur, to a degree beyond that of previous scholars. Next, and

---

55. [*1 Apol.* 14.5. AF]

not less important, is the discovery of Thackeray that the *Testimonium* shows occasionally the hand of the Greek reviser whom Josephus employed in the composition and correction of Books XVII. to XIX. of his *Antiquities*.[56] If this is a correct observation, it is vital and final for the question of authenticity. To use Shakespearian language, we have "two justices' hands to it." The passage in the *Antiquities* belongs to the *Antiquities*; *in its present form* it cannot belong to the *Jewish War*: that supposition is excluded by the joint authorship of the historian and his amanuensis.

Accordingly Thackeray was putting the case reasonably when he says:

> The criterion of style, to my mind, turns the scale in favour of the authenticity of the passage considered as a whole, if not in every detail. If the text has been mutilated and modified, there is at least a Josephan basis (Thackeray: *Lectures*, p. 141).

If the reader should ask for further information with regard to the hand of the assisting scribe, the following observation of Thackeray may be useful, over and above the general statement that Josephus' second assistant, whom he employed in this part of his book, was a Greek scholar who affected the style of Thucydides:

> The brevity of a passage of under a dozen lines does not give much scope for the mannerisms of the secretary. It does, however, contain one of his characteristic phrases not found in other parts of Josephus—the phrase, "to receive with pleasure." I infer, says Thackeray, that the amanuensis is still lending his aid.

The argument, then, appears to be final. The passage in dispute, allowing for some slight Christian changes, is genuine. It belongs to the eighteenth book of the *Antiquities*, and shows the hand of Josephus and a learned assistant. Whether there was a similar passage in the *Jewish War*, as the Russian text suggests, is another matter.

It requires no violent use of the imagination to suggest the manner in which the *Testimonium* was provoked. Josephus was attached to the Imperial Court, which was in the time of Domitian distracted by the invasion of a new religion. The Christian Faith was openly confessed by two of the heads of the Flavian clan, Titus Flavius Clemens and Flavia Domitilla his wife. Both of them paid the penalty of the Christian confession, one by his life, the other by her banishment. May we not then suppose that they had presented the case for Christ to the great Jewish scholar and politician, and could they have done it better than in the style which Paul employed to Agrippa, "Josephus, believest thou the prophets?"[57] The *Testimony Book* is of the prophets and

---

56. "Books XVII. to XIX. betray the idiosyncrasies and pedantic tricks of a hack in imitation of Thucydides" (*Lectures*, p. 108).

57. [Cf. Acts 26.27. AF]

de Christo. The situation is made for what Eisler calls the polemic against the Testimonies.[58]

Now let us turn back and see if we can get any clearer light on the complication which was introduced into the argument when Dr Eisler detected that the author of the *Acts of Pilate* had been imitating the Flavian Testimony, and when we observed further that there was a coincidence in thought and to some extent in language between the *Acts of Pilate* and the *Fourth Gospel*.

Three personalities are involved, whom we may call A, B and C. Of these A (the *Acts of Pilate*) is under the influence of B (the Josephan Testimony); the perplexity arises as to the connection between A and B on the one hand and C (the Fourth Gospel) on the other. Of these three personalities, two are certainly persons of distinction in the theological world; Josephus is eminent both theologically and politically; if Judaism had a political and religious leader in the latter part of the first century, it is Josephus. His religious position is also representative; he declines to admit the Messiahship of Jesus, but is a firm believer in the divine prophets, and is quite persuaded of the miraculous powers of Jesus, though he tries to find an explanation for them as the work of a Magician.

Our second personality is much more obscure. He represents the same doubts as to the real humanity of Jesus as Josephus does, or affects to do, and is equally persuaded with Josephus as to the reality of the miraculous works.

Our third personality is evidently a person of great authority in the early Christian community, whether he be an apostle or not. He is anti-Judaist and uses prophetical Testimonies against the Jews somewhat obscurely at times. His position controversially is one of antagonism to those who do not believe Jesus to be the Messiah, though they have seen marvellous works done such as never man had performed; and he confutes official Judaism which does not believe in the Christ, by means of prophecies in which they profess to believe, and scriptures which they spend their time in investigating, as well as by the miracles which they admit to have seen. The complex of opinions which he attacks is precisely that of the Flavian Testimony: and it would seem natural to infer the priority or, at least, the contemporaneity of the two writings. Compare the language of the Gospel, "Ye do not believe that I am (the Messiah)" (8.24); "though he had done so many miracles before them, they did not believe in him" (12.37), in spite of a prophetical Testimony on the point; "I did amongst them works such as no other had done" (15.24). No doubt the opinions of Josephus are representative of a general Jewish attitude, but they are grouped together in such a way as to make striking coincidence with the

---

58. Dr Plooij's work on these *Testimonies*, to which we referred above, will appear in 1932 in the *Verhandlingen der Kon. Akademie te Amsterdam, afd. Lett.* [*Studies*. AF].

Fourth Gospel. What all parties are agreed on is the Miracles; what they differ on, is the nature of the Miracle-Worker; the final Court of Appeal is to prophetical Testimonies. Dr Eisler's quotation from the *Acts of Pilate* is in order, and may affect the final restoration of the *Testimonium* to its non-Christian form.

Chapter 8

NICODEMUS

The investigations which have been recently re-opened on the Testimony of Josephus with regard to Jesus Christ[1] have done more than substantially to vindicate the authenticity of the statement attributed to the Jewish historian; they have re-acted upon the problems of the New Testament itself, and especially that great riddle for critics of the Gospel records, the origin and date of the Fourth Gospel. On the one hand we have restored to us a blurred page of a great historian, and to some extent may be said to have discovered a new Josephus; on the other hand we have discovered that the pages of the Fourth Gospel also need some rectification, and that we are on the way to the recovery of a new St John.

Let us see what is involved for us in these statements, and in what respect they constitute for us a new point of departure in Biblical and theological criticism.

The new material which has come to light, from which the new conclusions have been deduced, is of two kinds, first, documentary; and second, critical. The first block of new material is the discovery of a Russian version of the *Jewish War* of Josephus, a tradition of that great story which, though evidently much interpolated and corrupted, contains statements which cannot be neglected by the student who is desirous of a right understanding of Josephus and his work. The second accession of material is not altogether new, though from the neglect with which it was received on its first appearance it might be supposed to be the very opposite of new, namely the discovery that the main body of the New Testament writings, whether Gospels or Epistles, repose upon a prior documentary foundation, the lost document called *Testimonies against the Jews* with an alternative title of *Testimonies concerning the Christ*. This collection of Testimonies has acquired fresh importance, from the researches of the Dutch scholar, Dr Plooij,[2] who shows that, in its first form, the document referred to was extant in a Palestinian or North Syrian guise, being written in the Aramaic language, and under the influence of those Jewish explanations, current in the synagogues, which we know under their later title as the Biblical

1. [See Chapter 7. AF]
2. [Plooij, *Studies*. AF]

Targums. The critical study of this subject of the anti-Judaic Testimonies has led to the practical transfer of the main body of the collection which passes under the name of Cyprian from the third century to a date in the first century, earlier, as we have said, than the writings of the New Testament, to which it forms a prologue, the study of which is absolutely necessary for the textual critic or the exegete.

Our first statement, then, is two-fold. First, the researches of modern criticism, brought to a definite conclusion by Dr Robert Eisler,[3] have vindicated the authorship of the Flavian Testimony and restored it, approximately, to its non-Christian form; second, the researches into the anti-Judaic methods and materials of the early Christians, brought to a climax by Dr Plooij, who has carried out the speculations of earlier scholars to a final statement, have given us the necessary background for the development of the Christian doctrine.

The new situation in criticism has been created by placing the Testimony of Josephus side by side with the anti-Judaic Testimonies; when this is done, as Eisler was the first to detect, there is seen to be a connection between the two. Josephus is aware of the existence of the anti-Judaic document which the Christians employ in their propaganda, and expresses a measure of disagreement with it. If the Testimonies have a section to prove that Christ is called *Man and Angel*, he objects to the latter term while conceding the former. In so doing, however, he does not concede the obvious; he has a saving clause as to the propriety of calling the Messiah a man, when he has performed such miracles as are beyond human power. This statement the Christians made use of when transcribing the text of Josephus. It was certainly a very striking concession. The genuineness of the miracles is admitted; nor does it seem that it has ever been doubted by Jewish controversialists; we can see in the Gospel that it was the explanation of the miracles that was in debate, not the actual works of power. It was a dilemma for the observer, who thought the assistance of Beelzebub to be a more proper explanation than divine cooperation. Equally strange is the fact that in our time when at last the Jews have begun to write the Life of Christ for themselves, a writer so tinged with modern views as Klausner finds it admissible to concede the miracles.[4] With somewhat less of confidence, we may say that Josephus, while shaking his head at some things which he found asserted in the Christian Testimonia, admitted that the final appeal was to Moses and the prophets. There was certainly not so wide a gulf between Josephus and the early Christian advocates as to make an argument between them impossible. In this connection let it be noted that there was no need to stress, as we did in our recent Essay,[5] the language of Josephus

---

3. [Eisler, *IHCOYC*. AF]

4. [Joseph G. Klausner, *Jesus of Nazareth: His Life, Times, and Teaching* (trans. Herbert Danby; London: G. Allen & Unwin, 1925). AF]

5. [*Josephus*, printed in this volume. AF]

unduly, as to the "ten thousand things" which the prophets had foretold of the Christ, as though the enumeration were ironical, or perhaps a misunderstanding of a Semitic text. I am reminded by my colleague Miss Sherlock[6] that the Greek word μυρια (myria) can mean either ten thousand or simply "very many," according as the accent is placed on the first or second syllable: we may then with perfect propriety translate Josephus in the sense that the prophets had foretold many other things concerning the Messiah. It is not necessary even to make such a statement into a Christian affirmation, and insert in the Flavian Testimony a few words to the effect that "they say," for it is within the bounds of reasonable possibility that the Jews had themselves evolved a Testimony Book before the time of Christ, and that there are traces of this in the Gospel where reference is made as to "what the Scribes say" regarding either the Christ, or his forerunner, the Elijah of prophecy. In such a case the common ground might be much wider than we at first imagined: the polemic part of the Flavian Testimony might be further reduced. However that may be, the Testimony itself which is embedded in Josephus' works, in the *Antiquities* for certain (A.D. 94) and very likely in the *Jewish War* also (A.D. 75), is almost of the nature of an official document; for Josephus is the leading Pharisee in the literature of the first century, and the leading representative of Judaea in Rome.

This explains at once, what Eisler detected, the dependence of the apocryphal *Acts of Pilate* upon Josephus. The other Joseph, he of Arimathea, is made to quote the Flavian Testimony, with the Flavian hesitation and the Flavian affirmation, the hesitation as to whether it is proper to call the person *a man* who has done works that were more than human, and was in fact best described in modern terms as a *Super-man*. The importance of the reference to the *Acta Pilati* is great; it takes us into the world of half-formed opinion, where the indecision of the Jewish teacher is copied approvingly by the anonymous Christian writer, who has not reached a complete statement about the Christ, but is content with what is already being said in religious circles, both Jewish and Christian.

It was at this point that the writer of the Fourth Gospel comes on the scene, and represents Jesus as refuting in his own person the antagonistic statements of Josephus. Reference has already been made in our Essay to the passages where the words of Jesus occur. It is well to remind ourselves of them. If Josephus said of Jesus that "this was the so-called Christ (or Messiah)," a passage which the Christians altered by the omission of the word *so-called*, we can see why Jesus challenges the Jews because "Ye do not believe that I am he" (sc. the Messiah);[7] which incredulity is accompanied by an admission

---

6. [Helen Travers Sherlock, Rendel Harris's assistant during the last years of his life. AF]
7. [John 8.24. AF]

of the miracles on the part of those who were incredulous of his Messiahship; for "though he had done so many miracles before them they did not believe in him"; and again, "If I had not done among them the works which no other had done, they would not have had sin."

Now these quotations cover a wide tract in the Fourth Gospel; they range from 8.14 to 12.27, and to 15.18.[8] That takes in not only the irritating controversies between our Lord and the Pharisees, but the calm retrospect of the time of the Last Supper. Take them together, they agree with Josephus and the *Acta Pilati* in their description of the miraculous works of Jesus, and they contradict the opinion of Jews, including Josephus, as to whether He were the Christ or not. It would be easy to add other passages in which a challenging reference is made to the works done by Jesus: one of the most striking is John 10.17-18,[9] where it is said that "if I am not doing the works of my Father (ἐὰν μὴ ποιῶ τὰ ἔργα), do not believe me; but if I am so doing—I will not say, Believe me, but, You do believe the works." He leaves them on the horns of a dilemma. A very challenging form of appeal to anyone who had conceded the Works and had disavowed the Worker. How applicable this all is to the situation which is taken by Josephus in his *Testimonium* must be clear to every candid person. It suggests that the speeches of Jesus in the Fourth Gospel have been edited to meet a controversial exigency.

Nor is this all; of the two points in which we find Josephus expressing the direct negative, one, which has been already referred to, is the question whether Jesus is the Christ, which Josephus meets with the formula, "he that is called the Christ"; the other is the title of "Angel" which is given in the Christian *Testimonium*, to which Josephus takes exception; "Man, if you will, but not Angel." In the New Testament we have the Angelic Messenger replaced in the Epistle to the Hebrews by "*Apostle* and High Priest,"[10] with some evidence for an objection to the term *Angel* as being susceptible of a Docetic interpretation; in the Fourth Gospel we have a constant, repeated affirmation that Christ is the one whom God has sent. It is almost the favourite term in the Fourth Gospel, and is used by Jesus of himself, as well as by others to describe him. So that here also we have the affirmation repeated, where Josephus had suggested a negative. This is why we make the suggestion that there is matter in the Fourth Gospel, which is not only anti-Judaic, but definitely anti-Josephic, and we have to ask whether this does not mean that the Gospel is later in date than Josephus himself, and is, in some respects, particularly in the speeches reported, non-historical in character. If it should turn out that in the Fourth Gospel Jesus is made to reply to Josephus, the anachronism would re-act on the general question of the authorship, and it would be

8. [John 8.24; 12.37; 15.24. AF]
9. [John 10.37-38. AF]
10. [Heb. 3.1. AF]

8. Nicodemus

more difficult to decide how much of the work is a genuine contribution to history.

We are now going to examine a particular incident in the Gospel, the first appearance of the mysterious Pharisee named Nicodemus.[11] The portrait of Nicodemus and Christ's conversation with him is one of a pair of what we may call *Illustrated Dialogues*, containing Christian truths of the first magnitude. Nicodemus hangs adjacent to the Woman of Samaria,[12] and the conspicuous characteristic of the two is that they are *Duologues* rather than *Dialogues*. If the record of these conversations is historical, we can only say that the reporter of them is Jesus Himself: for when a private discourse is thus reported, no other person being behind the arras, we have to choose as reporter in one case either Jesus or Nicodemus, and in the other either Jesus or the anonymous Samaritan Woman. In the open air, at all events, an arras for a listener does not exist. The two portraits being evidently by the same hand, we arrive at the final decision that the artist is Jesus, and not either Nicodemus or the Woman. We have in that case dissected out what we may call a fragmentary *Gospel according to Jesus*, a portrait painted by Himself in two positions. If this could be maintained it would be easy to detect the meaning of either discourse; the one discourse is on the New Birth, the other on the New Worship. In which case Nicodemus and the Samaritan Woman are foils to set off fundamental doctrine of the First Period.

The matter, however, is not so simple as it looks. The Nicodemus portrait has been badly damaged and is broken at the lower end. It has been restored, and the restorer has put himself on the broken canvas. Any reader can satisfy himself that the record is broken; Jesus and Nicodemus disappear; perhaps Jesus is "left speaking," but the hand of the editor, with his favourite statement about witnessing what we have seen and telling what we actually know,[13] is already recognisable, and the completed discourse about the Serpent in the Wilderness is a highly evolved piece of allegory which belongs to a later date.[14] It is a pity that the story is left incomplete. One would have been glad to have it rounded off as neatly as the story of the Woman in the Fourth Chapter; for Nicodemus, though he does not appear in the Synoptic accounts, will turn up again in the Fourth Gospel, always with a sense of increasing devotion and discipleship. He will take Christ's part in the Sanhedrin, he will be the second of the chief mourners at the Burial.[15] But how, it will be asked, did the report get abroad of what happened in the secret session of the Sanhedrin? If this is historical, it would seem natural to assume that it was Nicodemus that

---

11. [John 3.1-21. AF]
12. [John 4.1-42. AF]
13. [John 3.11. AF]
14. [John 3.14. AF]
15. [John 7.50-52, 19.39. AF]

reported it, and that raises again a further question as to whether we were correct in assuming that it was Jesus' report of the Night Interview and not the report of Nicodemus. A worse perplexity remains behind. Let us turn back to the portrait of which we were first speaking. The picture hangs on a nail. The discourse in ch. 3 is in sequence with the closing verses of ch. 2.[16] These verses tell how Jesus, at some unexplained visit to Jerusalem, said to be a Passover festival, did so many miracles that many believed on him in consequence of what they saw; and it is this statement that is the prologue to the story of the Night Visit. There is no explanation of these remarkable miracles and consequent conversions. No account is given of a single miracle, and the Passover at which they happened is suspect on the side of chronology.

This is, however, a mere trifle. After all, we have no detailed account of Christ's marvels nor of his movements from Galilee to the South; what is more perplexing is that the terms in which Nicodemus addresses the Lord are closely connected with the Flavian Testimony as we observed it in the previous cases. Let us see what Nicodemus has to say, the great elect Pharisee of the Gospel narration. He calls the Master διδάσκαλος, a Teacher, not merely politely a Rabbi; this teacher has "come from God,"[17] then he is the Ἄγγελος of whom Josephus and the early Christian Testimonies speak, the former hesitating, the latter affirming. The proof of the *Angel* is the *Miracles*; they are super-human, they need God for their explanation. We see that we are in the Josephan sequence, with the terms Angel, Miracle-Worker, Teacher. When we recall the previous suspicions with regard to what the Fourth Gospel says of Jesus in language parallel to that of Josephus, we are obliged to ask whether the language of Nicodemus in the Gospel is not affected from the same source; the only difference between Pharisee Josephus and Pharisee Nicodemus being that the latter accepts Christ as the Angel, and the former accepts him as the Miracle-Worker only, denying him the title given in the Testimonia.

We might perhaps say that this makes Nicodemus into a lay figure, created for purposes of edification, but this may be too rapid a conclusion. The Fourth Gospel does not elsewhere give the impression that Nicodemus is a lay figure.

Josephus Again

Let us now see if we can carry the enquiry a little further. Is it possible to resolve certain other points of the enigma of the tradition of Josephus regarding the Christ? We have learnt a good deal already on the matter of the Flavian Testimony; but it is not yet clear whether this testimony is one or two. If the

---

16. [John 2.23-25. AF]
17. [John 3.2. AF]

Slavonic text is to be trusted, even without viewing it as a complete or trustworthy tradition, we have two Flavian Testimonies, not necessarily coincident at all points. Flavian A is our old-time friend of the *Antiquities*, Flavian B is the recently arrived visitor from the *Jewish War*; Flavian A belongs to the end of the first century; that would be quite certain, if, as Thackeray suggested, one could detect in it the touch of the amanuensis of the later books of the *Antiquities*; it appears to be the document which Justin Martyr set himself to refute in his *Apology* when addressing the Roman Senate, though that statement must not be made too positively. Flavian B is some twenty years earlier, and existed in two forms, one in Aramaic addressed to the Mesopotamian Jews, the other in Greek, addressed to Imperial Rome. We have made a strong case for the belief that the Russian Josephus has in it evidence of an ultimate Aramaic original, even if it be itself a clear translation from the Greek. We showed that the key to the understanding of the Flavian texts, whether one or both, was to observe the underlying motive of Josephus, in his attitude towards the Christian collection of proof-texts from Moses and the prophets, which defines the character of the Messiah, and his attitude towards Judaism. Josephus is regarding these prophetical Testimonies in a peculiar way; he at once owns and contradicts, he criticises without altogether disapproving, appears to admit the evidence of the miracles on the one hand, and of the prophets on the other, but speaks of Him that is "the *so-called Messiah*." We were able to confirm the accuracy of Eisler's reference to the *Book of Testimonies*, having reached the same result by a different road. We were able also to draw a further important conclusion as to the *Ecce Homo* of the Fourth Gospel,[18] by finding its prophetical origin.

We can now take another step in advance in the solution of the remaining difficulties. If we turn to the Russian text we shall find the following statement in Flavian B:—

> There appeared a certain man of magical power, if it is permissible to call him a man, whom certain Greeks call a Son of God, but his disciples call the true prophet, said to raise the dead and heal all diseases.

We stop at that point, in order to affirm that THOSE LAST WORDS ARE THE ACTUAL HEADLINE OF A SECTION IN THE CHRISTIAN *BOOK OF TESTIMONIES*. The proof is as follows: it was pointed out by me when I first wrote on the subject of Testimonies[19] that Justin Martyr in his *Apology* to the Roman Senate, quotes freely from the prophets concerning Christ, and amongst his quotations we find the following:—

---

18. [John 19.5. AF]
19. ["The Use of Testimonies in the Early Christian Church," *Expositor* 7th series, 2 (1906), pp. 385-409. AF]

ὅτι δὲ καὶ θεραπεύσειν πάσας νόσους καὶ νεκροὺς ἀνεγερεῖν ὁ ἡμέτερος χριστὸς προεφητεύθη, ἀκούσατε τῶν λελεγμένων. ἔστι δὲ ταῦτα. Τῇ παρουσίᾳ αὐτοῦ, ἁλεῖται χωλὸς ὡς ἔλαφος κτέ.

And that our Christ was foretold that he should *heal all diseases and raise the dead*, listen to what was said: "At his coming the lame man shall leap as an hart, etc."—Justin: *1 Ap.* 48.[20]

The same statement, introducing the prophecy of the thirty-fifth chapter of Isaiah, is repeated in an abbreviated form at a later point in the *Apology*:—

When the heathen "learnt that it was foretold that he should *heal diseases and raise the dead*," they dragged in Asklepios.—Justin: *1 Ap.* 54.[21]

Here then we have the headline of a section in the *Testimony Book*, and it is transferred bodily to the text of Flavian B, as being what the prophets have said and what the disciples say concerning Christ.

The importance of this discovery is obvious. Josephus, both in Flavian A and Flavian B, is regarding the Christian Testimonies: the antiquity of the collection is past question.

That is only a minor point; for our present purpose it is more important to have shown that the use of Testimony matter in Josephus is justified, and, as far as the evidence goes, the Flavian Testimony in the *Antiquities* is not independent of that in the *Jewish War*. In either case Jesus is the Wonder-Worker, in fact he has no other name in the Russian text, and we showed that this was the original of the θαυματουργός in the *Antiquities*, to which description of Jesus as Thaumaturge later Christians naturally objected.

It is evident that a much closer and more sympathetic study must be made of this Russian text. The terms describing Christ are ancient and significant. For instance, there is the *True Prophet*, which we recognise as the *Prophet of Truth* in certain collections of the Sayings of Jesus, and there is the admission that some say that "He is sent from God," which is one of the commonest terms used by Christ of Himself in the Fourth Gospel. It is implied in the address of Nicodemus to Jesus in the third chapter of the Gospel of John ("thou art come from God, a teacher");[22] and this at once raises the question of the relation of the Fourth Gospel to the Josephan traditions.

Our knowledge of the existence of a collection of early Christian Testimonies, of a pre-evangelic and Messianic type, and with a definite anti-Judaic temper, has increased in a number of ways our knowledge of the primitive beliefs of the Christian community and thrown light upon some obscurities in the Gospels. We have been able to confirm in some directions the speculations

---

20. [*1 Apol.* 48.1-2. AF]
21. [*1 Apol.* 54.10. AF]
22. [John 3.2. AF]

of Dr Eisler, who had also seen that the statements of Josephus with regard to Jesus Christ required a background for their proper intelligence in the Christian *Book of Testimonies*. It was an advantage to be able to see Josephus posing against the Testimonies, and a succession of early Christian writers contradicting Josephus, while the disputants on both sides appear to have been agreed on the miraculous character of the works of Jesus. We were able to recapture the controversial atmosphere of the first century, and to find out what certain people wanted to say and to persuade other people to believe, and what certain other people wanted not to have either said or believed. It became clearer, in the course of our enquiry, that it was not possible to reject altogether the statements contained in the Russian version of the *Jewish War*, and we deduced from this Slavonic tradition the conclusion that there was a Flavian Testimony to Jesus Christ belonging to this earlier writing of Josephus, and that the well-known Testimony in the *Antiquities* had not only been, to some extent, altered by Christian hands, but had actually undergone some change at the hand of Josephus himself. In some ways the Testimony in the *War* is more friendly than we could have expected: the writer is careful to say, that Jesus, except for His breach of the Sabbath Law, and some similar traditions, was of an upright character and harmless nature. "He did nothing shameful," says Josephus, "he did nothing by sleight of hand"; no conjurer of the common kind, this Wonder-Worker. Josephus of the time of the Jewish War, knew better than to say, as Celsus did later, that one could see these tricks done any day in the market-place, for twopence.

It will be seen that our estimate of the Russian document becomes more favourable the more we study it.

We are now going to show that the same document will assist us, not only to recapture early Christian mentality, and to some extent early Jewish mentality, for the period before A.D. 70, but that it will also restore to us the Jewish mentality for a period that antedates the Christian era.

We recall to our minds the steps by which we were able to establish the existence of the early Christian *Book of Testimonies*, which we have now tracked back from the pages of Cyprian and Lactantius, through the quotations of Tertullian, Irenaeus, and Justin, to a form in which we can still recognise the primitive document, very little changed in form or content. It was Messianic in character, and for the most part occupied in defining the marks by which the Messiah could be recognised. For instance, one of its leading sections was the proof that the Messiah "when he came," would "heal all diseases and raise the dead," the actual text being taken from the thirty-fifth chapter of Isaiah. The "coming of the Deliverer" was implied in the words, "Your God shall come ... *He will come* and save you. Then shall the lame man leap as an hart, etc." Christian Fathers who refer to this Testimony commonly prefix the words, ἐν τῇ παρουσίᾳ αὐτοῦ "at His coming," and it was the detection of this prefixed explanation by Irenaeus and Justin that opened our eyes to the fact that these two writers were not quoting Isaiah directly, but only a Testimony from Isaiah. (See what is said on this matter in my little book on *Testimonies*, Pt. 1.)

The early Christian emphasis on the Messianic "Coming," may be noted in a modification or expansion of the head-line, such as we find in Cyprian, to the effect that the Messiah is the one "qui venturus esset," as the "illuminator and salvator,"[23] where we can see the eyes of the blind being opened as in Isaiah, by the one who is to "come and save you."[24]

If the reader wants another Patristic specimen of the way in which Isaiah 35 was used Messianically, he may turn to Eusebius, *Demonstratio Evangelica* (6, 21), where he will find the παρουσία or "Coming," played upon in the following manner:—

κἐνταῦθα διαρρήδην Θεοῦ ἄφιξις θεοπίζεται σωτήριος·[25]

while the chapter is headed :

ἐμφανὴς Θεοῦ παρουσία,

and again

τῇ τοῦ Θεοῦ εἰς ἀνθρώπους παρουσίᾳ,[26]

and

τῇ εἰς ἀνθρώπους τοῦ Θεοῦ Λόγου παρουσίᾳ,[27]

and

διὰ τῆς τοῦ σωτῆρος ἡμῶν Ἰησοῦ Χριστοῦ παρουσίας, ὑφ' οὗ καὶ τυφλῶν ἀνεῴχθησαν ὀφθαλμοί, καὶ κωφοὶ τὴν ἀκοὴν παρειλήφασιν.[28]

What Eusebius, following the early Christian tradition, says about the "Coming of the Saviour," leads at once to the inference that the Messiah was described in the primitive Christian statement as ὁ ἐρχόμενος, *the Coming One*: it has not been sufficiently recognised that this title, for which we have New Testament evidence, is derived from the thirty-fifth chapter of Isaiah, by means of a collection of Messianic proof-texts.

Now see the importance of this recognition. When John the Baptist, apparently in a time of some spiritual discouragement, such as is natural to prison

23. [*Test.* 2.7. AF]
24. [Isa. 35.5; 35.4. AF]
25. [*Dem. ev.* 6.21.2. AF]
26. [*Dem. ev.* 6.21.5. AF]
27. [*Dem. ev.* 6.21.7. AF]
28. [*Dem. ev.* 6.21.2. AF]

8. Nicodemus

walls, and prison diet, sends disciples to enquire of Jesus, they are told to ask whether he is "the Coming One," or whether we are to look elsewhere, or elsewhen.[29] Jesus replies in the terms of the thirty-fifth of Isaiah, performing certain miracles and translating them into corresponding language of Testimony: "Tell John ... that blind men are recovering sight, lame men are walking, lepers are cleansed, deaf men are hearing, dead men are coming back to life, and *there is good news for the poor*."[30]

The language of Jesus is that of a written Testimony, to which language his acts correspond: it says clearly that "I am the Messiah." The importance of this Biblical recognition lies in the fact that there must have been a pre-Christian Book of Testimonies in which the Jews had recorded their own ideas and expectations of what Messiah would be like when he came. We shall now prove this, with the help of the Russian document, and prove it, not only for the Christian era, but for a time that is certainly anterior.

On the accession of Herod the Great to the throne of Judaea, there was much discontent over the assumption of the kingship by a foreigner, and this discontent became permanent, and was always more or less in evidence. Let us see what the Slavonic text says on the matter:—

> At that time the priests mourned and grieved together in secret. They durst not (do so openly for fear of) Herod and his friends.
> For (one Jonathan) spoke: "The law bids us have no foreigner for king. Yet we wait for *the Anointed, the meek one, of David's line*. But of Herod we know that he is an Arabian, uncircumcised. *The Anointed will be called meek*, but this (is) he who has filled the whole land with bloodshed. Under the *Anointed* it was ordained *for the lame to walk, and the blind to see, and the poor to become rich*. But under this man the hale have become lame, the seeing are blinded, the rich have become beggars, etc."[31]

Here Jonathan the priest is giving a series of Biblical Testimonies, which apply to *the Messiah, the Anointed*, and do not find verification in Herod. They are substantially the same Testimonies which Jesus sent back to John the Baptist; even the description of the "evangelisation of the poor" is not wanting (πτωχοὶ εὐαγγελίζονται).[32] We infer, then, that at the time of the accession of Herod there was in existence a series of collected *Testimonies concerning the Anointed*, and that there is some overlapping between this collection and the first Christian *Book of Testimonies*.

It is surprising, in view of these parallelisms and coincidences, to find that there are people who still believe that Jesus never affirmed himself to be the

---

29. [Matt. 11.3. AF]
30. [Matt. 11.4-5. AF]
31. [Part of the passage replacing the Greek text of *B.J.* 1.364-70. AF]
32. [Matt. 11.5. AF]

Messiah. It would be nearer the truth to say that he never affirmed himself to be anything else.

It seems impossible to neglect the Russian Josephus, when from a single passage we are able to throw so much light both on Jewish and on Christian beliefs.

The Magic of Jesus

The Russian text tells us clearly that whatever works of power were done by Jesus were accomplished by oracle rather than by miracle; the mechanics of the conjurer were non-existent. "Everything, whatsoever he wrought through some invisible power, he wrought through some word and as command." And again, "He himself did nothing shameful nor by sleight of hand, but by a word." The statements are too closely embedded in the narration to be subtracted as Christian interpolations. Moreover we can see that they are in accordance with the tradition of the New Testament itself and of later Christian traditions. In the New Testament Jesus commands unclean spirits and unruly winds, no machinery other than the word being applicable in either case. In the later traditions, as Dr Plooij reminds me, such as the Abgar story,[33] we have the correspondence between Jesus and Abgar opened by the latter with a statement that "I have heard of your cures that they are done without medicaments," after which Abgar recites the cures in what is evidently a transcript of Testimonies of the type which we have been studying. "Report says, that thou makest the blind to see again, the lame to walk, and cleansest lepers ... and thou raisest the dead." Abgar expresses his doubt whether Jesus is God come down from heaven or a son of God, and begs Jesus to pay a visit to himself and his city. Jesus replies by quoting an oracle that those *who have seen me will not believe in me*, and explains that he must fulfil his mission in Judaea and then return *to Him that sent me*. Here we have grouped together the Angel or Divine Messenger, the Miracle-Worker without machinery, and the Testimony from Isaiah to the same. It is clear that the account in the Russian Josephus is altogether in harmony with these traditions, and as we said there is no need to remove them from the text of Josephus on the ground that they are Christian interpolations.

There is, however, one direction in which difficulty arises. We quoted above the statement in the restored text of Josephus that the Messiah should "heal all diseases and raise the dead," which is identified as one of the leading Christian, and perhaps pre-Christian, Testimonies concerning the Messiah. It was not quite easy to find the words in question in the Russian text, and we suspected that the text had been expanded by Eisler from the Prologue to the *Letter of*

---

33. [*Epistle of Christ and Abgar.* AF]

Lentulus. Montefiore transcribes it without any mark of suspicion. It should have been bracketed. I do not mean that the passage is wrongly restored to the text, though everyone feels that Eisler is very easygoing in his insertions and omissions. In the present case there is ground for believing the restoration to be correct, whether it comes from Ps. Lentulus or not; for I do not think that either Eisler, or Montefiore who transcribes him, had any suspicion that a leading Christian Testimony had been put back into the text. For that reason we may approve the insertion. If it comes from the Prologue in the Lentulus letter, that is an unexpected argument for approving Eisler's treatment of the text. We certainly did not expect to acquire primitive material from a twelfth-century Latin text: but it is clear that we are on fresh trails in the early history of the Christian movement, and must keep our eyes open for new evidence from any quarter whence it may arise. Josephus may very well have recorded the fact that the disciples of Jesus said that he was "to heal all diseases and to raise the dead." We know on other grounds that they did so. The Christian tradition on the point is multiform and manifold.

Jesus As Pacifist

We are now coming in view of the principal contention of Eisler, viz., that Jesus was a Pacifist leader of the people, who, under pressure of his followers, became a Revolutionary, and instigated a revolt against Rome. We should like to have this matter fully discussed, and the evidence on one side and on the other, to be carefully restated. Montefiore in the *Hibbert Journal*[34] has done much in this direction, and has pronounced an adverse verdict to Eisler, with which most students will be disposed to agree. Our contribution to the evidence adds one important element to the final argument and decision. Whatever may be said of Eisler's treatment of the Gospels as being wilful and unworthy of exact scholarship, we have shown that outside of the Gospels, and in a definitely Jewish tradition, the newly-found Russian text of Josephus describes the priestly party in Jerusalem at the accession of Herod, as altogether non-resistant and pacifist. The Messiah whom they expect is to be *the Meek One*. He will not shed blood as Herod has been shedding. He will enrich the poor, instead of pauperising the rich. All the statements made by Jonathan the priest under this head have the force of oracles, their descriptions are based on prophetical authority. Even if the Law forbids an alien king, they will not lift a finger against him. That applies both to Herod and the Romans. If the Jewish pre-Christian Testimonies describe in this way a Pacifist Messiah, and if Jesus assumes the rôle of that Messiah, and endorses his prophetical

---

34. [Claude G. Montefiore, "Dr Robert Eisler on the Beginnings of Christianity," *Hibbert Journal* 30 (1931–1932), pp. 298-318. AF]

description, perhaps even deducing from it his own statement as to being "meek and lowly in heart," then we have the strongest case possible for the Christian statement concerning Christ as non-resistant. To prove Him anything else, the *onus probandi* will be upon Dr Eisler's shoulders. So far as we have gone, the new evidence is against his interpretation of the events.

The Messiah the Meek One

We have seen that the pre-Christian description of the Messiah, disclosed by the Jews at the time of the accession of Herod, included amongst other titles that of the *Meek One* who was to come; and it may perhaps be asked what was the oracle of the Old Testament which was being quoted and acted upon by the Jewish leaders. It must surely have been the prophecy of Zechariah (9.9), "Thy King cometh to thee; he is just and having salvation; he is meek, and rides upon an ass." This is certainly interpreted by the Jewish Priests in a pacifist, or at least an anti-zealot, sense; and it is in this sense that it must have been taken over by the Christian Testimonies. This is, however, the oracle of the Triumphal Entry:[35] from which we are entitled to affirm that this *Entry* was a Quietist Demonstration and not an incitement to Revolt against Rome.

A Further Trace of the Aramaic Josephus

It will be convenient to add at this point a note on the importance of the observation of Dr Plooij with regard to the parallel in language and ideas between the Russian Josephus and the Abgar correspondence. In the former we are definitely told that Jesus worked "by invisible power, by word and command ... He did nothing shameful, nor by sleight of hand, but by word alone." In the latter series of documents, Jesus is addressed as the Saviour "who does cures without drugs or herbs." Abgar, then, proceeds to quote the great Testimony of the thirty-fifth chapter of Isaiah, which report says that Jesus is fulfilling, concludes that Jesus must be either very God from Heaven, or a son of God, and begs that Jesus will come and heal him of his distemper. Evidently Abgar had his *Testimony Book* with the preface, "Your God will come ... he will come and save you. At his coming the lame man shall leap as a hart, etc." The passage in the prophet has become the motive for the message of Abgar, "I have concluded," says he, "that you are God, or God's representative, come and save me." To complete the parallel, one has only to add that Abgar was himself the lame man, and afflicted with gout! One more artificial fulfilment of prophecy.

---

35. [John 12.15. AF]

Returning now to the parallel between the Russian text and the Abgar story, we infer that there is an underlying agreement between them, in the Miracle-Worker who uses no medicaments but only the word of command. Now it is clear that the Abgar literature, being genuine Syriac, is drawing upon Syriac materials, and it follows, that if that literature is drawing on Josephus, it is the Aramaic Josephus that underlies the text, and not any Greek recension of the same. Nor should this surprise us; for Josephus sent his first draft of the *Jewish War* across the Euphrates, and could not have missed Edessa in its circulation.

The Russian text, then, which is substantially in agreement with Abgar, may have behind it the Aramaic text of the *Jewish War*.

We will leave the further elucidation of this interesting question to Dr Plooij. The whole problem of the Abgar literature appears to be involved.

Conclusion

From the study which has preceded we are entitled to make the following general statements:—

1. If we wish to understand the Gospels, we must get behind the Gospels.
2. If we wish to get behind the Gospels, we must study the first collection of Christian Testimonies concerning the Messiah.
3. If we wish to understand the early Christian Testimonies, we must get behind them; i.e.
4. We must study the Jewish collection of Messianic prophecies from which they are, in part at least, derived.

The Triumphal Entry with its Meek Messiah is only one of many Gospel incidents that are now made intelligible by the searchlight of the Testimonies. Jesus rode into Jerusalem, not on an ass, but upon a Testimonium.

Chapter 9

CORRESPONDENCE WITH HERBERT G. WOOD

LETTER 1

Rendel Harris to Herbert G. Wood, 11 January, 1910.[1]

Dear Boy,
[...] I am sorry we hadn't time to go further with the question of the Sacraments. It is quite clear that the N.T knows nothing of baptismal regeneration, or the Mass on an honest exegesis: but it is equally clear that they were both very early, and that the Catholic interpretations are really to a large extent borrowed from folk-lore. The problem is when did this influence become sensible. In order to settle this, I apply two methods of enquiry, first textual criticism, which greatly simplifies the problem, and then folklore analogies in other religions. It must be admitted as very singular that so many leading beliefs and practices of Christianity are paralleled from the anthropological side.

Take the Virgin Birth, for instance. If it did not originate in folk-lore, it certainly was affected by it: every Annunciation picture, in which the Angel offers the B. V. M a lily to smell, proves it; and so do the Apocryphal Gospels.

Christianity can never maintain its position if at every point it has to be picking off folk-lore accretions; unless we courageously affirm our right to revise our records as well as our rituals. It is a very large order. You will say the Quakers cut the knot. I am not by any means disposed to deny it. But there were many influences inviting drastic reform.

If, for example, we choose to drop the Second Advent, how can we establish an ordinance on the words 'Until he come'. The difficulties are not to be disguised. And they are not all of Paul's making. You see I am alive and thinking. So are you.

Happily the Lord is on our side when we think lowly and courageously.

And many of our old time difficulties have long since melted into natural air.

I wish thee could have stayed longer and gone into things more at leisure.
[...]
Rendel Harris

  1. ['Letters to H. G. Wood, 1906–39,' G Har 11, Woodbrooke archives. AF]

LETTER 2

Rendel Harris to Wood, 18 July, 1910.[2]

Dear Boy,
[...] I have had another turn at Schweitzer, have read all the earlier portions in the English as well as the concluding part.[3] The style is extremely difficult; the epigrams gorgeous; they lure one on from point to point, but I cannot call it lucid. But it is great criticism, and I agree that, if he is right in his emphasis on eschatology, it is all up with Modern Christianity. And we must not evade the eschatology if it is there and a part of his (Christ's) teaching. Neither does it seem possible, at this time of day, to accept it and systematise it.

My statements that the Odes of Solomon have no eschatology do not involve us in the belief in a religious school which ignored eschatology in the sense that it grew up without it and did not assimilate it. For Leendertz has just pointed out, in a very interesting little dissertation which he has sent me,[4] that all the eschatological terms are in the Odes, only atrophied or used for other than their original ends; such as the Dragon with Seven Heads, the Sealing of the Faithful, the Entrance into Paradise etc. And this makes it look as if the Odist had done what the Fourth Gospel did (perhaps a little later), had disentangled himself from his eschatology, or, as a Gentile, had never properly assimilated it. And this process of de-eschatologizing becomes an established fact, traceable on several lines of historical development. For this reason I have some thought of translating Leendertz' little brochure into English, and allowing his observations to make their proper impression. But this will not help us with the Jesus question; it will not make him the uneschatological mystical teacher that we are in search of; for although we may rescue the Saying that the 'Kingdom of Heaven is within you' from misinterpretation, and refuse to allow it and other sayings to be interpreted in an eschatological manner, it is very doubtful whether we have sufficient material to construct our Christ out of, when the eschatology has been subtracted from his teaching.

So you see I do not find Schweitzer as easy as I at first supposed: in any case it is, and must remain, a most important piece of constructive criticism, however much it may appear at first sight to be destructive only. And I mean to

---

2. ['Letters to H. G. Wood, 1906–39,' G Har 11, Woodbrooke archives. AF]
3. [Albert Schweitzer, *The Quest of the Historical Jesus: A Critical Study of its Progress from Reimarus to Wrede* (trans. William Montgomery; London: Adam & Charles Black, 1910). AF]
4. [J.M. Leendertz, *De oden van Salomo* (Amsterdam: Algemeene Doopsgezinde Societeit, 1910). AF]

read it over again with care, so as to see whether the obscure parts will yield a pabulum of digestible matter.

That is all I can say at the present. [...]

Rendel Harris

LETTER 3

Wood to Rendel Harris, 29 December, 1920.[5]

[...] I have just finished reading, though not studying the Testimonies.[6] My mind is full of speculations and questions: so I have taken a large sheet. But now I don't know where to begin. I find your primitive collection of Testimonies very elusive and Protean. I can't get hold of it and I am a bit suspicious that one little book is being over-worked and made to fulfil too many purposes. Yet your main contention that a collection or collections of Testimonies existed at least as early as Q and are/is used in many N.T. writings, I think you have established. And it is a most important conclusion. I am not satisfied with the further attempts to define it. I wish you would now go to work and reconstruct the primitive Testimony-book. Here are two main suggestions or cautions I should like to submit to thee. First, I think you press 'anti-Judaic' too hard. You admit a second line of interest in Testimonies, catechetical or evangelic or Christological. But the 'anti-Judaic' interest is assumed to be always more primitive and dominant. You yourself apparently argue that the use of Hab. in Rom. 1.[7] is later than the Testimony-book because it is not there used anti-Judaically as it was in the Testimony-book. Burch argues passim that the more anti-Judaic use of a passage is the more primitive. e.g. Cyp. I.21[8] preserves a more primitive because more anti-Judaic use of Is. VIII.23 than Matt. IV.15-16 (p. 63),[9] or the quotation in Matt. XIII.14-15 from Is. is secondary because it has lost its anti-Judaic edge. All these arguments I hold to be fallacious. You have no right to assume that the earliest Christian use of a passage is the most anti-Judaic. It is the same fallacy as the assumption that the most violent apocalyptic teaching must be the earliest. Then it is illegitimate to rule out a 'gathering of Testimonies on the basis of events in the life of Jesus,'[10] on the ground that the early possible motifs of Testimony-collections are anti-Judaism and Christology. Both these latter terms may cover a good deal of association of O.T. passages with events in the life of

5. [G Har 17, Woodbrooke archives. AF]
6. [Rendell Harris, *Testimonies*. AF]
7. [Hab. 2.4 in Rom. 1.17. AF]
8. [*Test.* 1.21. AF]
9. [*Testimonies*, 2. AF]
10. [*Testimonies*, 1.68. AF]

Jesus. But I also believe that this interest existed very early and not in a purely controversial form. Take such points as that it must be the son of David and must be born in Bethlehem. They are certainly not anti-Judaic. You may also call them Christological if you like; but I believe the early Christians were interested in the temporal literal fulfilment of prophecy in the events of the life of Jesus. I have very little doubt that Jn [unreadable reference. AF] represents a real factor in the formation of the earliest collections of Testimonies, and it is not anti-Judaism nor Christology. I am inclined to think you yourself underrate the appeal of the argument from prophecy to Gentile minds. That Justin makes so much of it in his Apology is surely significant and shows that the use of Testimonia was not always adversus Judaeos. So I question much, the equation, anti-Judaic=primitive. My second suggestion is this. I most like the chapter on Jesus and the Testimonies, and it seems to me to modify Burch's argument re the gospels. Why not go further along the line? Certain of the oldest parts of the Testimony-book go back to Jesus. They belong to the earliest strata of the gospels. If a later Testimony-book has affected their form in the gospels as they stand, yet their place in the gospels is not due to the Testimony-book, pace Burch. But why attribute all the rest of the Testimony-book to Matthew? Why may not Paul have contributed to the book as well as used it? And so of other N.T. writers, esp. the Evv. But take the case of Paul. I don't see any reason for believing that he derived 'the just shall live by faith'[11] from the Testimony-book. Your argument on that point is not convincing because you begin with Rom. x and do not start from Gal. Burch's argument on Gal. is weak. I cannot see a single serious point of contact between Gal. and Cyp. in his elaborate statement on p. 34.[12] I do not even see why Cyp. I.5.[13] may not be drawn from Gal. itself. So far I'm not convinced that there is any case of the Testimony-book in Gal. and I'm inclined to trace the earlier passages in Rom. to Paul's own original use in Gal. and not to Testimonies. The case re Rom. IX-XI. is much the most convincing. It is clear to me that in any case some of the elements, [unreadable word. AF] the stone passage[14] which you can trace most certainly to the original Testimony-book were so well-known before and apart from the Testimony-book that the references in the gospels need have nothing to do with the book itself. And it seems to me not unlikely that Paul and Apollos contributed more to the book than they took from it. It is a least a possibility that needs to be explored.

I am glad you are more cautious on the subject of Matthew the monk. I hesitate to express an opinion, but I doubt if you can retain your poem at all. I should not myself like to call the suspicion that Eus. knew the poem, a *strong*

---

11. [Rom. 1.17. AF]
12. [*Testimonies*, 2. AF]
13. [*Test.* 1.5. AF]
14. [Rom. 9.33. AF]

one. Assuming the connection in ideas between Eus. D.E.[15] and the poem, you have argued in Pt. I[16] that the poem embodies early matter derived from Hegesippus. If so, I should have thought it was at least as likely that Eus. is influenced by Hegesippus as that he knows the poem. Moreover the poem is attached to a collection of Testimonia which is influenced by Eus. Why then should not the prefatory poem be influenced by Eus. also? Then I would urge that a Byzantine poet must be allowed with Shadwell, to deviate into sense, and even if it is better than the other poems, it is not so good as to be impossible, a good deal later than Eus. So far I see no strong ground for believing Matt's Logia to be Testimonies, and no ground at all for supposing that the earliest collection of Testimonies was in five books. But I want to take up these points more in detail later, if I remain of this opinion on further enquiry.

One isolated point. P. 54 n.[17] If I understand you aright you interpret apostolum in your first quotation[18] to be Jesus. But is it not possible a reference to Acts II.37? Does not Peter spiritually circumcise the Jews at Pentecost? […][19] This is a sceptical outburst rather, but at least it will show that I am truly interested. […]

LETTER 4

Rendel Harris to Wood, 30 December, 1920.[20]

Dear Boy,
I am glad you have taken some time over *Testimonies* and have written such an excellent and necessary criticism. I should be glad if you put it in a magazine form and send it somewhere. If you will do this, I will return it to you.

C.F. Angus also wrote me about the difficulty that he found in restoring and visualising the primitive *Testimony Book*. I advised him to begin with Cyprian and see how far he could get in restoring the Latin of Cyprian and the general arrangement of Cyprian to an earlier form, say by comparison with Irenaeus, Justin etc. It is a splendid theme for a whole dissertation. We must not too hastily label everything that is a Testimony with the title Apostolic, but I am glad that you agree that the existence of a nucleus of *Testimonies* behind the N.T. is made out. It is curious that the otherwise conservative Dr Swete had already conceded the point. If that is right, we are open to discuss

---

15. [*Dem. ev.* AF]
16. [*Testimonies*. AF]
17. [*Testimonies*, 2. AF]
18. [Evagrius, *Altercatio legis inter Simonem Judaeum et Theophilum Christianum* 20. AF]
19. [A list of misprints in *Testimonies*, 2, follows. AF]
20. ['Letters to H. G. Wood, 1906–39,' G Har 11, Woodbrooke archives. AF]

details of authorship. We have certainly opened a new path in criticism and in homiletics, in the relations of the Church and the Synagogue, and in Christology. Would it be too sanguine to say that it is the most important forward step in recent years.

Now for a word or two on your particular objections.

The first relates to anti-Judaic character of the *Testimony Book*. It is quite likely that the original title was merely *Testimonies*, and that *adversus Judaeos* is a later connotation. I want, however, to make the hypothesis that the anti-Judaic element was there from the start. In that case, if we can confirm the hypothesis by making it elucidatory of passages in the N. T., we shall probably have to take some of the Testimonies back to Jesus Himself, and in that case and to that extent He is what I call an *anti-Judaist*. As a matter of fact the earliest N. T. Testimonies are suspect of anti-Judaism. For instance: Matt. 12.18 is not quoted because of its reference to the Servant but because of the mission of the Servant *to the Gentiles*. So is Greg. Nyss. p. 329.[21] But to be pro-ethnic is in the first preaching to be anti-Judaic; in that sense Jesus is anti-Judaic. In the same way the oft-repeated 'Eyes and no-eyes' passage from Is. 6[22] is clearly anti-Judaic to Paul, and we may therefore take ἐκείνοις τοῖς ἔξω of Mark[23] as referring to the Jews who do not believe. So with regard to the Stone: they understood that he had spoken the parable, (including the scripture proof) against themselves. The existence of an anti-Judaic nucleus in the reported Scripture-teaching of Jesus raises for us definitely the question of anti-Judaism and affects our whole judgement as to what went on in the great Propaganda. We must ask as I do, 'What about circumcision? What about sacrifice? What about the sabbath?.' The answer is not equally clear in all three cases; but I notice that Origen definitely says that our Lord abolished circumcision: (*not* St Paul, as commonly supposed). These are the questions that want to be investigated. I agree, however, with you that they need not exhaust the content of the Book of Testimonies. There is Christology and there is History in them: we must, if possible, put them in order of sequence. Does 'all things concerning me in Prophets and Psalms' mean Christology or History. The disciple appear to take both ways.

That is all this afternoon. I will try and send you some more presently.

Thine.

Rendel Harris

---

21. [Zacagni, *Collectanea*. AF]
22. [Isa. 6.9-10. AF]
23. [Mark 4.11. AF]

LETTER 5

Rendel Harris to Wood, 30 December, 1920.[24]

Dear H.G.

Continuing my letter of this morning, does it not seem that not only a certain group of the earliest Testimonies were anti-Judaic, but that Jesus is responsible for their anti-Judaism. I am studying just now for a reason which will appear later our Lord's discourse at Nazareth.[25] What made the people so angry unless it was the statement that prophets were sent to Gentile homes, while to Jewish homes properly so called, to none of them was Elias sent. If this is historical, it is natural that they should want to throw him over the Tarpeian rock. He was anti-Judaising. To continue with your questions; I think you have a right to ask for some place in a primitive collection, of Testimonies that are really historical, like the birth in Bethlehem. I must own to being perplexed over this passage, because it is said to be a testimony of the scribes both in Matt. and in John;[26] and this suggests the existence of a Messianic text-book among the Jews. The difficulty is that we find not a great deal in the Testimonies that can properly be called Messianic; and if the scribes were on this line, we ought to find a great deal. I think you are right in suggesting that a place for historical details may be wanted in the primitive collection.

As to the growth of the collection, it seems certain that it was affected by accretion and rejection. Some of the texts made untenable arguments and the Jews made short work of them. What about "the Lord reigned from the tree,"[27] which seems to be involved in Acts V.[28] But if we admit accretions it would be wrong to assume that neither Paul or Apollos could make additions from their own stores. Here the difficulty is that when one removes from Paul what we can, on other grounds, suspect to be primitive Testimony, there is not much left.

Entre nous I am a little sorry that I gave the chapter on Galatians to Burch. He is wanting in lucidity, and is tempted to make up for lack of lucidity by emphasis; so you can criticise him a little without destroying the main argument.

As to Matthew the Monk, I agree that the matter is largely speculative. I can't think the verses are late, but I can't make an adequate proof of their being early. But the whole Papias' problem is on another shelf from the proof of the Testimony Book, which we make on their own merits.

24. ['Letters to H. G. Wood, 1906–39,' G Har 11, Woodbrooke archives. AF]
25. [Luke 4.16-30. AF]
26. [Matt. 2.6; John 7.42. AF]
27. [Christian interpolation in Ps. 96.10: cf. Justin, *1 Apol.* 41.4. AF]
28. [Acts 6.30. AF]

Many thanks for the enclosed corrections which are being transferred to my standard copy.

I think you should now read Athanasius and Zaccheus,[29] to see what Testimonies are like when dramatised; I think you will get some illumination from this quarter.

You may have noticed that Robinson and Bernard are quite sure that the Testimony Book cannot be of apostolic origin. Each of them writes positively before seeing the book. That was not wise, to say the least.

To change the subject, let us now report on the Odes. We have now a lot of fresh proofs that the Odes depend on the Biblical Targum. You will be greatly interested. It opens a new field of view. Apparently the author was a converted Meturgeman from the Synagogue. I am to lecture on the subject the week after next.

Thine:
Rendel Harris

---

29. [*Dial. Ath.* AF]

BIBLIOGRAPHY

James Rendel Harris's Works*

Aaron's Breastplate (London: National Council of Evangelical Free Churches, 1908).
Rendel Harris and Seth K. Gifford (eds.), *The Acts of the Martyrdom of Perpetua and Felicitas: The Original Greek Text Now First Edited from a MS. in the Library of the Convent of the Holy Sepulchre at Jerusalem* (London: Clay, 1890).
The After-Glow Essays (London: University of London Press, 1933–35).
The Annotators of Codex Bezae (with Some Notes on Sortes Sanctorum) (London: Clay, 1901).
Rendel Harris (ed.), *The Apology of Aristides* (TS, 1; Cambridge: Cambridge University Press, 1891).
As Pants the Hart (London: Hodder & Stoughton, 1924).
The Ascent of Olympus (Manchester: John Rylands Library, 1917).
'Athanasius and the Book of Testimonies', *Expositor*, 7th series, 9 (1910), pp. 530-37; repr. in *Testimonies*, 1.87-93.
'Athena, Sophia, and the Logos', *BJRL* 7 (1922), pp. 55-72.
Boanerges (Cambridge: Cambridge University Press, 1913).
Caravan Essays (Cambridge: Heffer, 1929).
'Cod. Ev. 561.–Codex Algerinae Peckover', *Journal of the Society of Biblical Literature and Exegesis* 6 (1886), pp. 79-89.
Codex Bezae: A Study of the So-Called Western Text of the New Testament (TS, 2.1; Cambridge: Cambridge University Press, 1891).
The Cult of the Heavenly Twins (Cambridge: Cambridge University Press, 1906).
'Deissmann and the Holy Grail', *Expository Times* 35 (1924), pp. 523-24.
The Diatessaron of Tatian: A Preliminary Study (London: Clay, 1890).
The Dioscuri in Christian Legends (London: Clay, 1903).
'An Early Christian Psalter', *Contemporary Review* 95 (1909), pp. 414-28.
Evergreen Essays (Cambridge: Heffer, 1931–32).
Rendel Harris, Francis C. Burkitt, and Robert L. Bensly (eds.), *The Four Gospels in Syriac Transcribed from the Sinai Palimpsest* (Cambridge: Cambridge University Press, 1894).
Further Researches in the History of the Ferrar-Group (London: Clay, 1900).
'Glass Chalices of the First Century', *BJRL* 11 (1927), pp. 286-95.
The Guiding Hand of God (London: National Council of Evangelical Free Churches, 1905).
Josephus and his Testimony (Evergreen Essays, 2; Cambridge: Heffer, 1931).

---

*   This list includes only the works cited in this book.

Rendel Harris with Helen B. Harris, *Letters from the Scenes of the Recent Massacres in Armenia* (London: Nisbet, 1897).
'The Library of the Convent of the Holy Sepulchre at Jerusalem', *Haverford College Studies* 1 (1889), pp. 1-17.
Memoranda Sacra (London: Hodder & Stoughton, 1892).
'Methods of Research in Eastern Libraries' (Lecture no. 4, Haverford College Library Lectures, 1895; typescript, Rendel Harris Room, Woodbrooke Quaker Study Centre, Birmingham).
The Migration of Culture: Two Essays, with Maps (Oxford: Blackwell, 1936).
'A New Patristic Fragment', *Expositor*, 5th series, 1 (1895), pp. 448-55.
New Testament Autographs (Supplement to the *American Journal of Philology* 12 [1882], Baltimore).
Nicodemus (Evergreen Essays, 4; Cambridge: Heffer, 1932).
Rendel Harris and Alphonse Mingana (eds.), *The Odes and Psalms of Solomon* (2 vols.; Manchester: Manchester University Press, 1916–20).
Rendel Harris (ed.), *The Odes and Psalms of Solomon: Now First Published from the Syriac Version* (Cambridge: Cambridge University Press, 1909).
On the Origin of the Ferrar Group (London: Clay, 1893).
The Origin of the Leicester Codex of the New Testament (London: Clay, 1887).
'The Origin of the Prologue to St John's Gospel', *Expositor*, 8th series, 12 (1916), pp. 147-60, 161-70, 314-20, 388-400, 415-26.
The Origin of the Prologue to St John's Gospel (Cambridge: Cambridge University Press, 1917).
'Passive Resistance: A Letter from J. Rendel Harris to the Nonconformists of the County of Cambridge and the Isle of Ely', *The British Weekly* (1 December 1902).
Side-Lights on New Testament Research: Seven Lectures Delivered in 1908, at Regent's Park College, London (London: The Kingsgate Press, James Clarke, 1908).
'Spoken by Jeremy the Prophet', *Expositor*, 6th series, 12 (1905), pp. 161-71, reprinted in *Testimonies*, 1.53-60.
'Stichometry', *American Journal of Philology* 4 (1883), pp. 133-57, 309-31.
Stichometry (Cambridge: Clay, 1893).
'Stoic Origins of the Prologue to St John's Gospel', *BJRL* 6 (1922), pp. 439-51.
The Sufferings and the Glory (London: Headley Brothers, 1914).
Sunset Essays (Cambridge: Heffer, 1930–1931).
Rendel Harris with the collaboration of Henry V. Burch, *Testimonies* (2 vols.; Cambridge: Cambridge University Press, 1916–1920).
Ulysses to his Friends (private publication, 1917).
Union with God (London: Hodder & Stoughton, 1895).
'The Use of Testimonies in the Early Christian Church', *Expositor*, 7th series, 2 (1906), pp. 385-409.
Woodbrooke Essays (Cambridge: Heffer, 1927–28).

Other Works

Albl, Martin C., *'And Scripture Cannot Be Broken': The Form and Function of the Early Christian* Testimonia *Collections* (NovTSup, 96; Leiden: E.J. Brill, 1999).
—(ed.), *Pseudo-Gregory of Nyssa: Testimonies against the Jews* (Society of Biblical Literature Writings from the Greco-Roman World, 5; Leiden: E.J. Brill, 2004).

Alford, Henry (ed.), *The Greek Testament: With a Critically Revised Text, a Digest of Various Readings, Marginal References to Verbal and Idiomatic Usage, Prolegomena and a Critical and Exegetical Commentary* (4 vols.; F. & J. Rivington: London, 1849–61).
Anon, 'Dr Harris's Angus Lectures', *The Old Woodbrookers Magazine* 9 (1909), p. 68.
Anon, 'Dr Rendel Harris at Home', *The Christian Commonwealth* (7 March 1907).
Anon (ed.), 'Tauchnitz text of Josephus', *Flavii Iosephi iudaei opera omnia ad optimorum librorum fidem accurate edita* (6 vols.; Leipzig: Caroli Tauchnitii, 1850).
Backhouse, Margaret A., 'James Rendel Harris', in *London Yearly Meeting of the Society of Friends 1942: Reports and Documents Presented to the Yearly Meeting Together with Minutes and Index* (London: Headley Brothers, 1942), pp. 182-84.
Bacon, Benjamin W., *The Story of St Paul: A Comparison of Acts and Epistles* (London: Hodder & Stoughton, 1905).
Berendts, Alexander, and Konrad Grass (eds.), *Flavius Josephus. Vom jüdischen Kriege Buch I-IV: Nach der slavischen Übersetzung deutsch herausgegeben und mit dem griechischen Text verglichen* (Dorpat: C. Mattiesen, 1924–27).
Berger, Samuel, *Histoire de la Vulgate pendant les premiers siècles du moyen âge* (Paris: Hachette, 1893).
Birt, Theodor, *Das antike Buchwesen in seinem Verhältnis zur Literatur: Mit Beiträgen zur Textgeschichte des Theokrit, Catull, Properz und anderen Autoren* (Berlin: Hertz, 1882).
Bridges, Robert S., *The Spirit of Man: An Anthology in English and French from the Philosophers and Poets* (London: Longmans, 1916).
Browne, Edward G., *Traveller's Narrative Written to Illustrate the Episode of the Báb: Edited in the Original Persian, and Translated into English* (2 vols.; Cambridge: Cambridge University Press, 1891).
Burch, Henry V., *Jesus Christ and his Revelation: Fresh Evidence from Christian Sources and Josephus* (London: Chapman and Hall, 1927).
Burgon, John W., *The Revision Revised: Three Articles Reprinted from the 'Quarterly Review' to Which Is Added a Reply to Bishop Ellicott's Pamphlet in Defence of the Revisers and their Greek Text of the New Testament Including a Vindication of the Traditional Reading of 1 Timothy III. 16* (London: John Murray, 1883).
Caspari, Carl P., *Alte und Neue Quellen zur Geschichte des Taufsymbols und der Glaubensregel* (Christiania, 1879).
Cerfaux, Lucien, 'Vestiges d'un florilège dans I Cor., I, 18–III, 23?', *RHE* 27 (1931), pp. 521-34.
Charles, Robert H. (ed.), *The Book of Enoch: Translated from Professor Dillmann's Ethiopic Text, Emended and Revised in Accordance with Hitherto Uncollated Ethiopic Mss. and with the Gizeh and Other Greek and Latin Fragments Which Are Here Published in Full* (Oxford: Clarendon Press, 1893).
Christ, Wilhelm von, *Die Attikusausgabe des Demosthenes: Ein Beitrag zur Textgeschichte des Autors* (Abhandlungen der Königlich Bayerischen Akademie der Wissenschaften, 1. Classe, 16/3; Munich: Verlag der K. Akademie, 1882).
Ciasca, Agostino (ed.), *Tatiani evangeliorum harmoniae arabice* (Rome: Ex Typographia Polyglotta, 1888).
Collins, Anthony, *A Discourse of Free-Thinking: Occasion'd by the Rise and Growth of a Sect Call'd Free-Thinkers* (London, 1713).
Conybeare, Frederick C. (ed.), *The Dialogue of Athanasius and Zaccheus and of Timothy and Aquila* (Anecdota Oxoniensia; Oxford: Clarendon Press, 1898).

Cramer, John A. (ed.), *Catenæ in Sancti Pauli Epistolas ad Corinthios* (Oxford: e Typographeo Academico, 1841).
Cureton, William (ed.), *Spicilegium syriacum: Containing Remains of Bardesan, Meliton, Ambrose and Mara Bar Serapion* (London: F. & J. Rivington, 1855).
—*Remains of a Very Ancient Recension of the Gospels in Syriac Hitherto Unknown in Europe* (London: John Murray, 1858).
—*Ancient Christian Documents Relative to the Earliest Establishment of Christianity in Edessa and Neighbouring Countries, from the Year after Our Lord's Ascension to the Beginning of the Fourth Century* (London: Williams and Norgate, 1864).
Daubuz, Charles, *Pro testimonio Flavii Josephi de Jesu Christo libri duo* (London: R. Sare, 1706).
Davidson, Samuel, *An Introduction to the New Testament: Containing an Examination of the Most Important Questions Relating to the Authority, Interpretation, and Integrity of the Canonical Books, with Reference to the Latest Inquiries* (3 vols.; London: Samuel Bagster, 1848–51).
—*The New Testament: Translated from the Critical Text of von Tischendorf* (London: H. S. King, 1875).
Dieter, Melvin E., *The Holiness Revival of the Nineteenth Century* (Lanham, MD: The Scarecrow Press, 2nd edn, 1996).
Dobbin, Orlando T., 'The Vatican Manuscript', *Dublin University Magazine* 54 (1859), pp. 614-29.
Drummond, Henry, *The Greatest Thing in the World: An Address* (London: Hodder & Stoughton, 1890).
Drummond, James, *An Inquiry into the Character and Authorship of the Fourth Gospel* (London: Williams & Norgate, 1903).
Ehrman, Bart D., *The Orthodox Corruption of Scripture: The Effect of Early Christological Controversies on the Text of the New Testament* (New York: Oxford University Press, 1996).
Eisler, Robert, 'Jésus d'après la version slave de Joséphe', *RHR* 93 (1926), pp. 9-21.
—'The Newly Rediscovered Witness of Josephus to Jesus', *The Quest* 17 (1926), pp. 1-15.
—'The Present Position of the Slavic Josephus', *The Quest* 20 (1928), pp. 1-19.
—*IHCOYC BACIΛEYC OY BACIΛEYCAC: Die messianische Unabhängigkeitsbewegung vom Auftreten Johannes des Täufers bis zum Untergang Jakobs des Gerechten, nach der neuerschlossenen Eroberung vom Jerusalem des Flavius Josephus und den christlichen Quellen* (2 vols.; Religionswissenschaftliche Bibliothek, 9; Heidelberg: C. Winter, 1929–30). English translation by Alexander H. Krappe, *The Messiah Jesus and John the Baptist according to Flavius Josephus' Recently Rediscovered 'Capture of Jerusalem' and the Other Jewish and Christian Sources* (London: Methuen, 1931).
[Ellicott, Charles J., and Edwin Palmer], *The Revisers and the Greek Text of the New Testament: By Two Members of the New Testament Company* (London: MacMillan, 1882).
Falcetta, Alessandro, *James Rendel Harris (1852–1941): Uno studioso delle origini del cristianesimo ed un uomo spirituale* (BA diss., Università di Bologna, 1996).
—'A Testimony Collection in Manchester: Papyrus Rylands Greek 460', *BJRL* 83 (2001), pp. 3-19.
—'The Testimony Research of James Rendel Harris', *NovT* 45 (2003), pp. 280-99.
Farrar, Frederic W., *The Early Days of Christianity* (2 vols.; London: Cassell, Petter, Galpin, 1882).

—'The Revised Version and its Assailants', *Contemporary Review* 41 (1882), pp. 359-80.
Ferrar, William H., *A Collation of Four Important Manuscripts of the Gospels: With a View to Prove Their Common Origin and to Restore the Text of Their Archetype* (ed. Thomas K. Abbott; Dublin: Hodges, Foster, and Figgis; London: MacMillan, 1877).
Gaisford, Thomas (ed.), *Eusebii Pamphili episcopi Caesariensis eclogae propheticae* (Oxford: e Typographeo Academico, 1842).
Gardthausen, Viktor, *Griechische Paläographie* (Leipzig: Teubner, 1879).
—*Catalogus codicum graecorum sinaiticorum* (Oxford: e Typographeo Clarendoniano, 1886).
Gebhardt, Oscar von, *et al.* (eds.), *Patrum apostolicorum opera ... Editio minor* (Leipzig, 1877).
Gibson, Margaret D., *How the Codex Was Found: A Narrative of Two Visits to Sinai from Mrs. Lewis's Journals, 1892–1893* (Cambridge: MacMillan and Bowes, 1893; repr., Piscataway, NJ: Gorgias Press, 2001).
Goshen-Gottstein, Moshe H., *Syriac Manuscripts in the Harvard College Library: A Catalogue* (HSS, 23; Missoula, MT: Scholars Press, 1979).
Graux, Charles, 'Nouvelles recherches sur la stichométrie', *RevPhil* 2 (1878), pp. 97-144.
Grech, Prosper, 'Testimonia and Modern Hermeneutics', *NTS* 19 (1973), pp. 318-24.
Gregory, Caspar R., *Prolegomena* (vol. 3 of Konstantin von Tischendorf [ed.], *Novum Testamentum Graece ... Editio octava critica maior*; Leipzig: Giesecke & Devrient, 1894).
Grenfell, Bernard P., and Arthur S. Hunt (eds.), *The Oxyrhynchus Papyri*, III (London: Egypt Exploration Fund, 1903).
Gwatkin, Henry M., *Early Church History to A.D. 313* (2 vols.; London: MacMillan, 1909; 2nd edn, 1912).
Harris, Helen B. [obituary of], *The Annual Monitor for 1915* (Gloucester: John Bellows, 1914), pp. 106-16.
Harris, Henry W., *Life So Far* (London: Jonathan Cape, 1954).
Hatch, Edwin, *Essays in Biblical Greek* (Oxford: Clarendon Press, 1889).
Haverkamp, Sigebert (ed.), *Flavii Josephi quae reperiri potuerunt* (2 vols.; Amsterdam: R. & G. Wetstenius, 1726).
Hawkins, Hugh, *Pioneer: A History of the Johns Hopkins University, 1874–1889* (Ithaca, NY: Cornell University Press, 1960).
Heinichen, Friedrich A.H. (ed.), *Eusebii Pamphili Historiae ecclesiasticae libri* (3 vols.; Leipzig: C.G. Kayser, 1827–28).
Hewison, Hope H., *Hedge of Wild Almonds: South Africa, the Pro-Boers and the Quaker Conscience, 1890–1910* (London: James Currey, 1989).
Howe, George R., 'The Lighter Side of a Weighty Friend' (typescript, 'Biographical Material', G Har 4, Woodbrooke Quaker Study Centre archives, Birmingham).
Jones, Rufus M., *Haverford College: A History and an Interpretation* (New York: MacMillan, 1933).
Josephus, *The Jewish War, Books IV–VII* (trans. Henry St.J. Thackeray; vol. 3 of *Josephus*; trans. Henry St.J. Thackeray *et al.*; LCL; Cambridge, MA: Harvard University Press, 1928).
Keill, Heinrich, and Theodore Mommsen (eds.), *Plini Caecili secundi Epistularum libri novem. Epistularum ad Traianum liber. Panegyricus* (Leipzig: Teubner, 1870).
Kennedy, Benjamin H., *Ely Lectures on the Revised Version of the New Testament: With an Appendix Containing the Chief Textual Changes* (London: Bentley, 1882).

Kennedy, Thomas C., *British Quakerism 1860–1920: The Transformation of a Religious Community* (Oxford: Oxford University Press, 2001).
Kenyon, Frederic G., *Handbook to the Textual Criticism of the New Testament* (London: MacMillan, 1901).
Klausner, Joseph G., *Jesus of Nazareth: His Life, Times, and Teaching* (trans. Herbert Danby; London: G. Allen & Unwin, 1925).
Lambros, Spyridon P., *Catalogue of the Greek Manuscripts on Mount Athos* (Cambridge: Cambridge University Press, 1895–1900).
Lebreton, Jules, *Histoire du dogme de la Trinité des origines à Saint Augustin* (2 vols.; Paris: Beauchesne, 3rd edn, 1910).
Leendertz, J.M., *De oden van Salomo* (Amsterdam, 1910).
Liddon, Henry P., *The Divinity of Our Lord and Saviour Jesus Christ: Eight Lectures Preached before the University of Oxford in 1866, on the Foundation of the Late Rev. John Bampton* (London: Rivingtons, 1867).
Lipsiensis, Phileleutherus (Robert Bentley), *Remarks upon a Late Discourse of Free-Thinking in a Letter to F.H. D.D.* (London: J. Morphew, E. Curll, 1713).
Mai, Angelo (ed.), *Vetus et Novum Testamentum ex antiquissimo Codice Vaticano* (Rome: Josephus Spithöver, 1857).
Massuet, René (ed.), *Sancti Irenaei episcopi lugdunensis et martyris detectionis et eversionis falso cognominatae agnitionis seu contra haereses libri quinque* (Paris: Joannes Baptista Coignard, 1710; repr. in PG 7.1).
Ménard, Léon, *Histoire civile, ecclésiastique et litteraire de la Ville de Nismes: Avec des notes et les preuves, suivie de dissertations historiques et critiques sur les antiquités et de diverses observations sur son histoire naturelle* (7 vols.; Paris: Chaubert, 1750–1758).
Mill, John (ed.), *Novum Testamentum cum lectionibus variantibus* (Oxford: e Theatro Sheldoniano, 1707).
Moesinger, Georg (ed.), *Evangelii concordantis expositio facta a Sancto Ephraemo doctore syro* (Venice: Libraria PP. Mechitaristarum in Monasterium S. Lazari, 1876).
Moffatt, James, *The New Testament: A New Translation in Modern Speech, Based upon the Greek Text by von Soden* (London: Hodder & Stoughton, 1913).
Mommsen, Theodore (ed.), *Corpus inscriptionum latinarum*, III (Berlin: G. Reimerum, 1873).
Montefiore, Claude G., 'Dr Robert Eisler on the Beginnings of Christianity', *Hibbert Journal* 30 (1931–32), pp. 298-318.
Moule, Handley C.G., *Colossian Studies: Lessons in Faith and Holiness from St Paul's Epistles to the Colossians and Philemon* (London: Hodder & Stoughton, 1898).
The New Testament: The Authorised English Version with Introduction, and Various Readings from the Three Most Celebrated Manuscripts of the Original Greek Text by Constantine Tischendorf (Leipzig: Bernhard Tauchnitz, 1869).
The New Testament of Our Lord and Saviour Jesus Christ: Translated out of the Greek: Being the Version Set Forth A.D. 1611 Compared with the Most Ancient Authorities and Revised A.D. 1881 (Oxford: Oxford University Press, 1881).
Nickalls, John L. (ed.), *The Journal of George Fox* (London: London Yearly Meeting of the Religious Society of Friends, 1986).
Paley, Frederick A., *The Gospel of St John: A Verbatim Translation from the Vatican MS. with the Notable Variations of the Sinaitic and Beza MS., and Brief Explanatory Comments* (London: S. Sonnenschein, Lowrey, 1887).

Papadopoulos-Kerameus, Athanasios I., *Catalogue of the Manuscripts in the Smyrna Library of the Evangelical School* (Smyrna, 1877) [in Greek].
—*Jerusalem Library* (5 vols.; Saint Petersburg, 1891-1915) [in Greek].
Parker, David C., *Codex Bezae: An Early Christian Manuscript and its Text* (Cambridge: Cambridge University Press, 1992).
—*The Living Text of the Gospel* (Cambridge: Cambridge University Press, 1997).
Pickard, Irene S., *Memories of J. Rendel Harris* (private publication, 1978).
Plooij, Daniel, *Studies in the Testimony Book* (Verhandelingen der Koninklijke Akademie van Wetenschappen te Amsterdam. Afdeeling Letterkunde, NS, 32/2; Amsterdam: Uitgave van De N.V. Noord-Hollandsche, Uitgevers-Maatschappij, 1932).
Plummer, Alfred, *A Critical and Exegetical Commentary on the Gospel according to S. Luke* (ICC; Edinburgh: T. & T. Clark, 1896).
Pott, August, *Der griechisch-syrische Text des Matthäus: E 351 im Verhältnis zu Tatian ssc Ferrar* (Leipzig: Teubner, 1912).
Potter, John (ed.), *Clementis alexandrini opera quae extant* (2 vols.; Oxford: e Theatro Sheldoniano, 1715).
Price, Allan W., *The Ladies of Castlebrae: A Story of Nineteenth-Century Travel and Research* (Gloucester: Alan Sutton, 1985).
Reiske, Johann J. (ed.), *Demosthenis quae supersunt* (9 vols.; London: Black, Young & Young, 1822-27).
Report of the Proceedings of the Conference of the Society of Friends Held by Direction of the Yearly Meeting, in Manchester from the Eleventh to the Fifteenth of Eleventh Month, 1895 (London: Headley Brothers, 1896).
Routh, Martin J. (ed.), *Reliquiae sacrae* (5 vols.; Oxford: e Typographeo Academico, 2nd edn, 1846-48).
Ryle, H.E., *The Early Narratives of Genesis: A Brief Introduction to the Study of Genesis I-XI* (London: MacMillan, 1892).
Sakkelion, Ioannes, *Patmos Library* (Athens: Alexandros Papageorgios, 1890) [in Greek].
Sakkelion, Ioannes, and Alkiviados I. Sakkelion, *Catalogue of the Manuscripts of the National Library of Greece* (Athens, 1892) [in Greek].
Samir, Samir K., *Alphonse Mingana 1878-1937 and his Contribution to Early Christian Studies* (Birmingham: Selly Oak Colleges, 1990).
Sanday, William, 'The Greek Text of the New Testament', *Contemporary Review* 40 (1881), pp. 985-1006.
Schmithals, Walter, *Johannesevangelium und Johannesbriefe: Forschungsgeschichte und Analyse* (BZNW, 64; Berlin: de Gruyter, 1992).
Scholz, Johann M.A. (ed.), *Novum Testamentum Graece* (2 vols.; Leipzig: Fridericus Fleischer, 1830-36).
Schweitzer, Albert, *The Quest of the Historical Jesus: A Critical Study of its Progress from Reimarus to Wrede* (trans. William Montgomery; London: Adam & Charles Black, 1910).
Scrivener, Frederick H.A., *A Plain Introduction to the Criticism of the New Testament for the Use of Biblical Students* (Cambridge: Deighton, Bell, 1861).
—*Bezae Codex Cantabrigiensis: Being an Exact Copy, in Ordinary Type, of the Celebrated Uncial Graeco-Latin Manuscript of the Four Gospels and Acts of the Apostles* (Cambridge: Deighton, Bell, 1864).
—*A Full Collation of the Codex Sinaiticus with the Received Text of the New Testament* (Cambridge: Deighton, Bell; London: Bell & Daldy, 1864).
Sinclair, L., 'A List of Writings, etc., of James Rendel Harris (1852-1941)' (typescript, 1956, Rendel Harris Room, Woodbrooke Quaker Study Centre, Birmingham).

Soden, Hermann von (ed.), *Die Schriften des Neuen Testaments in ihrer ältesten erreichbaren Textgestalt: Hergestellt auf Grund ihrer Textgeschichte* (3 vols.; Berlin: Glaue, 1902–13).
Swete, Henry B. (ed.), *The Old Testament in Greek according to the Septuagint* (3 vols.; Cambridge: Cambridge University Press, 1887–91).
Taylor, Charles, *Sayings of the Jewish Fathers: Comprising Pirqe Aboth and Pereq R. Meir in Hebrew and English* (Cambridge: Cambridge University Press, 2nd edn, 1897).
Thackeray, Henry St.J., *Josephus: The Man and the Historian* (The Hilda Stich Stroock Lectures at the Jewish Institute of Religion; New York: Jewish Institute of Religion Press, 1929).
Tischendorf, Konstantin von (ed.), *Bibliorum Codex Sinaiticus Petropolitanus* (4 vols.; St Petersburg, 1862).
—*Novum Testamentum Graece ... Editio octava critica maior* (3 vols.; Leipzig: Giesecke & Devrient, 1869–94).
—*Evangelia apocrypha* (Leipzig: H. Mendelssohn, 2nd edn, 1876).
Tregelles, Samuel P. (ed.), *The Greek Testament: Edited from Ancient Authorities with their Various Readings in Full and the Latin Version of Jerome* (7 vols.; London: Samuel Bagster, C.J. Stewart, 1857–79).
Waddington, William H., *Édit de Dioclétien: Établissant le maximum dans l'empire romain* (Paris: Firmin Didot, 1864).
Weil, H., review of Christ, *Attikusausgabe*, in *Revue critique d'histoire et de littérature* 16 (1882), pp. 424-27.
Westcott, Brooke F., *The Gospel according to St John: The Authorised Version* (London: John Murray, 1882).
—*Some Lessons of the Revised Version of the New Testament* (London: Hodder & Stoughton, 1897).
Westcott, Brooke F., and Fenton J.A. Hort (eds.), *The New Testament in the Original Greek* (2 vols.; Cambridge: MacMillan, 1881).
Weymouth, Richard F., *The New Testament in Modern Speech: An Idiomatic Translation into Everyday English from the Text of 'The Resultant Greek Testament'* (ed. Ernest Hampden-Cook; London: James Clarke, 2nd edn, 1903).
Windisch, Hans, 'Die göttliche Weisheit der Juden und die paulinische Christologie', in *Neutestamentliche Studien für Georg Heinrici zu seinem 70. Geburtstag (14. März 1914) dargebracht von Fachgenossen, Freunden und Schülern* (ed. Adolf Deissmann and Hans Windisch; Leipzig: Hinrichs, 1914), pp. 220-34.
Wood, Herbert G., 'The First Director of Studies', in Robert Davis (ed.), *Woodbrooke 1903–1953: A Brief History of a Quaker Experiment in Religious Education* (London: The Bannisdale Press, 1953), pp. 19-30.
Wood, Herbert G., et al., 'The Doctor', *The Woodbrooke International Journal* 41 (1941), pp. 2-15.
Wood, Herbert G., et al., 'James Rendel Harris: 1852–1941', *The Friend* 99 (1941), pp. 115-19.
Zacagni, Lorenzo A. (ed.), 'Gregorii Nysseni de Judaeis', in *Collectanea monumentorum veterum ecclesiae graecae ac latinae* (Rome: Typis Sacrae Congregationis de Propaganda Fide, 1698; repr. in PG 46.194-234).
Zwaan, Johannes de (ed.), *The Treatise of Dionysius Bar Ṣalibhi against the Jews: Part I, the Syriac Text Edited from a Mesopotamian Ms (Cod. Syr. Harris 83)* (Leiden: E.J. Brill, 1906).

INDEXES

INDEX OF REFERENCES

BIBLE

Old Testament		1.29	155	8.14	110
Genesis		3.13	177	8.23	234
1.26	163, 165	3.15	147	11.1	103
3	79	3.16	151	19.12	204
3.22	136	3.18	122, 177	26.19	101
37.10	207	3.19-20	140	28.16	110, 111
49.10	105, 106	3.19	122, 137	29.13	205
		8	146, 155, 184	29.14	204, 205
Exodus				33.18	204
23.20	200, 202	8.2	146	35	106, 108
		8.12	142	35.4	101, 226
Numbers		8.17	129	35.5-6	101
24.17	103, 104	8.21-36	137	35.5	101, 226
		8.22-31	179	35.6	101
2 Kings		8.22-30	121	40.5	189
1.7-8	207	8.22-25	140	40.12	165
22.8	76	8.22-23	122	41.15	164
		8.22	128, 136, 141, 148, 150, 152, 153, 160, 165, 173, 182	41.20	164
Job				48.13	165
12.17	204			49.6	115
				49.8-9	115
Psalms				53.1	180
1.3	49			53.4	101
2.7	183	8.23-31	132	58.1	163
33.6	137	8.23	150	59.1	163
45	138, 139	8.24	183	64.5	49
45.1	119, 134, 138, 142	8.25	157, 183	65.1-3	113
		8.27	122, 182	66.1	163
45.10	142	8.30	122, 127, 153, 182	66.2	163, 167
96.10	237				
102.25	165, 168	8.31	183	*Jeremiah*	
104.24	123	8.35	122	11.19	109
110.3	112	8.36	129		
118.22	110, 111	9.1	134	*Daniel*	
143.5	168	9.10	129	3.57	168
				7.13	202
Proverbs		*Isaiah*			
1.17	207	1.2-4	154	*Habakkuk*	
1.28	154, 161	6.9-10	180, 237	2.4	234

Index of References

Zechariah		24.4	148	26	125
6.10-15	200	24.6	135, 157	27.9-10	109
6.12	201	24.7	149	27.9	114
9.9	230	24.8-12	148		
11.13	109	24.14	133	*Mark*	
		24.19	178	1.1	119
Malachi		24.21	178	1.2-3	107, 207
3.1	202	32.14-15	152	1.2	114, 202
		32.15	153, 161	1.6	206
Apocrypha		34.6	161	4.11	237
Wisdom of Solomon		34.13	161	6.2	178
1.1	145	42.15	157	6.3	125
1.7	154, 183	42.21	133	7.6-7	205
3.9	152, 161	43	135	7.6	108
4.15	152	44.31	157	7.32	108
6.22	161	51.26	178	7.37	108
7.22-24	172			9.19	125
7.22	129, 144, 172	*Baruch*		12.13-17	196
		3.29-37	153	14.49	125
7.25-26	171	3.35	115	16.9-20	92
7.25	161, 171-74				
		New Testament		*Luke*	
7.26	130, 146, 160, 161, 170, 174	*Matthew*		1.1	116
		1.1	119	1.15	207
		2.6	237	2.22	154
		2.15	116	2.36	96
7.27	130, 157, 161	3.4	96, 206	2.40	178
		3.5	206	2.52	178
7.29	146, 160	4.15-16	234	3.15	202
7.30	147	5.30	87	4.16-30	237
9.1-2	127	11.3	227	4.16	95
9.1	145	11.4-5	227	7.25	89
9.4	127, 145, 160	11.5	227	7.27	202
9.9	127, 145	11.10	202	9.41	125
9.10	127	11.28-30	178	11.31	177
9.17	128	12.18	237	11.49	121, 159, 177
16.12	145	12.42	177		
24.9	145	13.14-15	181, 234	20.20-26	196
		13.54	178	22.19-20	55
Sirach		13.56	125	22.19	58
1.4	128	17.25-27	187	22.31	57
1.9	128	17.26	188	22.43-44	55
1.14	129	21.33	149	22.43	58
2.16	152, 153	21.42	206	22.56	125
4.11	129	22.4	96	22.62	57
4.12	129	22.15-22	196	22.64	57
24.3–16.19	132	23.34	121, 177	22.68	57
24.3	133	25.6	59	23.5	196

Luke (cont.)		4.9	29	17.18	30
23.17	57	4.14	29	19.5	201, 223
23.34	57, 58	5.3-4	30	19.39	221
23.38	57	5.4	30, 186	20.3-10	126
24.4	57	5.12	29	20.30	31
24.6	57	5.16	29	21.25	26, 31
24.12	57, 126	5.17	159, 182		
24.31	57	5.19	125	Acts	
24.36	57	5.45–6.1	28	2.9	58
24.40	57	5.45	29	2.20	58
24.46	57	6.11	30	2.21	58
24.49	57	6.22	30	2.37	236
24.51	57	6.35	178	2.43	58
24.52	57	6.50–8.52	59	6.30	237
24.53	57	7.30	30	7.60	58
		7.42	237	8.37	59
John		7.46	30	9.12	58
1.1	118, 128	7.50-52	221	13.23	58
1.3	123, 128, 150, 156, 165, 168	7.53–8.11	26, 186	14.20-21	58
		8.5	28	15.32	58
		8.24	215, 219, 220	21.13	58
1.4-5	146			21.22	58
1.4	147	8.52	30	26.27	214
1.5	29, 147	8.59	30, 37	28.25	108
1.6	202	9.7	30	28.26-27	181
1.7-9	146	9.36	30	28.27	58
1.12-13	157	10.13	30		
1.12	157	10.26	30	Romans	
1.13	29, 157	10.31	37	1.17	234, 235
1.14	148, 149, 158	10.37-38	220	8.1	52
		11.40	30	8.29	182
1.15	157	12.15	230	9	205
1.16-17	151	12.37-40	180	9.28	52
1.16	151	12.37	215, 220	9.32-33	110
1.18	147, 150, 157	12.38-40	180	9.33	235
		13.10	30	10.15	52
1.27	29	13.14	30	11.6	52
2	222	13.24	30	12.17	52
2.2	29	13.32	30	13.9	52
2.23-25	222	14.4	30	14.6	52
3	222	14.5	30	14.21	52
3.1-21	221	14.6	177	14.23	51
3.2	222, 224	15.14	209	15.13	52
3.11	221	15.24	215, 220	15.32	52
3.13	29	16.16	30	16.1	52
3.14	221	17.5	125, 126	16.12	52
3.26	125	17.8	120	16.24	52
3.31	29	17.14	120	16.25	52
4.1-42	221	17.15	30		

Index of References

1 Corinthians		Philippians		Hebrews	
1	155	2.18	54	1.2-3	130
1.8	51	3.16	54	1.3	146, 147
1.18-20	204	3.21	54	1.5	183
1.24	120, 134,			2.7	203
	142, 173,	Colossians		2.16	203
	174, 179,	1.2	54	3.1	200, 201,
	199	1.6	54		220
1.27	51	1.12	54	4.12	120, 172
1.30	121, 143,	1.14	54	5.5	183
	179	1.15-18	135	5.7	203
2.15	51	1.15-16	182		
3.3	51	1.15	133, 135,	1 Peter	
7.5	51		144, 147,	1.22	47
8.6	168		157	1.23	47
10.19	51	1.16	143, 150	2.6-8	110
11.24	51	1.17	135, 144,	2.12	47
13.1-2	50		150, 168	3.5	47
15.13	51	1.18	135, 140,	3.7	47
15.26-27	51		150, 151	3.16	47
15.33	35	1.19	151, 152	4.5	47
		1.23	54	4.14	47
2 Corinthians		1.25	54	5.2	47
1.13	51	2.2	54	5.3	47
3.16	51	2.3	178	5.5	47
4.4	51	2.11	54	5.10	47
8.4	51	3.6	54		
9.4	51			2 Peter	
12.7	51	1 Thessalonians		1.5	87
12.11	51	1.1	49	1.12-13	47
		2.13	49	1.19	11
Galatians		2.16	49	2.10	47
1.11	53	3.2	49	3.10	48, 49
3.1	52	5.8	49	3.14	48, 49
Ephesians		2 Thessalonians		1 John	
1.1	53	1.2	50	1.2	125
1.3	53	1.8	50	2.1	122
1.15	53	1.12	50	4.3	45
1.21	183	2.4	50	4.21	46
3.14	53	2.14	50	5.7	46
3.18	53	2.16	50		
5.22	53	3.4	50	2 John	
5.30	53			12	18, 31
6.3	53	1 Timothy			
6.12	53	3.16	92	3 John	
6.19	53			13	18, 31

Jude
12   46
15   46

16   46
25   46

Revelation
5.1   22
19.13   120

OTHER ANCIENT LITERATURE

Pseudepigrapha
1 Enoch
10.19   211
42.1-3   161
42.1-2   155

Odes of Solomon
12.5   172
13.1   170
33   161
33.3   146
33.5-11   146
33.11   146

Jewish Authors
Josephus
Antiquities of the Jews
17–19   214
18.5.2   206
18.63.3   192
20.267   35

The Jewish War
1.364-70   227
2.110   203
2.174   193
2.175   193

Philo
De ebrietate
30   169
31   169

Rabbinic Writings
Pirqe Aboth
iii.23   153
vi.10   152

Early Christian and
Classical Writings
Athanasius
Orationes contra
Arianos
1.19.8-9   138
2.16   167
2.71.28-36   168

De decretis Nicaenae
synodi
17.3-7   166

De incarnatione
33–40   104
33.4   104
38.1   113
38.3   106
38.4   107
40.3   106

De sententia Dionysii
15.5-6   171

De synodis
16.2   167

Augustine
Confessions
9.10.24   177
10.27.38   176

Enarrationes in Psalmos
118.18.1   166

In evangelium Johannis
           tractatus
124.48.7   166

Sermones
23.5   166
143.14   166

Barnabas
11.6   49

Clement of Alexandria
Eclogae Propheticae
58   153

Paedagogos
1.12.2-3   165

Cyprian
Testimonies against
the Jews
1.3   154, 180
1.5   235
1.21   234
1.53-60   109
2.1   132, 135, 140
2.2   162
2.3   162
2.4   161, 180
2.5   197
2.7   226
2.13   180
2.16   110
2.17   110

Dionysius of
Halicarnassus
De Demosthenis dictione
57   37

Ephrem
Commentary on the
Diatessaron
14.16-17   189
14.17   188

Epiphanius
Ancoratus
31   55

Index of References

Panarion		Irenaeus		14.5	213
30.13.4	96	*Adversus haereses*		32.1	105
		3.21.10	164	32.2	105
Eusebius		3.9.2	101	32.12	103
De ecclesiastica		4. Praefatio	164	41.4	237
theologia		4.10.2	105	48.1-2	101, 224
1.20.81	159	4.20.1	164	49.1	113
		4.20.2-4	140	54.5	105
Demonstratio evangelica		4.33.11	100	54.7	105
5.1.1-4	144	4.35.1	75	54.10	224
5.1.7	144	5.17.1	184		
6.21.2	226	5.24.1	184	Juvenal	
6.21.5	226	5.28.4	164	*Satirae*	
6.21.7	226	5.33.3-4	73	1.4-5	21
Contra Marcellum		Jerome		Lactantius	
2.2.32	139	*De viris illustribus*		*Divinarum institutionum*	
2.2.37	139	18	74	*libri VII*	
3.2.16-17	153			4.13.10	104
		Justin Martyr			
Historia ecclesiastica		*Dialogue with Trypho*		Lucian	
1.2.3	122	11.1	174	*Vitarum auctio*	
3.27.3	158	12.2	181	9	22
3.39.13	73	15.7	113		
7.24.1-3	74	18.1	113	*Martyrium Sancti Pauli*	
		19.6	114	*et Julianae*	
Vita Constantini		32.5	205	22	175
4.37.1	24	33.1	181		
		34.2	198	Methodius	
Eustathius		52.1	106	*Convivium decem*	
De engastrimytho contra		52.2	106	*virginum*	
Origenem		54.1	106	3.3-4	157
21.11	37	61.1	137	3.8	160
		61.3-5	137		
Evagrius		63.2	106	Origen	
Altercatio legis inter		67.2	96	*Commentarii in*	
Simonem Judaeum et		67.4	96	*Romanos*	
Theophilum Christianum		76.2	106	7.13	183
20	236	78.11	205	10.43	44, 51
		126.1	137		
Hermas		128.1	198	*Commentarii in*	
Vision		129.3	136	*evangelium Joannis*	
4.2	83	129.4	136	1.22	159
		139	136	1.31.222	142
Isidore				1.39.287-290	142
Etymologiarum siue		*1 Apology*		2.12	166
originum libri		1.14	213	13.36	159
XX 6.12.1	64	1.30	212		

Contra Celsum		Pseudo-Clement		*Adversus Marcionem*	
5.39	183	*Epistula Clementis*		4.11.4	95
		1.3	78	33.6	205
Homiliae in Jeremiam					
15.4	166	*Homilies*		*Adversus Praxean*	
		16.11.1-2	163	6-7.4	141
De principiis		16.12.1	163	25.4	31
1.2.5	173				
		Pseudo-Cyprian		*De baptismo*	
Passio Perpetuae et		*De montibus Sina et Sion*		9.4	31
Felicitatis		13	170		
5.3	79			*De praescriptione*	
13	76	Pseudo-Gregory of		*haereticorum*	
		Nyssa		38.9	44
Photius		*Testimonia adversus*			
Bibliotheca		*Judaeos*		Theophilus	
235.304a	160	1.4	134	*Ad Autolytum*	
		4	114	1.7.3	137
Pindar		6.3	109	2.10.2	138
Olympionikai		22	154	2.10.4-6	138
1.33-34	94			2.10.6	138
		Tertullian		2.15.4	139
Pliny the Younger		*Adversus Hermogenem*		2.18.1-2	165
Epistles		45.1-2	165	2.18.2	139
3.9.37	69	45.1	141	2.22.2	139
3.14.5	70				
4.11.15	69				

PAPYRI

P.Oxy.
1.11-21   181

INDEX OF AUTHORS

Albl, M.C. x
Alexander, P.H. xii
Alford, H. 88, 144, 148, 149

Backhouse, M.A. 2
Bacon, B.W. 153
Bensly, R.L. 5
Berendts, A. 193
Berger, S. 97
Birt, T. 36, 39, 40, 64, 69
Bridges, R.S. 118, 123
Browne, E.G. 175
Browning, R. 76
Burch, H.V. 11, 193, 234, 235
Burgon, J.W. 48, 86, 88-94, 186
Burkitt, F.C. 5, 87, 112, 113

Caspari, C.P. 158, 159, 171
Cerfaux, L. 204, 205
Charles, R.H. 155
Christ, W. von 37, 38
Ciasca, A. 188
Collins, A. 84
Conybeare, F.C. 174
Coxe, H.O. 76
Cramer, J.A. 155, 156
Cureton, W. 163, 178, 187

Daubuz, C. 192
Davidson, S. 28, 87, 92
Dieter, M.E. 2
Dobbin, O.T. 25
Drummond, H. 80
Drummond, J. 99, 100

Ehrman, B.D. x
Eisler, R. 192-96, 198-200, 202, 209, 215, 216, 218, 219, 223, 225, 228-30
Ellicott, C.J. 91, 94
Falcetta, A. 1, 11
Farrar, F.W. 48, 90
Ferrar, W.H. 186

Gaisford, T. 142
Gardthausen, V. 40, 77, 81
Gebhardt, O. von 36
Gibson, M.D. 5
Gifford, S.K. 4
Goshen-Gottstein, M.H. 13
Grass, K.K. 193
Graux, C. 34-37, 39, 42, 43, 45
Grech, P. 12
Gregory, C.R. 185, 186
Grenfell, B.P. 102
Gwatkin, H.M. 111, 112

Harris, H.W. 1
Hatch, E. 99, 100, 107, 110
Hawkins, H. 3
Heinichen, F.A.H. 195, 196
Hewison, H.H. 7
Hort, F.J.A. 2, 3, 41, 44, 48, 49, 57, 84-86, 88-95, 97
Howe, G.R. 9
Hunt, A.S. 102

Jones, R.M. 3

Keill, H. 64
Kennedy, B.H. 91
Kennedy, T.C. 7
Kenyon, F.G. 186
Klausner, J.G. 218
Krappe, A.H. 194

Lambros, S.P. 81
Lebreton, J. 117
Leendertz, J.M. 233
Liddon, H.P. 122
Lynch, T.T. 176

Macdonald, D.B. 183
Mai, A. 18
Massuet, R. 100, 140, 164, 184
Ménard, L. 73
Mill, J. 87
Moesinger, G. 188
Moffatt, J. 121, 147, 148
Mommsen, T. 39, 64
Montefiore, C.G. 229
Moule, H.C.G. 135

Nickalls, J.L. 11

Paley, F.A. 124
Palmer, E. 91
Papadopoulos-Kerameus, A.I. 80
Parker, D.C. x, 4, 12
Pickard, I.S. 1
Plooij, D. 196-98, 200, 202, 204, 215, 217, 218, 228, 230
Plummer, A. 179
Pott, A. 187, 191
Potter, J. 153
Price, A.W. 5

Reiske, J.J. 38
Rossetti, C.G. 72
Routh, M.J. 156, 171
Ryle, H.E. 79

Sakkelion, A.I. 81
Sakkelion, I. 81
Samir, S.K. 14
Sanday, W. 86, 91
Schmithals, W. x
Scholz, J.M.A. 41
Schweitzer, A. 233
Scrivener, F.H.A. 18, 42, 43, 49, 62, 89, 185, 186
Sinclair, L. 1
Soden, H. von 186
Spenser, E. 161
Swete, H.B. 5

Taylor, C. 153
Thackeray, H.St.J. 194, 195, 198, 208, 213, 214, 223
Tischendorf, K. von 29, 41, 84, 87, 88, 209
Tregelles, S.P. 29, 48

Waddington, W.H. 40
Weil, H. 37
Wesley, C. 177
Westcott, B.F. 2, 41, 44, 48, 49, 57, 84-91, 93, 94, 124, 125, 131, 149
Weymouth, R.F. 87
Windisch, H. 118
Wood, H.G. 1, 2, 7, 8, 203

Zacagni, L.A. 109, 111, 114, 115, 237
Zigabenus, E. 122
Zwaan, J. de 111, 205

Printed in the United States
62493LVS00002B/140